Napoleon's contribution to Germany's development was immense. Under his hegemony, the millennium-old Holy Roman Empire dissolved, paving the way for a new order. Nowhere was the transformation more profound than in the Rhineland.

Based upon an extensive range of German and French archival sources, this book locates the Napoleonic episode in this region within a broader chronological framework, encompassing the Old Regime and Restoration. It analyses not only politics, but also culture, identity, religion, society, institutions and economics. It reassesses in turn the legacy bequeathed by the Old Regime, the struggle between Revolution and Counter-Revolution in the 1790s, Napoleon's attempts to integrate the German-speaking Rhineland into the French Empire, the transition to Prussian rule, and the subsequent struggles that ultimately helped determine whether Germany would follow its own *Sonderweg* or the path of its western neighbours.

DR MICHAEL ROWE is a Lecturer at the School of History, Queen's University, Belfast.

FROM REICH TO STATE

Napoleon's contribution to Germany's development was immense. Under his hegemony, the millennium-old Holy Roman Empire dissolved, paving the way for a new order. Nowhere was the transformation more profound than in the Rhineland.

Based upon an extensive range of German and French archival sources, this book locates the Napoleonic episode in this region within a broader chronological framework, encompassing the Old Regime and Restoration. It analyses not only politics, but also culture, identity, religion, society, institutions and economics. It reassesses in turn the legacy bequeathed by the Old Regime, the struggle between Revolution and Counter-Revolution in the 1790s, Napoleon's attempts to integrate the German-speaking Rhineland into the French Empire, the transition to Prussian rule, and the subsequent struggles that ultimately helped determine whether Germany would follow its own *Sonderweg* or the path of its western neighbours.

MICHAEL ROWE is a Lecturer at the School of History, Queen's University, Belfast.

NEW STUDIES IN EUROPEAN HISTORY

Edited by

PETER BALDWIN, University of California, Los Angeles
CHRISTOPHER CLARK, University of Cambridge
JAMES B. COLLINS, Georgetown University
MÍA RODRÍGUEZ-SALGADO, London School of Economics and
Political Science
LYNDAL ROPER, University of Oxford

The aim of this series in early modern and modern European history is to publish outstanding works of research, addressed to important themes across a wide geographical range, from southern and central Europe, to Scandinavia and Russia, and from the time of the Renaissance to the Second World War. As it develops the series will comprise focused works of wide contextual range and intellectual ambition.

For a full list of titles published in the series, please see the end of the book.

FROM REICH TO STATE

The Rhineland in the Revolutionary Age, 1780–1830

MICHAEL ROWE

CAMBRIDGE
UNIVERSITY PRESS

PUBLISHED BY THE PRESS SYNDICATE OF THE UNIVERSITY OF CAMBRIDGE
The Pitt Building, Trumpington Street, Cambridge CB2 1RP, United Kingdom

CAMBRIDGE UNIVERSITY PRESS
The Edinburgh Building, Cambridge, CB2 2RU, UK
40 West 20th Street, New York, NY 10011–4211, USA
477 Williamstown Road, Port Melbourne, VIC 3207, Australia
Ruiz de Alarcón 13, 28014 Madrid, Spain
Dock House, The Waterfront, Cape Town 8001, South Africa

http://www.cambridge.org

© Michael Rowe 2003

First published 2003

Printed in the United Kingdom at the University Press, Cambridge

Typeface Adobe Garamond 11/12.5 pt.   *System* LATEX 2$_\varepsilon$ [TB]

A catalogue record for this book is available from the British Library

ISBN 0 521 82443 5 hardback

To my mother

Contents

Preface

This book has been long in gestation, and in that time I have incurred innumerable debts. My thanks are due in the first instance to the British Academy, whose three-year studentship provided the necessary financial support for my doctoral research completed in Cambridge in 1996, and upon which much of this book is based. A smaller British Academy grant facilitated a subsequent follow-up visit to the Rhenish archives in 1998. Financial support for research in Germany in 1994/5 was provided by the European Commission-administered ERASMUS Inter-University Co-operation Programme, for which I offer my thanks. I must also record my gratitude to Nuffield College, Oxford, for the Prize Research Fellowship they awarded me from 1996 to 1999. This, together with grants from the College, allowed me to conduct additional archival research in Berlin in 1997, and to attend conferences around the world where I benefited from those exchanges that are so essential to academic scholarship. This book has evolved and matured through such exchange and discussion. With this in mind, my greatest debt of all is to Professor Tim Blanning, my doctoral supervisor, whose criticism and encouragement, not to mention practical assistance, has proved invaluable over the last nine years. I am also deeply grateful to Professor Wolfgang Schieder, for the welcome he extended me during my visits to Cologne, and to Dr Geoffrey Ellis and Dr Brendan Simms. Many other individuals, too numerous to mention by name, have assisted along the way – the archivists and librarians in Aachen, Berlin, Cambridge, Cologne, Düsseldorf, Koblenz, London, Oxford and Paris; the participants in the many seminars and conferences where I have presented my findings and floated ideas; and, most recently, my colleagues at the School of History, Queen's University Belfast, and especially Professor Peter Jupp. Finally, I would like to thank my wife, for her unfailing support, which has been moral, practical and professional. It goes without saying, I hope, that the responsibility for the various defects of this work is entirely my own.

Queen's University, Belfast   MICHAEL ROWE
July 2002

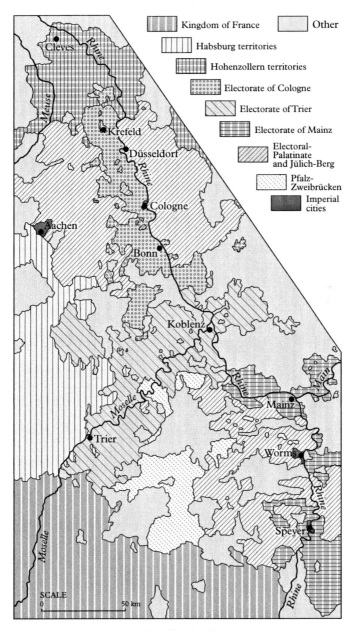

Map 1 The Rhineland in 1789

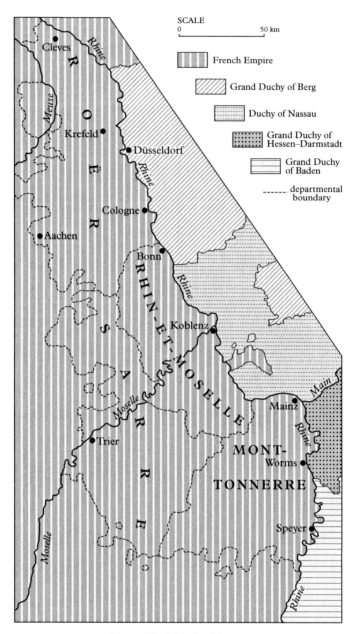

SCALE
0   50 km

French Empire

Grand Duchy of Berg

Duchy of Nassau

Grand Duchy of
Hessen–Darmstadt

Grand Duchy
of Baden

------ departmental
boundary

Cleves

Rhine

R
O
E
R

Meuse

Krefeld

Düsseldorf

Rhine

Cologne

Aachen

Bonn

RHIN-ET-MOSELLE

Rhine

Koblenz

S
A
R
R
E

Moselle

Main

Mainz

Trier

MONT-

Worms

Rhine

TONNERRE

Moselle

Speyer

Rhine

Map 2 The Rhineland in 1812

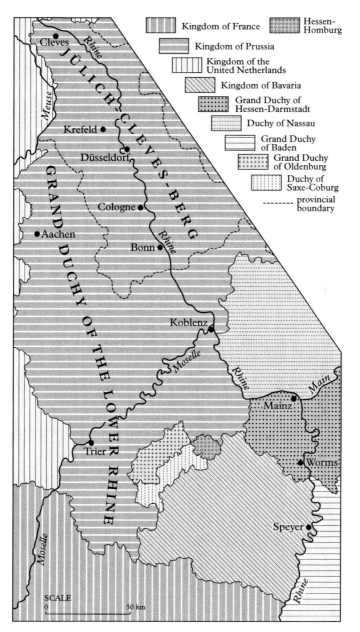

Map 3 The Rhineland in 1820

CHAPTER I

Introduction

This book is concerned with borderlands and transitions. Geographically, it examines a region bordering Germany and France; chronologically, it spans the Old Regime, French Revolution, Napoleon and Restoration. Two reasons justify this focus. First, the Rhineland experienced with unique intensity episodes that shaped modern Germany: the Enlightenment, French Revolution, Napoleon, Prussian reform movement and industrialisation. Each contributed to the development of the state. Second, the modern state that eventually triumphed represented only one of several competing forms that for centuries had co-existed in Europe.[1] Alternatives – the city state, the ecclesiastical state and universal empire – remained uniquely strong and able to command allegiances in the Rhineland until the late eighteenth century, when they were finally overthrown by outside forces. The transformation was completed in a generation.

The Rhineland was especially exposed to the French Revolution. This swept away old structures and created the modern state with its absolute claims to sovereignty. In itself, the state's triumphant progress is a familiar story, often recounted in different contexts. The eventual outcome never appears in doubt, despite resistance and continuities that persist for several generations before succumbing. Yet, such an account is incomplete. It represents the centre's perspective, epitomised by Napoleon's interior minister who impatiently expected government commands to flow to every locality with electric speed. It dismisses opposition as futile and obstructive to progress. It ignores that politics in Germany at least remained primarily local until the late nineteenth century. It ascribes to the locality the status of victim. It fails to recognise that historically peripheries have often ended

---

[1] For the comparatively slow development of the concept 'sovereign state' in Germany, see Hans Boldt and Reinhart Koselleck, 'Staat und Souveränität', in Otto Brunner, Werner Conze and Reinhart Koselleck (eds.), *Geschichtliche Grundbegriffe* (8 vols., Stuttgart, 1972–97), 6, pp. 1–6.

up dominating the centre and that they produce the small sparks that start great fires, to paraphrase Braudel.[2]

The Rhineland's historiography reflects its status as a borderland. It mirrors the present and reflects the past, with each generation of historian addressing contemporary concerns. The comparatively brief period of French dominance during the revolutionary era has attracted controversy ever since the departure of the last Napoleonic *grognard*.[3] Until the mid-twentieth century, competing French and German national agendas dominated. For Germans, the Rhine became a symbol of resistance to French imperialism, whilst generations of Frenchmen were taught that the river represented civilisation's frontier with barbarism. Rhinelanders, caught in-between, felt obliged to assert their essentially German culture against claims from both sides that they tended towards francophilia and ultramontanism.[4] Nationalistic stridency increased in times of Franco-German conflict, especially in the aftermath of the First World War, when historians sought to justify their countries' claims to the Rhineland by reference to Napoleonic rule a century earlier. Only those least preoccupied with contemporary politics and closest to the sources – local historians and archivists – then produced scholarly works that have withstood the tests of time.[5]

---

[2] Fernand Braudel, quoted by Raimondo Strassoldo, 'Centre-Periphery and System-Boundary: Culturological Perspectives', in Jean Gottmann (ed.), *Centre and Periphery. Spatial Variation in Politics* (Beverly Hills and London, 1980), p. 48.

[3] The historiography of the Rhineland in the revolutionary age is itself the subject of a number of articles and at least one doctoral dissertation. An accessible survey is provided by T. C. W. Blanning, *The French Revolution in Germany. Occupation and Resistance in the Rhineland 1792–1802* (Oxford, 1983), pp. 1–17.

[4] Justus Hashagen, for example, felt obliged to introduce his in other respects scholarly study of the Rhineland under French rule with an explicit refutation of accusations that Rhinelanders were somehow pro-French. Justus Hashagen, *Das Rheinland und die französische Herrschaft, Beiträge zur Charakteristik ihres Gegensatzes* (Bonn, 1908), p. 2. Such accusations were no more forthrightly expressed than by Heinrich von Treitschke, who compared Prussia's fight for German freedom with the 'weak willed population' of 'the crozier-ridden lands of the Rhine', who had 'become so foreign to the nation'. Heinrich von Treitschke, *History of Germany in the Nineteenth Century* (translated by Eden Paul and Cedar Paul, London, 1915), pp. 31–2, 59, 73, 107, 138, 146, 149, 200–3, 219. For the anti-Catholicism of the small-German school, see Helmut Walser Smith, *German Nationalism and Religious Conflict. Culture, Ideology, Politics, 1870–1914* (Princeton, 1995), pp. 27–34.

[5] Two representatives of the post-First World War nationalistic French genre are L. Engerand and Jean de Pange, listed in the bibliography. Equally nationalistic, though of greater scholarly worth, is Philippe Sagnac, *Le Rhin français pendant la Révolution et l'Empire* (Paris, 1918). On the German side, see the works by Herrmann Oncken, Alexander Conrady and Max Springer, also listed in the bibliography. Not all publications produced in the interwar period can be dismissed as crudely nationalistic. Max Braubach's contributions on the history of electoral Cologne, for example, remain of great value. See especially *Max Franz von Österreich, letzter Kurfürst von Köln und Fürstbischof von Münster* (Münster, 1925). Amongst the best products of *Landesgeschichte* are Carl Georg Bockenheimer's various publications on the history of Mainz and the numerous contributions published in the *Zeitschrift des Aachener Geschichtsvereins*. As for the professional archivist, a great debt is owed by historians of

Franco-German reconciliation in the 1950s and intellectual developments in the 1960s transformed Rhenish historiography. However, it remained heavily politicised, as it was now enlisted to endow the two German successor states with historical legitimacy. For West Germany, this required emphasis on links with the west, not the discredited Prussian east.[6] Observations such as that of Friedrich Engels the previous century, that the 'character trait of the Rhineland' was 'hatred of Prussianism', were helpful.[7] They played on the notion of Germany's essentially Janian character, the idea one encounters from Madame de Staël to A. J. P. Taylor that Germany possessed a benign western and barbaric eastern face. This justified Prussia's abolition (February 1947) and its replacement by a 'Prussia in the West' (Rhineland-Westphalia, in June 1946) as the new Federal Republic's core. It re-emerged in 1991, with the transfer of reunited Germany's capital to the Spree, in the form of well-worn clichés about Germany 'edging away from Anglo-Saxon & Latin influences'.[8] Politically, this view was exploited by the Federal Republic's first chancellor, Konrad Adenauer, with his vision of a reformed Germany firmly embedded within a western Europe defined by a common Christian heritage. A vision of Germany and Europe centred on Cologne cathedral. It is within this context that one must place Adenauer's reference to his native Cologne as embodying centuries-old western democratic traditions.[9]

For historians it was less medieval civic traditions and Christian heritage, and more the establishment in Mainz in 1792–3 of the first modern republic on German soil, that provided historical justification for membership of the Atlantic world discovered by Palmer and Godechot.[10] It was upon the Mainz Republic and its 'Jacobins' that the postwar generation of Marxist

the Rhineland to Joseph Hansen of the *Historisches Archiv der Stadt Köln*, whose vast collection of annotated documents from the 1780s and 1790s, first published in the 1930s, remains an invaluable source (Joseph Hansen (ed.), *Quellen zur Geschichte des Rheinlandes im Zeitalter der französischen Revolution 1780–1801* (4 vols., Bonn, 1931–8)).

[6] The 'inversed Prussianism' that arguably legitimised the Federal Republic ironically drew upon many of the previously accepted Borussian myths. For more on this, see Stefan Berger, 'Prussia in History and Historiography from the Nineteenth to the Twentieth Centuries', in Philip G. Dwyer (ed.), *Modern Prussian History 1830–1947* (Harlow, 2001), pp. 21–40 (and especially pp. 33–8).

[7] Engels is quoted from Jonathan Sperber, *Rhineland Radicals. The Democratic Movement and the Revolution of 1848–1849* (Princeton, 1991), p. 259.

[8] See, for example, the British press reaction to the move to Berlin, as reflected in *The Times*, 8, 11, 14, 17, 20, 21, 22 June and 12, 15 July 1991.

[9] Hans-Peter Schwarz, *Konrad Adenauer. A German Politician and Statesman in a Period of War, Revolution and Reconstruction* (2 vols., Oxford and Providence, 1995), I, p. 7. Also, Rudolf Augstein, *Konrad Adenauer* (London, 1964), pp. 17, 112.

[10] R. R. Palmer, *The Age of the Democratic Revolution. A Political History of Europe and America, 1760–1800* (2 vols., Princeton, 1959–64), and Jacques Godechot, *France and the Atlantic Revolution of the Eighteenth Century, 1770–1799* (New York, 1965).

historian – both East and West German – lavished attention in order to provide the German states with radical, democratic traditions. The resulting research blossomed in a profusion of publications in the 1960s and 1970s. These have added to our knowledge of one aspect of Rhenish history, but also distorted the overall picture.[11]

Since then, the eastern bloc's collapse and reunification have undermined the context within which *Jakobinerforschung* flourished. Jacobins were not especially prominent in the commemorations held in Rhenish cities in 1994 to mark the bicentenary of French rule. Nor, at a time of European integration, was nationalism. Rather, the commemorations stressed the French contribution to Germany's 'modernisation', though in a less critical way than the academic literature, which sandwiches the concept between qualifying inverted commas.[12] Absent, for example, was the nuance contained in the concept *Gleichzeitigen des Ungleichzeitigen* – the 'deficit of simultaneity' – that arguably distinguishes Germany's path to modernity.[13] Also absent were the sinister overtones associated with another concept linked to modernisation, '*Sozialdizplinierung*' – the state's disciplining of society and the individual – which runs through much of the recent scholarly literature in publications devoted to such areas as public administration, health reform, social relief, prisons and conscription.[14] The old question

---

[11] Amongst the important publications associated with this Marxist genre are: Heinrich Scheel, *Deutscher Jakobinismus und deutsche Nation: ein Beitrag zur nationalen Frage im Zeitalter der Grossen Französischen Revolution* (Berlin, 1966); Walter Grab, *Norddeutsche Jakobiner. Demokratische Bestrebungen zur Zeit der Französischen Revolution* (Frankfurt a. M., 1967); Axel Kuhn, *Jakobiner im Rheinland: der Kölner konstitutionelle Zirkel von 1798* (Stuttgart, 1976); and Helmut Haasis, *Deutscher Jakobiner: Mainzer Republik und Cisrhenan, 1792–1798* (Mainz, 1981). For a lively critique of '*Jakobinerforschung*', see T. C. W. Blanning, 'German Jacobins and the French Revolution', *The Historical Journal* 23 (1980), pp. 985–1002. More balanced in its assessment of the Jacobins is Franz Dumont, *Die Mainzer Republik von 1792/93. Studien zur Revolutionierung in Rheinhessen und der Pfalz* (Alzey, 1982). More balanced in its coverage overall, is Hansgeorg Molitor, *Vom Untertan zum administré. Studien zur französischen Herrschaft und zum Verhalten der Bevölkerung im Rhein-Mosel-Raum von den Revolutionskriegen bis zum Ende der Napoleonischen Zeit* (Wiesbaden, 1980).

[12] For the exhibitions in Aachen and Cologne, see, respectively, Thomas R. Kraus, *Auf dem Weg in die Moderne. Aachen in französischer Zeit, 1792/93, 1794–1814. Handbuch-Katalog zur Ausstellung im Krönungssaal des Aachener Rathauses vom 14. Januar bis zum 5. März 1995* (Aachen, 1994) and Historisches Archiv der Stadt Köln, *Die französischen Jahre. Ausstellung aus Anlaß des Einmarsches der Revolutions Truppen in Köln am 6. Oktober 1794* (Cologne, 1994).

[13] Wolfgang Hartwig, 'Der deutsche Weg in die Moderne. Die Gleichzeitigkeit des Ungleichzeitigen als Grundproblem der deutschen Geschichte 1789–1871', in Wolfgang Hardtwig and Harm-Hinrich Brandt (eds.), *Deutschlands Weg in die Moderne. Politik, Gesellschaft und Kultur im 19. Jahrhundert* (Munich, 1993), pp. 9–31. For an accessible, albeit brief recent discussion in English of the concept '*die Ungleichzeitigkeit des Gleichzeitigen*', and its implications for modernisation theories as pioneered by the German sociologist Max Weber, see Brendan Simms, *The Struggle for Mastery in Germany, 1779–1850* (London, 1998), p. 4.

[14] *Sozialdisziplinierung*, for example, provides the theme running through Josef Smets, *Les Pays rhénans (1794–1814): le comportement des Rhénans face à l'occupation française* (Bern, 1997). More specialised

of 'collaboration' and 'resistance', when its does arise, is now examined through sociological rather than national lenses.[15]

Though displaying distinct features, the Rhineland is an ideal region to test general theories and engage with wider debates concerned with Europe's development in the revolutionary period. Three debates are of particular relevance for this study. The first revolves around the nexus Reich, *Land* and *Stadt*, on the eve of its dissolution. For the first 150 years after its demise, and especially after German unification in 1871, the old Reich was dismissed by the bulk of historical literature. This instead focused upon Prussia's inexorable rise, for which the Holy Roman Empire merely provided a foil. It was only in the 1960s that the Reich's rehabilitation began.[16] This depended upon changing the criteria against which the Reich and its competitors, the territorial states, are judged. Previously, resource mobilisation – the size of armies and tax revenues – provided the yardstick. Today, in this less belligerent age, the emphasis is on conflict resolution. Measured against this criterion, the Empire does well as a surprisingly effective 'community of law and justice'[17] that retained public confidence until the bitter end. The revisionism has now extended so far as to elicit a warning from John Breuilly against naively replacing the distorted Borussian and Marxist teleologies with a new one, that discovers in the Empire a precursor of the European Union. This fear is exaggerated, as the extent to which the Reich proved capable of evolution remains controversial. However, historians have at least rediscovered the imperial reform debate of the 1780s and 1790s,

---

literature includes: (on the French administration) Sabine Graumann, *Französische Verwaltung am Niederrhein. Das Roerdepartement 1798–1814* (Essen, 1990); (on prisons) Norbert Finzsch, 'Zur "Ökonomie des Strafens": Gefängniswesen und Gefängnisreform im Roerdépartement nach 1794', *Rheinische Vierteljahrsblätter* 54 (1990), pp. 188–210; (public health provision) Calixte Hudemann-Simon, *L'Etat et la santé: la politique de santé publique ou "police médicale" dans les quatre départements rhénans, 1794–1814* (Sigmaringen, 1995); (poverty relief) idem, *L'Etat et les pauvres: l'assistance et la lutte contre la mendicité dans les quatre départements rhénans, 1794–1814* (Sigmaringen, 1997); and (on conscription) Josef Smets, 'Von der "Dorfidylle" zur preußischen Nation. Sozialdisziplinierung der linksrheinischen Bevölkerung durch die Franzosen am Beispiel der allgemeinen Wehrpflicht (1802–1814)', *Historische Zeitschrift* 262 (1996), pp. 695–738.

[15] For this approach applied on a European level, see Michael Broers, *Europe under Napoleon 1799–1815* (London, 1996).

[16] Karl Otmar Freiherr von Aretin led the rehabilitation of the old Empire with *Heiliges Römisches Reich 1776–1806* (2 vols., Wiesbaden, 1967). For a historiographical review of the early revisionism, see Gerald Strauss, 'The Holy Roman Empire Revisited', *Central European History* 11 (1978), pp. 290–301. In English, see especially: J. A. Vann, *The Swabian Kreis. Institutional Growth in the Holy Roman Empire, 1648–1715* (Brussels, 1975); John G. Gagliardo, *Reich and Nation. The Holy Roman Empire as Idea and Reality, 1763–1806* (Bloomington, 1980); and, more recently, Peter H. Wilson, *German Armies. War and German Politics, 1648–1806* (London, 1998), which convincingly argues that the Empire, at times, was even quite effective on the military front.

[17] To use John G. Gagliardo's apt formulation, employed in *Reich and Nation*, pp. 42–3.

and so extended back by fifty years the beginnings of Germany's modern constitutional development.[18]

The Rhineland formed the western extremity of the 'unique combination of centrifugal dispersion of political authority counterbalanced by the centripetal forces of imperial law and German culture'[19] that was the Empire. More than any other region apart from the south-west, it epitomised the values upon which the Empire rested. Its political landscape, dominated by ecclesiastical electorates, imperial cities, home towns, imperial abbeys, counts and knights, and a plethora of other entities that elsewhere had succumbed to early-modern state formation, survived so long thanks to the protective legal cocoon provided by the Reich. In that sense, the parochial depended upon the universal, a connection still evident in Cologne whose gothic cathedral boasts prebendal stools reserved for the Emperor and Pope. Historically, the Rhineland is rich in other sources that help us better understand the alternative order the Reich represented: its foundations, legitimacy and potential for reform.

Rehabilitation of the Reich has extended to encompass entities dependent upon it. These included the ecclesiastical states, the archetypal territorial unit in the pre-revolutionary Rhineland that earned it the unflattering sobriquet 'die Pfaffengasse' ('the priests' alley'). Worthy of ridicule and condemnation for their religious intolerance and lack of dynamism, earlier generations of nationalist historian identified their major failing as their inability to protect Germany's western marches from French expansionism.[20] However, as with the Reich, the adoption of criteria other than military power as a measure of success, including education, culture and general quality of life, has shed a more positive light on these states. They might have represented the antithesis of the Protestant work ethic, but (probably for that reason) commanded the allegiance of their subjects.[21] The same

---

[18] Horst Dippel, 'Der Verfassungsdiskurs im ausgehenden 18. Jahrhundert und die Grundlegung einer liberaldemokratischen Verfassungstradition in Deutschland', in idem (ed.), *Die Anfänge des Konstitutionalismus in Deutschland. Texte deutscher Verfassungsentwürfe am Ende des 18. Jahrhunderts* (Frankfurt a. M., 1991), pp. 8–9. The full reference to Breuilly is John Breuilly, 'The National Idea in Modern German History', in idem (ed.), *The State of Germany. The National Idea in the Making, Unmaking and Remaking of a Modern Nation-State* (London and New York, 1992), p. 3.

[19] Another pithy summary that encapsulates the essential nature of the Reich, on this occasion from T. C. W. Blanning, *Joseph II* (London, 1994), p. 9.

[20] Within this context, it is worth noting that German travellers returning from Paris during the French Revolution commonly held up the ecclesiastical Rhenish states as a foil to the dynamism and progressiveness of France. Uwe Hentschel, 'Revolutionserlebnis und Deutschlandbild', *Zeitschrift für historische Forschung* 20 (1993), pp. 321–44.

[21] Peter Hersche, 'Intendierte Rückständigkeit: Zur Charakteristik des geistlichen Staates im Alten Reich', in Georg Schmidt (ed.), *Stände und Gesellschaft im Alten Reich* (Stuttgart, 1989), pp. 147–8. In English, see above all T. C. W. Blanning, *Reform and Revolution in Mainz 1743–1803* (Cambridge, 1974).

applies to the imperial cities and home towns, entities that also previously faced condemnation as conservative bastions against 'movers and doers', but have more recently enjoyed some rehabilitation as a result of a separate debate over the origins of early German liberalism, discussed below.[22]

Research into the origins of German liberalism and constitutional development connects with another institution dependent upon the Reich for survival in the eighteenth century, the representative estates (*Landstände*). These, whose precise composition varied where they persisted, not only survived but experienced a revival before the French Revolution. They served to check the onward march of princely absolutism. Scholarly debate revolves around the extent to which they represented precursors of nineteenth-century parliaments. Opinions remain divided on this, and the danger of assessing the *Landstände* according to whether they resembled nineteenth-century assemblies needs to be recognised. Those who argue that they offered no prospect for further development point to their foundation upon the concept of a society of orders, and failure to embrace the notion of *individual* rights that underpins all modern constitutions. According to this line, the intervening phase of 'bureaucratic state absolutism' of the Napoleonic period that destroyed the old estates was, paradoxically, a necessary precursor for later liberal constitutional development. The alternative explanation asserts that whether or not the *Landstände* were open to reform depended upon the nature of the society they represented: in places like Württemberg, where the bourgeoisie provided the dominant element, the estates were more progressive than in the Mecklenburg duchies, dominated by the landed nobility. This explanation privileges the socio-economic over the institutional. Whether the *Landstände* were '*Reformfähig*' depends upon where one looks.[23] Certainly, the *Landstände* remained significant in the eighteenth-century Rhineland, and this did have implications for later developments, as this book will show.

Whether the order of Reich, *Land* and *Stadt* was '*Reformfähig*' in the late eighteenth century might appear pointless speculation. After all, did not Napoleon sweep aside this order, preparing the ground for the sovereign

---

[22] For an accessible and still useful example of the older, more negative literature on the home towns, see Mack Walker, *German Home Towns: Community, State, General Estate, 1648–1871* (New York, 1971).

[23] The volume of literature produced over the last twenty years that is devoted to the representative estates is considerable. Groundbreaking, in many respects, was the collection of essays in Karl Bosl and Karl Möckl (eds.), *Der moderne Parlamentarismus und seine Grundlagen in der ständischen Repräsentation* (Berlin, 1977). Amongst more recent contributions, see Eberhard Weis, 'Kontinuität und Diskontinuität zwischen den Ständen des 18. Jahrhunderts und den frühkonstitutionellen Parlamenten von 1818/1819 in Bayern und Württemberg', in idem (ed.), *Deutschland und Frankreich um 1800. Aufklärung – Revolution – Reform* (Munich, 1990), pp. 218–42; and Dippel, 'Verfassungsdiskurs'.

state? This might be considered especially true of the Rhineland, where Napoleonic hegemony was experienced most intensely. However, such a position is only defensible if it is accepted – as much of the literature does – that Napoleon was a revolutionary whose rule marked a new beginning. It is this study's contention that whilst French rule did result in momentous change, the new order that eventually emerged represented a synthesis that drew on the Old Regime's legacy. The older literature, which portrays the eighteenth-century Rhineland as a backward region distinguished by a conservative *Volkskultur*, tends to exaggerate the drama of French rule. The period of French domination can only be comprehensively assessed by placing it within the context of what happened before and after, as well as by looking at the principles of Napoleonic governance elsewhere in Europe.

This leads to the second great historiographical debate, that concerned with Napoleon. Napoleon has inspired a mass of research. One dimension of this concerns his location within the revolutionary tradition and in particular, on the social basis of his regime. Beginning in the 1970s, research on the so-called *notabilités* undermined the Marxist notion of 1789 as a bourgeois revolution, and instead demonstrated that the Napoleonic elite consisted of essentially the same fusion of elements that were already emerging into prominence under the auspices of the Old Regime.[24] A second, related area of research that has resulted in several important publications over recent years concerns the state-formation process. Based upon local as well as national archival resources and hence better informed on the perspective from below, this research questions the extent to which the Napoleonic state – an institution that appeared uncompromisingly formidable on paper – penetrated downwards in practice.[25] Though it ultimately imposed its will in the key areas that really mattered to Napoleon – taxation and conscription – it did so through a process of negotiation and adaptation as well as brute force. Napoleon emerges from these studies less as a revolutionary or counter-revolutionary than as a pragmatic manager who drew on dominant elements and traditions within a locality where they served his interests. With respect to the Rhineland, it might be believed that there were few

---

[24] Seminal for our understanding of the 'notables' is the survey into the departmental elites, Louis Bergeron and G. Chaussinand-Nogaret, *Les 'Masses de granit': cent mille notables du Premier Empire* (Paris, 1979). Also, see Geoffrey Ellis, 'Rhine and Loire: Napoleonic Elites and Social Order' in G. Lewis and L. Lucas (eds.), *Beyond the Terror: Essays in French Regional and Social History, 1794–1815* (Cambridge, 1983); and, most recently of all, Rafe Blaufarb, 'The *Ancien Régime* Origins of Napoleonic Social Reconstruction', *French History* 14 (2000), pp. 408–23.

[25] Two relatively recent studies on Napoleonic state formation from below stand out: Alan Forrest, *Conscripts and Deserters. The Army and French Society during the Revolution and Empire* (Oxford, 1989); and, more general in its focus, Isser Woloch, *The New Regime. Transformations of the French Civic Order, 1789–1820s* (New York and London, 1994).

such elements and traditions that might be profitably drawn upon. After all, did not the region historically represent the very antithesis of the demanding sovereign state that was Napoleonic France? Yet, it will be argued, Rhinelanders found much in the Napoleonic system they liked. It was not just that Napoleon was adept at rallying established elites – that in itself is not startling – but rather, that he allowed reinvigoration of practices, traditions and, more subtly, *mentalités* commonly associated with the old order. This was especially apparent in the area of law, conflict-resolution and those institutions that mitigated the authoritarianism also inherent in the Napoleonic style of government. Napoleonic institutions ultimately enjoyed such longevity in the region – the Code Napoléon remained in effect until 1900 – not because they swept away the previous order or imposed 'social discipline', but because they were in harmony with what went before.

Reappraisal of the Old Regime and Napoleon has implications for our understanding of developments following Napoleon's fall and hence connects with a third historiographical area, concerned with nineteenth-century Germany. Over the last decades, this has been especially focused on the middle class (*Bürgertum*) and its attendant ideology, liberalism, both of which were peculiarly strong in the Rhineland. Two projects begun in the 1980s, in Bielefeld (*'Sozialgeschichte des neuzeitlichen Bürgertums: Deutschland im internationalen Vergleich'*) and Frankfurt (*'Stadt und Bürgertum im 19. Jahrhundert'*) have contributed to our understanding. The second project – led by Lothar Gall – with its focus on the interaction between the historically rooted town burghers (*Städtebürgertum*) and the emerging middle class defined by wealth (*Besitz*) and education (*Bildung*), is especially interesting for this study.[26] It gives due weight to the contribution made by old civic traditions to Germany's modern political development. Early liberalism, according to this interpretation, was founded socially upon an amalgamation of the new middle classes and the *Städtebürgertum*, and hence represented an uneasy compromise between two value systems, the one based on individualism and private property and the other on notions

---

[26] The Frankfurt project, headed by Lothar Gall, examined seventeen cities, including Aachen and Cologne. Apart from specialised studies on the cities themselves, this project has also produced several edited collections that present the research findings. These include Lothar Gall (ed.), *Vom alten zum neuen Bürgertum. Die mitteleuropäische Stadt im Umbruch 1780–1820* (*Historische Zeitschrift* Beiheft 14, Munich, 1991); and idem (ed.), *Stadt und Bürgertum im Übergang von der traditionalen zur modernen Gesellschaft* (Munich, 1993). Also, more recently idem (ed.), *Bürgertum und bürgerlich-liberale Bewegung in Mitteleuropa seit dem 18. Jahrhundert* (*Historische Zeitschrift* Sonderheft Band 17, Munich, 1997), which includes an excellent survey of the current state of research on the emergence of the modern bourgeoisie and liberalism, Elisabeth Fehrenbach, 'Bürgertum und Liberalismus. Die Umbruchsperiode 1770–1815', pp. 1–62.

of commonweal and civic autonomy. The first, 'newer' value system pre-dominated in north German liberalism, the second 'older' ingredient in the south, with the divide running through the Rhineland. What united both was a shared hostility to the nobility as well as to the *arbitrary* exercise of power by the prince. This socially broad-based liberal ideology emerged at the end of the eighteenth century, and dissolved under the pressures of the second great revolution, the industrial, which hit Germany with full force in the mid-nineteenth century. Thereafter, liberalism degenerated into an elitist class ideology of the upper bourgeoisie that withered electorally in the face of new mass movements, political Catholicism and socialism.

Gall's thesis of a socially broad-based liberalism is not universally accepted. Doubts centre on the ability of the old *Städtebürgertum* to liberate itself from a social vision centred on privileged orders. According to this critique, the emergence of modern liberalism depended upon the rise of a new elite that defined itself through wealth and talent rather than through ancient civic affiliations.[27] This study draws on and seeks to contribute to this debate, a debate of especial significance for a region whose political culture was dominated by the *Bürgertum* in the nineteenth century. On its conclusions rest our assessment of how deeply rooted and hence how durable its values were. To this end, this book is divided into three parts. The first examines developments under the Old Regime and ends with consideration of the French Revolution's impact, the Revolutionary Wars, and the establishment in Mainz of the first modern republic on German soil. The second focuses on the Napoleonic episode, exploring how Bona-partism functioned in practice, the degree of continuity and change, social, economic and cultural developments, attempts by the French to mould identity, and military conscription. The third, finally, examines the transition from French to Prussian/Bavarian rule, including an assessment of German nationalism, debate over the French legacy, and the successor states' attempts to integrate their new trans-Rhenish territories on their own terms.

---

[27] For this point of view, see Fehrenbach, 'Bürgertum und Liberalismus', pp. 16–22. For an intermediate position, see Michael Stolleis, who argues that the old *Bürgertum* did not make the switch to modern individualism, but that its self-perceptions nonetheless developed into a new form. Michael Stolleis (ed.), *Recht, Verfassung und Verwaltung in der frühneuzeitlichen Stadt* (Cologne, 1991), p. xiii. Much of the debate hinges around changing perceptions of commonweal and private property. For this, see Winfried Schulze, 'Vom Gemeinnutz zum Eigennutz. Über den Normenwandel in der ständischen Gesellschaft der Frühen Neuzeit', *Historische Zeitschrift* 243 (1986), pp. 591–626.

PART I

1780–1801: Enlightenment, revolution, occupation

CHAPTER 2

Land, Stadt *and Reich*

Rivers convey ideas as well as merchandise, Victor Hugo observed during his Rhineland tour of 1838–9.[1] Though essentially a geographical expression, the 'Rhineland' encompasses a distinct if diverse historico-cultural space, albeit one whose precise limits have varied over time. Like many, Hugo was especially captivated by the central stretch of the river, the Middle Rhine, which flows between Bingen and Bonn. Enclosed by rocky hills, this segment presents the familiar panorama of ruined castles and vineyards clinging precariously to terraces. Less known are the upper reaches of the Rhine, between Basel and Mainz, where the wide and shallow river valley is bordered by the Black Forest in the east and Vosges in the west, and the lower reaches north of Bonn, where the Rhine undergoes its second metamorphosis as it merges with the great northern European plain.[2]

The Rhine has moulded its surrounding landscape and shaped the civilisation that developed along its banks over the last two millennia. Rome, whose legions stood on its banks for the first four centuries after Christ, left its indelible mark in the form of cities – notably, Moguntiacum (Mainz), Confluentia (Koblenz), Colonia Agrippina (Cologne) and Augusta Treverorum (Trier) – and the Church. These survived Roman rule and the subsequent Frankish epoch that closed with the Carolingian Empire's collapse in the ninth century. They survived over the following centuries, within the framework of the Holy Roman Empire. Architecturally, Romanesque abbeys and cathedrals attest to the medieval Church's vitality. Institutionally, it was reflected in the concentration of three archbishoprics within the region: Mainz, Cologne and Trier. These combined spiritual and temporal power and, together with the only significant secular ruler, the Counts Palatine, were elevated to electors in the fourteenth century. Concurrently, Rome's other great legacy, the cities, also witnessed a highpoint

---

[1] Victor Hugo, *Le Rhin. Lettres à un ami* (2 vols., Paris, 1912, Nelson edn), 1, pp. 189–90.
[2] Étienne Juillard, *L'Europe rhénane. Géographie d'un grand éspace* (Paris, 1968).

in their fortunes based upon lucrative commerce flowing along the Rhine. As imperial strength diminished, these two powers – the cities and archbishops – came into conflict. In Mainz, the archbishops emerged as victors, but in Cologne they fled the city and established themselves in nearby Bonn. In Trier, the outcome was indecisive.

Rhenish prosperity declined in the early modern period. America's discovery hastened the shift of economic gravity towards the Atlantic and away from the trade route connecting the Low Countries and north Italy. The religious wars following the Reformation reinforced economic decline. Only after their termination with the Westphalian Peace (1648) could the reconstruction begin. Louis XIV's wars proved a temporary setback to this, but uninterrupted regeneration followed in the eighteenth century. Politically, the region now occupied the margins. With the beginning of Austro-Prussian rivalry in 1740 and the 'diplomatic revolution' of 1756 that ended centuries of Franco-Habsburg conflict, great-power struggle shifted towards east-central Europe. France accepted the status quo in Germany and responded with subtle gravitation towards Prussia rather than direct intervention when this was threatened by the Habsburgs in the 1770s and 1780s.[3] The Rhineland's demotion to the strategic periphery was confirmed when the ecclesiastical electorates finally dropped out of the European arms race at the beginning of the eighteenth century.[4]

The Rhineland's medieval territorial order thereby survived into the 1780s. The ecclesiastical electorates covered the larger part of the 8,500 square mile territorial patchwork of the German-speaking left bank. To the south lay Mainz, the bulk of whose 3,200 square miles and 300,000 mainly Catholic inhabitants were clustered along the Lower Main valley rather than the Rhineland proper. Its ruler, Friedrich Karl Joseph zu Erthal (1774–1802), was a vain prince who entertained ambitions in keeping with his dignity as imperial chancellor, placing him second in the Reich's hierarchy after the Emperor himself. To the west, occupying the Moselle's banks, was Trier, with an area and mainly Catholic population comparable in size to Mainz. Trier's last elector, Clemens Wenzeslaus (1768–1802; d. 1812), was a Saxon Wettin who enjoyed familial ties with the Habsburgs and Bourbons (he was an uncle of Louis XVI of France). His elevation as elector in 1768 was celebrated as reinforcing the Vienna–Versailles alliance. To the north of Trier lay Cologne, which like Mainz straddled the Rhine. Its left-bank possessions encompassed 1,025 square miles containing 200,000 overwhelmingly Catholic souls. Its elector on the eve of the French Revolution, Max Franz

[3] Eckhard Buddruss, *Die französische Deutschlandpolitik 1756–1789* (Mainz, 1995).
[4] Peter H. Wilson, *German Armies. War and German Politics, 1648–1806* (London, 1998), pp. 29–30, 66, 90–3, 104–6, 162, 282–3.

(1784–1801), was the youngest brother of Emperor Joseph II (1765–90) and a model enlightened prince. Of the numerous secular territories, the most significant was the Wittelsbach agglomeration, including the duchies of Jülich and Berg in the Lower Rhine, and the Rhineland-Palatinate and Pfalz-Zweibrücken along the Middle Rhine. After 1777, all these territories with the exception of Pfalz-Zweibrücken were governed from Munich by Elector Karl Theodor (Elector Palatine, 1742–99). Pfalz-Zweibrücken, a cluster south of the Moselle containing 80,000 mainly Protestant inhabitants, remained under a cadet Wittelsbach branch in the shape of the eccentric Duke Karl II August (1775–95). His main achievement was Schloß Karlsberg, a vast set of pavilions whose construction bankrupted the duchy and triggered the eighteenth-century equivalent of IMF intervention in the form of a Reich investigative commission. The other great dynasty with a sizeable stake in the Rhineland were the Hohenzollerns. Their possessions included the duchies of Cleves and Geldern, and Lordship of Moers, together with a substantial bloc straddling the Lower Rhine containing a confessionally mixed population of about 125,000. Apart from these territories, the Rhineland boasted four of the Reich's fifty-one imperial cities: Cologne (population: 45,000) and Aachen (27,000), both overwhelmingly Catholic and located in the north, and predominantly Protestant Speyer (5,000) and Worms (6,000) in the south. Finally, the left bank counted nearly 100 additional quasi-sovereign (*Reichsunmittelbar*: enjoying unmediated relations with the Emperor) entities, ruled over by imperial counts, abbots, abbesses and lords, whose populations were measured in the thousands if not hundreds.

Historical development lent Rhenish political culture distinct features. However, before these are examined, it is logical to analyse the socio-economic context. As noted, shambolic territorial arrangements and surviving medieval forms did not prevent the Rhineland from experiencing economic recovery in the eighteenth century. Population grew rapidly in the century, surpassing the pre-Thirty Years' War level in the 1720s and rising by a total of 30 per cent until it reached the 1.5 million mark on the eve of French rule. Demographic pressure became acute in some areas. The Palatinate produced almost 10,000 (over 5 per cent of population) emigrants between 1776 and 1785 alone, most of whom settled in Poland, Transylvania, Russia and the Americas.[5] Population increase meant greater demand for agricultural products and higher prices; this, combined with

[5] Walter Rödel, 'Demographische Entwicklung in Deutschland und Frankreich', in Helmut Berding, Etienne François, and Hans-Peter Ullmann (eds.), *Deutschland und Frankreich im Zeitalter der Revolution* (Frankfurt a. M., 1988), pp. 28–38.

physiocratic appreciation of agriculture and an inflow of new ideas from Britain and the Netherlands, stimulated improvement, though this was uneven. Whilst most of the region adhered to the three-field system, areas with richer soil along the alluvial plane of the Lower Rhine practised crop rotation, whilst in the barren Eifel a two-field system persisted. However, the manorial system had disappeared throughout as long ago as the twelfth century. Instead, a varied pattern of tenancy dominated the landscape in which personal, non-monetary obligations played a comparatively small role, though they were more common in the south.[6] In the north, hereditary tenure was common, a form that created a degree of certainty and hence investment. Hereditary tenants could divide the land freely and sub-let, something that encouraged flexibility in response to market pressures. About one-third of agricultural land, including most Church land, was however subject to fixed-term tenancies that generally ranged from six to twenty-four years. These did not usually allow for further sub-division, but rather preserved larger units (200 acres or more). Generally, such tenancies included obligations on the tenant to ensure that the land did not deteriorate. Arguably, fixed-term tenure stimulated productivity in that it allowed landlords to benefit from rising prices by periodically increasing rents.[7]

New methods, including greater use of fertilisation, boosted productivity. Fertilisation required livestock, which in turn depended upon well-tended pastures, new fodder crops and stall feeding. When in place, a virtuous circle ensued that allowed for the transition from the three-field system to crop-rotation. In practice, this was limited to the Lower Rhine, with its rich pastures, whilst stall feeding was only common in parts of the Middle Rhine where pastures were lacking. Dairy farming, which was concentrated near urban centres, was a relatively commercialised sector and employed up-to-date methods introduced from the Netherlands. Elsewhere, arable farming, with the cultivation of cereals and especially rye, predominated. The flat lands between Aachen and Cologne were especially productive. Here a wealthy class of tenant farmer prospered through the export of surpluses to the Netherlands. Apart from cereals, there were scattered pockets of market

---

[6] There was a tendency in the Middle Rhine towards a greater exploitation of feudal dues in the last decades before the French invasion. Roger Dufraisse, 'L'Influence de la domination française sur l'économie du Palatinate', in idem, *L'Allemagne à l'époque napoléonienne. Questions d'histoire politique, économique et sociale* (Bonn and Berlin, 1992), pp. 105–10.

[7] Volker Henn, 'Die soziale und wirtschaftliche Lage der rheinischen Bauern im Zeitalter des Absolutismus', *Rheinische Vierteljahrsblätter* 42 (1978), pp. 242–5; also, idem, 'Zur Lage der rheinischen Landwirtschaft im 16. bis 18. Jahrhundert', *Zeitschrift für Agrargeschichte und Agrarsoziologie* 21 (1973), pp. 173–88.

gardening as well as commercial crops of tobacco and flax, not to mention the vineyards of the Moselle and Middle Rhine.

Agriculture depended ultimately upon geography and climate, but it is important not to overlook institutions. Legally, equal inheritance was the norm for most of the Rhineland with the exception of the far north, where impartible inheritance predominated. Some have linked this to the greater political radicalism of the south compared with the north.[8] However, one should not exaggerate the distinction. Studies from elsewhere in Europe suggest that neither type of inheritance was common in its pure form, and that pragmatic considerations rather than law dictated practice. The pattern of agriculture determined inheritance, not the reverse. This would remain so even after the French Revolution, when a diversity of systems of preferential partibility survived irrespective of the Napoleonic code. In any case, in areas like the Rhineland with widespread leasehold, inheritance made little impact on the size of farms, which was determined primarily by economic considerations.[9] These dictated that isolated farmsteads and larger holdings should represent the norm in the north, and village settlements and smaller farms dominate the south. Nor should it be assumed that parcelisation necessarily represented an impediment to improvement. Even in the Palatinate, where parcelisation was acute, development proceeded thanks to government encouragement and demographic pressure. It was one of the first regions in Germany to experiment with cultivation of the potato. In the decades before the French invasion, the Palatine government successfully encouraged land reclamation, all-year stall-feeding, the use of mineral fertilisers and enclosure, and established model farms that cultivated clover, turnips and potatoes, which it then made a concerted effort to introduce from the 1760s onwards. A similar effort was made with tobacco in the 1770s. Comparable government-led attempts at innovation and improvement occurred elsewhere, especially in Mainz.[10]

Inevitably, there was resistance to innovation. Peasants uprooted new crops and hacked down apparently useless novelties such as mulberry trees. More fundamentally, legal complexities, common rights and obligations deriving from the dispersal of plots, and the tithe, obstructed the new

---

[8] Thomas Theuringer, *Liberalismus im Rheinland. Voraussetzungen und Ursprünge im Zeitalter der Aufklärung* (Frankfurt a. M., 1998), p. 53.

[9] Lutz K. Berkner and Franklin F. Mendels, 'Inheritance Systems, Family Structure, and Demographic Patterns in Western Europe, 1700–1900', in Charles Tilly (ed.), *Historical Studies in Changing Fertility* (Princeton, 1978), pp. 214–20.

[10] Mainrad Schaab, *Geschichte der Kurpfalz* (2 vols., Stuttgart, 1988–92), 2 (*Neuzeit*), pp. 221–8; T. C. W. Blanning, *Reform and Revolution in Mainz 1743–1803* (Cambridge, 1974), pp. 91–3, 185–7.

crops and methods.[11] Nor was an inequitable fiscal system helpful. For though taxes were comparatively low, they fell disproportionately on the land. Worse, they weighed excessively on a proportion because large tracts enjoyed exemption thanks to privileged status or because of out-of-date land cadastres. Electoral Cologne's most recent land survey had been completed in 1669. This had assessed property not according to area but commercial value, something likely to change after a century. Furthermore, land brought under cultivation after 1669 was not assessed at all, whilst a further one-third was recorded as exempt from tax because it was owned by the nobility or Church which, with its 90,000 acres, was the greatest landowner.[12] Though tax exemption benefited tenants through lower rents, it nonetheless provoked mounting criticism with the arrival of ideas associated with French physiocracy, which held the peasantry as the economic foundation of the state. Especially influential was Gaspard de Réal's publication *Science du gouvernement* (1761–4), which argued that the Church should share the tax burden for the common good. Yet, despite institutional weaknesses, the Old Regime bequeathed the French a thriving agricultural sector that was capable of further adaptation and increasingly commercialised.

A healthy agricultural sector contributed to the Rhineland's emergence by the late eighteenth century as one of Germany's most advanced manufacturing regions. That said, manufacturing was still limited to unevenly spread pockets. It was largely absent from electoral Cologne, Mainz, Trier and the Palatinate, but predominated in Jülich and Berg, Aachen and the Prussian enclave of Krefeld. Berg, located on the right bank, experienced the most dramatic economic development. There, religious tolerance combined with abundant natural resources proved a winning combination. Meanwhile, Jülich's natural advantages – high population density (cheap labour), nearby highlands dotted with sheep (wool), moors covered in peat (fuel), and lime-free water (needed for the washing, dyeing and fulling process) from the Rur – facilitated the development of a thriving textile sector centred on Monschau. Nearby Aachen inadvertently provided know-how in the form of Lutherans escaping discrimination. Above all, commercial freedom encouraged prosperity. To quote one contemporary:

The general well-being of this land has resulted from the freedom of commercial action, and from the factories and businesses which have developed in this freedom. Trade and factory business have risen to a peak since 1742, and particularly in the

---

[11] Henn, 'Bauern', pp. 252ff.
[12] Karl Essers, *Zur Geschichte der kurkölnischen Landtage im Zeitalter der französischen Revolution (1790–1797)* (Gotha, 1909), pp. 22–33, 100, 105, 124.

last ten years, because of an undisturbed freedom of trade. It is a peak which the other German states will strive in vain to reach, so long as they continue to allow monopolies, controlled markets, and the like. Commercial freedom, which many a foreign country would make such a show of, is enjoyed here by every manufacturer and merchant without fuss and without advertisement. Here there is no inspection by excise-officers and such like.[13]

Not all industrial development resulted from economic liberty, however. The spectacular success of the von der Leyens in Krefeld, for example, depended largely upon support from the Prussian state. The von der Leyens were Mennonites who found refuge in Krefeld in the 1650s, after being driven from Berg. In 1763, their textile business employed 2,800 individuals, and by 1794 their capital amounted to 1,279,000 *Reichsthaler*. Monopoly rights first conceded under the Austrian occupation during the Seven Years War and subsequently confirmed by Berlin partly accounted for their success.[14]

The von der Leyens' success can also be accredited to the absence of guild restrictions in Krefeld. Economic histories are uniformly negative in their appraisal of the guilds. Certainly, by the eighteenth century their original function as guarantors of quality had receded behind self-interested obstruction of competition. However, their influence was declining in the eighteenth century. Many were heavily indebted and faced attack on several fronts, as will be examined below. At the imperial level, legislation (in 1731) diminished their social and political role within the Reich, whilst Joseph II further undermined their position in his domains in the 1780s. In addition, many individual territories sought to limit guild autonomy, whilst elsewhere businessmen undermined them from within.[15] New, lucrative niche sectors ranging from tobacco to eau de Cologne developed outside the guilds, often under enterprising immigrants. The same was true with the putting-out system employed by the textile industry. In short, the guilds no longer

[13] E. F. Wiebeking, *Essays on the History of the States of the Palatinate, with Particular Reference to the Duchy of Jülich and Berg, 1742–92* (Heidelberg and Mannheim, 1793), quoted in Max Barkhausen, 'Government Control and Free Enterprise in Western Germany and the Low Countries in the Eighteenth Century', in Peter Earle (ed.), *Essays in European Economic History 1500–1800* (Oxford, 1974), p. 225.

[14] Wilhelm Kurschat, *Das Haus Friedrich & Heinrich von der Leyen in Krefeld. Zur Geschichte der Rheinlande in der Zeit der Fremdherrschaft 1794–1814* (Frankfurt a. M., 1933), passim.

[15] For Mainz's guilds, see Friedrich Schmitt, *Das Mainzer Zunftwesen und die französische Herrschaft. Ein Beitrag zur Charakteristik ihres Gegensatzes* (Darmstadt, 1929), pp. 9, 12–16, 19, 28–41. For those of Aachen, Michael Sobania, 'Das Aachener Bürgertum am Vorabend der Industrialisierung', in Lothar Gall (ed.), *Vom alten zum neuen Bürgertum. Die mitteleuropäische Stadt im Umbruch 1780–1820* (*Historische Zeitschrift* Beiheft 14 Munich, 1991), pp. 187–8.

proved a serious hindrance within the region as a whole, though they might hold back individual towns and cities.

One reason for this was the Rhineland's territorial fragmentation. Fragmentation might be considered inimical to economic development. Yet, in an era of porous borders (even the Reich's frontier with France was properly policed only after 1789) fragmentation encouraged development. Certainly, it failed to prevent the establishment of business connections that transcended frontiers and the formation of a *regional* economic elite. It failed to prevent, for example, the marriage of the daughter of Aachen's most important cloth manufacturer, Esajas von Clermont, to Friedrich Heinrich Jacobi, a prominent Düsseldorf merchant and councillor for industrial affairs; or the establishment of familial ties between the Lutheran manufacturing aristocracy of Monschau and the economic elites of Aachen, Burtscheid, Krefeld, Berg and Mark; or the marriage of Palatine merchant families into Krefeld's manufacturing elite. Larger firms, like families, transcended borders. Monschau's largest enterprises, for example, had branches extending into Prussian, Palatine and Austrian territory. The putting-out network of the von der Leyens extended well beyond the Prussian enclave of Krefeld into Jülich-Berg and electoral Cologne. Territorial fragmentation encouraged economic liberalism by making the alternative impractical. It encouraged competition for investment, which resulted in policies beneficial for business, including greater religious tolerance and favourable tax regimes. For example, in much of Germany, tax was substantially derived from excise duties levied on commerce passing through town gates; this was impractical in the Rhineland, partly because so much industry was located in the countryside, but also because territorial fragmentation meant that trade could be diverted towards towns with the most competitive tax regimes. In the Prussian enclaves, for example, peasants purchased goods in neighbouring territories where taxes were lower. Over time, fiscal competition resulted in lower taxes everywhere and harmonisation between town and country, and a shift to direct property taxes.[16] The advantages of territorial fragmentation were recognised by enlightened contemporaries, such as Franz Wilhelm von Spiegel, curator of Bonn university, who ascribed Germany's cultural renaissance to inter-territorial competition; or the future Mainz Clubbist Georg Forster, who praised fragmentation because it stimulated competition and therefore reform; or Niklas Vogt, an early liberal, who argued that the state's role was to guarantee freedom rather than itself instigate improvements, and that fragmentation helped preserve

---

[16] Barkhausen, 'Government', pp. 212–73.

freedom.[17] In conclusion, the political and social structures of the old-regime Rhineland were more conducive to economic development than they have generally been credited for.

Contemporaries blamed the lack of manufacturing in the ecclesiastical states on the persistence within them of sectarian bigotry and baroque religiosity. The linkage is unproven and arguably territorial fragmentation mitigated the worst confessional discrimination. Certainly, vibrant popular piety distinguished the *Pfaffengasse*. In towns and cities, religious brother-hoods gave institutional expression to this and served as points of social orientation. Closely associated with the guilds, they provided material and spiritual relief and sponsored public festivals that bound civic culture to religion.[18] In the countryside, quasi-religious peasant superstitions persisted within a few leagues of enlightened beacons like Bonn and Mainz universities. As late as the early nineteenth century, there was a reported case of a suspected witch being lynched in the Lower Rhine.[19]

More commonly, bigotry expressed itself in religious intolerance. The Rhineland, though mainly Catholic, included sizeable Protestant and Jew-ish communities. Protestants predominated in the Palatinate and formed a sizeable group in the Lower Rhine. The legal status of all confessions varied significantly. Only Zweibrücken extended religious tolerance to Jew, Calvinist, Lutheran and Catholic alike; only Krefeld tolerated Mennonites, a minority that had suffered persecution almost everywhere else. In the other Hohenzollern possessions and Wittelsbach Jülich-Berg, each town and vil-lage decided for itself the creed it adopted. In contrast, in the imperial city of Cologne, only Catholics could become burghers after 1617. However, by the 1780s, about 400 Protestants lived there, of whom twenty-four were amongst the seventy-one highest tax-payers. Though debarred from public office, they socialised freely with the elite. Jews, in contrast, were excluded from the city after 1424. In nearby Bonn, electoral Cologne's capital, Jews enjoyed toleration, but not Protestants. In the imperial city of Aachen, the tiny Protestant minority of fifty families was excluded from public of-fice and forbidden from celebrating religious services. Instead, Protestants celebrated services outside the city gates, though these were occasionally

---

[17] For Spiegel and Forster see Joseph Hansen (ed.), *Quellen zur Geschichte des Rheinlandes im Zeitalter der französischen Revolution 1780–1801* (4 vols., Bonn, 1931–8), I, pp. 478–83. For Vogt, see Theuringer, *Liberalismus*, pp. 278–80.

[18] Jonathan Sperber, *Popular Catholicism in Nineteenth-century Germany* (Princeton, 1984), pp. 30–3.

[19] Wilhelm Schmitz, *Die Misch-Mundart in den Kreisen Geldern (südlicher Teil), Kempen, Erkelenz, Heinsberg, Geilenkirchen, Aachen, Gladbach, Krefeld, Neuss und Düsseldorf, sowie noch mancherlei* (Dülken, 1893), p. 125.

disrupted by Catholic youths. Yet, despite sectarianism, Aachen's city council successfully enticed thirty-six wealthy Protestant families into settling in the city between 1750 and 1790. Electoral Mainz allowed Protestants to settle in its cities from the 1650s, though it did not grant them full civic rights. Their baptisms and marriages could only be celebrated by Catholic priests, for example. Conditions for Protestants and Jews in Mainz improved in the 1780s: Jews received the same rights as Christians with respect to judicial procedures in 1783, and full economic and religious tolerance in 1784. Mainz also admitted Jewish children to Christian schools, and after 1786 both Protestants and Jews were allowed to graduate from the university.[20]

Religious tolerance formed one component in a series of reforms associated with the Catholic Enlightenment. This movement largely stemmed from the belief amongst many in the Catholic elite that a cultural gap had opened up between themselves and Protestant Germany, and that this needed to be closed.[21] A simplified liturgy, greater independence from Rome, ecumenicalism and secularisation, plus religious toleration, lay at the heart of the agenda. A minority of ordained clerics employed in the universities of Bonn, Trier and Mainz, together with a number of theology students, dominated the radical fringe; many would later rise to prominence in the Mainz republic.[22] Jansenism influenced the theological component of this movement, which enjoyed support in the highest of places within the electorates from the 1760s. The official journal of electoral Mainz, the *Mainzer Monatsschrift*, became the leading organ of the Catholic Enlightenment. It frequently published articles attacking feast-days, pilgrimages and religious shrines.[23] Amongst those influenced by Jansenism was the suffragan archbishop of Trier, Nicolas Hontheim. In 1763, he published *De statu ecclesaie* under the pseudonym Febronius, which set out the tenets of what was subsequently labelled 'Febronianism': a simplified liturgy, the eventual union of Protestants and Catholics, and the establishment of a German National Church under the Archbishop of Mainz as *Primas Germaniae* with only

---

[20] Hansen, *Quellen*, 1, pp. 87, 225–7, 325. Also (for Cologne), Gisela Mettele, 'Kölner Bürgertum in der Umbruchszeit (1776–1815)', in Gall, *Vom alten zum neuen Bürgertum*, pp. 234–5, 243; and (for Aachen), Sobania, 'Aachener Bürgertum', pp. 183, 189.

[21] For an example of this sentiment, see Eulogius Schneider's lecture upon his appointment as professor of arts at Bonn, delivered on 23 April 1789. It was entitled 'On the current situation and constraints on literature in Catholic Germany' ('*Über den gegenwärtigen Zustand und die Hindernisse der schönen Literatur im katholischen Deutschland*'), and is reproduced in Hansen, *Quellen*, 1, pp. 346–61.

[22] *Ibid.*, 1, pp. 857 n. 2, 1035–45. Marxist historians, unsurprisingly, have glossed over the clerical origins of Rhenish radicalism, as noted by Theuringer, *Liberalismus*, pp. 272–3.

[23] Peter Wende, *Die geistlichen Staaten und ihre Auflösung im Urteil der zeitgenössischen Publizistik* (Lübeck and Hamburg, 1966), p. 34.

tenuous links to Rome. Mainz's Elector, Friedrich Karl, was attracted by Hontheim's arguments, though as Aretin dryly comments, proved 'a couple of sizes too small' to carry them through.[24] Nonetheless, he implemented various enlightened reforms that outraged orthodox opinion, such as the secularisation of several monasteries in order to fund education. He also ordered that mass should be celebrated in German and not Latin, though this was abandoned after vigorous protests from both the people and the Papal nuncio in Munich.[25] 'Febronianism' lent a new significance to disputes over the responsibilities of the Papal nunciature and over other issues that bedevilled relations between Rome and the German hierarchy in the 1780s. The climax came in 1786, when the German archbishops gathered at Ems came close to proclaiming a German National Church, but then drew back when Mainz's delegation went too far by proposing the abolition of celibacy. Rome did not forget this episode and had its revenge in 1802, when Pope Pius VII compelled the Rhenish prelates to 'voluntarily' give up their left bank holdings so as to conform with the Napoleonic Concordat.[26]

Part of the imperative behind the Catholic Enlightenment was economic. The dynamism of areas on their doorstep spurred the imperial cities and ecclesiastical electorates to consider measures to emulate their success, and a debate ensued over the connection between religious practices and economic progress. Numerous religious holidays, enlightened Catholics argued, restricted growth and should be diminished. The same applied to religious discrimination. This issue assumed greater importance after Joseph II introduced religious tolerance in his dominions in October 1781. Other Catholic territories such as Frankfurt followed, and France introduced greater religious equality in November 1787. This emboldened proponents of tolerance in the Rhineland. In late November (1787), Cologne's Protestant minority successfully petitioned the city council for permission to found a church and school in the city, arguing this would help attract enterprising Protestant refugees from the Netherlands, which was then experiencing civil war. Exactly the same consideration lay behind Trier's decision the previous February to extend toleration. Meanwhile, the Palatinate encouraged the settlement of Mennonites, Jews and Anabaptists as a means of encouraging manufacturing activity outside the control of

---

[24] Karl Otmar Freiherr von Aretin, 'Friedrich Karl. Der letzte Kurfürst-Erzbischof von Mainz', in Christoph Jamme and Otto Pöggeler (eds.), *Mainz – 'Centralort des Reiches'. Politik, Literatur und Philosophie im Umbruch der Revolutionszeit* (Stuttgart, 1986), pp. 77, 85, 92–3.

[25] Blanning, *Mainz*, pp. 163–94, 207–9.

[26] Hansen, *Quellen*, I, pp. 113–14, 561–3. Also, Karl-Georg Faber, *Andreas van Recum 1765–1828. Ein rheinischer Kosmopolit* (Bonn, 1969), pp. 20–49.

the guilds.[27] Yet even before the extension of formal toleration, Protestant and Catholic elites socialised in such institutions as Masonic lodges. Most Rhenish towns and cities boasted at least one lodge by the 1780s, and these allowed minorities to mingle with the established elite. Protestant manufacturers in stolidly Catholic Aachen and Cologne, for example, viewed their membership of the cities' lodges as the first step towards political emancipation. Even leading Mennonite families in the Lower Rhine, who had been distinguished by their austere dress and aloofness in the seventeenth century were, a hundred years later, culturally indistinguishable from other notables in their embrace of 'enlightened sociability'. They too merged into a new class whose interaction in the proliferating societies of the 1770s and 1780s contributed to the emergence of a well-informed, secular public sphere before which current political issues were critically judged. This was especially important in the territorially fragmented Rhineland, where 'cosmopolitanism' acted as an antidote to stifling localism and bigotry, and where there was a craving for news on foreign improvements which might be applied locally.[28]

Most Rhenish lodges followed the hierarchical French structure in their organisation. Reading societies, in contrast, through their procedures, introduced a small (under 2 per cent of the population) but influential number of Rhinelanders to annual secret elections to office, clearly defined membership criteria, debating rules and transparent administration, principles and conventions that two generations later lay at the heart of demands for constitutional reform. Indeed, some Rhenish radicals in the 1790s argued that their constitutional model be adopted for society as a whole.[29] The first such societies appeared in the region in the 1750s. Those of Bonn, Koblenz and Trier boasted separate rooms for reading and discussion, and subscribed to French, English and Italian as well as German journals. They reflected the new social value attached to cultured comportment as opposed to courtly elegance. Most, however, dedicated themselves to the propagation of useful knowledge rather than radical politics. Mainz's society proved a notable exception, and many of its members later joined the 'Jacobin' Club

---

[27] Hansen, *Quellen*, I, pp. 89–92, 114–17, 167–8, 209–13.

[28] Winfried Dotzauer, *Freimaurergesellschaften am Rhein. Aufgeklärte Sozietäten auf dem linken Rheinufer vom Ausgang des Ancien Régime bis zum Ende der Napoleonischen Herrschaft* (Wiesbaden, 1977), passim. Also, Hansen, *Quellen*, I, pp. 41–75, 1035–45 (for the *Illuminati*). For the special importance of sociability within the confines of a small territory, see Andreas Hofmeister-Hunger, 'Provincial Political Culture in the Holy Roman Empire. The Franconian Margravates of Ansbach and Bayreuth', in Eckhart Hellmuth (ed.), *The Transformation of Political Culture. England and Germany in the Late Eighteenth Century* (London, 1990), pp. 149–64.

[29] The importance of the reading clubs in this respect is convincingly argued by Theuringer, *Liberalismus*, pp. 142ff., 157.

established during the French occupation of 1792/3. However, even the less overtly political societies met the craving for news that contemporaries agreed gripped Germany following the Seven Years War.[30]

Education determined the social breadth of this craving and more particularly the ability of ordinary Rhinelanders to follow the conflict fought out in the press between proponents of reform and conservatives. The Rhineland enjoyed a comparatively high literacy rate, thanks to good public education. This possibly represented the Old Regime's most important legacy. Crowning the educational edifice were the universities of Bonn, Cologne, Mainz and Trier. Their importance in the Rhineland's late-eighteenth-century political development was without parallel in Britain and France, where the old saying 'out of scribblers and students are world rulers made' ('*Aus Schreiber und Studenten werden der Welt Regenten*') would have then been unimaginable. In the mid-eighteenth century, the impetus for university reform that spread from Halle and Göttingen reached the Rhine, where higher education was still dominated by Thomist-Aristotelian scholasticism. However, the need to stem the growing tide of students heading for the reformed Protestant universities forced change.[31] This was especially the case with Mainz, whose emergence as an intellectual centre owed much to the elector's *ex-officio* function as imperial chancellor. This office demanded university-educated officials and jurists capable of administering imperial responsibilities, something especially important following Friedrich Karl's election given his determination to play a leading role in German politics. So, brushing aside opposition from a conservative cathedral chapter, Friedrich Karl embarked upon reform partly funded through the dissolution of some monasteries. By the eve of the French Revolution, Mainz university – or 'Catholic Göttingen', as it became known – was a leading centre of Kantian thought.[32]

Substantial reform was also completed in the university of Trier. There, intellectuals influenced by the doctrines of Febronius and Kant began to enter the faculties. Concurrently, bright young students from Trier went to Göttingen supported by electoral scholarships and subsequently returned imbued with the latest philosophical ideas. Less, in contrast, was achieved

---

[30] Klaus Gerteis, 'Bildung und Revolution: Die deutschen Lesegesellschaften am Ende des 18. Jahrhunderts', *Archiv für Kultur-Geschichte* 53 (1971), pp. 130–2, 136–7. A list of the journals subscribed to by the reading societies of Mainz, Koblenz and Bonn is provided by Hansen, *Quellen*, 1, pp. 17, 36, 216.

[31] Notker Hammerstein, *Aufklärung und katholisches Reich. Untersuchungen zur Universitätsreform und Politik katholischer Territorien des Heiligen Römischen Reichs deutscher Nation im 18. Jahrhundert* (Berlin, 1977), pp. 10ff.

[32] *Ibid.*, pp. 142–58. For Kantian intellectual influences in Mainz, see Hansen, *Quellen*, 1, pp. 659–62.

in the university of Cologne, due to the stubborn opposition from the Jesuits and the imperial city's council. Cologne's elector finally gave up his attempts at reforming this institution and instead founded a new academy in Bonn in 1777 (elevated by Joseph II to a university in 1786) using funds released by the dissolution of the Jesuit order. Bonn, like Mainz, quickly developed into a centre of radical thought and attracted Kantians fleeing from the unpropitious surroundings in Cologne. From Bonn they engaged throughout the 1780s and early 1790s in a bitter and public dispute over a range of issues with their orthodox opponents who remained ensconced in the imperial city, and who included the cathedral chapter and resident Papal nuncios Bellisomi (1776–86) and Pacca (1786–94).[33]

Both sides became increasingly vociferous and coherent in denouncing their opponents' agenda and availed themselves fully of the press. The 1770s in Germany witnessed the emergence of a *political* press. This not only informed the reading public of daily occurrences as before, but now engaged in continuous dialogue on the issues of the day.[34] This development extended to the Rhineland in the 1780s. Those on the 'Josephist', 'enlightened' side in particular availed themselves of German- and French-language journals such as the *Bönnische Intelligenzblatt*, *Gazette de Bonn*, *Le Nouvelliste politique d'Allemagne* and *Kölnischer Staatsboth* to engage their orthodox opponents.[35] Through these publications, they appealed to the elite that increasingly populated the Masonic lodges and reading societies. The views of their orthodox enemies were less well represented in Rhenish journals, but could be found in media such as satirical rhymes circulated in pamphlet form. These were generally more successful in reaching a wider audience. Indeed, those supporting an orthodox stance made a virtue out of necessity by skilfully exploiting the widening gap between high and popular culture to portray themselves as representatives of the people.

The educational gap between the enlightened elite and sceptical masses should not be exaggerated, though it possibly flattered some to do just that. That the gap was not a chasm was largely due to the well-developed school system in the Rhineland, where university reform did not come

---

[33] For Trier, Hansen, *Quellen*, 1, pp. 125–6; also Kyösti Julku, *Die revolutionäre Bewegung im Rheinland am Ende des Achtzehnten Jahrhunderts*, vol. 1: *Die Anfänge der revolutionären Bewegung von etwa 1770 bis zum Beginn der Revolutionskriege* (Helsinki, 1965), pp. 113–16; and Hammerstein, *Aufklärung*, pp. 136–41. For Cologne and Bonn, Hansen, *Quellen*, 1, pp. 45*, 30–2, 138–9, 157–8, 346, 662, 703 n. 1.

[34] H. E. Bödeker, 'Journals and Public Opinion: the Politicization of the German Enlightenment in the Second Half of the Eighteenth Century', in Hellmuth, *Transformation*, pp. 423–45.

[35] A full list of Rhenish journals published in the 1780s, arranged by place of publication and including notes on editorial policies, is provided in Hansen, *Quellen*, 1, pp. 23*–52*.

at the expense of primary and secondary education as would later be the case under Napoleon. Rather, the universities stood at the apex of a system that theoretically provided for compulsory education for children aged up to eleven (Trier), twelve (Mainz) or fourteen (Cologne). Attendance rates averaging 70 per cent were amongst the highest in Europe. This impressive achievement predated the Enlightenment. What was new from about the 1770s was the belief that education was the state's concern. Rousseau's *Discours sur l'économie politique* (1755) in particular encouraged governments to take a keener interest in the quality and status of teachers. In Mainz, Elector Emmerich Joseph (1763–74) founded a state school commission and teacher-training academy in 1770. Over the following two years he embarked upon a programme to improve urban and rural schools. In Trier, Clemens Wenzeslaus followed with the creation of a school commission in 1780 and teacher-training institute in 1784, whilst in electoral Cologne, Max Franz founded a teacher-training institute in 1783 and a school commission in 1786. Once established, no new teacher could practise without first attending a course at these institutes, whilst existing teachers were encouraged to attend specially designed summer courses. At the same time, teachers' status was improved through higher pay and bans on demeaning supplementary occupations.[36]

Such efforts produced some of the highest literacy rates in Europe. An official survey conducted in Trier in 1788 recorded that 91 per cent of the 7,000 schoolchildren included in the investigation could read and write. The survey concluded that almost all children aged between seven and twelve attended school, though most did so only between the beginning of November and early May, when they were not needed in the fields. Each parish had at least one teacher, and the rural teacher-to-pupil ratio was a not unimpressive 1:50. As in the other electorates, Trier's reforms of the 1780s built upon a strong base and therefore concentrated on quality enhancement through such measures as the propagation of the advanced pedagogical methods pioneered by Felbiger.[37]

Proponents of Enlightenment assumed that improved public education would lead to increased support for their own agenda. This was the belief of a new generation of authors that appeared in the 1780s who attempted

---

[36] *Ibid.*, I, pp. 10–12, 31, 83–4, 117–28.

[37] Etienne François, 'Die Volksbildung am Mittelrhein im ausgehenden 18. Jahrhundert. Eine Untersuchung über den vermeintlichen "Bildungs-Rückstand" der katholischen Bevölkerung Deutschlands im Ancien Régime', *Jahrbuch für westdeutsche Landesgeschichte* 3 (1977), pp. 278–93, 303. Also, Erwin Schaaf, 'Sozioökonomische Funktionen der Volksschule und Gewerbeschule im Raum Trier-Koblenz vom aufgeklärten Absolutismus bis zur Mitte des 19. Jahrhunderts', *Jahrbuch für westdeutsche Landesgeschichte* 4 (1978), pp. 281–312.

to propagate radical politics amongst a wider audience.[38] However, the assumption was not necessarily justified. If anything, the stress placed by enlightened educational theory on the need to teach pupils according to the role they would fulfil as adults reinforced the concept of a society of orders to a greater extent than the earlier religious emphasis on educating children for membership of a common community of belief characterised by a basic equality.[39] Certainly, educational reform enhanced the prestige of the ecclesiastical states in the eyes of the enlightened elite. It demonstrated their ability to reform and gave enlightened Catholics a new confidence. This was reflected in 1785, when Philipp Anton von Bibra, Mainz's leading minister, sponsored an essay competition on the weaknesses of the ecclesiastical states and how these might be overcome. The resulting list of perceived weaknesses contained in the essays appears disheartening at first glance: non-hereditary rule harmed long-term development; the selection process for electors encouraged bribery, foreign pressure and the imposition by cathedral chapters of selfish conditions binding winning candidates; the ecclesiastical states functioned as a Papal Trojan Horse in Germany; the 'dead-hand' of church ownership of large estates caused economic underdevelopment, proof of which was provided by widespread mendicancy; revenues were squandered on degenerate courts and clerical drones; clerical influence was pernicious to education, enlightenment and religious tolerance; and so on. Yet nowhere was the status of the ecclesiastical states questioned. Instead, the remedies suggested included the secularisation of a few monasteries to finance improvement and the collection of statistics. Significantly, some identified the elective principle and role of the cathedral chapters as strengths that guarded against despotism.[40]

Over the centuries, not only the Church but also towns and cities shaped the Rhineland. These came in a variety of forms and can be categorised according to the degree of independence they enjoyed from territorial rulers. The so-called *Residenzstädte* – literally, 'residence cities' – containing princely courts enjoyed the least independence. Mainz, Koblenz and Bonn fell into

---

[38] One of the most important 'enlightened' publications aimed at the wider Rhenish public was, J. B. K. von Schönebeck, *Das Gesetzbuch der reinen Vernunft, oder kurze Darstellung dessen, was die Vernunft allen Menschen zur Regel ihres Betragens und zur Sicherung ihrer Glückseligkeit vorschreibt* (Bonn, 1787). Schönebeck briefly held the chair in botany in Bonn before becoming editor of the pro-reform *Bönnische Intelligenzblattes*. Hansen, *Quellen*, 1, pp. 179–201.

[39] Theuringer, *Liberalismus*, pp. 72, 79ff, 109ff., 120–2.

[40] Wende, *Staaten*, pp. 9, 16–38. Notably, Friedrich Carl von Moser, whilst recommending the secularisation of the ecclesiastical states, argued in favour of the preservation of the elective principle as a defence against absolutism. Friedrich Carl von Moser, *Über die Regierung der geistlichen Staaten in Deutschland* (Frankfurt a.M. and Leipzig, 1787), pp. 176–8.

this category. At the opposite extreme came the imperial cities (*Reichsstädte*), entities that in centuries past had won their independence from princely rule and now recognised no secular authority other than the Emperor. The Rhineland boasted four *Reichsstädte*: Aachen, Cologne, Speyer and Worms. Finally, between these extremes came numerous semi-autonomous 'home towns', ranging in size from about 1,000 to 10,000 inhabitants and accounting for roughly a quarter of the region's population. Each category – the *Residenzstädte*, *Reichsstädte* and home towns – enjoyed certain characteristics, as did individual cities within those categories. They also shared commonalities, including a predilection for political conflict between magistracies and burghers. At least twenty-one Rhenish cities, including Cologne, Aachen, Trier and Koblenz, experienced such conflict in the years immediately preceding the French Revolution.[41]

An increasing socio-economic and cultural gap between the mass of burghers and urban elites (sometimes misleadingly labelled 'patrician') largely accounted for rising political conflict. The decline of the burgher-dominated craft guilds lay at the heart of this. These were threatened on three fronts. Economically, their role diminished as merchant-manufacturers bypassed restrictive practices. In a territorially fragmented region, this was relatively easy: entrepreneurs simply moved their establishments to jurisdictions beyond the guilds' reach. By the late eighteenth century even this inconvenience was unnecessary, as merchant-manufacturers found ways of undermining the guilds from within or surreptitiously establishing workshops within city walls. Many a sumptuous merchant-manufacturer's town house concealed workshops discreetly behind rococo façades and representational rooms. Politically, the guilds lost ground. Officially, according to faded medieval charters that served as civic constitutions, sovereignty resided with the guilds. Civic rights were derived through them. Of course, only a minority enjoyed such rights – in Cologne about 4,000 out of 40,000 inhabitants. However, by the eighteenth century, the magistracies had largely escaped from the supervision of the guilds. In Trier, for example, the guilds lost control of the city council in the second half of the seventeenth century after selling their seats to wealthy businessmen, whilst in Aachen, merchant-manufacturers purchased guild membership in order to influence their policies from within.[42] Finally, guild-dominated urban culture was challenged by the new elitist culture

---

[41] Klaus Müller, 'Städtische Unruhen im Rheinland des späten 18. Jahrhunderts. Ein Beitrag zur rheinischen Reaktion auf die Französische Revolution', *Rheinische Vierteljahrsblätter* 54 (1990), pp. 166–9.
[42] Joachim Kermann, *Die Manufakturen im Rheinland 1750–1833* (Bonn, 1972), pp. 118–60.

of enlightened sociability that bridged confessional and territorial barriers, but also widened the social gap.

Though weakened, the *Zunftbürger* remained imbued by civic republicanism.[43] They too were exposed to an expanding public sphere and new political ideas. This is unsurprising given that the artisan craft sector was in part export-orientated and depended upon a degree of intercourse with the wider world. Trade has always encouraged the diffusion of ideas from abroad. Cologne, for example, though it enjoyed a justified reputation for superstition and bigotry, also possessed the best-developed newspaper press in the Rhineland thanks to its position as the region's leading commercial centre. New ideas from outside combined with old republican values emboldened the *Zunftbürger*. As the existing constitutional mechanisms proved inadequate, burghers in many cities started forming 'deputations' to challenge magisterial control. Such a deputation formed in Cologne in 1779 and set itself the task of restoring the imperial city's ancient liberties. To this end, it requested and received permission in 1784 from Vienna to translate the city's two key constitutional texts – the *Verbandbrief* (1396) and *Transfixbrief* (1513) – into German so that their contents would be more widely known and less prone to magisterial 'misinterpretation'. Three years later, the deputation led opposition to the city council's decision to extend toleration to Protestants. This might appear to confirm the inherent hostility of the *Zunftbürgertum* to enlightened progress. This, certainly, was the interpretation of pro-reformers viewing events from outside. However, the perspective from within Cologne's medieval walls was different. There, the deputation's resistance appeared justified on constitutional rather than religious grounds. The city council, the deputation argued, was acting arbitrarily in unilaterally altering Cologne's constitution. Significantly, this opinion was shared by the impeccably enlightened elector, Max Franz, whose own rights as archbishop had similarly been infringed. Opposition to toleration was not necessarily 'unenlightened'.[44]

Nor was conflict always determined socially, despite the apparently clear-cut division between the *Zunftbürgertum* and rising elite. This is illustrated

[43] Hartmut Zückert, 'Republikanismus in der Reichsstadt des 18. Jahrhunderts', *Aufklärung* 4 (1989), pp. 53–74. Also, Hans-Christoph Rublack, 'Political and Social Norms in Urban Communities in the Holy Roman Empire', in Kaspar von Greyerz (ed.), *Religion, Politics and Social Protest. Three Studies on Early Modern Germany* (London, 1984), pp. 33–4.

[44] The conflict in Cologne over toleration can best be followed in the relevant documents in Hansen, *Quellen*, I, pp. 67–8, 89–90, 209–14, 217–95, 342–3, 371, 386–92, 400, 404, 407, 451, 560, 663, 786, 925. Also, Ingrid Nicolini, *Die politische Führungsschicht in der Stadt Köln gegen Ende der Reichsstädtischen Zeit* (Cologne and Vienna, 1979), passim, and Barbare Becker-Jákli, *Die Protestanten in Köln. Die Entwicklung einer religiösen Minderheit von der Mitte des 18. bis zur Mitte des 19. Jahrhunderts* (Cologne, 1983), pp. 16–35, 55–69.

by examination of the conflict that rocked another imperial city, Aachen, in the 1780s. There, bitter constitutional conflict – the so-called 'Great *Mäkelei*' – embroiled the somewhat misleadingly labelled 'New' and 'Old' parties. Analysis reveals that the two parties were socially indistinguishable. The division was essentially political. As in Cologne, conflict centred on accusations of corruption and mismanagement levelled against the incumbent ('Old Party') administration and demands by the opposition ('New Party') for more accountable government. The 'New Party's' agenda, though formulated by a small elite dominated by businessmen and freemasons, appealed to a socially broad-based coalition. Both sides legitimised their position by claiming to act on behalf of the *Bürgerschaft* – all those with civic rights – from which they variously solicited supportive petitions. Matters in Aachen finally came to a head in 1786, when the 'Old Party' declared itself victorious in a bitterly contested election. This sparked riots during which a mob stormed the city hall and forcibly installed a 'New Party' administration.[45]

An interpretation of urban conflict based upon social reductionism appears even less convincing following research that uncovers the surprising degree of social mobility within the Reich's cities. This discovery extends even to Cologne, overturning the caste-like reputation of its ruling clique. Dominated by about 250 great merchant families, this 'clique' readily assimilated wealthy newcomers. Throughout the eighteenth century, if not earlier, Cologne willingly accorded civic status to the wealthy and talented, and provided institutions for their integration. The same was true of Aachen, where a special guild for professionals (the *Gelehrtenzunft*) allowed a new elite to participate in old civic culture.[46]

Disputes between burgher deputations and magistracies frequently ended up in the Reichshofrat in Vienna, which served as a constitutional court for imperial cities. Johann Jacob Moser, writing in 1772, estimated

---

[45] The older literature, including Jeffry Diefendorf, *Businessmen and Politics in the Rhineland, 1789–1834* (Princeton, 1980), ignores the social breadth of 'New Party' support, and instead focuses on the tiny elite of businessmen. Theuringer, *Liberalismus*, p. 351, and Sobania, 'Bürgertum', pp. 193–4, 200–6, redress the balance. What can be conceded is that businessmen tended to dominate the 'New Party' leadership, whilst members of the judicial elite were better represented amongst the 'Old Party' hierarchy. Carl Horst, 'Die Aachener Mäkelei 1786–1792. Konfliktregelungmechanismen im alten Reich', Sonderdruck aus *Zeitschrift des Aachener Geschichtsvereins* 92 (Aachen, 1985), p. 115.

[46] Wolfgang Herborn, 'Der Graduierte Ratsherr. Zur Entwicklung einer neuen Elite im Kölner Rat der frühen Neuzeit', in Heinz Schilling and Hermann Diederiks (eds.), *Bürgerliche Eliten in den Niederlanden und in Nordwestdeutschland. Studien zur Sozialgeschichte des europäischen Bürgertums im Mittelalter und in der Neuzeit* (Cologne, 1985), pp. 337–74; Joachim Deeters, 'Das Bürgerrecht der Reichsstadt Köln seit 1396', in *Zeitschrift der Savigny-Stiftung für Rechtsgeschichte* 104 (1987), pp. 1–3, 32–3, 50, 75. More generally, Mettele, 'Bürgertum', pp. 235–49, and for Aachen, Sobania, 'Bürgertum', pp. 188–93, 195–6.

that the imperial courts were then examining cases involving thirty-one of the fifty-one *Reichsstädte*.[47] One contemporary blamed this prevalence of conflict on the participatory political culture of the cities, where 'the burgher likes to have a voice in the government, and out of natural vanity believes that he is as well – nay, better – qualified to understand it than his neighbour'. Another blamed the lack of openness in government: if only magistracies acted more transparently, then a hundred cases before the courts would end.[48] Conflict often centred on financial accountability. Another frequent demand made by burgher deputations was for a greater separation of powers, especially between what today would be classified the judiciary and executive. This agenda – open government, transparent procedures, financial accountability, an independent judiciary – hardly reflected the political backwardness of the *Zunftbürger*, but rather pre-empted the standard package of demands presented by nineteenth-century liberals.[49] As seen in Aachen, such demands attracted a broad social coalition.

Imperial cities, with their histories, traditions and republican sentiments, functioned as independent states and were represented in the Reichstag. Other towns and cities belonged to a particular territorial state. Despite this subordinate position, many enjoyed wider influence within the so-called *Landstände*, or representative estates. These essentially medieval institutions comprised the representatives of the '*Land*', a term without equivalent in English. A '*Land*' was defined by its peculiar (and supposedly ancient) customs and laws rather than by geography. It might not necessarily coincide with the dynastically defined territory of the prince. For example, dynastic agglomerations like Prussia, the Habsburg Monarchy and Wittelsbach holdings encompassed many 'lands'. Alternatively, a particular 'land' might be divided amongst several princely possessions. Such was especially the case in fragmented regions like the Rhineland. Whatever

---

47 Johann Jacob Möser, *Von der Reichsstättischen Regiments-Verfassung (= Neues Teutsches Staatsrecht, Bd. 18)* (Frankfurt a. M. and Leipzig, 1772), pp. 420–68. For the at times ambiguous role of the Reichshofrat in conflict resolution, see Christopher R. Friedrichs, 'Urban Conflicts and the Imperial Constitution in Seventeenth-Century Germany', *Journal of Modern History* 58 (supplement), (1986), pp. 98–123. Also, Aretin, *Reich*, 1, p. 90–4.

48 Both quotes are taken from Theuringer, *Liberalismus*, pp. 345–53, 361–6.

49 Many scholars remain unconvinced of any progressive political potential in the home towns and imperial cities. Press, for example, argues that the 'legalisation' of conflict resolution froze all further development within the imperial cities. Volker Press, 'Die Reichsstadt in der altständischen Gesellschaft', in Johannes Kunisch (ed.), *Neue Studien zur frühneuzeitlichen Reichsgeschichte (Zeitschrift für historische Forschung* Beiheft 3, Berlin, 1987), pp. 14–16, 23–4. For another sceptical interpretation, see Etienne François, 'Villes d'Empire et Aufklärung', in Pierre Grappin (ed.), *L'Allemagne des lumières. Périodiques, correspondances, témoignages* (Metz, 1982), pp. 9–24.

the position, those '*Landstände*' that survived into the eighteenth century perceived themselves as representing the interests of the '*Land*'.

Thanks to the Reich's protective legal cocoon, representative estates survived early-modern princely absolutism in much of Germany. More than that, they actually revived in the eighteenth century, something attributable to international developments. In the later seventeenth century, Habsburg emperors depended upon the German princes for military support against the Ottomans and Louis XIV, and hence used imperial institutions to weaken the estates because these obstructed 'resource mobilisation'. Following the diminution of the Ottoman and French threat, Habsburg policy changed. The turning point came in 1714, when the Reichshofrat ruled that the estates enjoyed the right to approve taxation. Thereafter, mounting Habsburg fears of the princes provoked further rulings that favoured the estates, including dramatic interventions in Mecklenburg in 1727 that saw the duke briefly removed from office, and Württemberg, where the estates emerged much strengthened and subsequently earned the oft-quoted accolade from Charles James Fox as the only 'parliament' (apart from Westminster) worthy of the name.

In the Rhineland, only two of the larger territories, Mainz and the Palatinate, lacked estates. To the north, estates survived in the Hohenzollern possessions of Cleves, Moers and Geldern despite efforts to bring them to heel. They continued to meet regularly until the French occupation in the 1790s. In neighbouring Jülich and Berg, the Wittelsbach dukes made even less progress in weakening the estates. As with the Hohenzollern possessions, this was partly because of the duchies' peripheral status within a wider dynastic agglomeration. Interestingly, a memorandum drawn up in 1742 for the new duke, Karl Theodor, warned that whilst he might exploit the Palatinate at will because of the extinction of its estates, in Jülich-Berg he must tread carefully. In neighbouring electoral Cologne, the estates not only approved taxation but ran the financial administration. Moving still further south, Trier's estates deserve special attention for their assertiveness under the last elector, Clemens Wenzeslaus. Nor should the plethora of smaller territories be forgotten, which enjoyed analogous institutions whose rights were likewise protected by the imperial courts.[50]

---

[50] For Cleves and Jülich-Berg, see F. L. Carsten, *Princes and Parliaments in Germany. From the Fifteenth to the Eighteenth Century* (Oxford, 1959), pp. 258–347. For electoral Cologne, Essers, *Landtage*. For the smaller mini-states, Helmut Gabel, *Widerstand und Kooperation. Studien zur politische Kultur rheinischer und maasländischer Kleinterritorien (1648–1794)* (Tübingen, 1995). For contemporary recognition that territories with representative estates enjoyed lower taxation, see Anton Klebe, *Reise auf dem Rhein durch die teutschen und französischen Rheinlander nach Aachen und Spaa* (2nd edn, Frankfurt a. M., 1806), p. 50.

Traditionally, the *Landstände* comprised the clergy, nobility and towns, but by the eighteenth century a more varied picture existed. In some areas, such as Moers, peasants were represented, though in most cases the towns and cities, which invariably controlled hinterlands, claimed also to speak for rural populations. This was significant, as it reinforced the sense amongst the towns and cities that they represented the people as a whole, and not just those enjoying civic rights. Such was the case in electoral Cologne, for example, whose estates comprised four curia: the cathedral chapter, representatives of the imperial counts, the imperial knights, and representatives of the cities, who together convened regularly in Bonn as they had done since 1463. In Jülich and Berg, the nobility and cities were represented, and convened annually in Düsseldorf for six weeks throughout the seventeenth and eighteenth centuries. In other territories, especially those of the Middle Rhine (notably Trier), the 'unmediated' nobility had no territorial representation, leaving a bicameral structure of cities and clergy. In Protestant *Länder*, in contrast, the clergy disappeared as an independent estate following the Reformation, leaving a bicameral division of towns and nobles. Variations similarly distinguished the procedures of the different *Landstände*, though most appear to have convened regularly and often annually.[51] They were an institution and not an event, to adopt Conrad Russell's memorable phrase. In electoral Cologne, at least, they deliberated in secret, with the public admitted only to their ceremonial opening. The elector feared they might become a public tribunal and sought to prevent the circulation of reports on their deliberations. However, in electoral Cologne, at least, news of their proceedings did invariably leak out and formed the basis for pamphlets that circulated whenever they were in session.[52]

The most significant power the *Landstände* held was that of the purse. Taxation and the sale of public property required their consent. They also generally enjoyed the right to petition the ruler. Beyond that, their significance, legacy and whether they represented a precursor to nineteenth-century constitutional developments, remains debatable. The influential conservative, Friedrich von Gentz, argued during the debates over Germany's reordering following Napoleon's fall that representation through estates (which he and his employer, Metternich, supported) was incompatible with modern forms of representation. This interpretation has tended to stick. Certainly, there were institutional discontinuities. However, a

---

[51] Gustav Croon, *Der Rheinische Provinziallandtag bis zum Jahre 1874. Im Auftrage des Rheinischen Provinzialauschusses* (Bonn, 1974), pp. 21–6.
[52] Essers, *Landtage*, passim.

different conclusion is reached when focusing on the perspective from below.[53] This approach has shed light on how the estates connected with the communities they represented through consultation, petitions and reporting, and how through this certain principles, such as voting by head and accountability, were disseminated. The estates formed but the tip of a broader consensus-building pyramid. Throughout the Rhineland, as in Justus Möser's Osnabrück, this contributed to a peculiarly 'corporatist' slant to the Enlightenment fundamentally opposed to absolutism.[54]

This in itself does not overturn the argument that the *Landstände* were fundamentally different from later representative institutions, based on equal citizenship and individual rights. Analysis of the Rhenish case does not entirely overturn this conclusion, though it does suggest that some of the estates increasingly viewed themselves as representatives of all the people and not simply a particular privileged order. This was evident in Trier, for example, where the *Landtag* in 1780 started referring to its members as 'the people's representatives' ('*des volckes Repräsentanten*') and claimed to speak on behalf of all inhabitants over the entire electoral territory. This represented a fundamental shift in the *Landtag*'s self-perception.[55] Developments in electoral Cologne were less dramatic, though significantly at an institutional level, various committees and conferences bridged the division between the orders represented in the four curia. Such institutional arrangements reinforced the notion that, collectively, the *Landstände* represented more than the sum of their parts.[56]

The estates' self-perception as the representatives of the '*Land*' was reinforced by the Rhineland's territorial order. All the larger territories were either elective monarchies (the three ecclesiastical electorates) or (the Hohenzollern and Wittelsbach possessions) '*Nebenländer*' – peripheral territories geographically separated from the dynastic core to which they were loosely bound through personal union. What characterised both was that neither enjoyed close emotional bonds to a particular dynasty. Instead, and with the possible exception of the Protestant elite in Cleves, Rhenish

---

[53] The two pioneering studies that adopt this new perspective from below are Peter Blickle, *Landschaften im Alten Reich. Die staatliche Funktion des gemeinen Mannes in Oberdeutschland* (Munich, 1973); and Karl Bosl, *Die Geschichte der Repräsentation in Bayern. Landständische Bewegung, landständische Verfassung, Landesausschuß und altständische Gesellschaft* (Munich, 1974).

[54] Jonathan B. Knudsen, *Justus Möser and the German Enlightenment* (Cambridge, 1986), pp. 11, 61–2.

[55] Theuringer, *Liberalismus*, pp. 337–9, 359.

[56] Essers, *Landtage*, pp. 6–7, 14–22, 156–8. More generally, also, Rudolf Vierhaus, 'Land, Staat und Reich in der politischen Vorstellungswelt deutscher Landstände im 18. Jahrhundert', *Historische Zeitschrift* 223 (1976), pp. 41, 59–60. Peter Blickle, 'Kommunalismus, Parlamentarismus, Republikanismus', *Historische Zeitschrift* 242 (1986), p. 540.

loyalties centred on the '*Land*', not the '*Staat*'.[57] The ecclesiastical electors, it was sometimes claimed, lacked the same commitment to their subjects as hereditary rulers because they had no heir to pass their legacy to. This was not necessarily justified; it hardly seemed applicable to rulers of Max Franz's calibre, for example, who represented a paradigm of conscientiousness and dedication to public service. The accusation concerning commitment might more realistically have been levelled against the rulers of the *Nebenländer*, who neglected their peripheral territories and concentrated their reforming zeal on the core. This was the case in the Hohenzollern holdings, for example, which escaped the centralising reforms imposed elsewhere in Prussia during the eighteenth century. In the west, the reforms foundered on the colourful but generally lethal reef of opposition from the estates backed by imperial law, and because Berlin lacked the will to overcome this.[58] Though perhaps welcome in the short term, such a lack of commitment over the longer term increased the perception of the ruler as being somehow foreign to the *Land*, and this in turn made any arbitrary acts by him or his officials appear all the more illegitimate. It also reinforced the view that there existed a hierarchy of laws, with the old laws of the *Land* – '*altrechtliche Verfassungsgefüge*' – possessing a far higher status than mere ministerial ordinances or police decrees. With the appearance of a new political vocabulary following the outbreak of the French Revolution, some started to equate '*altrechtliche Verfassungsgefüge*' with the '*pouvoir constituant*' – the power to make constitutional law. At least this was the connection made by one venerable defender of the old estates in Württemberg, Ludwig Uhland, whose political career spanned the disappearance of the old order and who finished as a left-wing deputy in the Frankfurt parliament in 1848.[59]

Ultimately, the *Landstände* reflected the societies they represented, and it was the balance within those societies that determined the estates' response to the challenges they faced. In a region like Mecklenburg, dominated by the landed nobility, it was hardly surprising that the *Landstände* should

[57] In Trier this was symbolised by the 1650 ruling according to which public officials needed to swear a triple oath of loyalty to the elector, the cathedral chapter and the estates. Theuringer, *Liberalismus*, pp. 117–18.

[58] Horst Carl, *Okkupation und Regionalismus: die preußischen Westprovinzen im Siebenjährigen Krieg* (Mainz, 1993), pp. 412–41. More specifically on the Hohenzollern duchy of Geldern see Heinrich Holthausen, *Verwaltung und Stände des Herzogtums Geldern preußischen Anteils im 18. Jahrhundert* (Geldern, 1916).

[59] Gerhard Dilcher, 'Vom ständischen Herrschaftsvertrag zum Verfassungsgesetz', *Der Staat* 27 (1988), pp. 163–5, 170ff., 187–93. Gerhard Oestreich, 'Zur Vorgeschichte des Parlamentarismus: ständische Verfassung, landständische Verfassung und landschaftliche Verfassung', *Zeitschrift für historische Forschung* 6 (1979), pp. 65, 75–6, 78.

represent privileged landed interest, and that their victory should cement an out-of-date socio-political order. Elsewhere, in territories like Uhland's Württemberg, where urban representatives carried greater weight, the estates contributed to rather than hindered developments that might loosely be labelled 'modern'.[60] Such was also the case in the Rhineland, a region shaped less by a landed nobility than by burghers and clerics.

The revival of the *Landstände* in the eighteenth century occurred within the legal framework provided by the Empire: imperial law – the 'palladium of our constitution', according to Max Franz[61] – and the imperial courts based in Wetzlar (Reichskammergericht) and Vienna (Reichshofrat) that administered it. The imperial courts served as appellate courts for the territorial courts (*Hofgerichte* and *Austrägalgerichte*) scattered throughout the individual states. On matters concerning fundamental principle, a final appeal could be made from the imperial courts to the Reichstag. By the eighteenth century, the Reichshofrat emerged as the more popular court, because of its relatively simple procedures. Thanks partly to reforms by Joseph II, the number of cases heard by this court rose dramatically, increasing from 2,000 in 1767 to almost 3,400 in 1779.[62] As we have seen, many of these cases emanated from the imperial cities, entities with a strong sense of imperial patriotism (*Reichspatriotismus*) that served to further Habsburg influence in Germany. However, the number of cases brought before the imperial courts from rural areas also increased. This was partly a result of the agricultural revolution, which disrupted existing relationships and caused disputes.[63]

Recent research illustrates the effectiveness of the imperial courts and overturns earlier criticism centred on huge backlogs of cases, inordinately

---

[60] The modernising potential (or lack of it) of the estates has attracted much debate. Amongst the more significant contributions are the following: Vierhaus, 'Land'; Volker Press, 'Landstände des 18. und Parlamente des 19. Jahrhunderts', in Helmut Berding and Hans-Peter Ullmann (eds.), *Deutschland zwischen Revolution und Restauration* (Düsseldorf, 1981), pp. 133–57; Winfried Schulze, 'Vom Gemeinnutz zum Eigennutz. Über den Normenwandel in der ständischen Gesellschaft der frühen Neuzeit', *Historische Zeitschrift* 243 (1986), pp. 591–626; Dilcher, 'Herrschaftsvertrag'; Eberhard Weis, 'Kontinuität und Diskontinuität zwischen den Ständen des 18. Jahrhunderts und den frühkonstitutionellen Parlamenten von 1818/1819 in Bayern und Württemberg', in idem (ed.), *Deutschland und Frankreich um 1800. Aufklärung – Revolution – Reform* (Munich, 1990), pp. 218–42; Andreas Schwennicke, 'Der Einfluß der Landstände auf die Regelungen des Preußisches Allgemeinen Landrechts von 1794', in Günter Birtsch and Dietmar Willoweit (eds.), *Reformabsolutismus und ständische Gesellschaft. Zweihundert Jahre Preußisches Allgemeines Landrecht* (Berlin, 1998), pp. 113–29.

[61] Max Franz to Friedrich Karl, 5 April 1790. Quoted from John G. Gagliardo, *Reich and Nation. The Holy Roman Empire as Idea and Reality, 1763–1806* (Bloomington, 1980), p. 113.

[62] Aretin, *Reich*, I, pp. 97–103.

[63] Bernhard Diestelkamp, *Rechtsfälle aus dem alten Reich: denkwürdige Prozesse vor dem Reichskammergericht* (Munich, 1995), p. 125.

long proceedings, the failure to reach verdicts, and the inability to enforce rulings. Amongst the weaknesses previously identified was the *privilegium de non appellando*. This was enjoyed by the larger German states, and prevented their subjects from seeking redress in the imperial courts. However, this *privilegium* never prevented the imperial courts from hearing complaints of a denial to grant justice, and such cases accounted for three-fifths of the cases brought annually to the Reichshofrat and Reichskammergericht. As for enforcement, this varied greatly between territories. Larger states were largely immune. Smaller states, as predominated in the Rhineland, were more vulnerable, as the courts might authorise a potentially hostile, powerful neighbour to enforce their rulings. In such entities, imperial law provided a deterrent against the arbitrary exercise of judicial power ('*Kabinettsjustiz*') of the kind that Prussia witnessed during the notorious Müller-Arnold case (1779), and instead encouraged regular, standard judicial procedure. According to a contemporary jurist, Joseph Schick, the majority of cases brought before the imperial courts hinged around the question of due process and judicial independence. Certainly, the Reichskammergericht became increasingly outspoken in its judgements against '*Kabinettsjustiz*' in the 1780s, something linked to the penetration of that court by the radical *Illuminati*. Similarly, the Reichshofrat, whose rulings were increasingly informed by natural law, and which took on a more theoretical and even quasi-constitutional form in the late eighteenth century, also proved more willing to strike down examples of *Kabinettsjustiz*. Consequently, its prestige rose and the volume of appeals it received increased.[64] Amongst those Rhenish rulers on the receiving end of imperial rulings on account of their arbitrariness was Count Karl Magnus of the Rheingrafschaft, who in 1778 was sentenced by Joseph II to ten years' penal confinement for 'irresponsible misuse of authority', and the Bishop of Speyer, Count August von Limburg-Styrium, who was fined by the Reichskammergericht in 1787 for 'infringing the civic freedom' of the burghers of Speyer. Thus the imperial courts affirmed the concept of the *Rechtsstaat*.[65]

---

[64] *Ibid.*, pp. 28, 33ff., 160–2, 170–2. Also, Hanns Gross, *Empire and Sovereignty. A History of the Public Law Literature in the Holy Roman Empire, 1599–1804* (Chicago and London, 1975 reprint), pp. 29–42.

[65] For individual cases of imperial intervention against arbitrary rulers, Eberhard Weis, 'Ländliche und städtische Unruhen in den linksrheinischen deutschen Gebieten von 1789 bis 1792', in idem (ed.), *Deutschland*, pp. 115–16. For the broader constitutional implications, see Thomas Würtenberger, 'Staatsverfassung an der Wende vom 18. zum 19. Jahrhundert', in *Wendemarken in der deutschen Verfassungsgeschichte (Der Staat. Zeitschrift für Staatslehre, öffentliches Recht und Verfassungsgeschichte* Beiheft 10, 1993), pp. 86–7, 106. For the effect of court interventions on the ground, see Gabel, *Widerstand*.

The French Revolution set in train events that brought about the Reich's dissolution. News of the Bastille's fall travelled quickly up the Rhine from Strasbourg and dominated the regional press from 20 July 1789 onwards. Leading newspapers such as the *Mainzer Zeitung, Kurtrierische Intelligenzblatt* and *Kölnischer Staatsboth* generally welcomed events. In this, they reflected educated opinion as expressed by prominent intellectuals like Georg Forster, who wrote on 30 July of philosophy's triumph in France. Accompanying press reports of widespread violence in France dented initial optimism, but was blamed as the inevitable consequence of centuries of Bourbon despotism. However, very soon – within weeks – the first negative commentaries began to appear accompanied by warnings not to follow the French example.[66]

Fears that the revolutionary contagion might spread created something akin to the *Grande Peur* over the summer. Alarmist reports of unrest in areas bordering France appeared in Cologne's newspapers in August, conjuring up visions of rampaging peasants burning property and assaulting clergymen and forestry officials.[67] These reports, though exaggerated, contained some truth in that unrest did surface in various localities. In September, it erupted in Annweiler and Bergzabern in the duchy of Zweibrücken close to Alsace. In Annweiler, conflict revolved around how communal fields were leased by the town council, and complaints that the process was rigged. Local councillors arrested some of the more vocal critics, thereby sparking both protests and petitions to the ducal government. This responded sympathetically and matters quickly quietened down. Significantly, Annweiler would remain loyal to the duke during the first French occupation in 1792/3. Ducal conciliation also kept the rest of Zweibrücken relatively quiet. For example, a cull of wild animals and the sale of their meat at low prices soothed popular discontent over forestry rights and hunting policy. Elsewhere, rulers attempted to forestall unrest with similar concessions. Generally, they were successful, despite rural discontent that was worst in the Middle Rhine and especially in the electorate of Trier. Everywhere forestry infractions multiplied, though they were most common in relatively poor areas such as the Hunsrück.[68] Peasants in the vicinity of Trier staged a brief tax strike,

---

[66] Hansen, *Quellen,* 1, pp. 380–5.   [67] *Ibid.,* pp. 412–14.

[68] Georg Forster, writing in 1790, even warned that the wood shortage might spark a Europe-wide revolution. Joachim Radkau, 'Holzverknappung und Krisenbewußtsein im 18. Jahrhundert', *Geschichte und Gesellschaft* 9 (1983), pp. 513–43. For a contemporary Rhenish source on rural conflict, see the chronicle of Johann Peter Delhoven reproduced in H. Cardauns and R. Müller (eds.), *Die rheinische Dorfchronik des Joh. Peter Delhoven aus Dormagen (1783–1823)* (Cologne, 1926). Also, Hansen, *Quellen,* 1, pp. 451, 531–2.

whilst in Boppard, a small town at the other end of the electorate, a long-festering conflict over forestry rights provoked sinister threats to 'follow the Parisian example'. Electoral officials feared for their safety to the extent of requesting the evacuation of their families. Meanwhile, within the city of Trier, signs of radicalisation appeared with the circulation of pamphlets calling for resistance to the elector.[69] Moving north, large-scale, intimidating demonstrations directed against the magistracy rocked Cologne in October, with discontented burghers threatening to deal with the mayor 'in the French manner'.[70] Here, as elsewhere, disaffected groups played upon the authorities' fears to force concessions in existing disputes. They employed threatening references to events in France, used revolutionary rhetoric and displayed revolutionary symbols such as cockades that now bloomed in a variety of colours. Popular political awareness undoubtedly reached new heights. The imperial secretary in Koblenz reported to Vienna in September 1789 that the common people avidly read newspapers, whilst Johanne von Müller wrote to his brother shortly thereafter of the 'all pervasive spirit of renewing liberty' that existed in Jülich, Cologne and Trier. Where would it all end, he asked.[71] The previous trend towards conflict resolution through legal channels, it appeared, was being superseded by direct action.

Yet, popular demonstrations never quite transcended the bounds within which conflicts had been fought previously.[72] They remained sporadic and less radical than in France; blood-curdling threats were never carried out. Calls for an overthrow of the existing order enjoyed no popular support even in places racked by conflict like Aachen. The preconditions for revolution were not there. The pocket-sized Rhenish territories proved better able to spot trouble early and take remedial action in the form of concessions, relief or application of military force. The small Rhenish armies, though useless at fighting wars, were well suited for dealing with internal trouble; and, should they fail, imperial forces stood ready to intervene. Not that the Reich's contribution to peace was limited to its military capacity. Greater was the ongoing contribution made by its institutions of conflict resolution.

[69] *Ibid.*, pp. 367–8, 394, 556–7, 575, 613–15. Also on Trier, Alois Schumacher, *Idéologie révolutionnaire et pratique politique de la France en Rhénanie de 1794 à 1801. L'exemple du pays de Trèves* (Paris, 1989), pp. 20–1.

[70] Hansen, *Quellen*, I, pp. 401 n. 1, 417.

[71] Imperial secretary in Koblenz to the imperial vice-chancellor, Colloredo, September 1789 and Johanne von Müller to his brother, March 1790, quoted from Hansen, *Quellen*, I, pp. 440–2 and 561 n. 2 respectively.

[72] This conclusion applies even to the serious disturbances that occurred in Mainz in August 1790 when apprentices from the guilds briefly gained control of the city. The limited political objectives of the guilds are revealed in Schmitt, *Zunftwesen*, pp. 41–7.

The contrast with France, where it took violent revolution to end despotism, was not lost on contemporaries. It was obvious to the peasants of the county of Saarbrücken, for example, who, in the summer of 1789, responded to the arbitrariness of their local ruler not through revolution but by appealing to the Reichskammergericht. Within months the court found in their favour and issued an official warning to the count, who accepted a compromise that was celebrated outside Saarbrücken's town hall that November.[73]

Imperial intervention, in the form of an arbitration commission, similarly defused the ongoing political crisis in Aachen. Crucially, this intervention did not aim at simply restoring the old order but rather attempted to reach consensus over a new constitutional document. To this end, the commission consulted widely and solicited detailed reform proposals. Several radical draft constitutions were submitted, and one of these – drawn up by the Prussian diplomat Christian Wilhelm von Dohm – served as the basis (albeit, in modified form) for Aachen's revised *'Gaffelbrief'* of 1792 approved by the Reichskammergericht. This document started from the principle that the burgher of Aachen was 'a free man, subject to no one but only the laws of the Empire and this city', and its provisions represented an attempt to graft new principles concerning personal freedom and the inviolability of private property onto existing structures. Above all, it transformed Aachen's guilds from closed trade-based institutions into 'political' bodies open to all enjoying civic rights, a development Thomas Würtenberger correctly describes as 'revolutionary'.[74]

Though never implemented because of the French invasion and internal opposition, Aachen's new *Gaffelbrief* demonstrated the ability of the Reich to embrace reform.[75] Even radicals like Franz Dautzenberg (who submitted his own proposed constitution for Aachen) and Niklas Vogt believed in the Holy Roman Empire's progressive potential; Dautzenberg praised the imperial constitution as the 'the first bulwark of German freedom',[76] whilst Vogt described it as

the best support, the scaffolding, behind which the most beautiful construction of civic freedom can emerge. – So, we keep the scaffolding standing for the moment, and progressively establish a better balance between burgher, estates and states.

---

[73] Hansen, *Quellen*, I, pp. 412–14, 471–4, 501–5.
[74] Würtenberger, 'Staatsverfassung', pp. 93–5, 115.
[75] Though, as Horst Carl stresses in his study of the Aachener *Mäkelei*, the scope for intervention by the imperial courts in future conflicts within the imperial cities was much restricted by the *'Wahlkapitulation'* extracted by the territorial princes from Leopold II in 1790. Carl, 'Mäkelei', pp. 177–9.
[76] Hansen, *Quellen*, I, p. 583.

We increasingly enlighten them as to their interests and position through the application of science and publicity. – Then, finally, we dismantle the Gothic scaffolding.[77]

This sentiment was shared by the last generation of thinkers who contributed to the genre of political writing known as '*Reichspublizistik*' (publications concerned with the reform of imperial institutions). They included Carl Friedrich Häberlin and Nikolaus Thaddäus von Gönner, both of whom attempted to update the Reich through the application of new concepts emerging from France. Häberlin, for example, linked the imperial *maietas* with the revolutionary concept 'nation', before concluding that the Reich encouraged freedoms which the French only achieved through Revolution. Gönner went even further, legitimising the Emperor's authority as an expression of the 'general will'.[78]

The apparent effectiveness of the Empire contrasted with the failure of France to arrive at a durable internal settlement contributed to a sense of *Reichspatriotismus* in the Rhineland in the early 1790s. Opponents of the Revolution exploited this and introduced a new ingredient by connecting it with more obviously national sentiments. Increasingly, there appeared in the conservative press national stereotypes that contrasted such German virtues as loyalty ('*deutsche Treue*'), honesty and steadfastness with French collective violence and superficiality. It is unclear whether such arguments struck a popular chord, though it is indicative that the anti-revolutionary press felt them worth making. In this context it was fortuitous that 1789 should mark the centenary of Louis XIV's devastation of the Palatinate, an atrocity that remained alive in the region's collective memory. Of course, the anniversary could be 'spun' in different ways, with the blame pinned either on the French people or, as pro-revolutionaries preferred, on the Bourbons. Another opportunity to exploit francophobia presented itself with the dispute that erupted between the German princes and new French government over the status of Alsace. When, in August 1789, the French Constituent Assembly abolished feudalism throughout France, it quite naturally included Alsace within this legislation. This infringed the treaty rights enjoyed by German princes in the region. The anti-revolutionary press within the Rhineland interpreted the resulting conflict not primarily in social (nobles versus peasants) or ideological (historical rights versus national sovereignty) terms, but rather, as a national conflict.[79]

---

[77] Theuringer, *Liberalismus*, pp. 307–10.   [78] Gross, *Empire*, pp. 455–75.
[79] Hansen, *Quellen*, I, pp. 374, 422–3, 435, 475, 639, 733–4, 796, 807.

The diminution of the French military threat in the Revolution's first years probably reinforced anti-militarist rather than chauvinistic sentiment within the Rhineland. In any case, Austria and Prussia posed a potentially greater threat following their rapprochement at Reichenbach in July 1790. In response, some commentators argued for greater unity between the smaller German states.[80] Prussia in particular represented princely absolutism at a time when France (and also neighbouring Liège) appeared to be adopting a system of limited monarchy. Such an interpretation, of course, rested upon misunderstanding.[81] It was an interpretation that emboldened elements within the Rhenish *Landstände* to press their own demands more forcefully. Mainz's elector, Friedrich Karl, recognised the danger this posed when he warned Max Franz in April 1790 that the greatest revolutionary threat in the *Reich* came from territories where the 'third estate' enjoyed an established institutional position.[82] The warning reached Max Franz at a time when electoral Cologne's estates (which convened between February and August 1790) were engaged in bitter dispute over the contentious issue of fiscal equality. Since 1777, the city curia had been calling for greater equality, but in 1790 the tone became more threatening. The other three curia who opposed the cities also resorted to polemical accusations. Hostile pamphlets circulated accusing the cities' representatives of being 'adherents of the party of upheaval', whilst on the other side numerous pamphlets appeared urging the cities to 'get the clergy and nobility to pay like the peasant', and demonstrating how the historical justifications for noble tax exemption no longer applied.[83]

Successful political management and limited concessions by Max Franz prevented an open breach in electoral Cologne, though the issue remained unresolved at the time of the French occupation in 1794. In Trier, in contrast, the confrontational policies of Clemens Wenzeslaus and chief minister von Duminique, who reversed the previous reform course, provoked trouble

---

[80] Hansen, *Quellen*, 1, pp. 481, 483, 582, 590, 902, 1059–60 n. 2; also, Gagliardo, *Reich*, pp. 132–4. Whether such arguments reflected the emergence of a specifically regional identity is a moot point, though it is worth mentioning in this context that the word '*Rheinländer*' first became common in the 1780s as the collective for the German-speaking inhabitants of the Rhine. Hansen, *Quellen*, 1, p. 353 n. 3.

[81] Rhenish press coverage of the French Revolution was surprisingly uneven. Whilst the humiliation of the Bourbons and acts of revolutionary violence attracted sensationalist reporting, such fundamental reforms as the abolition of the old provinces in favour of uniform departments or the details of the 1791 constitution attracted no attention. Hansen, *Quellen*, 1, pp. 47*, 545–7, 665–6, 688–9, 846, 932–3, 949.

[82] Friedrich Karl to Max Franz, 11 April 1790. *Ibid.*, 1, pp. 601–3.

[83] *Ibid.*, 1, pp. 548–58, 702, 777; Essers, *Landtage*, pp. 6–7, 38–44, 57–8, 60, 62, 80, 84, 98, 103.

with the *Landstände*. The electoral government restricted religious tolerance, closed reading societies, imposed strict censorship, issued threatening
circulars against disturbers of the peace, and employed military force to
suppress demonstrations. However, the issue that finally brought matters
to a head was the welcome extended by the elector to the French *émigrés*.[84]
The first wave of *émigrés* reached the Rhine in the summer of 1789. Most
did not settle but moved on, so that at the beginning of 1791 the French
ambassador in Koblenz counted only a dozen *émigrés* in the city plus a
few more in Trier. This position changed in February 1791 when Friedrich
Karl of Mainz, ever concerned to raise his international profile and much
to the annoyance of Emperor Leopold II, offered hospitality to the French
princes Artois and Condé. Over the following months, numerous followers
settled in the region. Their presence and arrogance greatly aggravated the
domestic political conflict within the electorate of Mainz at a time when
Friedrich Karl's government, like that of Clemens Wenzeslaus, was engaged
in a clampdown that resulted in a purge of Kantians. Radicals like Georg
Forster lumped together what they termed the German 'aristocratic party'
and the French *émigrés*, and feared that together they would bury reform
in the name of counter-revolution.[85]

Not to be outdone, Clemens Wenzeslaus offered *émigrés* hospitality in
Koblenz, a city that soon earned the nickname '*Klein-Versailles*' on account
of its transformation over the summer of 1791 into the headquarters of
the comtes de Provence and d'Artois.[86] These ensconced themselves in
Schloß Schönbornlust, a palace that Clemens Wenzeslaus placed at their
disposal. Here they established a government-in-exile, replete with ministers, mistresses, guards and sycophants jockeying for positions that would
be claimed upon the triumphal return to Versailles. Rhinelanders looked
on with bemusement at the antics within this exiled court, and the arrogant
contempt with which the *émigrés* treated locals. The Habsburg representative in Koblenz reported that the number of impregnated local girls and
general decline in morals in those areas where *émigrés* settled made it appropriate to rename the 'French disease' the 'aristocratic disease'. Several
Rhenish journals reached the opposite conclusion, and lumped together
the *émigrés* with their revolutionary opponents as joint examples of French

---

[84] Hansen, *Quellen*, I, pp. 345–6, 401–4, 439, 502, 520, 691.
[85] *Ibid.*, pp. 767, 774, 778–81, 791.
[86] Max Franz, in contrast to his counterparts in Trier and Mainz, refused hospitality to the *émigrés*
and more generally criticised the provocative counter-revolutionary course embarked upon in the
southern electorates. He even spent part of 1791 in Vienna so as to avoid having to receive the French
princes in Bonn. Emperor Leopold II refrained from maintaining an embassy in Koblenz after 1791
for similar reasons; his representative in the region was henceforth based in Bonn.

immorality. Certainly, the *émigrés'* behaviour hardly provided an appealing advertisement for counter-revolution, and their unpopularity rubbed off on the elector.[87] Worse, the *émigrés'* military preparations throughout the summer of 1791 led to rumours of French retaliation in a repeat performance of Louis XIV's devastation of the Palatinate. Trier's estates, in their self-declared role as defenders of the *Land*, accused Clemens Wenzeslaus of sacrificing the interests of his subjects and linked his hospitality to the *émigrés* with his preferment of foreign-born nobles more generally, whilst the city of Trier interpreted the refusal of *émigrés* to obey the city council as part of a wider electoral plot to undermine its ancient liberties. The *émigré* controversy was only resolved in November 1791, when Clemens Wenzeslaus and Friedrich Karl bowed to intense French pressure and ordered the dispersion of *émigrés*. However, with the outbreak of the Revolutionary Wars in 1792, the *émigrés* were allowed to return in preparation for the predicted promenade to Paris.[88]

Before turning to the Revolutionary Wars, it is appropriate to re-emphasise the main points raised in this chapter. The Rhineland's civilisation was an ancient one. Its cities and 'lands' in the eighteenth century were governed according to conventions that dated back centuries. Conflicts often extended back as far. Yet this chapter has failed if it has conveyed an impression of stagnation. Thanks in part to its location on the geopolitical periphery, the Rhineland in this period experienced an economic recovery and the beginnings of industrialisation. Territorial fragmentation assisted rather than undermined this. Certainly, development was uneven and some territories proved more successful than others. However, even places such as the imperial city of Cologne proved more adaptable to change than has been conceded previously by historians.

The Rhineland, as an important European trade artery, has always been a receptacle of influences from abroad. The eighteenth century was no exception, and ideas associated with the Enlightenment left their mark. Within the Rhenish context, the Enlightenment should be seen primarily as a religious reform movement motivated partly by an inferiority complex vis-à-vis Protestant Germany. The historiography as a whole has underestimated this

---

[87] *Ibid.*, I, pp. 16*, 157, 232–3, 273–4, 778–81, 791–4, 811–12, 818, 830–5, 844, 850–1, 876–7, 957, 962. For the argument that the *émigrés* indirectly contributed to a radicalisation of political culture in the Middle Rhine, see Josef Smets, 'Freiheit, Gleichheit, Brüderlichkeit. Untersuchungen zum Verhalten der linksrheinischen Bevölkerung unter der französischen Herrschaft', *Rheinische Vierteljahrsblätter* 59 (1995), pp. 79–122.

[88] Hansen, *Quellen*, I, pp. 41*, 635, 923, 934–5, 941–2, 947–8, 971–2, 998–9, 1002, 1008–10, 1012–14, 1017; 2, p. 51*.

dimension. Orthodox Catholicism opposed the Catholic Enlightenment, and the two sides engaged in bitter debate in the final decades before the Revolution. Neither side emerged triumphant at the time of the Bastille's fall. Both sides made full use of the public sphere to whose development they contributed. Both sides also employed the ancient but reinvigorated conflict-resolution structures available within the Holy Roman Empire.

Conflict between Enlightenment and Orthodoxy tended to obscure an older set of disputes that persisted in the region and engaged a broader social spectrum. These generally pitted magistracies against burghers, and princes against estates, and revolved around a myriad of particular issues that varied in detail from locality to locality, but which tended to increase as a consequence of economic development. Often, the conflict between Enlightenment and Orthodoxy superimposed itself on top of these older struggles as protagonists sought to gain advantage by legitimising their position through association with a set of transcendental beliefs. Such occurred in Aachen, for example, in the conflict between the 'Old' and 'New' parties; the same was true of the centuries-old struggle that pitted the archbishops of Cologne against the imperial city. Failure to unravel different layers of conflict leads to a misunderstanding of motives and the misapplication of labels such as 'progressive' or 'reactionary' to factions in disputes that cannot be understood in those terms.

All existing conflict, whether it be between the enlightened and orthodox, the magistrate and burgher, or the prince and representative estate, would soon be overwhelmed by the revolutionary and Napoleonic tidal waves. Viewed from a longer-term perspective, the conflicts of the Old Regime often appear farcically trivial. Certainly, their detail might attract the specialist's attention, but why should they be of wider interest, for they would soon be overtaken by events? Arguably, the conflicts in themselves were of little consequence. More important was the political culture they reflected, reinforced and bequeathed. This culture was not founded upon new institutions associated with enlightened sociability, which appealed to a restricted elite. Rather, it was based upon the older conflict-resolution mechanisms found within the Reich and its territories. These mechanisms – including the imperial courts and commissions, representative estates and burgher deputations – extended further down the social spectrum and further back in time. Until recent decades, the historiography has dismissed them as ineffectual. Even now, they are blamed for blocking Germany's development and are contrasted negatively with the enlightened absolutist rulers, who drove through far-reaching reform from above. This negative appraisal is inaccurate, because institutions such as the imperial courts and representative estates proved capable of adapting new concepts and political ideas, and countenancing reform, though admittedly within strict limits. More fundamentally, they provided a mechanism through which a substantial proportion of Rhinelanders became familiar with the use of consensus-forming, representational and judicial mechanisms to blunt the arbitrary exercise of power, whether it be revolutionary or counter-revolutionary. This enlightened absolutism failed to do.

CHAPTER 3

French invasion and exploitation

The territory that lies between Paris and Saint Petersburg as well as Moscow will soon be made French, municipal and Jacobin. (Pierre Gaspard Chaumette, president of the Paris commune, 16 November 1792)[1]

It took two decades before Napoleon briefly justified Chaumette's prediction, minus the Jacobin ingredient. Initially, the Rhineland enjoyed strategic and ideological front-line status following the French declaration of war on Austria in April 1792. The Austrians and Prussians first held the initiative, advancing and capturing Verdun on 2 September. Then the French, under Dumouriez, managed to redeploy and block the Prussians at Valmy (20 September), a battle that condemned Europe to a generation of war. The French, exploiting their numerical superiority, followed up Valmy by invading the Reich: one army, under Custine, entered the Palatinate, whose cities fell quickly, whilst a second, under Dumouriez, advanced into the Netherlands, pushed aside the Austrians at Jemappes (6 November), captured Brussels and invaded the Lower Rhine.[2]

As the situation deteriorated, Austria attempted to mobilise the military potential of the Holy Roman Empire. This proved difficult. Officially, France was not at war with the Reich, as she had declared war on the Habsburgs as kings of Hungary. The Reich as a whole lacked the internal consensus to resort to force, and this French diplomats exploited. Opposition to the war was led by France's old allies, the Wittelsbachs, but was a sentiment that extended widely. In electoral Cologne domestic opposition to war from the estates prevented mobilisation. Legally, such opposition could only be overcome with an imperial declaration of war, something that would forbid neutrality and require all to contribute

[1] Jean Favier et al., Chronicle of the French Revolution (London, 1989), p. 304.
[2] T. C. W. Blanning, The French Revolutionary Wars 1787–1802 (London and New York, 1996), pp. 71–82, 88–91.

their fair share to the imperial contingents the Reichstag might authorise. So, the newly elected Emperor Francis II initiated the cumbersome process for an imperial declaration of war in autumn 1792 – the opening Reichstag debate took place on 22 October – but ran into opposition. The Wittelsbachs dragged their feet. They continued to host a French embassy in Munich and, more outrageously, allowed revolutionary troops to march through their territory and capture Speyer. This was too much, and provoked threats from Austria and Prussia. The Reich's smaller states took note and speculated grimly of the dangers posed by an Austro-Prussian victory. On 22 March 1793 the Reichstag finally agreed to declare that France had placed itself in a state of war, a formula short of a full declaration of war.[3]

The Reichstag's tortuous proceedings gained wider significance through their diffusion amongst the general public via a flood of pamphlets and newspapers. Briefly, the Reichstag became the focus for German politics. This contributed to a growing sense of imperial patriotism, a well-established sentiment that had existed during the Turkish wars and struggle against Louis XIV. It was now increasingly given a cultural dimension and exploited by Habsburg propaganda.[4] Yet swelling *Reichspatriotismus* never translated into sufficient troop contingents. Indeed, advances by the First Coalition – bolstered by the adhesion of Britain and Spain – in 1793 diminished the need for additional effort from the Rhenish states, who argued they had already suffered enough from the partial French occupation of 1792/3. Electoral Cologne's estates, the imperial cities of Aachen and Cologne and the Palatinate all proved niggardly in making any useful contribution, whilst most of Mainz's little army had been destroyed when the French captured Speyer. The quibbling over contributions and gothic legal technicality contrasted starkly with the heroic mobilisation then being organised by Lazare Carnot in France.[5]

---

[3] Joseph Hansen, *Quellen zur Geschichte des Rheinlandes im Zeitalter der französischen Revolution* (4 vols., Bonn, 1931–8), 2, pp. 7, 48, 93 n., 156, 159–60, 167, 179, 183 n. 1, 221–3, 230–2, 291–3, 303–4, 309–13, 325–5, 329–2, 333–5, 353–5, 381, 428 n. 4, 440, 495–7, 550, 805–10, 826, 829 n. 2.

[4] Karl Härter, *Reichstag und Revolution 1789–1806. Die Auseinandersetzung des immerwährenden Reichstags zu Regensburg mit den Auswirkungen der Französischen Revolution auf das alte Reich* (Göttingen, 1992), pp. 21–3. For more on the emergence of German national sentiment in this period, see T. C. W. Blanning, *The French Revolution in Germany. Occupation and Resistance in the Rhineland 1792–1802* (Oxford, 1983), pp. 247–52. Justus Hashagen, *Das Rheinland und die französische Herrschaft. Beiträge zur Charakteristik ihres Gegensatzes* (Bonn, 1908), pp. 85–91, 102. Arnold Berney, 'Reichstradition und Nationalstaatsgedanke (1789–1815)', *Historische Zeitschrift* 140 (1929), p. 62. John G. Gagliardo, *Reich and Nation. The Holy Roman Empire as Idea and Reality, 1763–1806* (Bloomington, 1980), p. 12.

[5] Hansen, *Quellen*, 2, pp. 353 n. 1, 612–13, 664 n. 1, 670–2, 805–10, 830, 835ff., 843ff., 882ff., 892 n. 2, 912–13.

Carnot seized the advantage back for France in late 1793. In response, Francis II proposed mass Reich mobilisation, but this encountered decisive Prussian-led opposition. Given his later enthusiasm for popular insurrections, it is significant that Berlin's chief official in the Rhineland, Freiherr vom Stein, fully shared his government's reservations about arming the people. The other Rhenish princes entertained similar fears. These were not unjustified: in the Palatinate, peasants responded to the call to arms with demands for the abolition of noble privilege, whilst in Trier the estates rejected a planned levee of 6,000 conscripts, a proposal that provoked calls for rebellion. Electoral Cologne's estates resisted approving military contingents, and pressed their own demands for an end to clerical and noble privilege. The government, like its counterparts elsewhere, suspended mobilisation rather than make concessions. Only in the summer of 1794 did official attitudes change, but by then it was too late.[6]

For France, military success raised the question over the future location of the eastern frontier. The theory that peace depends upon nations possessing borders determined by natural features gained ground in the eighteenth century and unexpected conquests presented the new Republic with the prospect of acquiring such frontiers. At the very least, military success opened new options with regards to the Reich. Essentially, there were three alternatives: continuity with the relative disengagement of Louis XVI, but with France allied to Prussia, not Austria; the division of the Reich between Austria, Prussia and France along the lines of the Polish partitions; or French support for the medium-sized German states at the expense of the smallest territories and ecclesiastical entities, to counterbalance Prussia and Austria. This last option, which was eventually followed, enjoyed the advantage of conforming to France's traditional strategic policy whilst at the same time satisfying ideological demands.[7]

---

[6] For Stein's opposition to a *levée en masse*, Wilhelm Steffens, 'Die linksrheinischen Provinzen Preußens unter französischer Herrschaft 1794–1802', *Rheinische Vierteljahrsblätter* 19 (1954), pp. 405–6. For the situation in electoral Cologne, see Max Braubach, *Max Franz. Letzter Kurfürst von Köln und Fürstbischof von Münster* (Vienna, 1961), pp. 278–80, 290–1, 303–4; and Eduard Hegel, *Geschichte des Erzbistums Köln*, vol. 4, *Das Erzbistum Köln zwischen Barock und Aufklärung vom Pfälzischen Krieg bis zum Ende der französischen Zeit 1688–1814* (Cologne, 1979), pp. 490–1. More generally, Roger Dufraisse, 'Les Populations de la rive gauche du Rhin et le service militaire à la fin de l'Ancien Régime et à l'époque révolutionnaire', *Revue Historique* 231 (1964), pp. 117–19.

[7] Eckhard Buddruss, 'Die Deutschlandpolitik der Französischen Revolution zwischen Traditionen und Revolutionärem Bruch', in Karl Otmar Freiherr von Aretin and Karl Härter (eds.), *Revolution und Konservatives Begarren. Das alte Reich und die Französische Revolution* (Mainz, 1990), pp. 145–54. Sydney Seymour Biro, *The German Policy of Revolutionary France. A Study in French Diplomacy during the War of the First Coalition 1792–1797* (Cambridge, Mass., 1957), pp. 1–6, 21–4.

Georges-Jacques Danton expounded the new policy to the Convention on 31 January 1793: 'The limits of France are marked by nature and we will reach them on the four corners of the horizon: the banks of the Rhine, the shores of the ocean, the line of the Alps. To there must extend the boundaries of our Republic.' Not that this policy went unopposed. Some, including Carnot, believed that insistence on natural frontiers would prolong the war and endanger the Revolution. French territorial objectives subsequently remained ill-defined during the Jacobin Terror. Maximilian Robespierre never spoke of natural frontiers and with foresight feared that generals might use conquered territories as bases from which to intrigue against the Republic. He rejected the feasibility of exporting revolution and instead focused upon its preservation at home. The internationalism of the early Revolution evaporated. Chauvinism now triumphed in Paris and claimed the heads of various foreign radicals including their self-appointed leader, the Rhinelander Anacharsis Cloots, guillotined in March 1794. In conquered territories, the Committee of Public Safety decreed (on 18 September 1793) brutal exploitation.

This was the position inherited by the Jacobins' successors, the Thermidorians. They approached the question of frontiers with characteristic pragmatism. The issue became pressing as French armies again pushed forward and completed the occupation of the Austrian Netherlands and Rhineland by the autumn of 1794. The following year witnessed a debate in the Convention over Belgium's future. Deputies paid lip service to self-determination, but the debate quickly turned to the advantages that would accrue from territorial expansion, including an appreciation of the revolutionary paper-currency (*assignats*). Such considerations took precedence over any other principles: as Merlin de Douai concluded on the government's behalf, 'in order to indemnify itself for the evils and costs of the most unjust of all wars as well as to place itself in a state to prevent their recurrence by new means of defence, the French Republic can and must either retain these lands through right of conquest or through treaty as it sees fit, without consulting the inhabitants'. During the debate, the Convention also spent some time considering the Rhineland's future in discussions closely followed in that region's press. Amongst the plethora of justifications deputies presented for annexation were that the Rhine alone provided a sufficient defensive barrier, that the region had been part of Roman Gaul, that its inhabitants were destined to be French, that the Rhenish electorates had sent contingents to fight the Republic, that after years of sacrifice it was absurd to respect 'miniature sovereigns' with their 'Golden Bulls', that

Rhinelanders were mature enough to enjoy liberty, and that the tyranny of priests was worse than the tyranny of princes. Only a minority opposed annexation. Rather, the general sentiment was summed up by the dictum espoused by one deputy: 'The first right is to preserve oneself; the highest justice is to obtain and conserve the means.' However, the French did not annex the Rhineland in 1795, but signed an agreement – the Treaty of Basel – with Prussia that marked the first step in its acquisition. Berlin agreed to cede its Rhenish territories to France in return for compensation.[8]

Prussia's defection coupled with German suspicions that Austria was pursuing the war for selfish dynastic reasons increasingly undermined imperial defence. The creation, following Basel, of a north German neutral zone under Prussian guarantee greatly hampered the military efforts of those states, like electoral Cologne, that remained committed to the war but whose territories lay within that zone. Furthermore, Berlin's example encouraged other less committed states to enter into their own agreements with France. The Wittelsbachs in particular were tempted to follow the Prussians, though they were deterred by possible Habsburg retaliation. Bavaria's future king, Max Joseph of Pfalz-Zweibrücken, in particular strove for an understanding with France. He extended peace-feelers through a Rhenish go-between, Andreas van Recum, who would later serve as a Napoleonic sub-prefect and legislator. As part of these dealings, Max Joseph appears to have allowed the French to capture the strategically important fortress of Mannheim in September 1795. Certainly, the Austrians suspected treachery and arrested two Palatine ministers following the recapture of the fortress; the resulting controversy became a sensation in Germany. Recum kept low whilst carefully filing away incriminating material proving Max Joseph's involvement for possible future use.[9]

Whilst Vienna's policy remained under the direction of Franz Maria Thugut, a statesman who viewed revolutionary France as a menace to civilisation, Austria stood firm.[10] Indeed, following much effort, the Habsburg position within the Reich improved in late 1795. It was only in 1796, following defeats by Bonaparte in Italy, that Vienna approached the negotiating table. Another débâcle, at Rivoli (14 January 1797), produced the armistice of Loeben (18 April) followed by the Peace of Campo Formio

[8] For the debate in the Convention, see Hansen, *Quellen*, 3, pp. 651–6. For a full text of the Treaty of Basel, see Alexandre de Clercq, *Recueil des traités de la France* (23 vols., Paris, 1861–1919), 1, pp. 232–6.
[9] Karl-Georg Faber, *Andreas van Recum 1765–1828. Ein rheinischer Kosmopolit* (Bonn, 1969), pp. 51–8, 61–2, 81–92, 124–5, 131–3.
[10] Karl A. Roider Jr., *Baron Thugut and Austria's Response to the French Revolution* (Princeton, 1987), pp. 170–230.

(17 October). To the fury of proponents of natural frontiers, Bonaparte, who conducted negotiations without reference to Paris, focused on territorial gains in Italy and failed to secure the Rhine. Instead, the parties decided to convene a special international congress at Rastatt in 1798 to decide on that frontier.

The vagaries of revolutionary politics as much as the course of war determined French policy in the Rhineland. The occupation itself can be divided into four phases. The first, lasting from autumn 1792 to spring 1793, involved only the southern portion of the region, and is associated with the 'Republic of Mainz'. The second opened with France's occupation of the entire left bank in autumn 1794. It was characterised by exploitation. The third phase, from March 1797 to September 1797, was bound up with Lazare Hoche. The fourth, finally, started in November 1797 and involved the administrative integration of the occupied lands into France. It ended with Napoleon's seizure of power in 1799.

The French army that occupied Mainz on 21 October 1792 professed liberation. Official instructions from Paris promised security and freedom. Implicit from the beginning, of course, was the assumption that Rhinelanders receive fraternity only if they opted for liberty, but the French held high hopes of this. Initial signs from the Palatinate, where peasant discontent was apparent, were encouraging. The new soundbite, 'peace on the cottages, war on the palaces', seemed to strike a chord amidst reports of peasants plundering noble fields and wine cellars, expelling old-regime officials, and spontaneously planting liberty trees.[11] However, very quickly – within weeks – the French discovered that discontent with the Old Regime did not mean adherence to revolution. Disappointed, the French engaged more actively in propaganda, which was provided primarily by the minority of local radicals. When this failed, the French sought out scapegoats and found them in the old-regime officials whom they had initially kept on. So, a month into the occupation of Mainz, they abolished the old administrative structures and created new ones staffed by radicals. They also 'municipalised' the city governments of Worms and Speyer, though this did not involve a major change in personnel. It was at this point that the French confronted the difficulty of reconciling their long-term political objective of propagating revolution, which meant favouring radicals, with the short-term requirements of the army, which were best met through co-operating with the established elite.

---

[11] Franz Dumont, *Die Mainzer Republik von 1792/93. Studien zur Revolutionierung in Rheinhessen und der Pfalz* (Alzey, 1982), pp. 61–6, 79–80. Hansen, *Quellen*, 1, p. 414; 2, pp. 562–4, 785–6.

For nowhere in the Rhineland, the French discovered, were the radicals numerous enough to represent a sound basis of government.[12]

The French nonetheless forged ahead in their attempts to win political commitment to revolution. A stark choice now presented itself which excluded any possibility of a 'middle way' between revolution and counter-revolution. In Mainz, these two extremes were represented by registers, one in black, decorated with chains representing slavery, and a second in red denoting freedom. The French expected all adult male inhabitants of Mainz to sign one of the registers. Subsequently, the new administration of the 'Republic of Mainz' despatched commissioners into the countryside to gather signatures in favour of 'reunion' with France, and on 15 December the Convention in Paris decreed that elections be held in the occupied territories. All males over twenty-one could vote provided they swore to be 'faithful to the people and the principles of liberty and equality'. The authorities treated those who abstained as counter-revolutionaries.[13]

As we shall see when examining reactions to French rule in detail, few Rhinelanders were prepared to commit themselves even under pressure. The final realisation by the French that they were dealing with a hostile population in Germany came in early December 1792, when occupied Frankfurt was liberated by a Prusso-Hessian relief force with the active assistance of the civilian population. Arguably, this event was as important as Valmy: Valmy exploded the myth that revolutionary France would collapse in the face of invasion; events in Frankfurt disillusioned the French of the notion that they would be welcomed as liberators. Nor was Frankfurt a one-off, as civilians also assisted in the expulsion of the French from Aachen on 2 March 1793.[14] Shortly thereafter Mainz also fell to the Coalition, and France again faced invasion. The new Jacobin Republic responded with an unparalleled degree of mobilisation, declaring total war (23 August 1793). In 1794, with the army swollen to over a million men, the Republic seized the initiative. On the north-eastern front, the decisive victory came at Fleurus on 26 June 1794, leading to the reoccupation of Belgium. The Battle of Aldenhoven in October, the first engagement where the Republic

---

[12] *Archives Parlementaires de 1787 à 1860. Recueil complet des débats législatifs et politiques des chambres françaises. Imprimé . . . sous la direction de MM. I. Mavidal et E. Lurent, etc.* 1st series (1787–99), (Paris, 1868–), 52, pp. 651–5. Dumont, *Mainzer Republik*, pp. 89–90, 121–6. For Speyer, see Jürgen Müller, *Von der alten Stadt zur neuen Munizipalität. Die Auswirkungen der Französischen Revolution in den linksrheinischen Städten Speyer und Koblenz* (Koblenz, 1990), p. 104.

[13] T. C. W. Blanning, *Reform and Revolution in Mainz 1743–1803* (Cambridge, 1974), p. 280.

[14] For Frankfurt, see Hansen, *Quellen*, 2, pp. 621–2. For Aachen, see *ibid*., pp. 775–7. In retaliation, the French Convention, acting on Robespierre's initiative, decreed on 25 September 1793 that Aachen would be torched when recaptured.

fielded more than 100,000 men, resulted in the occupation of most of the Rhineland: Cologne, Bonn, Krefeld, Koblenz and Cleves all quickly fell. Only Mainz, facing its third siege in two years, held out.

Two French armies now occupied the Rhineland: the Sambre-Meuse in the north and Rhin-et-Moselle in the south. Together, they numbered between 136,000 and 187,000 troops between 1794 and 1797, a colossal burden on a civilian population of 1.6 million souls at most.[15] Disillusioned by their experience of 1792/3, the French now treated Rhinelanders as an exploitable enemy. The scale of exploitation reflected military requirements. The Sambre-Meuse army alone consumed 182 head of cattle, 850 sheep, 210,000 pounds of bread and 400,000 pounds of fodder *per day*. In any three-month period, it required 250,000 quintals (1 quintal = 48.95 grams) of wheat, 250,000 quintals of rye, 11,250 quintals of rice, 1.2 million pints of brandy, 300,000 pints of vinegar, 1.5 million pounds of salt, 1.62 million quintals of hay, 1.8 million quintals of straw for fodder, 720,000 quintals of straw for bedding, 1,080,000 bushels of oats and 50,000 head of cattle. The Rhineland needed to provide the bulk of these vast quantities, as Paris had redirected Belgian supplies to supply the exhausted French market. Thus, between 22 September and 21 October 1794, the French extracted 154,405 quintals of wheat, 145,827 quintals of rye, 8,461 head of cattle and 9,778 sheep from the region between the Meuse and the Rhine. The occupation authorities in Aachen estimated that in the first ten months alone, the region north of the Moselle provided supplies amounting to 227,030,000 *livres*, supplies that were either unpaid for or else extracted in return for worthless *assignats*. Worse, much requisitioned produce never reached the army, but perished in depots thanks to mismanagement by military commissariats. Competition for scarce food supplies had predictable consequences: the price of bread tripled following the occupation, and during the terrible 'hunger winter' of 1794/5, when temperatures hit −17°C and vital waterways froze, soldiers and civilians alike teetered on the brink of starvation.[16]

The French demanded cash as well as produce and imposed huge monetary contributions, totalling 150 million *livres* between 1794 and 1799. They seized local notables as hostages to ensure these were met. They also took over feudal dues and tithes which they extracted more rigorously than

[15] The figures for the size of the French occupation forces are taken from Blanning, *Germany*, p. 84.
[16] Peter Wetzler, *War and Subsistence. The Sambre and Meuse Army in 1794* (New York, 1985), pp. 33–5, 93–5, 117–8, 136. One bushel in this context equals 13 litres dry, the equivalent of 0.358 of an English bushel; a French pound, as used here, is equivalent to 489.5 grams, or 1.08 English pounds. Also, Hansen, *Quellen*, 3, pp. 771–2, 762.

before. Confiscation of religious endowments destroyed public health, welfare and poverty relief systems. Local communities, crushed by the burden, took out loans at disadvantageous interest rates, shifting a proportion of the costs onto future generations. As late as 1797–8, five-sixths of tax revenue went to the French army. Or at least in theory, for much of the cash raised was siphoned off by corrupt officials. In addition, Paris despatched special extraction committees to requisition strategic raw materials to augment the Republic's resources. Forced billeting, aggravated by the lack of an equitable system, was an additional burden, whilst towns unfortunate enough to contain French general officers needed to provide generous table money. The French also requisitioned labour for work on fortifications and logistics. The short-term impact was hardship and misery. The longer-term damage to the Rhenish economy was mixed, though a few sectors – notably forestry and livestock farming – took decades to recover. Some concerns, including the largest in the region, the von der Leyen textile business in Krefeld, remained profitable until 1797, and prudent manufacturers moved their portable capital across the Rhine to escape seizure. Businessmen nonetheless remained popular targets for hostage taking, but simultaneously their importance in meeting French demands gave them a public profile they had not previously enjoyed.[17]

Occupation also threatened the Rhineland's cultural heritage. In June 1794, the Committee for Public Education in Paris ordered the attachment to the army of 'experts' responsible for identifying valuable cultural objects in occupied territories. The painter Jacques-Louis David was earmarked for such a post in Belgium and the Rhineland, but was dropped following Thermidor. His less eminent colleagues proved thorough enough: from Aachen they collected numerous books and manuscripts, the marble sarcophagus of Charlemagne, and other collections. From Cologne, they took twenty-five boxes of books, manuscripts and engravings, plus Roman artefacts and works by Dürer and Rubens. The 'extraction' mission was only wound down after spring 1795, having bagged over 50,000 volumes of books and numerous other objects. Many other objects had already been

---

[17] For French exploitation of the Rhineland, see Blanning, *Germany*, pp. 75–6, 89, 99–102, 118, 123ff., 136–9, 156–8, 210, 281–2. For the impact of the occupation on the Rhenish economy, see Marieluise Schultheis-Friebe, 'Die französische Wirtschaftspolitik im Roër-Departement 1792–1814' (Bonn D.Phil., 1969), p. 47. For the response of the business elite, Jeffry M. Diefendorf, *Businessmen and Politics in the Rhineland, 1789–1834* (Princeton, 1980), p. 52; Wilhelm Kurschat, *Das Haus Friedrich & Heinrich von der Leyen in Krefeld. Zur Geschichte der Rheinlande in der Zeit der Fremdherrschaft 1794–1814* (Frankfurt a. M., 1933), pp. 72–4. For the collapse of the poverty-relief structures, Calixte Hudemann-Simon, *L'Etat et les pauvres: l'assistance et la lutte contre la mendicité dans les quatre départements rhénans, 1794–1814* (Sigmaringen, 1997), pp. 40–3.

evacuated in the other direction by the electors, including the shrine of the Magi (by Nicolas of Verdun) from Cologne. Tragically, many of these treasures were subsequently sold, dispersed or melted down to finance the war. The French, meanwhile, requisitioned plundered ecclesiastical buildings and turned them into depots or prisoner-of-war camps. Teaching in Bonn, Cologne and Trier universities, which had resumed following the occupation, was disrupted by the ongoing war and the loss of endowment income. Mainz university remained closed, due to the siege. The French abolished all four universities in early 1798.[18]

Cultural disruption was not the main concern of ordinary Rhinelanders under occupation. Apart from pressure on scarce resources came military brutality. At worst, troops ran amok, inflicting atrocities against civilians that foreshadowed Napoleon's war in Spain. Many French officers were themselves shocked by what they saw, but there were limits to what they could do following the disintegration of military justice after 1792–3. Those who attempted to enforce discipline faced possible denunciation as counter-revolutionaries. The short-lived civil administrations established by the French between 1794 and 1797 proved incapable of controlling the army, which now justified Robespierre's worst fears of 'praetorianisation'. The restoration of the primacy of civilian government would come only in 1800, thanks to a general, Napoleon Bonaparte. As for civilians, open resistance was hardly an option, given the massive military presence. When resorted to, it triggered uncompromising retaliation, as experienced by the towns of Kusel and Westhopfen, which the French razed to the ground.[19]

Such dramatic confrontation between occupier and occupied mercifully proved exceptional. Most Rhinelanders accepted the advantages of some degree of co-operation, as will be seen. As for the French, they recognised the need for local collaboration. Upon occupying the region in 1794, they decreed that natives make up three-quarters of the local administration. The Republic had a right to talent, which it 'requisitioned' like everything else. In the south, where the military situation remained precarious, the Rhin-et-Moselle army simply took over the existing administrative structures. In the

[18] For the extraction commission, see Ferdinand Boyer, 'Les Conquêtes scientifiques de la Convention en Belgique et dans les Pays Rhénans (1794–1795)', *Revue d'Histoire Moderne et Contemporaine* 18 (1971), pp. 355–7, 366–7, 373. For the cultural impact on the archdiocese of Cologne, see Hegel, *Erzbistums Köln*, 4, pp. 487, 512–13.

[19] Blanning, *Germany*, pp. 91–8, 203, 302–3. The fullest account of the many ad hoc administrative structures erected by the French remains Ludwig Käss, *Die Organisation der allgemeinen Staatsverwaltung auf dem linken Rheinufer durch die Franzosen während der Besetzung 1792 bis zum Frieden von Lunéville (1801)* (Mainz, 1929).

north, under the Sambre-Meuse army – which, unlike the Rhin-et-Moselle army, was solidly republican – the French created new institutions, but depended upon local personnel. This was especially true of the judiciary, where local lawyers alone could make sense of the myriad Rhenish laws.[20]

The various short-lived administrative structures the French experimented with after 1794 hardly coped with meeting immediate military requirements, let alone laying down any long-term foundations. By 1797, the Rhineland was utterly exhausted and demoralised. Stein, reporting to Berlin, complained bitterly of French maladministration, something that would only end with a full restoration of the Old Regime.[21] Stein was hardly an impartial observer, but his assessment resembled that of the Sambre-Meuse army's new commander, General Lazare Hoche. Hoche was one of a fresh breed of political general whose coming Robespierre had dreaded. He identified 'misguided extremism' and 'false political and administrative principles' as the cause of all ills, and recommended the return not only of the personnel but also the institutions of the Old Regime as alone possessing legitimacy and popular confidence. 'Experience should have corrected our mania of wanting to municipalise Europe,' he concluded, noting that after their experience of occupation, it would be pointless trying to reconcile Rhinelanders to the Revolution.[22] Paris accepted Hoche's recommendations and, on 12 March 1797, reintroduced the old structures.

Hoche's concept proved fundamentally flawed, as it was founded on misunderstanding. Most Rhinelanders believed the restoration of old institutions heralded the imminent restoration of the Old Regime in its entirety. This demoralised the minority of radicals who genuinely supported French rule. The French government obviously had no such intention, but rather favoured a 'Cisrhenan Republic' under French protection. Carnot, who dominated the Directory at this time, outlined these plans to Hoche in August. More fundamentally still, Hoche misunderstood the nature of old-regime governance in believing it might function outside the legal structure

---

[20] For the requisitioning of native administrative talent, see Hansen, *Quellen*, 3, pp. 4, 230, and Archives Nationales, Paris (AN), D. XLII, 7, fo. 380. For the dependence of the French on local lawyers, see Marcel Erkens, *Die französische Friedensgerichtsbarkeit 1789–1814 unter besonderer Berücksichtigung der vier rheinischen Departemente* (Cologne, Weimar and Vienna, 1994), pp. 137–9. For a recent contribution on French administrative policy in general in the occupied Rhineland, see Jörg Engelbrecht, 'Grundzüge der französischen Verwaltungspolitik auf dem linken Rheinufer (1794–1814)', in Christof Dipper, Wolfgang Schieder and Reiner Schulze (eds.), *Napoleonische Herrschaft in Deutschland und Italien – Verwaltung und Justiz* (Berlin, 1995), pp. 79–91.

[21] See especially Stein's memorandum of 10 January 1797. Erich Botzenhart (ed.), *Freiherr vom Stein. Briefe und amtliche Schriften* (8 vols., Stuttgart, 1959–70), I, pp. 442–3.

[22] Hoche to the Executive Directory, 2 February 1797. Longy, *La Campagne de 1797 sur le Rhin* (Paris, 1909), p. 462. Hansen, *Quellen*, 3, pp. 878–9.

guaranteed by the Reich or independently of the various consensus-building and conflict-resolution mechanisms. These mechanisms, of course, represented the antithesis of arbitrary governance inherent under any military occupation. The two were impossible to reconcile. This fundamental conflict became apparent when Aachen's magistracy responded to Hoche's policy by angrily challenging its legality on the grounds it had not been confirmed by the Reichskammergericht.[23] Hence, Hoche's strategy was doomed even before the two events that sealed its fate: the Fructidorian coup of 4 September, which resulted in a reshuffle of the Directory and a shift towards the annexationist faction led by the Alsatian Director Reubell and, on 19 September, Hoche's own death. The following month, France and Austria signed the Treaty of Campo Formio.

At Campo Formio, Austria agreed to evacuate Mainz whilst the Prussians reaffirmed cession of their Rhenish possessions in return for compensation. The details would be decided at the forthcoming Rastatt negotiations. Paris sought to pre-empt these with the administrative incorporation of the Rhineland into France. To this end, in November 1797 the Directory created the civilian post of *commissaire du gouvernement* for the Rhineland and appointed the Alsatian François Rudler as its first commissioner. Rudler reorganised the entire civil, judicial and financial administration along French lines, starting with the division of the region into four departments, the Roër, Rhin-et-Moselle, Sarre and Mont-Tonnerre. Rudler did not, however, extend any democratic elements as existed in France proper. Instead, he abolished the old-regime institutions through administrative fiat. On a single day alone in early 1798, Rudler issued no less than 625 decrees and orders to this end. Thus the French swept away the structures of the Old Regime.[24] There was greater continuity with respect to personnel. Of the 900 officials employed in the new departments, over 60 per cent were natives of the region. Of the rest, a significant proportion were Alsatian, whose bilingualism together with the patronage of Reubell – in whose 'patrimony' the Rhineland was said to be – afforded them an advantage.[25] Most natives originated from the university-educated elite, having commonly studied law or cameralism at a Rhenish or German university, and

[23] Luise Freiin von Coels von der Brügghen (ed.), 'Das Tagebuch des Gilles-Leonard von Thimus-Goudenrath, 1772–1799', *Zeitschrift des Aachener Geschichtsvereins* 60 (1939), pp. 185–6.

[24] As well as Käss, *Organisation*, see also Sabine Graumann, *Französische Verwaltung am Niederrhein. Das Roërdepartement 1798–1814* (Essen, 1990), pp. 18–45, and Roger Dufraisse, 'L'Installation de l'institution départementale sur la rive gauche du Rhin (4 novembre 1797–23 septembre 1802), in idem, *L'Allemagne à l'époque napoléonienne. Questions d'histoire politique, économique et sociale* (Bonn and Berlin, 1992), pp. 77–104.

[25] AN, F^{1c}43, nos. 19–27.

a majority had previously served in the administration or judiciary. Even in the commercially dynamic Roër, only 9 per cent of officials originated from the economic elite. Above all, it was within the judiciary, with its professional requirements, that the degree of continuity was greatest and native predominance most pronounced.[26]

As in France itself, new structures did not end conflict. Rather, they simply institutionalised the various battles – ideological, political, social, economic – that had been raging since before the French Revolution. If anything, the administrative structures of directorial France actively encouraged discord. In particular, the practice of attaching politically committed republican commissioners to oversee the regular administration, which was dominated by old-regime officials (or 'vile egoists, who only covet public employment in the hope of serving personal interests', as the Roër's commissioner, Anton Dorsch, preferred to describe them) aggravated existing conflicts. In Aachen, relations between the magistracy and local commissioner degenerated into fisticuffs.[27] French institutions connected essentially local conflicts that had been raging for decades with the far broader ideological struggles that continued to destabilise directorial France. The various factions of different ideological hues that came and went with bewildering frequency in the coups that rocked Paris in these years fought out their battles by proxy in the Rhineland.

Matters reached a head after the Prairial putsch of 18 June 1799, which ideologically pushed the Directory to the far left. The neo-Jacobin regime despatched a new commissioner, Lakanal, to the Rhineland together with the full panoply of extremist legislation including the infamous 'Law of Hostages' of 24 Messidor VII (12 July 1799). Lakanal proceeded to establish denunciation committees to root out 'counter-revolutionaries' holding public office. 'Has there been a police state, Citizen minister,' the Roër's departmental administration complained to Paris, 'since the destruction of the Venetian oligarchy that has resorted to such measures?'[28] Under these pressures, the occupation dissolved into disorder. In Koblenz, for years a

---

[26] Karl-Georg Faber, 'Verwaltungs- und Justizbeamte auf dem linken Rheinufer während der französischen Herrschaft. Eine personengeschichtliche Studie', in *Aus Geschichte und Landeskunde. Forschungen und Darstellungen. Franz Steinbach zum 65. Geburtstag gewidmet von seinen Freunden und Schülern* (Bonn, 1960), pp. 350–88. Graumann, *Verwaltung*, pp. 156–60, 164, 166, 176–7. Erkens, *Friedensgerichtsbarkeit*, pp. 149–51.

[27] AN, F^{1b}II Roër 1, (nos. 69–70, 72, 76).

[28] Central administration in Aachen to the minister of justice, 11 October 1799, AN F^{1c}III Roër 3, nos. 5 and 8; also, F^{1c}43, nos. 398–400. Philippe Sagnac, *Le Rhin français pendant la Révolution et l'Empire* (Paris, 1917), pp. 218–19. For Lakanal's hatred of Reubell, which had repercussions in the Rhineland, see J. R. Suratteau, 'Reubell', in Albert Soboul (ed.), *Dictionnaire historique de la Révolution Française* (Paris, 1989), pp. 898–903.

centre of tension between radicals and conservatives, matters spiralled out of control in October 1799 when the radical-controlled municipality orchestrated a campaign of harassment against moderates. As was often the case, the army distrusted the radicals, and in Koblenz the garrison commander, General Leval, retaliated at their provocations by declaring a state of siege and dissolving the town council amidst widespread popular rejoicing. A mini White Terror ensued. Despite attempts to seal off the city, news of the affair reached Lakanal in Mainz who rescinded Leval's orders, though significantly he confirmed the general's abolition of the town council. French policy had turned full-circle since those heady days in late 1792, and Rhenish radicals emerged the losers, simultaneously 'persecuted by the military, intimidated by their fellow-citizens, and abandoned by their [French] superiors'.[29]

Throughout Europe, the revolutionary wars and terrorism in France widened the gulf between radicalism and conservatism. Both sides became more ideologically coherent. Rhenish radicalism – often misleadingly labelled 'Jacobinism' – came to prominence with the Republic of Mainz, whose rise and fall was inextricably bound with the French occupation. However, its ideological roots extended deeper, into the Catholic enlightenment centred on the university in the 1780s. In that decade, proponents of reform – university professors like Matthias Metternich, Felix Blau, Anton Joseph Dorsch, Andreas Hofmann, Rudolf Eickemeyer – looked to the elector to carry forward their agenda. After 1789, they became disillusioned that progress might occur within the existing framework. It was less the Revolution that caused this than the Old Regime's response to it, which in Trier and the Palatinate as well as in Mainz resulted in a reversal of the previous course. Only in electoral Cologne was an open breach between the regime and radicalism avoided thanks to Max Franz's moderation. These differing official responses to the Revolution possibly contributed to the distinction apparent in the nineteenth century between a southern Rhineland marked by a radicalism suspicious of princely government and a more moderate north.

Persecuted, many radicals opted to leave the Rhineland after 1789 and settle in nearby Alsace. In 1792, they returned in triumph to Mainz in the French baggage train.[30] Almost immediately, they established a French-style 'Club', named 'Society of the Friends of Liberty and Equality' ('*Gesellschaft der Freunde der Freiheit und Gleichheit*'). The Club first met on

---

[29] Blanning, *Germany*, pp. 278–81. [30] Blanning, *Mainz*, pp. 267–70.

23 October 1792, in the electoral palace. Twenty members signed up that evening. Over the following weeks membership expanded, peaking at about 500 in December. This represented about 6 per cent of those in Mainz eligible to join, a figure that compares not unfavourably with the 8–10 per cent achieved by Jacobin Clubs in French towns and cities. In order to ensure a modicum of ideological cohesion, the Club's rules required new applicants to win the support of six existing members and swear an oath to 'live free or die'. Yet, despite a promising start, the Club never developed into a committed mass movement. Above all, it never attracted support from the guilds, who feared the extension of revolutionary legislation (the Le Chapelier law of 14 June 1791) banning corporations. Instead, it was dominated by university-trained professionals, who made up just under one-third of the membership. Within this group, a small number of personalities, collectively known as the 'Clubbists', set the tone. They included the professors Metternich, Blau, Dorsch, Hofmann and Eickemeyer, as well as the doctor Georg Wedekind and, most famously, the naturalist and philosopher Georg Forster, a figure of international renown who had accompanied Captain Cook on one of his expeditions. Significantly, a majority of 'Clubbists' were 'foreigners', something that provided ammunition to their opponents: Metternich was a native of Trier, Hofmann of Würzburg, Forster and Wedekind of Göttingen. Each brought different talents to the enterprise: Metternich, who recognised the need to engage the peasantry, emerged as the Club's propagandist; Wedekind, whose sister translated Thomas Paine's *Rights of Man* into German, became the leading political theorist; and Dorsch, who subsequently headed the government of the Republic of Mainz, distinguished himself as an organiser.[31]

A set of fundamental beliefs bound these personalities. Central was the notion that democracy alone could guarantee liberty. Drawing on Kant and Rousseau, the Clubbists believed that people need only obey laws granted by themselves as an expression of the common will. Private 'egoisms' must be subordinated to these laws. In constitutional terms, the Clubbists favoured representative rather than direct democracy, though they argued that legislators must be bound closely to the electorate – consisting of males over twenty-one, excluding dependants such as servants – through a two-year electoral cycle and plebiscites. They insisted upon judicial independence. Absent from their concept was any notion of 'loyal opposition' or 'parties'; those favouring a different constitution could expect neither liberty nor

---

[31] For profiles of the leading Clubbists, see Dumont, *Mainzer Republik*, pp. 130–5, 205–9; Blanning, *Mainz*, pp. 283, 291, 295–6. Also, Hansen, *Quellen*, 2, p. 499.

fraternity. As for equality, the Clubbists shared the then common assumption that socio-economic equality automatically follows from legal and political equality. They rejected state redistribution of wealth and favoured economic liberalisation in the belief that this would encourage Rousseau's '*heureuse médiocrité*' of craftsmen and farmers. As for religion, the Clubbists condemned the Catholic Church as part of the Old Regime and favoured a return to the simpler liturgy supposedly followed by early Christianity. Their entire programme, the Clubbists conceded, could only be achieved through 'reunion' with France, and their belief, along with the rest of Germany's intelligentsia, in the existence of a German *Kulturnation*, did not alter this conclusion. Rather, they clung to a cosmopolitan and voluntarist conception of the nation state that made a distinction between culture and power. If the Russian tsars and Habsburg emperors could rule over many nationalities, Georg Forster asked rhetorically, why might not France be able to extend its political principles to the Rhine whilst accepting that its inhabitants spoke in a different tongue?[32]

How far this agenda attracted popular support is hard to gauge. Membership figures for the Club alone reveal little as to why Rhinelanders joined. A better source is the electoral investigation into collaboration that followed Mainz's recapture in early 1793. This reveals that for many, Club membership stemmed less from ideological than pragmatic considerations. Fear, reinforced by peer pressure, was a motivator for many. Dependants and the vulnerable – public employees, Jews, those reliant on public poor relief – in particular felt less able to resist pressure to publicly proclaim revolutionary sympathies. Commercial gain motivated others, such as the coffee-house owner who donned a Phrygian cap to gain business from French officers. Others blamed a few too many *Schoppen* of wine for their brief flirtation with revolutionary politics. Certainly, all 'collaborators' under investigation had a strong incentive to play down the ideological significance of their actions, just as their enemies emphasised the opposite in the flood of denunciations submitted to the electoral commission. Arguably, it was in the interests of the electoral authorities themselves to minimise the importance of revolutionary ideology so as to be able to portray committed 'Clubbists' as an isolated minority. However, even taking these considerations into account, the investigation exposed a whole range of possible motives for adherence to the Republic of Mainz.[33]

---

[32] *Ibid.*, 2, pp. 533, 584–6; Dumont, *Mainzer Republik*, pp. 170–9.

[33] Karl H. Wegert, *German Radicals Confront the Common People. Revolutionary Politics and Popular Politics 1789–1849* (Mainz, 1992), pp. 26–37.

The Republic of Mainz encompassed a substantial rural hinterland. The 'Clubbists' sought to exploit rural discontent by flooding the countryside with fly-sheets, pamphlets and revolutionary theatre directed against the Old Regime. Attacks against the profligate electoral court touched a raw nerve in the countryside, where suspicion of urban culture ran deep. A minority of priests preached reform and stressed the Christian basis of the Revolution. In places, 'clubs' of peasants gathered spontaneously, to read revolutionary pamphlets from Mainz and complain about the existing order.[34] However, as with the city of Mainz, it is important to consider the precise nature of rural agitation. Certainly, the countryside was riddled with conflict on the eve of occupation. The peasant's life depended precariously on the cycle of seasons and weather, upon which he relied for his livelihood. Suspicion of new ideas emanating from the cities was well ingrained. Yet deep-rooted conservatism did not necessarily signify satisfaction with existing realities. Conflict over common usages and rights, such as access to wood, were rife and on the increase. Such conflict, for example, lay behind the apparently revolutionary eruption in Bergzabern in 1792/3. Jacobin terminology, perhaps transmitted through the radical poems of Eulogius Schneider, which at least one contemporary eyewitness noted were read by humble day labourers, were employed in Bergzabern and elsewhere to give expression to grievances. However, the grievances remained the same as before, and the agitation in Bergzabern and elsewhere was directed by individuals with a long history of insubordination rather than a new generation of revolutionaries.[35]

Overall, the geographical extent of rural 'Jacobinism' was limited mainly to the Palatinate, and the Clubbists were privately disappointed at the poor response to their blandishments. They responded initially with yet more propaganda, purges of administrative personnel and pressure to force people to commit themselves. Most opted for the status quo. This became apparent in the elections for the new Rhenish National Convention in February 1793. The electoral arrangements gave all males over twenty-one the vote on condition they swore an oath to be 'faithful to the people and

---

[34] Almost all of the Clubbist publications are printed in Heinrich Scheel (ed.), *Die Mainzer Republik* (2 vols., Berlin, 1975–81).

[35] Dumont, *Mainzer Republik*, pp. 181–93. Wegert, *German Radicals*, pp. 43–51, 54–74. Thomas Theuringer, *Liberalismus im Rheinland. Voraussetzungen und Ursprünge im Zeitalter der Aufklärung* (Frankfurt a. M., 1998), p. 192. A minority in Bergzabern established a revolutionary municipality and Jacobin Club, and then petitioned the Convention in Paris for incorporation into the French Republic. Several nearby small localities followed suit, and met with (brief) success when the Convention decreed their 'reunion' with France on 14 March 1793. The course of events can best be followed in Hansen, *Quellen*, 1, p. 414; 2, pp. 562–4, 785–6.

the principles of liberty and equality'. Despite pressure to vote, the elections proved a disaster on account of the minuscule turnout. In Mainz, only 400 out of the city's 30,000-plus-strong population bothered to vote; only 100 out of 900 rural communities voted.[36]

This, together with the outburst of public fury against leading Clubbists following the fall of Mainz, finally disillusioned Rhenish radicals as well as the French of the notion that they would win large-scale popular support. The French, as noted above, responded by retreating into a chauvinistic siege mentality. This, coupled with the descent into Terror, presented Rhenish radicals with an awful dilemma. For having burned their bridges with the Old Regime, they were limited to two choices: either withdraw from political life or else continue to support the French irrespective of their policies in the hope of change in the future. Most chose the second option and, following the French reoccupation of the Rhineland in the summer and autumn of 1794, found employment in the administration. There, they enjoyed no control over the policies they found themselves implementing, policies geared solely at exploitation and that through association earned for them and their agenda ever greater popular hostility. Yet, only the continued occupation guaranteed they would escape the kind of retribution some of their number experienced following Mainz's fall in 1793. Hence their terror in early 1797 when the truce of Loeben suggested the Rhineland would return to its pre-war status.

The radicals' insecurity increased with Hoche's policy of restoring old-regime structures. However, salvation presented itself in August 1797 with the prospects of an independent 'Cisrhenan' Republic, and radicals rallied around this cause earning for themselves the label '*Cisrhénan*'. This label is misleading, as the territorial objective was incidental to their thought. Of greater importance was the evolution of their constitutional ideas. Here, the legacy of the Mainz Republic's fall and popular hostility, together with the radicalisation of the Revolution and brutality of the occupation, had all left their mark. Shocked by the excesses of the Terror, Rhenish radicals had travelled the same ideological journey as many of their French counterparts. They too now rejected the radical democracy of the Jacobin constitution of 1793 as 'premature by many centuries', and instead favoured the French constitution of 1795 with its restricted franchise. Above all, their political thought was informed by Kantian ethics, which provided the basis for their critique of the Revolution to date. The Revolution, they argued, had failed to fuse morality and liberty, as demonstrated by the behaviour of the

---

[36] Blanning, *Mainz*, pp. 280, 289, 299–300.

French occupation. The Rhineland, with its unshakeable Kantian ethics, could make a unique contribution to humanity, they argued, by making the French Revolution moral.

An ex-priest and journalist, Johann Baptist Geich, and a lawyer, Christian Sommer, helped translate *Cisrhénan* philosophy into a political programme. Geich, in his writings, rejected the restricted liberal view of the state and instead supported active state promotion of morality. This meant compulsory state education to prepare all for liberty. Geich hoped that the French would employ German Kantians, including Schelling and Fichte, in the newly established central schools in the region that replaced the universities. Thus, Geich argued, would the Rhineland bridge the gap between Kant and the Revolution. Sommer's contribution came in his proposed constitution for the city of Cologne. Sommer was much influenced by the French constitution of 1795. His suspicion of democracy was reflected in his exclusion of the poor from the franchise and employment of complex, indirect electoral arrangements. In this, Sommer's draft resembled the later Napoleonic constitution. In the short term, enlightenment needed protection from the ignorant masses as well as from counter-revolutionary princes. Over the long term, the free education Sommer's constitution guaranteed for all would extend enlightenment to society as a whole.[37] More immediately, the *Cisrhénans* put their faith in propaganda activities such as liberty-tree plantings to educate the masses.[38]

Synthesising the Revolution and Kantian ethics proved a hopeless ideal given the Directory's notorious immorality, something an increasing number of *Cisrhénans* including the young Joseph Görres recognised. Like the Clubbists, they never managed to appeal beyond a small minority. According to Görres – who, through his periodicals, *Das rote Blatt* and *Der Rübezahl,* emerged as the most prominent *Cisrhénan* – their number never exceeded 2,000. In Bonn, they numbered 140 at most, or 3.5 per cent of the adult population. In Koblenz, the other centre of their activities, there were 300 *Cisrhénans* (again, equivalent to 3.5 per cent of the adult population), composed mainly of university-trained professionals.[39] Their

---

37 Horst Dippel, 'Der Verfassungsdiskurs im ausgehenden 18. Jahrhundert und die Grundlegung einer liberaldemokratischen Verfassungstradition in Deutschland', in idem (ed.), *Die Anfänge des Konstitutionalismus in Deutschland. Texte deutscher Verfassungsentwürfe am Ende des 18. Jahrhunderts* (Frankfurt a. M., 1991), pp. 17, 22, 68–113. Theuringer, *Liberalismus,* pp. 311–19.

38 Hansen, *Quellen,* 4, pp. 48–50, 619, 642–4. Wolfgang Hans Stein, 'Die Ikonographie der rheinischen Revolutionsfeste', *Jahrbuch für westdeutsche Landesgeschichte* 15 (1989), pp. 194–212.

39 For Görres's estimate, see Max Braubach (ed.), *Joseph Görres, Gesammelte Schriften,* vol. 1: *Politische Schriften der Frühzeit, 1795–1800* (Cologne, 1928), p. 589. Hansgeorg Molitor, *Vom Untertan zum Administré. Studien zur französischen Herrschaft und zum Verhalten der Bevölkerung im Rhein-Mosel-Raum von den Revolutionskriegen bis zum Ende der Napoleonischen Zeit* (Wiesbaden, 1980), pp. 147–51.

isolation made them completely dependent upon the French. Their proclamation of a Rhenish Republic in Cologne on 17 September 1797 remained
stillborn because of Paris's change of policy in favour of annexation.[40] They
now had little choice but to support this, and were exploited by the French
who wished to use evidence of favourable public opinion to justify territorial claims during the Rastatt conference. Hence, they were instructed in
early 1798 to organise a petitioning campaign throughout the Rhineland
calling for 'reunion' with the Republic. Predictably, this ended in failure:
under 15 per cent of those eligible to sign did so and of these a sizeable
proportion were Frenchmen; entire communities simply refused to submit
any signed address at all, and the few successful results represented the fruit
of vote rigging and intimidation.[41]

Motives for adherence to radicalism ranged from the ideological to the
pragmatic. The same was true of counter-revolution. Whilst the French
occupation catapulted Rhenish radicals to positions of prominence and
endowed them with an administrative and propaganda machine, it also
tainted them through association with all the hardships inflicted by the
revolutionary army. Such hardships remained at the forefront of ordinary
people's concerns judging from such contemporary sources as the petitions
submitted by afflicted communities to the occupation authorities. Violence,
requisitioning, billeting, forced loans and forced labour were amongst the
litany of burdens endured. They were inevitable in a region that served as
a base of operations for military forces that were equivalent numerically
to over ten per cent of the population. Military occupation was not, of
course, unprecedented in Rhenish history. The Hohenzollern duchies had
experienced occupation by Austro-French forces within living memory,
during the Seven Years War. In terms of intensity and destructiveness,
Louis XIV's devastation of the Palatinate was worse than the 1790s, but
that was small comfort for those alive at the time.

The extent to which Rhinelanders blamed radical politics for their suffering, as opposed to 'the French', is hard to discern. Certainly, conservative
propaganda connected radicalism with the sufferings of occupation. Whilst
native Clubbists and *Cisrhénans* used what little influence they enjoyed
with the French to mitigate the occupation, for ordinary Rhinelanders
oppression at the hands of the revolutionary army was associated with revolutionary politics. This was especially the case when it came to religion,
and specifically the Roman Catholic Church, an institution that provided

[40] Jacques Droz, *L'Allemagne et la Révolution française* (Paris, 1949), pp. 217–47.
[41] Josef Smets, 'De la coutume à la loi. Le pays de Gueldres de 1713 à 1848' (Montpellier III Doctorat
d'Etat, 1994), pp. 468ff.

a target for the anti-clericalism of the French army. It was quite natural that ordinary Rhinelanders should associate the desecration of their churches and the suppression of manifestations of popular piety with earlier attempts by radicals to dismantle the entire paraphernalia of the Baroque Church. Just as religion lay at the heart of ideological disputes in the 1770s and 1780s, so in the 1790s it occupied centre stage. Not that Rhinelanders perceived the French Revolution as fundamentally anti-clerical from the very start. However, with Pius VI's condemnation of the Civil Constitution of the Clergy in 1791 and the increasing vociferousness of revolutionary anti-clericalism, Rhinelanders were confronted with a choice between their faith and the new ideology. Inevitably, the vast majority opted for the former. Rhenish Protestant responses to the Revolution, in contrast, were initially more positive. Did it not herald the defeat of Catholic absolutism and the liberation of their co-religionists in Alsace? As for the Jewish minority, the sources are obscure, though one might assume a similar response as for Protestants. Certainly, the anti-revolutionary press made much of popular unease in Alsace over moves to emancipate the Jews.[42]

With the occupation, Rhinelanders experienced revolutionary anti-clericalism at first hand. This assumed a variety of guises: the desecration of churches, the requisitioning of ecclesiastical buildings and their conversion to profane use, the harassment or suppression of religious services and processions, and not least the prominence of radical ex-priests amongst native collaborators. All this offended Catholic sensibilities and turned most clergymen into proponents of counter-revolution. This had serious political repercussions, as first became apparent in the elections to the Rhenish Convention in February 1793, when the line adopted by the parish priest usually proved decisive in persuading people to abstain. Of course, Rhenish culture and religion remained so inextricably linked that it is difficult to abstract opposition to revolution motivated by religious faith alone. In a place like the city of Cologne, where popular civic culture and religion were interconnected and where urban republican perceptions centred on notions of the city as a Catholic bastion against irreligious enlightened absolutism, French anti-clericalism posed a threat on several fronts. Through its disruption of the Church's infrastructure it threatened salvation. Beyond that, it threatened the city's cultural life, identity, dignity and independence. These essentially secular considerations were felt more acutely after the French authorities established their headquarters in Bonn and recruited former electoral officials. For Cologne, Bonn as the *Residenzstadt* of the

---

[42] Hansen, *Quellen*, i, pp. 774 n.1, 784, 786, 804–5.

archbishops was perceived historically as a location from which challenges emanated. On these grounds alone Cologne's burghers felt justified in objecting to the French.[43] The French, in contrast, ignored such subtleties and simply lumped together all opposition as 'counter-revolutionary'.

As for inter-confessional relations, the French occupation threatened to undermine the delicate balance established by the Westphalian settlement of 1648. This ignited sectarian feuds. Catholic communities forced to take out loans to meet French demands found themselves dependent upon Protestant and Jewish creditors, and became resentful. Jealousies arose where religious minorities found their public status radically improved under the occupation. Such was the case in Aachen, where the Protestants' rise to prominence created Catholic resentment, or Worms, where Lutherans complained as previously excluded Calvinists and Catholics entered high office.[44] At times, common suffering and shared disgust at French de-Christianisation united all confessions. The Rhineland escaped the worst of de-Christianisation in 1793/4, but did receive a heavy dose in 1798 and 1799. Administrative incorporation in 1798 brought with it a raft of anti-clerical measures previously implemented in the Republic, including the ban on monasteries taking novices, the abolition of the tithe and sequestration of Church property, the ban on public religious processions and their replacement with the revolutionary fest-cycle, and the abolition of religious education in the newly established central schools.[45] Radical Rhenish officials often went further in venting their anti-clericalism through rigorous enforcement of this legislation. Yet at least the region experienced nothing comparable to neighbouring Belgium, where 8,000 priests were arrested and deported after 1797.[46]

Apart from religion, attitudes towards the old-regime secular authorities greatly influenced Rhinelanders' choices under occupation. These attitudes included loyalty and fear. Fear as a disincentive to collaboration fluctuated in intensity with shifting military fortunes and the likelihood of the princes' return. This possibility ended only in 1801, with the Peace of Lunéville that legitimised French rule in international law. Before then, collaboration with the French could be construed as treason not only against the princes, but the Reich itself. Emperor Francis II issued several warnings (notably, on

[43] Hashagen, *Rheinland*, pp. 47–50, 72. Hansen, *Quellen*, 3, p. 735.
[44] For Catholic resentment of Protestants in 1790s Aachen, see Albert Huyskens, 'Die Aachener Annalen aus der Zeit von 1770 bis 1803', *Zeitschrift des Aachener Geschichtsvereins* 59 (1939), pp. 10, 51, 62.
[45] Hegel, *Erzbistums Köln*, 4, pp. 488–90.
[46] Martyn Lyons, *France under the Directory* (Cambridge, 1975), p. 107.

19 December 1792 and 30 April 1793) threatening punishment for 'persons
lacking German [*sic*] spirit and heart...who have volunteered or allowed
themselves to be used as tools for seducing the people', and 'criminals against
us, the German Reich and their Fatherland'.[47] Such threats carried weight
following the reversal of French military fortunes in late 1792, and at various
times in 1795, 1796 and 1799, when it appeared they might be expelled. The
beginning of the downward spiral in the fortunes of the Club in Mainz
coincided with the reversal of French military fortunes at Frankfurt, and
the rough treatment subsequently meted out to those Clubbists who failed
to escape before the surrender of the French garrison to the Prussians on
23 July 1793 served as a warning to all future would-be collaborators that
the punishment of princes was mild compared to the mob's vengeance.[48]

Initially, the princes viewed 'collaboration' pragmatically. As the French
stood poised to invade a second time in 1794, they issued statements per-
mitting local officials to remain in post and continue to shoulder public
responsibilities under occupation. 'It is far better,' Max Franz reasoned,
'[that the administration] should be in the hands of old established families
than *sansculottes*.' Clemens Wenzeslaus allowed his officials to stay behind
whilst Friedrich Karl promised not to punish individuals compelled to
take a French oath so long as they remained loyal 'in their hearts'. The
Palatine government even threatened to discipline officials who abandoned
their posts.[49] The princes nonetheless distinguished between disinterested
service to mitigate the occupation and ideological commitment to revolution. Clemens Wenzeslaus, for example, threatened such commitment with
severe punishment, whilst Max Franz forbade local attempts to negotiate
neutrality agreements with the French or enter into other special arrangements. Such threats succeeded in undermining the occupation according to
reports from the French representatives-on-mission. Many Rhinelanders refused public positions for fear of retribution should the French suffer defeat,
and the electors' supporters were forever spreading rumours of this eventuality. Only reassurances as to the permanence of French rule would remedy
this. Under these circumstances, it is hardly surprising that shrewd operators

---

[47] Hansen, *Quellen*, 2, pp. 668–9, 728–32, 848–50.

[48] For the last days of the Republic of Mainz, see Blanning, *Mainz*, pp. 281–2, 285.

[49] For Max Franz's attitude, see Braubach, *Max Franz*, pp. 308, 311, 385–7 and Hansen, *Quellen*, 2,
pp. 618–21. For Clemens Wenzeslaus, Hansen, *Quellen*, 3, pp. 280–2, 295 n. 2. For the Palatine
government, see the electoral order no. 2398 of 14 July 1794. Johann Josef Scotti, *Sammlung der
Gesetze und Verordnungen, welche in den ehemaligen Herzogthümern Jülich, Cleve und Berg und
in dem vormaligen Herzogthum Berg über Gegenstände der Landeshoheit, Verfassung, Verwaltung und
Rechtspflege ergangen sind. Vom Jahr 1475 bis zu der am 15. April 1815 eingetretenen Königlich Preußischen
Landes-Regierung* (Düsseldorf, 1821), part 2, p. 742.

like the von der Leyens of Krefeld and van Recums of the Palatinate should hedge their bets and maintain cordial relations with both the French and the princes.[50]

Whilst the vast majority of Rhinelanders remained behind, the princes and their courts, plus many nobles and clerics, emigrated across the Rhine in face of the French. Max Franz evacuated to Mergentheim, Clemens Wenzeslaus to Augsburg and Friedrich Karl to Aschaffenburg. The French gave *émigrés* two weeks to return or else face the confiscation of their property, though later they relaxed these provisions slightly. Subsequently, many returned to reclaim their possessions. However, for the vast majority who opted to remain behind, the princes' flight reinforced the perception that they were alien to the 'land'. This sense of abandonment turned to resentment when the exiled princes started issuing threats against those co-operating with the French.[51] Patriotism towards the *Land* ('*Landespatriotismus*') dictated engagement with the occupier in the community's interests, and in order to prevent worse being imposed by 'foreigners', be they Protestants, Catholics or burghers from a rival town; for, as a representative of one of Cologne's old families wrote, to be ruled by the French was a small evil compared to being governed by the wrong sort of German.[52] According to this view, it was better that trusted locals of standing serve as interlocutors with the French. Throughout the region, such individuals emerged. They organised petitions and managed the distribution of the burdens of occupation, often acting without reference to the exiled governments. The chronicler of Dormagen – a small town north of Cologne – recorded how the local mayor, on his own authority, managed demands from the French army, organised patrols to counter plundering by isolated bands of soldiers, ensured the town's provision of firewood in winter, dealt with outbreaks of disease caused by troop movements, bribed key officials to lighten requisitioning, and travelled to the French army

---

[50] For the assessment of the representatives-on-mission, see Hansen, *Quellen*, 3, pp. 380–2, 440. For later French assessments of the problem, see Rudler (government commissioner in the Rhineland) to Lambrechts (minister of justice), 15 December 1797, AN, F^{Ie}41, no. 18; the central administration of the department of Mont-Tonnerre to Shée (government commissioner in the Rhineland), 12 April 1800; and Shée to Abrial (minister of justice), 14 April 1800, respectively, AN, F^{Ie}43, nos. 367, 369. For the von der Leyens, Kurschat, *Leyen*, pp. 33, 45–52, 58–9.

[51] Those issued by Clemens Wenzeslaus were especially threatening, and provoked resentment. Hansen, *Quellen*, 3, pp. 280–2. For a similar sense of abandonment in the Prussian territories, see Johann Adolf Kopstadt, *Ueber Kleve. In Briefen an einen Freund aus den Jahren 1811 und 1814* (Frankfurt a. M., 1822), pp. viii–x.

[52] Theresa von Wittgenstein to her brother-in-law, Franz von Coels, 5 April 1801, Historisches Archiv der Stadt Köln (HASK), Bestand 1123, Kastennr. 22, dossier 'Johann Jacob v. Wittgenstein (Briefe). Abschriften aus dem Archiv v. Coels-Aachen, nos. 1814ff'.

headquarters at his own expense to negotiate reductions in Dormagen's quota of men to be requisitioned for work on fortifications, fix the price of supplies, and reroute two army columns. Such activity preserved Dormagen from the worst effects of the occupation and, as the chronicler shrewdly observed, it was useful for the French themselves to have influential natives as interlocutors.[53] In many areas, local businessmen achieved greater prominence, as they possessed the resources and connections to meet the army's demands whilst alleviating the burden on the general population. This was the case with the von der Leyens, for example, who insured the supply of bread not only to their own workers but initially to the whole community, and who imported coal from the right bank to guarantee fuel supplies over winter. Their efforts were facilitated by easy access to senior French officers billeted on their luxurious mansions, which served as headquarters of the Sambre-Meuse army.[54]

Staatspatriotismus – loyalty to a larger dynastic state – superseded *Landespatriotismus* only in the Prussian territories of the Lower Rhine. In places like Cleves, the Protestant elite remained attached to the Hohenzollerns, though Catholic loyalties were less clear. Even here, the transition from *Landespatriotismus* to *Staatspatriotismus* was a relatively new development. As recently as the Seven Years War, the same elite had shown little attachment to the Prussian cause and had happily co-operated with the Franco-Austrian occupation. However, since then many leading families had been ennobled under Frederick William II (1786–97). Hence their attachment to Prussia and preference for emigration rather than collaboration.[55] This choice was much encouraged by Stein, who evacuated his provincial administration to the right bank, from where he lost no opportunity to undermine French rule. He did this even after the apparent normalisation of Franco-Prussian relations at Basel, of whose secret provisions he remained ignorant. Stein threatened collaborators with trial for high treason under the recently introduced Prussian law code, the Allgemeines Landrecht (ALR); he instructed Rhinelanders to oppose all French demands unless threatened with force; he sponsored a secret

---

[53] H. Cardauns and R. Müller (eds.), *Die rheinische Dorfchronik des Johann Peter Delhoven aus Dormagen, 1783–1823* (Cologne, 1926), pp. 92, 97–9, 117, 128, 131–2, 134–5, 140, 145, 159–60, 165, 168. For a recent study that looks at this more generally, see Uwe Andrae, *Die Rheinländer, der Revolution und der Krieg 1794–1798* (Düsseldorf, 1994), pp. 21–5, 28, 31–3, 36–41, 45–6.

[54] Kurschat, *Leyen*, pp. 33, 45–52, 58–9, 77–81.

[55] Horst Carl, *Okkupation und Regionalismus. Die preußischen Westprovinzen im Siebenjährigen Krieg* (Mainz, 1993), pp. 412–16. For contemporary accounts, Kopstadt, *Kleve*, pp. viii–x; Adolf Klein and Justus Bockemühl (eds.), *1770–1815. Weltgeschichte am Rhein erlebt. Erinnerungen des Rheinländers Christoph Wilhelm Heinrich Sethe aus der Zeit des europäischen Umbruchs* (Cologne, 1973), p. 34.

anti-French society; his subordinates continued to run what amounted to a parallel government in Cleves and turned the city into 'a ferment of royalism' in the words of commissioner Rudler.[56] Far from restraining Stein, Berlin reaffirmed its claims to the region. In November 1797, Prussia's new king, Frederick William III (1797–1840), included the Rhenish territories in his review of the royal administration throughout the kingdom. Stein's provincial authorities sent Berlin reports on the 'conduct' of public officials from the end of 1797.[57] Further Prussian provocation increased following French defeats in the early stages of the second Revolutionary War. In the summer of 1799, Berlin massed 20,000 Prussian troops in Wesel. Though the deployment was precautionary – only in the event of the Anglo-Russian expedition in the Low Countries succeeding would the Prussians cross the Rhine – it suggested the imminent return of the Old Regime, and with it the punishment of collaborators as promised in a number of Prussian ordinances circulated at this time. Pro-Prussian newspapers and agents stepped up their attacks against the French, spread rumours of Berlin's adherence to the Second Coalition, and gave publicity to Frederick William III's generous aid to flood victims along the Rhine as evidence of his ongoing commitment to the region. These activities increased popular opposition to the occupation: people refused to pay their taxes to the French but instead paid them to the Prussians, they ripped French decrees from public places, and subjected known collaborators to daily harassment and nocturnal catmusic. The occupation authorities remained too fearful to intervene and were in any case constrained by foreign ministry instructions to avoid any confrontation that might provoke Prussia.[58]

---

[56] Botzenhart, *Stein. Briefe*, 1, pp. 442–3. For the relevant articles of the ALR, see *Allgemeines Landrecht für die Preussischen Staaten von 1794. Textausgabe* (Frankfurt a. M., 1970), p. 672; Steffens, 'Provinzen', pp. 406–8, 410; Georg Mestwerdt, *Zur clevischen Geschichte aus der Zeit der französischen Herrschaft, 1795–1798* (Cleves, 1895), p. 11; Klein, *1770–1815*, pp. 36–7; Rudler to Lambrechts, 24 December 1798, AN, F^{1e}43, no. 156. Also, Hauptstaatsarchiv, Düsseldorf (HStAD), Roër dept., 19 (ministry of the interior), fol. 5. For the complicated status of the Hohenzollern territories, see Rudler's earlier letter to Lambrechts (minister of justice) of 17 December 1797, AN, F^{1e}44, dossier 'Divisions & organisations'.

[57] HStAD, Kleve-Kammer, 3577.

[58] For French reports on Prussian agitation, see HStAD, Roër dept. 2745, nos. 2–6, 9–12. See also: Lambrechts's report to the Executive Directory, 18 January 1799 (AN, F^{1e}43, no. 130); Dorsch to Lambrechts, 20 June 1799 (AN, F^{1e}III Roër 3, no. 3); and Dorsch to Marquis (Lakanal's predecessor as government commissioner for the four Rhenish departments), 4 July 1799, (AN, F^{1e}44, dossier 'Divisions & organisations'). For French military reports, General Wirion (commander of the *gendarmerie* in the four Rhenish departments) to the ministers of war and police, 18 October 1799, Archives de l'Armée de Terre, Vincennes (AG), B^{13}111, dossier '18 October 1799', unfoliated (13, 14). For the foreign policy dimension, see Otto (French chargé d'affaires in Berlin) to Talleyrand, 24 September 1799, and Lakanal to Lambrechts, 12 October 1799, AN, F^{1e}43, nos. 143, 152. Also, Dorsch to Marquis, 4 July 1799, AN, F^{1e}44, dossier 'Divisions & organisations'. For the Prussian

Prussia, through its status as a Great Power and the *Staatspatriotismus* it engendered, retained a degree of influence unmatched elsewhere in the occupied Rhineland, where politics devolved back to the *Land* and city. Here, institutions, traditions and political culture provided an alternative both to revolution and counter-revolution, political extremes that smacked of arbitrariness and absolutism. Instead, as the imperial representative in Mainz, von Schlick, noted in his despatches to Vienna, Rhinelanders preferred a moderate course of reform founded upon existing structures.[59] However, the ideological challenge posed by revolution and counter-revolution forced those championing moderate reform to develop and refine their ideas. The result was a series of constitutional proposals that foreshadowed nineteenth-century developments whilst drawing on older traditions.

Nowhere were such traditions stronger than in the imperial cities. These drew on deep-rooted republican sentiments that made them impervious to revolutionary blandishments. Such traditions centred on a deeply ingrained legal culture that emerged in part as a result of centuries of struggle against princely and episcopal interference. A comparable urban political culture existed in the neighbouring Netherlands and proved equally difficult for the revolutionaries to subvert.[60] What were the French to do when Aachen's burghers confronted them with the observation that their constitution was already democratic and that it had been since 1450; or when their counterparts in Speyer reminded them that they had been republicans for centuries; or when Cologne's representatives, armed with their medieval *Gaffelbriefe*, gloried in their constitution allegedly granted them by ancient Rome? The burghers of Aachen, Cologne and Speyer made their bold claims not as an afterthought, but at the head of all their communications with the French. Nor did they do so pragmatically, only to withdraw the claims when it was politic to do so, or in return for concessions; rather, they insisted on them stubbornly, throughout.[61] Centuries of resistance

---

parallel administration, see AN, F^{1e} 43, nos. 127, 130, 144–5, and HStAD, Roër dept. 2745, fols. 9–12. Even after Brumaire, Lakanal's successor was instructed to treat the Prussian duchies with special '*ménagement*'. Instructions to Dubois-Dubais (government commissioner in the Rhenish departments) from Abrial, 11 December 1799, AN, F^{1e} 43, no. 122. For the wider context, see Brendan Simms, *The Impact of Napoleon. Prussian High Politics, Foreign Policy and the Crisis of the Executive, 1797–1806* (Cambridge, 1997), pp. 94–6, 152–3, and Thomas Stamm-Kuhlmann, *König in Preußens großer Zeit. Friedrich Wilhelm III der Melancholiker auf dem Thron* (Berlin, 1992), pp. 165–73.

[59] See especially Schlick's despatch to Reich's vice-chancellor Colloredo of 2 November 1792, penned in Würzburg whilst Mainz languished under French occupation. Hansen, *Quellen*, 2, pp. 557–9.

[60] Simon Schama, *Patriots and Liberators. Revolution in the Netherlands 1780–1813* (2nd edn, London, 1992), pp. 14–15.

[61] Hashagen, *Rheinland*, pp. 9–24, 29–45.

to electors and bishops had produced a deeply ingrained *mentalité* that made it impossible for them to distinguish between the obviously fraudulent revolutionary concept of *liberté* and the older but tangible notion of rights. Such sentiment was weaker in the *Residenzstädte*, where it had been undermined by direct princely rule; and it was, of course, these cities – Bonn, Koblenz and Mainz – that were the centres of radicalism in the 1790s.

It might be argued that hostility to the French in defence of historic rights represented the last gasp of a defunct system. However, in the short term at least, the French threat led to a closing of ranks between magistracies and guilds in favour of the status quo. This occurred in Cologne, whose guilds feared the extension of French legislation suppressing corporations and whose magistracy feared the loss of power. The latter recognised the advantages of guild support, which would enable it to portray itself as a popular government in its dealings with the occupation authorities. Significantly, the word 'guild' was translated into 'section' in its communications with the French in order to better appeal to their political sensibilities.[62]

It was not only in the imperial cities that attempts were made to steer a course between revolution and counter-revolution. Histories of the Republic of Mainz have generally focused on the radical political agenda of the Clubbists to the exclusion of alternatives. These looked to existing institutions as the basis for constitutional development. Amongst the proposals circulating widely in Mainz following the Elector's flight, according to Schlick, was one package calling for the formation of a *Landtag* representing peasant, noble, burgher and clerical estates and enjoying fiscal responsibility, the immediate replacement of Friedrich Karl with his radical coadjutor, Dalberg, the participation of popular representatives in the nomination of future electors, and the establishment of a civil list to support the head of state.[63] Possibly, Schlick was referring to the ideas propounded by the canon Schumann and his circle. Schumann was much influenced by Friedrich Carl von Moser, a thinker who saw the potential for reformed ecclesiastical states to provide a barrier against absolutism. Moser's proposals centred on the secularisation of the cathedral chapters in the ecclesiastical states. It was the chapters that both elected the electors and represented a check on their powers. Their development according to Moser's vision would have transformed the ecclesiastical states into elective constitutional

---

[62] Hansen, *Quellen*, 3, pp. 366ff. Gisela Mettele, 'Kölner Bürgertum in der Umbruchszeit (1776–1815)', in Lothar Gall (ed.), *Vom alten zum neuen Bürgertum. Die mitteleuropäische Stadt im Umbruch 1780–1820* (Munich, 1991), pp. 249–63.

[63] Schlick to Colloredo, 2 November 1792. Hansen, *Quellen*, 2, pp. 557–9.

monarchies where the representative element would have dominated the executive.[64]

A better-known set of constitutional proposals from occupied Mainz in this period emanated from Daniel Dumont. These were not unsolicited, but were the outcome of a request from Custine to Mainz's guilds. Custine viewed the guilds in political rather than economic terms, and treated them as the people's representatives early in the occupation. Mainz's guilds collectively delegated the task of drafting a response to the merchants' guild, which entrusted the task to the businessman Dumont. Dumont's draft proceeded from the principle that rejected the simple transplantation of the French constitution because it was ill suited to the German character. Beyond that, his document contained provisions for a constitutional monarchy with executive power limited by an elected assembly of the 'nation of Mainz' holding the power of the purse, a two-year legislative cycle, an end to clerical and noble privilege, and the reservation of public office for natives. Dumont drew on both the French constitution of 1791 and the traditional division in urban Germany between burghers (with civic rights) and *Beisassen* (those without) in his distinction between 'active' citizens enjoying full political rights and 'passive' citizens. Mainz would remain part of the Holy Roman Empire, but its constitution would come under French guarantee.[65]

The Clubbists contemptuously rejected Dumont's proposals. They were especially dismissive of his identification of a unique German character and his attachment to the Reich, which they contested was irredeemably defunct.[66] The French eventually expelled Dumont from Mainz. Before then, in November 1792, the later Napoleonic mayor of Mainz, Macke, an individual who enjoyed a measure of popular trust, organised a petition to Paris requesting that the French not impose their own constitution, but modify that already in existence in Mainz. Over a three-day period in November, Macke negotiated with the guilds, the majority of whom supported the despatch of the petition. What was significant in these discussions was the guilds' lack of ideological attachment to the elector; if the French offered them a better settlement, so much the better. What

---

[64] Theuringer, *Liberalismus*, p. 371. For more on this important potential of the cathedral chapters see Friedrich Carl von Moser, *Über die Regierung der geistlichen Staaten in Deutschland* (Frankfurt a. M. and Leipzig, 1787), pp. 176–8. Also, Wende, *Die geistlichen Staaten*, pp. 42–7.

[65] Hansen, *Quellen*, 2, pp. 569–73.

[66] For attempts to combine republicanism within the framework of the Holy Roman Empire, see Monika Neugebauer-Wölk, 'Reich oder Republik? Pläne und Ansätze zur republikanischen Neugestaltung im Alten Reich 1790–1800', in Heinz Duchhardt and Andreas Kunz (eds.), *Reich oder Nation? Mitteleuropa 1780–1815* (Mainz, 1998), pp. 21–50.

also emerges is that the guilds, far from restricting themselves to parochial politics, took a keen interest in the wider territorial settlement, something they recognised would have a great impact on their own future. Unfortunately for them, pragmatism did not exist amongst the French, for whom the petition came as an unpleasant surprise. The occupation authorities abolished the guilds on 25 February 1793, from which time on their former members were implacable foes of French rule. Yet whilst they welcomed the expulsion of the French that summer, they equally feared an aristocratic reaction with the return of the Old Regime, and were disappointed that the elector continued with his previous policy of whittling away at their autonomy. Their agitation for constitutional reform in Mainz continued, albeit underground.[67]

Mainz lacked the political focus that representative estates provided. Such was not the case in electoral Cologne and Trier, where relations between elector and estates were at times fraught. Max Franz suspected that Cologne's estates were prepared to exploit the threatened French invasion to strengthen their political position, and took care to dissolve them before evacuating Bonn because it would be 'extremely dangerous' to have them assembled under enemy occupation.[68] In Trier, the breach between prince and estates was more serious. Conflict centred on the elector's counter-revolutionary policies, which the estates feared would provoke French retribution. They openly called for neutrality following the outbreak of war. Matters came to a head with Custine's capture of nearby Mainz in October 1792. Trier's estates dreaded the imminent occupation of Koblenz which Parisian newspapers had threatened with destruction on account of its status as the *emigrés'* headquarters. To prevent this, the estates petitioned Clemens Wenzeslaus to allow them to declare neutrality, something he rejected before abandoning Koblenz to its fate. The elector's flight reinforced the sentiment that the estates alone represented the interests of the *Land*. With this in mind, one of their representatives, Lassaulx, travelled to Custine's headquarters in Mainz and, on behalf of the people, distanced himself from the elector. In the event, the assurances Lassaulx eventually extracted from Custine proved unnecessary, as Koblenz was saved by a Hessian relief force. Lassaulx returned home and was promptly imprisoned. Despite a successful appeal to the Reichskammergericht, he remained incarcerated whilst the government initiated an investigation into his alleged treason. It

---

[67] Friedrich Schmitt, *Das Mainzer Zunftwesen und die französische Herrschaft. Ein Beitrag zur Charakteristik ihres Gegensatzes* (Darmstadt, 1929), pp. 58, 62–4, 67, 69–70, 77, 79–80, 82, 87, 90, 97.

[68] Hansen, *Quellen*, 3, pp. 79–80, 255. Braubach, *Max Franz*, pp. 286, 389. Hegel, *Erzbistums Köln*, 4, pp. 483–5.

accused Lassaulx, and by implication the estates, of exploiting the war to introduce a version of the French constitution of 1791 and of wishing to share 'sovereignty' ('*landesherrliche Gewalt*'). Though later released, Lassaulx remained under investigation until the French occupation in October 1794. The fundamental question of whether Trier's estates represented specific groups or the people as a whole, as they themselves asserted in January 1793, remained a matter of dispute. The same was true elsewhere in Germany, where the estates increasingly saw themselves as popular representatives and, in a few instances – as, for example, when Bavaria's estates entered into independent peace negotiations with the French general Moreau in 1796 – acted on that basis.[69] Ultimately, this resurgence of the estates proved a false dawn. Napoleonic state formation, whether direct or indirect, swept aside the old estates in favour of princely or bureaucratic absolutism. However, whilst Napoleon and his German allies might change institutions overnight, *mentalités* proved harder to eliminate.

The French might have exploited the estates' revival. Equally, they might have played on the fear of many Germans of an Austro-Prussian partition that would have resulted in the imposition of absolutism. Yet France's gravitation towards the extreme ideological left after 1792 precluded such policy options. However, the collapse of the French constitution of 1791 in no way discredited the Rhenish preference for a form of government where arbitrary executive power was contained by a system of representation and law. Rather, events in France were interpreted in the region as the consequence of decades of absolutism that made Frenchmen temperamentally unsuited to constitutional government, a perception confirmed in the first years of the occupation.[70] Matters changed with the arrival of Hoche and with him the delegation of greater administrative responsibility to natives. This, together with talk of a *Cisrhénan* Republic, reopened the constitutional question, including the role of the estates. This was because the estates, where present, had formerly enjoyed the right to approve taxation and, in some areas, had even run the fiscal machinery. Given that Hoche's main objective was the extraction of money – he demanded a 'contribution' of 12 million *livres* from the region – his policy of devolution and restoration

---

[69] For Germany generally and Bavaria in particular, see Eberhard Weis, 'Kontinuität und Diskontinuität zwischen den Ständen des 18. Jahrhunderts und den frühkonstitutionellen Parlamenten von 1818/1819 in Bayern und Württemberg', in idem (ed.), *Deutschland und Frankreich um 1800. Aufklärung – Revolution – Reform* (Munich, 1990), p. 222. The conflict between the elector and estates of Trier can best be followed in the documents published by Hansen. Hansen, *Quellen*, 2, pp. 166–8, 424–7, 446–9, 454, 481–91, 529 n. 1, 627, 664 n. 1, 721–2, 786–98, 875–6.

[70] *Ibid*., 2, pp. 231–7, 689, 705; 3, pp. 839–47.

inevitably raised fundamental questions relating to equality, legitimacy and representation.

This was especially the case in electoral Cologne and Trier. In the former, which Hoche assessed at 1,751,680 *livres*, the city curia responded to the general's initiative by naming a representative, the Bonn law professor Johann Jakob Schmitz, to negotiate with the exiled Max Franz over an appropriate response. Schmitz argued that all groups must contribute to meeting French demands, irrespective of their privileged status. Even before 1797, the extraordinary costs of the war had made clerical and noble fiscal privilege politically unacceptable. Such privilege, its opponents argued, went against both imperial law, which stated that extraordinary taxes imposed following the declaration of a *Reichskrieg* must be levied equitably irrespective of existing privileges, and natural law. Acceptance of fiscal equality brought with it wider constitutional implications. Since the clergy (as opposed to the cathedral chapter) were not represented amongst Cologne's estates, Schmitz suggested they should unite with the 'people' in the fourth estate, sharing the same burdens and privileges. Max Franz, together with the cathedral chapter and clergy, accepted Schmitz's proposal. Max Franz distrusted Hoche, but supported the restoration of institutions on the left bank as a prelude to their subordination to himself. However, he instructed that the estates could only reconvene following his return. On no account were there to be formal negotiations between the estates and Hoche, but only informal contacts between the French and individual notables that carried no wider constitutional implications.[71] The noble curiae rejected Schmitz's proposals out of hand, to which he replied that if nobles wished to return from exile, they would need to accept modifications to their status ('... *dem Adel, wenn er als Adel zurückkommen sollte, machen wir ... eine solche Rechnung, daß er aufhören muß, Freiherr zu sein, wenn er Bürger sein will*'). The nobles responded by playing on Max Franz's fears of revolution, and accused the cities of colluding with the *Cisrhénans*. This was not the case. However, the cities, through the extension of their estate to encompass the clergy, certainly hoped for a redistribution of power in their favour. The collapse of Hoche's policy in September 1797 meant that Schmitz's plan remained on paper.[72]

---

[71] *Ibid.*, 3, pp. 935–42. HStAD, Kurköln II, 3254, nos. 13–16, 37–40. Also, Braubach, *Max Franz*, pp. 386–90. Similar tensions emerged between the local estates and government – in this case, the Prussian – in the Hohenzollern duchies as a result of Hoche's initiative. Steffens, 'Provinzen', pp. 422–5, 438.

[72] Karl Essers, *Zur Geschichte der kurkölnischen Landtage im Zeitalter der französischen Revolution (1790–1797)* (Gotha, 1909), pp. 34–7, 78ff., 106, 118–25.

In Trier, Hoche's initiative also resulted in interesting developments involving the estates. These reconvened in March 1797 to discuss Hoche's proposals, despite the determination of the elector to have nothing to do with the general. In an unprecedented move, they proposed co-operation with their counterparts in electoral Cologne and Jülich-Berg in order to present a united Rhenish front. Trier's estates aimed at regaining fiscal control from the occupation authorities and to this end proposed the establishment of a central council on which would be represented all classes – the nobility, clergy and third estate (cities) – who contributed to meeting French demands. As before, the syndic Lassaulx, together with his colleague Hetzrodt, emerged as proponents of radical reform. Lassaulx, writing in 1797, argued that the majority of Rhinelanders rejected revolution. However, thanks to the propaganda war between the French and their opponents, they were also more aware of their civic rights and liberties than before and, according to Lassaulx, hoped that peace would lead to a new constitution and not a restoration of fiscal and legal inequalities. Above all, constitutional methods alone would fill Rhinelanders with confidence.[73]

Following Hoche's death and Campo Formio, Trier's estates renewed their efforts to form a common front with their northern counterparts at the forthcoming Rastatt conference. In furtherance of this, Lassaulx sent a political memorandum to Clemens Wenzeslaus in which he argued that politics had changed fundamentally since the outbreak of the revolutionary war. Unlike earlier conflicts, this war was an '*Opinionenkrieg*', a war in which public opinion was important. Only radical reform, he argued, would counter *Cisrhénan* propaganda that exploited popular fear of a return of aristocratic privilege. 'The spirit of the age has advanced so far that superstition and stupidity can no longer overcome genuine enlightenment,' he warned, 'and only those states [will] remain standing whose form of government is founded upon justice and fairness.' Lassaulx proposed the creation of a neutral, independent Rhineland, linked to France through a free-trade agreement. Internally, this state would end fiscal and judicial privilege, and the noble monopoly over public offices, and reorganise the system whereby the *Land* was represented. In this last point, Lassaulx's proposal approached, conceptually, the notion of a *Staatsbürgertum*. The estates would no longer represent particular interests, but cover the entire territory of the state and represent all groups. Lassaulx's proposals were subsequently reaffirmed.[74]

---

[73] Hansen, *Quellen*, 4, p. 376; also 3, pp. 846, 920–3, 931–6, 1204–9; 4, 85ff., 155–6, 202–5.
[74] *Ibid.*, 4, pp. 372–87.

Nothing, of course, came of this, as the Rhineland's destiny was determined elsewhere. Yet the various proposals illustrate the state of German political thought in this transitional period. Whether they were forward- or backward-looking has divided historians. Hashagen, writing a century ago, described Dumont's proposal in Mainz as the first significant formulation of Rhenish liberalism. More recently, Dumont's namesake, Franz Dumont, has similarly emphasised the progressive, modern, forward-looking dimension of the document, especially with its stress on the division of powers. Others, notably Horst Dippel, have played down the progressive nature of this and similar hybrids because of their failure to list fundamental rights and the absence within them of any notion of progress so crucial to later liberal thought. Certainly, none of the Rhenish documents produced in the 1790s advocated complete economic liberalism or the abolition of corporate restrictions; in their terminology, they went out from the basis of restoring ancient liberties and to varying degrees included the Holy Roman Empire in their provisions.[75] Yet reference to the constitutional texts themselves refutes accusations of anachronism. For example, a reading of Dumont's proposal of 1792 or that of Lassaulx in 1797 does reveal an unmistakable vision of progress and betray a confidence that they conformed with the spirit of the age that one finds in later constitutional proposals put forward by Rhenish liberals like David Hansemann during the *Vormärz*.[76] Equally important in giving these documents a radical edge was the immediate context in which they were drafted. Though nullified by changes in French policy in the short term, the notion of limited government founded upon a socially inclusive concept of *Bürgertum* and self-administration, was made more attractive over the longer term by the experience of arbitrary military government in the 1790s. It appeared more feasible with the irreversible emigration of the electors and their 'foreign' courts in 1794, and the subsequent elevation by the French military of local elites – an amalgamation of relatively 'new' groups such as businessmen and well-established elements – to fill their place.

This chapter has attempted to guide the reader through difficult terrain. One way of making sense of this period is to reduce it to a struggle between revolution and counter-revolution. This struggle engulfed much of Europe

---

[75] Hashagen, *Rheinland*, p. 387. Dumont, *Die Mainzer Republik*, p. 222. Dippel, 'Verfassungsdiskurs', pp. 20–1, 31. Also, more recently, Theuringer, *Liberalismus*, pp. 306–7, 320–1.

[76] See, for example, David Hansemann's memorandum on the state of Prussia of December 1830, in Joseph Hansen (ed.), *Rheinische Briefe und Akten zur Geschichte der politischen Bewegung 1830–1850* (2 vols., Bonn, 1919–42), I, pp. 12–78.

in the 1790s. Nor was it contained within the chronological confines of the revolutionary decade, but rather represented the culmination of a longer ideological struggle between the radical Enlightenment and its opponents. A commonly posed question in the historiography of the Rhineland is which side attracted the support of ordinary people. The impression hopefully conveyed by this chapter is that few sided with the radicals, especially after these developed into 'Jacobins' and became tainted through association with the French occupation. However, it has been stressed that counter-revolution similarly failed to attract a broad following. Rather, moderate reform built upon existing foundations, appealed to the majority.

The preceding paragraph describes a political spectrum, stretching from revolution to counter-revolution. Moderate reform is located in-between. The intention of this chapter is not to present such a misleading image. For arguably the choice that presented itself in the 1790s was less one between revolution and counter-revolution, than between arbitrary government and government constrained by law, custom and consensus. Certainly, this appears to be how most Rhinelanders adjudged the choice that confronted them. Revolution, almost by definition, fell into the 'arbitrary' camp. Few forces more arbitrary can be imagined than the French revolutionary army, especially in the period between Robespierre's fall and Brumaire. At least before Thermidor, the French army was controlled to an extent by the fearsome Jacobin People's Representatives-on-Mission, and after Brumaire by a strengthening of the civilian administration. Between those dates, the descent of the French army resembled the arrival of a biblical plague of locusts. What it meant to be occupied by the French has been covered at greater length and more eloquently elsewhere. That the overwhelming majority of Rhinelanders should shrink back in horror and reject everything the revolutionary army represented is hardly surprising. More surprising is the attempt made by some historians to prove the contrary.

More controversial, perhaps, is the argument that counter-revolution similarly smacked of arbitrariness in the eyes of the majority. In reality, the threat from this quarter appeared the greater at times. Such was the case, for example, in 1791, when French *émigrés* settled in large numbers in the region. Equally threatening in its arbitrariness was the ongoing political clampdown in response to the French Revolution, even though its main victims were an unrepresentative minority of radical intellectuals. After the summer of 1792, counter-revolution, like revolution, meant resource mobilisation on an ever-greater scale. At a territorial level, counter-revolution brought with it the threat of the Reich's partition between Austria and Prussia. Poland's fate heightened fears of such an eventuality. Hence, the prospect of counter-revolution triumphant was not without its dangers, though the threat of this receded rapidly with the beginning of the French occupation.

The majority of Rhinelanders saw the choices open to them less in terms of a spectrum between revolution and counter-revolution, with a 'third way' in-between. Rather, they saw two incompatible systems of rule: their own – or, more accurately, an idealised version of their own – which operated within the constraints imposed by imperial law, local custom and consensus, and an arbitrary system dominated by princes and revolutionaries. These appeared to be the alternatives in the 1790s, and it was not clear which would emerge triumphant from the revolutionary wars. Ultimately, of course, the latter would triumph, but at times in the decade after the Bastille's fall it did appear that those institutions and sentiments that underpinned the former might emerge reinvigorated from the conflagration. The flight in 1792/4 of the princes and their courts, for example, not only provoked much resentment, but also created something of a vacuum which the French occupation authorities filled only with the assistance of local elites who found themselves thrust, albeit reluctantly, into positions of responsibility. To an extent, military occupation resulted in the devolution of power back to the *Stadt* and *Land*. Of course, few expected French military occupation to last and instead expected some form of restoration. However, what form that restoration would take remained to be seen. Everything was left to play for.

PART II

1801–1813: Napoleon

CHAPTER 4

The Napoleonic method of government

[We] committed a great error when, being too rigorous with regards to political opinions, we did not choose a certain number of functionaries from the classes of former magistrates and rich proprietors of these lands: by this means we would have inspired more confidence in the people and prevented the great dilapidation committed by those individuals who supplied no guarantee, either to the public treasury or to their fellow citizens.[1]

News of Napoleon's coup of Brumaire received a mixed reception in the Rhineland. Talleyrand's agent in the region reported that the majority joyfully welcomed the new regime with great 'hope that the equity of the members of the government will make cease the vexations which they have suffered, and of which they are still the victim despite protests'.[2] Commissioner Lakanal, who was to blame for the vexations, reported that the coup aroused no disquiet, but that Napoleon's creation of a Commission consulaire exécutive aroused concern of a military dictatorship. The commissioner was obviously expressing his own fears and the justice minister was sufficiently concerned to write: 'Your sense of civic duty and your talents assure me that you share the general opinion, and that the consuls can count you amongst those who will strive to insure the success of all that has been done up to now, and all that remains to be done.'[3]

Napoleon quickly removed Lakanal and embarked upon the process of winning Rhenish loyalties. This necessitated overcoming past ideological battles and creating a new image for the regime. Given Bonapartism's pragmatism, it was easy to select a variety of images for different audiences. For the Rhineland, the challenge was simpler given the total discredit into

---

[1] Archives Nationales, Paris (AN), F^{Ie}43, no. 411, 'Tableau des quatre nouveaux départemens, depuis leur organisation jusqu'à ce jour, présenté le 21. Vendémiaire (13 Oct. 1800)'.

[2] AN, F^{Ie}43, no. 121.

[3] Lakanal to the justice minister (17 November 1799) and the minister's reply (19 November), AN, F^{Ie}43, nos. 186, 189.

which previous French regimes had fallen.[4] Napoleon quickly distanced himself from these by removing revolutionary symbols. The theme of order restored recurred in all public pronouncements. Typical was that of Aachen's garrison commander delivered on the first Bastille Day following the coup:

After this day of predilection [14 July 1789], let us bless the sacred days of the last 18 and 19th Brumaire; bless them, I say, because in regenerating us they have crushed all those heads of the poisonous Hydra, of cabals, of fierce passions and of intrigues which by cowardly and specious subterfuge prolonged the civil and foreign war, which sowed discord everywhere, striving to hide the trace of the path which must lead us to concord, to pacification and true fraternity. Thus did the monster of calumny and of denunciation, which swelled daily, make its *unworthy converts*. Fatal cause of the loss of so many innocent heads, sacrificed at the whim of its *infamous caprice*.[5]

Symbols and speeches in themselves failed to end ideological conflict. Only the establishment of international peace and legitimisation of French rule in international law could do that. Whilst the War of the Second Coalition continued to rage, the permanency of French rule remained doubtful and, as Lakanal's successor, Henri Shée, reported in April 1800, encouraged counter-revolutionary agitation and intimidation of collaborators.[6] Even after Brumaire, German newspapers and propaganda pamphlets smuggled across the Rhine continued to predict the Old Regime's return.[7] For their part, Rhinelanders persisted in sending declarations of 'continued loyal attachment to the good cause' to their princes, though in reality these had by now given up hope of regaining their territories.[8] The conclusion of the war on French terms at the Peace of Lunéville (9 February 1801) established France's *de jure* sovereignty over the left bank, something of no mean importance in a region whose inhabitants were much impressed by legality. Rhinelanders had little option now but to take the oath the French demanded, though there was some last-minute resistance in the Prussian duchies.[9] Most made their peace with the new regime, with the exception of Cleves's noble elite and some

[4] This observation is not to deny the persuasiveness of much recent research that has rehabilitated aspects of the Directory. Martyn Lyons, *France under the Directory* (Cambridge, 1975), and Malcolm Crook, *Napoleon Comes to Power: Democracy and Dictatorship in Revolutionary France, 1795–1804* (Cardiff, 1998).

[5] AN, F^{Ic}III Roër 4, 1, nos. 92–3.

[6] Shée to Abrial, 29 April 1800, Joseph Hansen, *Quellen zur Geschichte des Rheinlandes im Zeitalter der französischen Revolution 1780–1801* (4 vols., Bonn, 1938), 4, p. 370.

[7] Dorsch (commissioner of the Roër) to Abrial, 26 April 1800, AN, F^{Ic}III Roër 3, no. 13.

[8] Hauptstaatsarchiv Düsseldorf (HStAD), Kurköln II, 2869, nos. 3–12.

[9] HStAD, Kleve Kammer, 3377, nos. 85, 104, 106, 125.

Palatine noble families who remained in Hohenzollern and Wittelsbach service respectively.[10] The French treated the small number of Rhenish imperial counts, including the Metternichs, as sovereigns and 'annexed' their estates. In compensation, they received secularised property on the right bank.[11] In contrast, the French viewed other nobles including the imperial knights as private individuals and lifted the sequestration on their properties on condition they return and adopt French citizenship. Most returned, 'rallied' and, as we shall see, entered Napoleonic service.

The conclusion of the Concordat with Pius VII in 1801 further reinforced the sense of harmony restored. Propaganda reinforced this over the following years, culminating in the series of officially sponsored obsequious addresses from Rhenish cantons welcoming Napoleon's assumption of the imperial dignity in 1804: 'Men and things have been put back in their place,' declared one; 'Disabused of systems which have successively made their unhappy progress, he [Napoleon] senses the necessity of returning to the principles and the foundations of social order which the experience of centuries has confirmed,' trumpeted a second; 'Europe will be consolidated upon its ancient foundations,' and 'A happy calm will now truly succeed the terrible storms of fifteen years of agitation and of torment,' stated another two. And so on.[12] The new monarchical theme was demonstrated in 1804 when Napoleon visited Cleves, where he drank a toast to the King of Prussia and renamed the main street *Königsstrasse* ('King's Street').[13] By the end of the Empire, official almanacs located the Bonapartes, or the 'fourth dynasty' (following the Merovingians, Carolingians and Capetians), within the ancient monarchical tradition.[14] Things had come full circle.

It took more than an image makeover to rectify the ills Shée discovered upon taking up his post. In a series of damning reports, he painted a bleak picture of administrative chaos and incompetence. Government had collapsed in many areas, he concluded. Everywhere, officials were resigning whilst the administration languished in 'the most complete stagnation', and was 'as without life and without energy as . . . without good will'. Only introduction of the prefectoral system would improve the situation, as it was cheaper and required less personnel than the bloated bureaucracy set up by the

[10] For the Palatine nobility, see Marcel Dunan, *Napoléon et l'Allemagne. Le système continental et les débuts du royaume de Bavière 1806–1810* (Paris, 1942), pp. 59–60.
[11] Alan Palmer, *Metternich. Councillor of Europe* (London, 1997 pbk edn), pp. 25, 39.
[12] AN, F¹ᶜIII Roër 3, no. 31–4.
[13] Justus Hashagen, *Das Rheinland und die französische Herrschaft. Beiträge zur Charakteristik ihres Gegensatzes* (Bonn, 1908), p. 109.
[14] *Almanach du Roër* (Aachen, 1813), pp. 33ff.

Directory. Only such a radical solution would facilitate a purge of existing personnel, only one-third of whom Shée classified as 'good'. The rest, composed mainly of left-wing extremists or, to quote Shée, 'conspirators who crept in during the first precipitous organisation made without local knowledge... ignoramuses who dishonour their office... rascals, who only serve in order to tyrannise the people', would be replaced by individuals with good mores and local knowledge.[15]

Napoleon responded quickly by decreeing the introduction of the prefectoral system in the Rhenish departments on 14 May 1800.[16] The First Consul, through councillor of state Roederer, subsequently outlined his thoughts on the new territories' integration to the Corps Législatif:

The introduction of every French law in a land which not only differs from France, but which contains within itself areas with varying customs and laws, must no longer be attempted without consideration, nor enacted with violence and precipitation! Changes in the law must be preceded by education, by persuasion, and with the authority provided by positive examples. One surely knows today the costs of premature reform. Furthermore, one senses that even the most useful changes still need to be made agreeable to a people whose affection is too recent not to require special care.[17]

These sentiments provided a welcome contrast to neo-Jacobinism. Yet, despite the rhetoric, the new prefectoral system as established in 'old France' by the law of 28 Pluviôse VIII (17 February 1800) and supplementary consular decree of 17 Ventôse VIII (8 March 1800) was hardly distinguished by its responsiveness to local concerns. Rather, it reinforced the centralisation of power through a strict hierarchical chain that ran from Paris (ministers) to the departments (prefects), districts (sub-prefects) and municipalities (mayors), and along which instructions supposedly sped with the rapidity of electricity.[18] Napoleon concentrated responsibility for each administrative tier in the hands of an individual official. As in the army, the emphasis was on swift executive action. Official correspondence was confined to strict hierarchical guidelines: officials could only correspond with the next tier, and letters sent in contravention of this were returned unopened.[19] Significantly, the new constitution (Article 75) put an end to

---

[15] Hansen, *Quellen*, 4, pp. 1268–78.

[16] Napoleon first consulted with Talleyrand over the foreign policy ramifications of such a step. Napoleon to Talleyrand, 10 May 1800, Napoleon I, *Correspondance de Napoléon Ier publiée par ordre de l'empereur Napoléon III* (32 vols., Paris, 1858–69), 6, p. 261.

[17] AN, 29 AP 75, no. 182.

[18] Felix Ponteil, *Napoléon Ier et l'organisation autoritaire de la France* (Paris, 1956), p. 47.

[19] Anton Keil, *Handbuch für Maire und Adjuncten, für Polizey-Commissare, Gemeinde-Räthe, Steuer-Empfänger und Vertheiler, Spital- und Armenverwalter, Pfarrer, Kirchen-Räthe und Kirchenmeister,*

damaging denunciations by ordering that legal proceedings against civil servants could only be initiated by the Council of State.[20]

Napoleon, as First Consul and then Emperor, crowned the executive pyramid. He was advised by the Council of State, which also served a quasi-legislative function and as a supreme administrative court. It represented the main forum for policy formulation. Immediately beneath the apex stood the ministers and senior ministerial staff, whose function was strictly executive. Rhinelanders, as provincials, could hardly aspire to such exalted positions, which were dominated by natives of the Seine basin. Rhenish notables, like other provincials, remained apart from the governing elite in Paris, which monopolised the highest posts and dominated institutions like the *école polytechnique*.[21] However, Napoleon's expansion of the auditorships of the Council of State as a nursery for the next generation of councillors, ministers and prefects created opportunities for financially and mentally well-endowed young men from throughout the French Empire. The number of auditorships rose from sixteen in 1805 to 452 in 1813, and eventually provided one-fifth of the 300 or so Napoleonic prefects. Napoleon specifically encouraged young notables from the new departments to serve as auditors in order to imbue them with an imperial culture that resembled enlightened absolutism. The response of Rhenish notables was disappointing. They did not share Stendhal's great ambition of joining the auditors. They were unwilling to shift their loyalties from the *Land*. Unlike in Italy, Napoleon did not resort to compelling Rhenish notables into joining, but reserved a number of auditorships for them. These were open to twenty-two- to twenty-seven-year-olds with an income of at least 6–7,000 francs. Only relatively impoverished Rhinelanders came forward, however, seeing in the auditorships a means of social mobility. Such, of course, was not Napoleon's intention.[22] Those handful of suitable Rhinelanders who did eventually join served with their colleagues throughout the Grande Empire.

Feld- und Forsthüter und Geschäftsmänner. Zweyte ganz umgearbeitete und vermehrte Auflage (2 vols., Cologne, 1811–13), 2, pp. 684–5.

[20] L. Duguit, H. Monnier and R. Bonnard, *Constitutions et lois politiques de la France depuis 1789* (Paris, 1952), p. 116.

[21] Geoffrey Ellis, 'Rhine and Loire: Napoleonic Elites and Social Order', in G. Lewis and C. Lucas (eds.), *Beyond the Terror: Essays in French Regional and Social History, 1794–1815* (Cambridge, 1983), pp. 240–1, 244. Jerry Shinn, *Savoir scientifique et pouvoir social. L'Ecole polytechnique, 1794–1914*, (Paris, 1980), p. 18. During the Directory, about half the bureaucrats within the central ministries originated from the Paris region. Clive Church, 'The Social Basis of the French Central Bureaucracy under the Directory 1795–1799', *Past & Present* 36 (1967), p. 63.

[22] Charles Durand, *Les Auditeurs au conseil d'état de 1803 à 1814* (Aix-en-Provence, 1958), pp. 76–83. For the Roër department, see HStAD, Roër dept. 2688 1c, nos. 12, 17, 34. For the Rhin-et-Moselle department, see Landeshauptarchiv Koblenz (LHAK), Bestand 256, 184, nos. 1–4.

Exuding imperial arrogance, their self-perceived mission was to 'civilise' the barbarian and bumpkin. They stood at the cutting edge of empire building and represented an embryonic pan-European governing class.[23]

The prefects formed the Napoleonic administration's backbone. Their responsibilities ranged from public security to opening the hunt. They were tightly bound to the interior minister and in that sense functioned as executors of policies they had no role in formulating. In practice, they represented more than that. Vitally, they served a ceremonial function designed 'to win for it [the administration] the respect which [it] must claim, and the *éclat* and the appropriate dignity', to quote Alexandre Méchin's first circular after taking up his post in the Roër.[24] Ceremonial might be considered an almost incidental function, but it assumed a more fundamental role in Napoleon's mind. It was especially important in the Rhineland, according to one memorandum, where it could enhance the civilian administration's prestige after years of humiliation. Only this would entice notables to 'rally'.[25] The first prefects needed to use their own prestige to protect their native subordinates from the arrogance of *French* soldiers, who in the 1790s contemptuously treated all Rhinelanders like conquered subjects. If this continued, the councillor of state Dauchy warned Napoleon following his fact-finding tour in 1802, notables would join their exiled rulers across the Rhine.

Judging by official correspondence, the first tranche of prefects successfully completed their mission, but only after fighting what one document termed an 'open war' with the army and other French-dominated institutions over the question of competence and respect.[26] Ceremonial, precedence and brilliant uniforms all figured prominently in this struggle which though seemingly trivial was of great importance. For, to quote one characteristically patronising formulation, ordinary Rhinelanders were 'naturally docile and respectful towards authority', but needed 'external symbols to recognise it'; 'the multitude judges their [officials'] power by their dress, and cannot believe that a modest sub-prefect, shabbily dressed and poorly paid, can be superior to an official of the tax, domainal or customs administration, richly clothed, who incurs great expense and whose carriage spatters with mud the pedestrian sub-prefect'.[27] To this end, Napoleon minutely

---

[23] Michael Broers, *Europe under Napoleon 1799–1815* (London, 1996), pp. 134, 200–1, 263–5.

[24] *Recueil des actes de la préfecture de la Roër* (Aachen 1803–13) (1803), pp. 9–12.

[25] Undated memoir from Méchin to the councillor of state, Dauchy, AN, AFIV 1025, Dossier 3, no. 13.

[26] General Lagrange to Napoleon, 13 June 1803, AN, AFIV 1025, dossier 'senatorie de Liège', no. 17.

[27] For more on this, see Michael Rowe, 'Between Empire and Home Town: Napoleonic rule on the Rhine, 1799–1814', *The Historical Journal* 42 (1999), pp. 652–3.

regulated official etiquette (laws of 28 Pluviôse (16 February 1800) and 8 Messidor VIII (26 June 1800)). Whilst official regulations banned priests from publicly wearing clerical attire, they prescribed elaborate uniforms for mayors, adjuncts, local police and, after July 1804, the presidents of departmental and district electoral colleges, and presidents of cantonal assemblies. Other regulations (notably the imperial decree of 24 Messidor XII (12 July 1804)) regulated the official hierarchy. Significantly, these accorded primacy to civilians over the military: mayors preceded the *commandants de place*, and prefects the departmental military commanders. Honorary positions held by local notables also enjoyed elevated positions: presidents of the departmental electoral colleges came immediately after the archbishop but *before* the prefect, whilst the presidents of the *arrondissement* colleges came before the sub-prefects. Further provisions regulated the number of honour guards different official grades might expect and, for the more senior echelons, the number of gun salutes and duration of church-bell ringing during their inspection tours.[28]

Emphasis on ceremonial display might be ridiculed as the obsession of a parvenu regime or even the militarisation of society by a dictatorship. In reality, it represented one element in a range of measures aimed at restoring order. From the Rhenish perspective, these measures represented less the militarisation of civilian life than the re-establishment of the primacy of civilians over the soldiery. Beyond that, they demonstrated a determination to co-opt the local elite. Hence, for example, the importance Napoleon accorded to the prefects' ability to sustain the appropriate lifestyle enabling them to interact socially with the wealthiest *propriétaires*. As Roederer stated to the Tribunate in 1801, 'it is necessary that he [the prefect] can mix with influential persons possessing social connections whose significance is greater than one wished to believe over the last ten years'.[29] Napoleon reversed the pay cuts for public officials introduced during the War of the Second Coalition and established generous new scales for prefects (up to 12,000 francs) set according to the population of the towns in which they were located on the grounds that this best reflected living costs. Napoleon disapproved of prefects lacking adequate personal fortunes, whom he suspected of being prone to avarice, parsimony or even corruption, all of which reflected badly on the government.[30]

[28] Keil, *Handbuch*, i, pp. 67–8.
[29] *Archives Parlementaires de 1787 à 1860. Recueil complet des débats législatifs et politiques des chambres françaises. Imprimé... sous la direction de MM. I. Mavidal et E. Laurent, etc.*, 2nd series (1800–1860), (Paris, 1862–), i, p. 171.
[30] Simon, the Roër's first prefect, fell into this category. Jollivet (government commissioner in the Rhenish departments) to the minister of the interior, 14 August 1801, AN F^{1b}II Roër 1, dossier

Karl Ludwig von Keverberg, representative of a prominent Lower Rhenish noble family, listed knowledge of local language and mores, and possession of connections with influential families, as amongst the attributes prefects required.[31] Though without doubt in possession of these talents himself, Paris refused Keverberg's request for a prefecture along the Rhine and instead granted him one elsewhere. Critics hostile to Napoleonic rule held up the prefectoral corps as an example of French discrimination against Germans on the grounds that not one incumbent of a Rhenish prefecture originated from the region. In reality, this conformed with the policy of appointing outsiders to prefectures as the surest means of guaranteeing government interests. All provincials, not only Rhinelanders, were in practice discriminated against, though uniquely in the Rhineland natives of Alsace, Lorraine and Belgium were over-represented through their provision of a third of the eighteen prefects who served in the region. In contrast, only four Rhinelanders served as prefects elsewhere in France, though another two held equivalent positions in the grand duchy of Berg and kingdom of Bavaria. Counting these, Rhinelanders were not much worse off than provincials from south-western France.[32] It might be surmised that had Napoleonic preponderance in Germany continued Rhinelanders, like neighbouring Alsatians, would have been ideally placed to benefit from Napoleon's need for bilingual talent.

Rhinelanders were better represented amongst the sub-prefects. Sub-prefects supervised the local administration, including conscription. They provided the prefects with regular reports and chaired various committees.

'Préfet- renseignements sur le' (no. 8). To put the salaries of prefects in perspective, it is worth noting that judges in civil courts received 1,000–2,400 francs, and appeal court and criminal court judges 2,000–4,200 francs. Councillors of state received 25,000 francs, archbishops and tribunes 15,000, bishops 10,000, and army colonels 5,000 to 6,750 francs. Humble parish priests received a modest 500 francs annually, whilst the average daily pay for a labourer in the manufacturing sector was about 1 franc 33 centimes. Cologne's welfare bureau calculated that 1 to 1.2 francs per day was the minimum required to sustain a five-head family. For judicial and administrative salaries, see Sabine Graumann, *Französische Verwaltung am Niederrhein. Das Roerdepartement 1798–1814* (Essen, 1990), pp. 148–71, 298–307. For military salaries, see J. P. Bertaud, 'Napoleon's Officers', *Past & Present* 112 (1986), p. 99. For the clergy, see Jakob Torsy, *Geschichte des Bistums Aachen während der französischen Zeit (1802–1814)* (Bonn, 1940), pp. 124–5, 143. For the humble, see Wilfried Feldenkirchen, 'Aspekte der Bevölkerungs- und Sozialstruktur der Stadt Köln in der Französischen Zeit (1794–1814)', *Rheinische Vierteljahrsblätter* 44 (1980), pp. 201–4. The regime's suspicion of those of insufficient social standing extended to candidates for inferior posts in the municipalities, as revealed in the comments on mayoral candidates in documents such as AN, F^{IC}III Roër 2, no. 67, 'Liste des soixante treize personnes les plus marquantes du département de la Roër, parmi lesquelles on peut faire un choix pour la présidence des collèges electoraux de département et d'arrondissement', August 1809.

[31] Keverberg to Lameth (prefect of the Roër), 11 November 1806, AN, F^{Ib}II Roër 3, 'Sous préfet de Clèves'.

[32] Rowe, 'Empire', p. 654.

How far they expanded their role beyond functioning as letter-boxes passing on communications between the prefectures and *mairies* depended on their own personalities and the willingness of individual prefects to accord them a wider role.[33] Whilst only five out of the initial batch of eleven sub-prefects appointed on the left bank in 1800 were Rhenish, subsequent appointments favoured natives so that by the end of Napoleonic rule Rhinelanders represented a clear majority. Within the sub-prefectoral corps in particular, Napoleon favoured those who appeared 'likely to render dignity to their office', as one circular put it. Hence the corps provides a good measure of '*ralliement*': the rallying of the old elite, who could best render dignity. Whilst only one of the initial batch of native appointees was of noble origin, half of the twelve subsequent appointments were ex-nobles; the first appointees included radicals inherited from the Directory, but after 1804 Napoleon was able to replace these with old-regime personnel.[34]

Elsewhere, former radicals experienced marginalisation. After Brumaire, 'anarchist' became an epithet bandied about to ruin their career prospects. Rhinelanders, when petitioning the French for employment, obviously emphasised those qualities they believed would impress. Significantly, under Napoleon, applicants stressed loyal service to the Old Regime rather than association with the occupation authorities in the 1790s.[35] Yet it took time before representatives of the established elite felt sufficiently confident to 'rally'. For example, in Cologne Abraham Schaaffhausen, one of the region's richest men, rejected his nomination as *maire* in November 1800 as did the two favoured contenders for adjunct; and when Schaaffhausen's alternative, the ex-*Bürgermeister* Johann Jakob von Wittgenstein, was offered the post, his brother-in-law wrote him: 'As I hear, you are being threatened with the position of mayor. I do not wish that on you.'[36] The thesis that a newly emerging, thrusting *Bürgertum* was clamouring for public positions was certainly not universally applicable. Given recent experiences, many

---

[33] Graumann, *Verwaltung*, pp. 69–70. An account of the activities of a Rhenish sub-prefect, Karl Ludwig von Keverberg of Cleves, is provided by Gustav Mücke, *Die geschichtliche Stellung des Arrondissements und seines Verwalters zur Zeit der napoleonischen Herrschaft, dargestellt an dem Leben und Wirken Karl Ludwig von Keverbergs als Unterpräfekt in Cleve* (Bonn, 1935).

[34] Roger Dufraisse, 'Les notables de la rive gauche du Rhin à l'époque napoléonienne', *Revue d'histoire moderne et contemporaine* 18 (1970), pp. 759–60. See also AN, F^{1e}43, no. 383, 'Etat indicatif des personnes que le commissaire du gouvernement croit les plus propres à remplir les places, de préfets, sous préfets, secrétaires généraux et conseillers de préfecture, maires & adjoints de police dans les quatre départements', 22 May 1800.

[35] *Ibid*.

[36] For Schaafhausen, Historisches Archiv der Stadt Köln (HASK), FV4373, nos. 2–4, 6, 102–3. For Wittgenstein, see HASK, Bestand 1123, Kastennr. 22, Paket betr. J. J. von Wittgenstein, Haes, Cramer, v. Biegeleben, etc.

viewed public service as an unpleasant distraction. They were not willing to 'rally' at any price. Yet, by the end of the Consulate, an increasing number judged the benefits of 'rallying' outweighed the costs. Such was the case with Wittgenstein, who accepted his nomination as *maire* in 1803 by the municipality that recommended him because the 'choice of the old magistrates of this ancient, small republic as present-day officials will apply a salutary balm to the wounds inflicted by the evils of war on this worthy commune, and will give to the government the unlimited confidence on the part of its *administrés*'.[37] The following year, another ex-*Bürgermeister* of Cologne, Reiner von Klespe (whose father and grandfather had also served as *Bürgermeister*), accepted his nomination as sub-prefect of Cologne. His pompous installation ceremony took place in October 1804.[38] The French appointed a third former *Bürgermeister* of Cologne, Johann Dumont, prefectoral councillor.

Cologne's old elite flourished under Napoleonic rule. This was not surprising given its success over previous decades at reinvigorating itself and amalgamating new elements. It presented a united front to the French, and was unchallenged by disaffected rivals who might have provided an alternative basis of rule in the city. Such was not always the case elsewhere. For example, in Aachen, the established elite had been divided politically in the last decades of the Old Regime and proved far less successful at integrating new elements. Hence, French rule marked something of a new beginning as that quintessentially Napoleonic process of 'amalgamation' produced a new ruling elite of 'notables'. This comprised a fusion of old and new elements that for the first time in centuries saw economic and political power in the city united. Aachen's three Napoleonic mayors collectively personified the new fusion: the first, Kolb, a cloth manufacturer, freemason, Protestant and recently settled immigrant, typified the new element; the second mayor, Lommessen, in contrast, as a member of a well-established family who had initially fled Aachen in the face of the French invasion, represented the old; the third, Guaita, a needle manufacturer and descendant of Italian migrants who had settled in Germany in the early eighteenth century, combined elements of the new and old. What united all three was their vast wealth: Kolb boasted a fortune of 300,000 francs, Lommessen 400,000, and Guaita an undisclosed but vast sum. A similar mix of personalities dominated the city council. Middling burghers who had dominated the

---

[37] HASK, Bestand 1123, Kastennr. 18 (Verschiedene Verwaltungs- und Prozeßsachen der Stadt Köln, 18. Jahrhundert).
[38] HASK, Bestand 1134, no. 12.

old city council, in contrast, now found themselves excluded.[39] Unlike in Cologne, Napoleonic rule in Aachen marked a break. Interestingly, native Frenchmen were marginal in both cities. Even their houses were located in different quarters to those favoured by the native elite.[40]

Wealth and talent were prerequisites for membership of the Napoleonic elite. In Aachen, these criteria were met by an amalgamation of new and old; in Cologne, they were met by the old. In Mont-Tonnerre, a surprising number of ex-Clubbists fulfilled the necessary prerequisites. Nineteen of Mont-Tonnerre's sixty-five highest tax-payers and four of its six representatives to the Corps Législatif were former radicals.[41] Napoleonic rule on the Middle Rhine betrayed a more radical tinge than further north, something reinforced by the fact that a former member of the Committee of Public Safety, Jeanbon Saint-André, served as Mont-Tonnerre's prefect throughout the period.

Despite the variations, there was a distinct tendency towards 'aristocratisation' as the Consulate gave way to the Empire. Napoleon intended to found his regime on masses of granite, not grains of sand. Thus, he reversed the social atomisation of the revolutionary decade in favour of corporations, albeit ones based on new foundations. Napoleon's creation of the Légion d'Honneur in May 1802 represented a move in this direction.[42] Another important step was the establishment of the imperial nobility – Napoleon's 'tinsel aristocracy', to quote Martyn Lyons – in 1808.[43] Attached to the newly created imperial titles of duke, count, baron and knight were endowed estates which were transmissible, undivided, to heirs. The Rhenish nobility increasingly joined other notables in accepting positions and imperial

---

[39] Michael Sobania, 'Das Aachener Bürgertum am Vorabend der Industrialisierung', in Lothar Gall (ed.), *Vom alten zum neuen Bürgertum. Die mitteleuropäische Stadt im Umbruch 1780–1820* (Munich, 1991), pp. 218–22. Thomas Kraus, *Auf dem Weg in die Moderne. Aachen in französischer Zeit 1792/93, 1794–1814. Handbuch-Katalog zur Ausstellung im 'Krönungssaal' des Aachener Rathauses vom 14. Januar bis zum 5. März 1995* (Aachen, 1994), pp. 178–82, 500–3. In other cities, such as Speyer, a similar process of amalgamation occurred. Jürgen Müller, *Von der alten Stadt zur neuen Munizipalität. Die Auswirkungen der Französischen Revolution in den linksrheinischen Städten Speyer und Koblenz* (Koblenz, 1990), pp. 136–8.

[40] Claudia Erdmann, *Aachen im 1812. Wirtschafts- und sozialräumliche Differenzierung einer frühindustriellen Stadt* (Aachen, 1986), pp. 142–52.

[41] Dufraisse, 'Notables', p. 769.

[42] Cologne's new mayor, Wittgenstein, was one of the first Rhenish recipients of this decoration in October 1804. For his inauguration ceremony, see HASK, FV1045, nos. 5, 6, 8, 10, 12. For the text of the oath sworn by Wittgenstein, see HASK, Bestand 1123, Kastennr. 22, dossier 'Französische Ehrenlegion betreffend'.

[43] Martyn Lyons, *Napoleon Bonaparte and the Legacy of the French Revolution* (Basingstoke, 1994), p. 161.

titles.[44] 'Aristocratisation' culminated at the highest levels with Napoleon's marriage to the Habsburg archduchess, Marie-Louise, in 1810. News of the impending dynastic match immediately sparked rumours in the Rhineland that Napoleon would reverse the entire revolutionary legacy: in Aachen and Cologne, people spoke of the imminent celebration by Napoleon of a mass in memory of Louis XVI, the expulsion of ex-conventionnels, including the prefects Lameth and Jeanbon Saint-André, the banishment of native 'patriots', and the outbreak of a second revolution that would devour those associated with the first.[45]

Napoleon's regime was socially exclusive and politically inclusive. It welcomed wealth and talent. As time passed, it assumed an aura of permanency that had eluded its predecessors, and the conclusion of peace with the other powers and the Catholic Church won it prestige. Prosperity gradually returned. Talented and wealthy Rhinelanders increasingly 'rallied'. Yet they did so on their own terms, for '*ralliement*' represented a compromise between two parties rather than the imposition of somebody's will on another. A variety of motives accounted for 'rallying'. For the young Keverberg, for example, Napoleon as an enlightened reformer represented the successor of Frederick the Great. For others, he represented the restorer of order and Christianity, whilst another group saw in him defence against counter-revolution. Bonapartism was all things to all men.[46] There were also gradations of '*ralliement*', ranging from full ideological commitment to pragmatic considerations. Napoleon learnt the lesson of the revolutionary decade by accepting this and providing a range of institutions through which individuals might determine their intimacy with the regime. For the majority, '*ralliement*' was about positioning oneself on a spectrum rather than choosing between the extremes of fanatical commitment and outright opposition. Hence the futility of categorising Rhinelanders as 'collaborators' or 'resisters'. How, for example, should one label the banker Schaaffhausen, who refused his appointment as Cologne's mayor, engaged in smuggling activities, but who also bought sizeable secularised properties? As we shall

---

[44] Wittgenstein was one of those few Rhinelanders – about half a dozen – awarded a knighthood, and with it a new coat of arms consisting of the old family shield overlaid with Napoleonic symbols. HASK, Bestand 1123, Kastennr. 22, dossier 'Entlassungs und Pensions-Versuch des bürgermeister Joh. Jacob von Wittgenstein betreffend'.

[45] Ernest d'Hauterive (ed.), *La Police secrète du Premier Empire: Bulletins quotidiens adressés par Fouché à l' Empereur, 1804–1810* (5 vols., Paris, 1908–64), 5, p. 359 (police report of 29 March 1810). See also Ladoucette to Count Réal, 10 March 1810, and Georgéon to Count Réal, 15 March 1810, AN, F⁷8390, dossier 'Situation'.

[46] Rowe, 'Empire', pp. 655–7.

see, the Prussians attempted just such a categorisation of Rhinelanders following the end of French rule, though without much profit.

Public service, it might be surmised, represented an unambiguous commitment to the new regime. This would assume that those who entered public service did so primarily to serve the state. An examination of the interface between the state and society – the municipalities – presents a different picture. The municipalities formed the lowest level of the administration. In conformity with Napoleonic practice, they were administered by individual *maires* assisted by *adjoints* and councils. It was another peculiarity of Napoleonic governance that rural and urban municipalities enjoyed the same status, irrespective of the discrepancies in their relative size, and that a *maire* responsible for a few hundred souls should have the same duties as his counterpart in Aachen, Mainz or Cologne, with populations measured in the tens of thousands. Nor were mayoral duties inconsiderable, though they were well summed up by one of Cologne's *adjoints* in 1803 as interpreting the paternal views of the government whilst representing the interests of the community.[47]

A handbook, published in German and running into two volumes and 1,300 pages, elaborated on this. Mayoral responsibilities ranged from political police duties, such as the investigation of publishers and bookshops to enforce the censorship laws, the surveillance of suspect individuals and posting of secret agents, to the more mundane examination of stagecoach passenger lists, supervision of workers' pass books and organisation of nocturnal patrols to protect isolated hamlets, a duty that sometimes incurred personal risk. Mayors were also responsible for the management of communal property, supervision of public works, maintenance of order and hygiene on the streets and setting the price of meat and bread. Amongst their most vital duties was the maintenance of civil registers recording births and deaths, upon which conscription and taxation ultimately depended. Mayors who failed to maintain the registers faced fines of 100 francs and those who deliberately falsified them a life sentence of hard labour.[48]

The mayoral guidebook represented an ideal that was rarely met. Instead, local notables served on their own terms, something the government had little choice but to accept. For example, officially mayors served unremunerated, but in practice they often awarded themselves handsome sums ostensibly to cover expenses. Cologne's mayor, for example, received

---

[47] HASK, FV4378, nos. 11–14.
[48] Keil, *Handbuch*, 2, pp. 58–61. One Rhenish mayor was sentenced to branding and twenty years in irons for forgery in 1807, though he subsequently received an imperial pardon. *Moniteur* 116 (26 April 1807).

a 'gratification' of 6,000 francs annually, something approved by the prefect because it was supported by the city council, which argued it was important for the city's dignity that its representative compete with other dignitaries. The interior minister, whilst reaffirming that the 'legal and general' principle was that mayors serve without pay, accepted they might receive compensation for costs incurred in the 'interests of their communes'. The councillor of state, Jollivet, quite openly advised the mayors of Cologne and Mainz to budget for their salaries under the heading '*frais de représentation de la Mairie*', rather than '*traitement*' or '*indemnité*', so as to avoid trouble.[49] Napoleon occasionally complained about this and observed in 1810 that mayors often received more generous salaries than prefects.[50] Yet, this was the price for attracting suitable candidates.

It was not only with respect to remuneration that local practice conflicted with official regulations. Given the reputation of Napoleonic France for rigorous centralisation, it is surprising to discover the extent to which older practices persisted, even in the largest cities. In Cologne, for example, the superior French authorities encountered difficulties in penetrating the workings of the ex-imperial city, controlled by the old elite. The ex-*Bürgermeister* Klespe and Wittgenstein, as sub-prefect and *maire* respectively, together sabotaged government attempts to farm out the collection of local tax (larger cities had the right to impose duties on selected goods entering their gates) so as to keep it under local control. More seriously, they conspired to cover up serious instances of anti-government protest in order to prevent intrusive investigations.[51] They pre-selected candidates for the city council by presenting the government with nominees who had no intention of taking up their posts should they be chosen, thereby giving their preferred choices a free run.[52] Contrary to Napoleonic procedure, Wittgenstein closely involved the city council in the administration, as had been the practice in the past. From at least 1805 onwards, the council became a near permanent fixture of Cologne's administration and councillors even started referring to themselves as 'Senator', as they had done previously; and whilst initially the mayor at least respected current form by convening the council 'in accordance with a decision of the prefect', in later years he dropped even this pretence.[53]

[49] HASK, FV4373, nos. 93, 97–8, 101, 109–11. The mayor of Mainz received an annual 'remuneration' of 4,000 francs.
[50] Napoleon to the interior minister, 17 September 1810, Napoleon I, *Correspondance*, 11, pp. 123–4.
[51] HStAD, Roër dept., 3009, nos. 44–53. Also, Lameth to the minister of the interior, 27 September 1807, F^{1b} II Roër 3.
[52] HASK, FV4377, no. 4.
[53] Gisela Mettele, 'Kölner Bürgertum in der Umbruchszeit (1776–1815)', in Gall, *Bürgertum*, pp. 262–3.

Whatever the difficulties the government experienced in the cities, they paled when it came to the hundreds of rural municipalities. Some of these were very small, with populations in the low hundreds. It was difficult to find suitably qualified mayors for these entities. As late as June 1802, two years after their creation, the interior minister reported to Napoleon that only a few mayors had been nominated in the Rhenish departments.[54] Dauchy reported in the same year that few suitable candidates accepted their nomination, that prefects were forced to employ special commissioners and that local government in the region was in a state of '*la plus grande irrégularité*'. In France, the appointment of a special commissioner – who was paid for by the locality on which he was imposed – was viewed as punishment. In the Rhineland it was greeted as liberation from an unprofitable distraction.[55] Mayoral candidates with the appropriate talent simply did not exist in sufficient numbers in the rural municipalities. Most who were eventually appointed were ill-qualified farmers, and only a tiny fraction – under 13 per cent in the Roër – belonged to the constitutionally defined group of 'notables' (the top 600 tax-payers in the department), though the proportion was slightly higher – 18 per cent – in the cantonal *chefs-lieux* (the equivalent of market towns). Few rural mayors – under one-fifth – bid for nationalised property, accounting for under 400 of the 9,000 lots sold in the Roër.[56] Even in a wealthy district like Aachen, only a tiny minority – ten out of 188 in one list – were classified as '*riches*' or '*très aisés*'. Most were '*aisés*' (sixty-five), '*médiocres*' (ninety) or lacked any fortune (twenty-three), and their average private income as a whole was well below 1,000 francs. Some rural mayors were so poor they even doubled up as church sextons, a position that placed them under the parish priest. Poor mayors not only undermined the state's dignity, but were impossible to discipline through fines. The threat of dismissal carried few fears, as neither mayors nor their deputies gained much through service, though unofficially many seem to have deducted expenses from communal budgets. So, whilst the prefectures regularly expressed alarm, there was little they could do.[57]

The viability of the smaller Napoleonic rural municipalities was questionable, and not only in terms of personnel. Financially, many were crushed by debts inherited from the revolutionary wars. Municipalities relied upon local direct taxes for funding, but the government restricted these to a level the prefects complained was inadequate, especially given Napoleon's instruction that they use a proportion of their revenues to pay off 10 per cent

---

[54] Report presented by the minister of the interior to the consuls, 10 June 1802, AN F[1c]43, no. 106.
[55] AN, AFIV 1025, dossier 3, no. 13.   [56] Rowe, 'Empire', pp. 660–1.
[57] Lameth to the minister of the interior, 11 September 1807, AN, F[1b]II Roër 3.

of their huge debts every year.[58] The lack of adequate revenue forced rural communities back onto their own resources when it came to the repair of local infrastructure or assistance for the needy. Some municipalities illegally imposed additional charges, contrary to government instructions.[59] As charges had often been usual in the past, an unsuspecting public continued to pay without complaint.[60] Over time, parallel administrations emerged, with their own budgets under local rather than central control. On their own authority, they defended local interests by, for example, preventing the enclosure and sale of communal property to speculators and notables from outside, or enforcing old restrictions on the sale of basic commodities, such as firewood and peat, to outsiders so as to prevent local shortages.[61] The extent to which prefects knowingly tolerated such abuses is less clear; certainly, they warned their superiors against too strict an interpretation of procedural guidelines for fear of provoking mass resignations and a collapse of local government.[62]

The small rural municipalities represented the weakest link in the administrative chain. Their limitations damaged not only the state, but also the interests of urban notables who, through the purchase of secularised properties, increasingly had an interest in the elimination of barriers dividing town and country. Through the departmental councils which they dominated, they agitated for greater central control over rural areas. In particular, they recommended the re-establishment of the cantons as an additional tier between the municipalities and *arrondissements*.[63] Napoleon refused this, but did allow the consolidation of the smallest communes into larger *mairies* containing perhaps a dozen villages and hamlets. Consolidation proceeded unevenly, however, with only the Rhin-et-Moselle making substantial progress by grouping its 828 communes into ninety *mairies*.[64] However, it quickly became obvious that this apparent solution brought new problems. As the mayors of the enlarged *mairies* were unable to personally

[58] AN, F[1c] 44, dossier 'Impositions extraordinaires'.
[59] Prefectoral circular of 3 April 1801, HStAD, Roër dept. 1520, 41. See also the circulars of 7 July 1806, 6 October 1807, 16 October 1812 and 28 July 1813, *Recueil* (1806), p. 554, (1807), (1812), pp. 249–53 and (1813) p. 200 respectively.
[60] Report from the 1st section of the interior ministry to the minister, 8 April 1804, AN, F[1b]II Roër 2.
[61] HStAD, Roër dept., 2746, 7–12; AN, F[1b]II Roër 3, 'Vente de Tourbe'.
[62] Méchin to the finance minister, 5 February 1804, AN, F[1b]II Roër 2. For the Prussian discovery of these parallel administrations after 1814, see Rüdiger Schütz, *Preußen und die Rheinlande. Studien zur preußischen Integrationspolitik im Vormärz* (Wiesbaden, 1979), pp. 125–7.
[63] See, for example, the Roër's departmental council of July/August 1802, AN, F[1c]V Roër, nos. 6, 12. Also, Jordans to Count Réal, 21 April 1810, with accompanying report, AN, F[7] 8390, dossier 'Situation'.
[64] LHAK, Bestand 241, 2043, nos. 5, 8.

administer outlying areas, they instead relied upon semi-official '*syndics*' or '*Bourgemeister*' to supervise these. Paris enjoyed neither control over the appointment of nor disciplinary powers over these individuals.[65] Yet, as one prefect (Lezay-Marnesia of Rhin-et-Moselle) admitted, the whole administration would collapse without them as it was 'impossible' to apply 'literally' the law of 28 Pluviôse VIII – the law that formed the entire basis of Napoleonic administration – in a department where whole villages were devoid of persons who understood French.[66] In other departments, where no consolidation occurred, municipalities themselves combined unofficially to employ French-speaking secretaries to perform public functions.[67] This resulted in a pernicious circle: ministers sent demands to the prefects which were then forwarded to the mayors via the sub-prefects; the mayors only responded when the local French-speaking secretary was available. In the meantime, sub-prefects imposed penalties on the municipalities for failing to meet deadlines, the mayors responded by resigning, and the whole administration ground to a halt.[68] Eventually, Paris discovered what was going on, and was sufficiently fearful that local government was in the hands of unscrupulous middle men to authorise mayors to use German.[69] More generally, the novelty of French methods exposed citizens to the tricks of self-styled '*gens d'affaires*' who wandered about, claiming they enjoyed special connections with higher authorities whom they could influence, for a sum.[70]

Analysis of the municipalities questions the extent to which the Napoleonic regime managed to impose its will locally. However, the municipalities together with the sub-prefects, prefects and interior minister to whom they were subordinate, represented but one column of a more impressive edifice. Running parallel to this column were others linking the departments to the centre, and no judgement on the effectiveness of Napoleonic governance can ignore these. They included the various agencies subordinate to the finance ministry. Of these, the customs administration (*direction des douanes*) was the least popular. It arrived on

---

[65] LHAK, Bestand 256, 120, nos. 71–80, 89–92.

[66] Lezay-Marnesia to the procurator general of the imperial court in Trier, 13 October, 23 October 1812, *ibid.*, nos. 117–20, 129–34.

[67] AN, F⁷8390, dossier 'Situation'.

[68] AN, AFIV 1025, dossier 3, 'Rapport aux Consuls de la République sur la situation des quatre départements de la rive gauche du Rhin, formant la 26ᵉ Division Militaire, par le Cᵉⁿ Dauchy, Conseiller d'Etat', 15 April 1803.

[69] *Recueil* (1810), p. 15.

[70] Prefectoral circulars of 22 November 1802 and 16 February 1810, *Recueil* (1802), pp. 71–2 and (1810), p. 29 respectively. See also HStAD, Roër dept., 199, no. 36; *ibid.*, 1549, no. 33.

the Rhine in 1798, along with France's eastern tariff barrier which it policed. The *direction* included a hierarchy of directors and inspectors that supervised the paramilitary 'brigades' of customs men who patrolled the frontier. Napoleon established three customs 'directions' in the Rhineland, based at Mainz, Bonn and Cleves. Each employed between 600 and 700 agents, which translated into one *douanier* per 1.5 kilometres of frontier. Subsequent reinforcement increased this to one per kilometre. The customs administration was almost wholly French, with Rhinelanders providing less than 3 per cent of all employees. This is unsurprising, as the existing personnel had quite naturally been kept on when the agency moved eastwards in 1798. Nonetheless, the national imbalance hardly endeared the customs service to locals, most of whom thoroughly hated it on account of its association with all the negative aspects of Napoleon's Continental System.[71]

The finance ministry also ran the agency responsible for the collection of direct taxes (*direction du recouvrement des impositions directes*). This organisation was responsible for the tax rolls that were based upon data collected by the municipalities. The upper echelon of the *direction* consisted of the tax directors, who were usually French. The more humble tax controllers, in contrast, included Frenchmen and Rhinelanders, with former radicals prominent amongst the latter. Yet another equally unpopular fiscal agency collected the registration fees for official documents and stamped paper, the patent tax, taxes on playing cards, and also managed national properties (*régie de l'enregistrement et des domaines nationaux*). In terms of revenue collected, this was the most important agency. Its departmental heads (directors) were all Frenchmen, and subordinate places were occupied by Frenchmen and a minority of Rhinelanders. In 1804, some of their duties were taken over by a new administration for the collection of indirect taxes (*régie des droits réunis*) including those on tobacco and alcoholic drinks. The *régie des droits réunis* gained an especially nasty reputation for violating the privacy of homes. Overall, it can be concluded that any type of tax-collector was always likely to be unpopular, but that matters were little helped by the fact that most were Frenchmen, especially at the senior levels.[72] Napoleon was aware of this and (in 1804) instructed his long-serving finance minister, Gaudin, to reserve more places for Rhinelanders: 'These lands can only

---

[71] Roger Dufraisse, 'La Contrebande dans les départements réunis de la rive gauche du Rhin à l'époque napoléonienne', *Francia* 1 (1973), p. 523.

[72] Graumann, *Verwaltung*, pp. 112–31. Hansen, *Quellen*, 4, pp. 521 n. 2, 959 n. 3. For contemporary German resentment at Frenchmen monopolising lucrative posts, see J. W. von Archenholz, 'Briefe über den gegenwärtigen Zustand der deutsch-französischen Rheinländer', *Minerva* 1 (1802), pp. 13, 26, 27, 241–2, 477.

become entirely French with the efforts of the finance minister,' he wrote, 'who, with a large number of positions at his disposal, is well placed to allow them to enjoy the benefits of government.'[73] Napoleon subsequently reiterated these intentions publicly during his visits in 1804 and 1811, but there is little evidence that they were acted upon.[74] The financial administrations remained predominantly 'French'. This was inevitable, as the government felt it could best trust 'outsiders' to carry out sensitive duties. Of course, in the Rhineland, such a distinction overlay significant cultural differences, with the result that oppressive, exploitative bureaucrat became synonymous with 'Frenchman', just as after 1815 it became synonymous with 'Prussian'.

Native Frenchmen also dominated the army officer corps including the divisional and departmental commands.[75] The main internal security force, the paramilitary gendarmerie, was in contrast mixed. Indeed, the government set great store on achieving the optimal national balance within it. Whilst senior officers were all native Frenchmen, German speakers made up a quarter of junior ranks. 'Thus has the government reconciled political considerations with those upon which the good of the service is founded,' wrote the Rhenish brigades' commander; natives provided local knowledge whilst simultaneously 'contract[ing] that spirit of fraternity...which we seek to establish with our new brothers'.[76] Partly for this reason, the gendarmerie was less unpopular than the *douaniers*. It even won grudging recognition for its suppression of banditry that had plagued the Rhineland in the 1790s. Nonetheless, its commanders often expressed dissatisfaction at the lack of support they received from the municipalities and the judiciary.[77]

The gendarmerie was responsible for order in the countryside. In towns with populations greater than 5,000, police commissioners appointed by Napoleon but subordinate to the municipalities kept order. These, like other municipal officials, were always local. However, Napoleon became dissatisfied with their performance and in March 1811 decided to augment them with special police commissioners (*commissaires spéciaux de police*) whom he despatched to the larger cities located on the Empire's frontiers, including Mainz and Cologne. The commissioners corresponded directly with the police minister. In Cologne, long accustomed to governing itself,

---

[73] Napoleon I, *Correspondance*, 9, pp. 509–10.

[74] *Kölnische Zeitung*, 27 September 1804. For the 1811 visit, see Johann Daniel Ferdinand Neigebaur, *Darstellung der provisorischen Verwaltung am Rhein von Jahr 1813 bis 1819* (Cologne, 1821), p. 284.

[75] Hansen, *Quellen*, 4, p. 549.

[76] Brigadier-General Wirion's circular to the central administrations of the four Rhenish departments, 23 August 1798, LHAK, Bestand 256, 804, nos. 1–68.

[77] Georgéon to Count Réal (head of the 1st imperial police district), 8 May 1810, AN, F⁷8390, dossier 'Situation'.

the appointment of a special commissioner was considered an attack on the city's autonomy. Bitter conflict ensued. Matters came to a head in August 1812, over a dispute as to whether the municipality or the police ministry should furnish the commissioner's new offices. At one point a local court, with the municipality's backing, issued a summons to the commissioner on the grounds that he had defrauded a local furniture supplier. Naturally, nothing came of these proceedings, but the commissioner complained subsequently to his superiors that the municipality was continuously undermining his authority.[78]

It was characteristic of the region that recourse should be made to the courts to resolve political conflict. Such had been the case under the Reich. Such was the case now, with the new French judicial institutions. These gained widespread acceptance. They were not viewed as an imposition or as serving the state's interests, but rather as a defence against injustice be it committed by individuals or the state itself. The fact that the judiciary was dominated by locals reinforced this perception. This dominance was especially apparent at the lowest tier that came into regular contact with the people: of the 259 Justices of the Peace (JPs) and notaries in the Rhenish departments in 1800, only twelve originated from outside the region, and of these, eleven came from Belgium or Alsace-Lorraine.[79] JP courts tried minor civil cases for which they could impose modest fines, and less serious police infractions, which attracted larger fines or even short custodial sentences. In cantons (the circumscription of a JP court) located on the frontier, JPs were inundated with cases related to smuggling but, much to the government's fury, proved lax in this area. After 1810, Napoleon transferred these cases to more reliable special courts. From Rhinelanders' perspective, the JP courts enjoyed several advantages: their proceedings were mainly oral so they circumvented the provision introduced in 1798 that official documents be drawn up in French; their proceedings were relatively quick and therefore cheap, as cases needed to be resolved within four months or were else quashed; the JP courts attempted prior mediation, though in practice this degenerated over time into little more than a formality. Indeed, in 1805, the Council of State seriously considered abolishing this facility, though it was eventually enshrined in the Code de procédure civile. As for the JPs

---

[78] AN, F⁷ 6343, nos. 657–68.
[79] Karl-Georg Faber, 'Verwaltungs- und Justizbeamte auf dem linken Rheinufer während der Französischen Herrschaft. Eine personengeschichtliche Studie', in *Aus Geschichte und Landeskunde, Forschungen und Darstellungen. Fritz Steinbach zum 65. Geburtstag gewidmet von seinen Freunden und Schülern* (Bonn, 1960), p. 359. For the original lists of personnel in the Roër, see HStAD, Microfilm A54 ('Etat des services des fonctionnaires').

themselves, recent research overturns the previously held view that they were mainly former radicals. Professional ability, not political considerations, determined appointments and nominations. This too accounts for their prestige.[80]

The JPs survived the major reorganisation of justice in 1802. This established a new hierarchy of courts: JPs at the cantonal level; courts of first instance in the *arrondissements*; criminal tribunals in the departments (replaced by *cours d'assises* in 1810); and appeal courts, covering several departments. As with the JPs, appointments to the rest of the judiciary were made on the basis of professional ability. The law of 22 Ventôse XII (13 March 1804) required all judicial personnel to have passed an exam in a law school, reversing the revolutionary attempt to deprofessionalise justice. In the courts of first instance, Rhinelanders outnumbered Frenchmen amongst the judges (the proportion was four-to-one in the Roër in 1803), though the number of Frenchmen tended to increase over time. The national balance was close to even in the criminal tribunals.[81] In all four departments, many former radicals found employment in these higher courts. This was not on account of their political background but in virtue of their talents as jurists.[82]

As we shall see, following the collapse of Napoleonic rule the Prussians initiated an enquiry into the French judicial system and concluded that its popularity lay less with the actual laws than with its procedures. In particular, Rhinelanders appreciated the independence of the judiciary, its separation from the administration, its oral and public proceedings and, above all, that trial was by jury. Juries provided the ultimate protection against arbitrary actions by the state and diminished the chances of conviction for socially acceptable crimes such as smuggling or conscription fraud. Of course, this hardly endeared them to Napoleon, who had great misgivings about juries. Nonetheless, he accepted their preservation for ordinary cases whilst creating a new range of supplementary special courts to try cases involving matters of direct concern to the state where juries might acquit. These included the fearsome special tribunals (*tribunaux spéciaux*) introduced in October 1801. Composed of judges and military officers appointed

---

[80] Marcel Erkens, *Die französische Friedensgerichtsbarkeit 1789–1814 unter besonderer Berücksichtigung der vier rheinischen Departements* (Cologne, Weimar and Vienna, 1994), pp. 161, 164–87, 189–91, 214–16, 228, 250.

[81] Graumann, *Verwaltung*, pp. 182–8, 192–3. For the French law school in Koblenz, see Luitwin Mallmann, *Französische Juristenausbildung im Rheinland 1794–1814. Die Rechtsschule von Koblenz* (Cologne and Vienna, 1987).

[82] Roger Dufraisse, 'Sarre', 'Mont-Tonnerre', 'Rhin-et-Moselle' and 'Roër' in Louis Bergeron and Guy Chaussinand-Nogaret (eds.), *Grands Notables du premier empire* (vol. 3, Paris, 1978), pp. 45–154.

by Napoleon, these tried cases including murder, forgery of coins, attacks against the purchasers of nationalised properties, bribery of recruitment officers and rebellion. They functioned without juries and their sentences, against which there was no appeal, were carried out within twenty-four hours. The special criminal courts (*cours de justice criminelle spéciale*; after 1810, *cours spéciale ordinaire*) tried similar crimes, and were also composed of a mixture of judges and military officers who sat without juries. After 1810 they were complemented by the non-jury customs courts (*tribunaux ordinaires des douanes* and *cours prévôtales des douanes*). Given their unpopularity, it is not surprising that judges serving on these courts fled into the French interior in the face of the Allied invasion in early 1814.[83]

The non-jury special courts disappeared in 1814, unmourned. Fortuitously shorn of its authoritarian elements, the French legal system subsequently became a surrogate constitution. A broad social spectrum united in its defence. Serving or retired judicial personnel led this defence out of conviction or professional necessity. Amongst them were Christoph Wilhelm Sethe and Georg Friedrich Rebmann, both of whom we shall encounter later. Sethe in particular played a crucial role after 1814 as head of the Prussian commission that decided in favour of the preservation of French judicial forms, whilst Rebmann deployed his journalistic talents after the Restoration in countering the wave of nationalism that sought 'de-Napoleonisation'. Previous episodes had shown them the strengths of the institution they were now defending. For Sethe, this episode came in 1813, whilst he was senior procurator in the grand duchy of Berg. During the serious uprising of that year, Sethe used his position to mitigate the repression that followed. As a consequence, Sethe faced condemnation from his superiors and was even summoned by Napoleon to Paris, where he was told the Emperor could have him shot. 'Then he will have to shoot the law first,' Sethe is said to have replied. Rebmann, as a superior judge in Mont-Tonnerre on the left bank, found himself in an analogous position following the abortive uprisings in Germany against French rule that accompanied the Austrian War of 1809. When followers of one of these uprisings – that led by the Prussian major Schill – were arrested, Napoleon determined they should be tried as common criminals and not combatants. However, Rebmann, in whose court they appeared, successfully employed technicalities to spin out proceedings until the collapse of French rule.[84]

[83] Graumann, *Verwaltung,* pp. 169–71, 194–6. LHAK, Bestand 241, fascicles 1029, 1247, 1255.
[84] For Sethe, see *Allgemeine Deutsche Biographie* (56 vols., Leipzig, 1875–1912), 30, pp. 152–3; also, Adolf Klein and Justus Bockemühl (eds.), *1770–1815. Weltgeschichte am Rhein erlebt. Erinnerungen*

Both episodes illustrated the authoritarian tendencies of Napoleonic governance. However, their real significance comes in their demonstration of the institutional strength of the Napoleonic state, the importance accorded to the rule of law (Sethe was, after all, not shot), and the guarantees this provided against arbitrary government.

'Power is based upon opinion,' Napoleon once stated. 'What is a government not supported by opinion? Nothing.'[85] Authority might come from above, but confidence emanated from below, in Sieyès's formulation. Allowing this confidence expression without creating a force that might claim sovereignty was the challenge that faced Napoleon following the Directory's overthrow. Napoleon wished to tap the power generated by popular legitimacy, but not release it uncontrolled. To this end, he introduced a complex set of institutions that ran parallel to the executive branch of government. These included a hierarchy of electoral colleges, starting with the cantonal assemblies at the bottom, followed by the district (or *arrondissement*) and departmental electoral colleges. The cantonal assemblies comprised one-tenth of all citizens, and they chose the electors who sat in the colleges. After 1802, the departmental electors could only be chosen from the top 600 tax-payers in the department. For the average department, this meant an annual income of at least 3,000 francs or 60,000 francs in capital assets.[86] The cantonal assemblies also nominated JPs. The district and departmental electoral colleges nominated candidates for the hierarchy of advisory councils. They also selected a national list of candidates for the Tribunate (until 1807) and Corps Législatif. The Senate, which together with the Tribunate and Corps Législatif represented the legislative branch, chose members of the two other houses from this national list.

The complexity of this electoral system poses questions as to its worth. Certainly, it fails to meet the criteria demanded of modern representational systems. It was supposed to give the Napoleonic regime popular legitimacy whilst avoiding any dangerous concentration of power within any particular

des Rheinländers Christoph Wilhelm Heinrich Sethe aus der Zeit des europäischen Umbruchs (Cologne, 1973). For Rebmann and the Schill episode, see N. S. Wraskaja, *A. G. F. Rebmann. Leben und Werke eines Publizisten zur Zeit der grossen französischen Revolution* (Heidelberg, 1907), p. 147. For Rebmann more generally, Karl-Georg Faber, *Die Rheinlande zwischen Restauration und Revolution. Probleme der Rheinischen Geschichte von 1814 bis 1848 im Spiegel der zeitgenössischen Publizistik* (Wiesbaden, 1966), pp. 46–55.

[85] Jacques Ellul, *Propaganda. The Formation of Men's Attitudes* (translated from the French by Konrad Kellen and Jean Lerner; with an introduction by Konrad Kellen, New York, 1968), p. 123.

[86] Ellis, 'Rhine and Loire', p. 238.

body. Beyond that, the system as a whole provided additional links that bound the departments to the centre.[87] It also provided checks against arbitrary acts by subaltern officials. Certainly, Napoleon took the electoral/representative system seriously; for example, he described the departmental electoral colleges as being 'of great importance for public order'.[88] This was because the various electoral colleges, assemblies and councils represented something of an early-warning mechanism. Whilst Napoleon never willingly suffered public criticism, he nonetheless was open to advice and above all betrayed an insatiable appetite for information. This the colleges and councils provided. In that sense, to dismiss them simply as a constitutional sham misses their point.

This conclusion certainly holds true if we include the prefectoral councils (*conseils de préfecture*) in our analysis. These councils comprised four or five members, depending upon the department's size. They included a mixture of local notables and outsiders who, unlike their counterparts on the departmental and district councils, were appointed by Napoleon and not selected by the electoral colleges. They were also paid. In some respects they should be classified as part of the executive hierarchy. However, they resembled the other councils in that their primary function was to provide the government with information on local conditions. This was especially important in the Rhineland, where local knowledge of the manifold laws and complex procedures of the former electorates was vital to the smooth running of the administration. Arguably, this lent the Rhenish prefectoral councils greater significance than their counterparts elsewhere. In addition to supplying the prefect with such information, the councils (which sat permanently) functioned as an administrative court. In this capacity, they heard appeals from individuals for a reduction in their tax assessment, ruled on claims against the administration, and in disputes between private contractors and the state. They also dealt with disputes relating to the nationalised properties, something that figured greatly in the activities of the Rhenish councils. The rulings of the prefectoral councils could only be reversed by the Council of State. Prefects attended their meetings and held the casting vote in cases of division. Napoleon took particular care in his appointment of prefectoral councillors, and generally opted for individuals with prior administrative or legal experience. In the Rhineland, radicals predominated amongst the first

[87] Newly elected Rhenish senators and legislators (no Rhinelanders entered the Tribunate) were inundated by congratulations upon their nomination by individuals and localities placing themselves under their 'protection'. Stadtarchiv, Aachen (StAA), Bestand RAII (Allgemeine Akten), 248, no. 56; HASK, FV4347.

[88] Napoleon to Cambacérès 12 August 1807, Napoleon I, *Correspondance*, 14, p. 487.

appointments, but after 1804 old-regime officials and wealthy businessmen came to the fore. Half of those appointed in 1800 were native Rhinelanders and this proportion subsequently increased.[89]

In contrast, the departmental, district and municipal councils did not sit permanently, but only convened for two weeks per year apart from extraordinary sessions occasionally ordered by the government. However, as we have seen from Cologne, it appears that some municipal councils at least sat for longer periods if not permanently without authorisation, and that they in practice played a greater role than official regulations entitled them to.[90] The official duties of the departmental, district and municipal councils included the sub-division of the tax burden and the supervision of prefectoral, sub-prefectoral and municipal accounts. They also provided annual reports to the interior minister on their localities and presented petitions to the government.

These were the structures provided for the expression of confidence from below. Whether Rhinelanders availed themselves of these is another matter. There is anecdotal evidence that at least some welcomed the colleges and councils as facilitating a 'real and significant participation in the governance of the state', to quote one contemporary.[91] The *cahiers de vœux* submitted by the councils did not confine themselves to obsequious statements of loyalty but often employed surprisingly critical language when highlighting various deficiencies, and as such represent an important historical source. Set against this evidence are the statistics indicating low voter turnout in elections and high levels of absenteeism amongst councillors. For example, in Cologne's first elections, held in August 1803, eight days passed before the required number (50 per cent) of cantonal assembly members voted to validate proceedings.[92] Overall, the average voter participation in the Roër's forty-three cantons was, at 52.6 per cent, barely above the level required, with three cantons in the district of Cologne and two in Aachen falling below the necessary threshold.[93] The prefect blamed the low turnout on the complex and novel voting procedures, and the fact that the elections took place when the greatest part of the population was working in the fields. Elections held subsequently showed no improvement: in 1809, six

[89] Graumann, *Verwaltung*, pp. 59–62. Dufraisse, 'Notables', pp. 759–60. For the Rhin-et-Moselle's council, see LHAK, Bestand 241, 1,073.

[90] AN, F^{IC}III Roër 1, nos. 130–2. See also the prefectoral circulars of 6 October 1802, *Recueil* (1803), part 1, p. 23, and November/December 1802, part 2, p. 24.

[91] Graumann, *Verwaltung*, p. 101.

[92] AN, F^{IC}III Roër 1, 96, 'Procès-Verbal-Général dressé sur les opérations de l'assemblée cantonale de la première section de la ville de Cologne [3 to 12 Aug. 1803]'.

[93] HStAD, Roër dept. 1601, nos. 7–8.

of the Roër's cantons failed to vote at all.[94] Despite the best efforts of the cantonal presidents, attendance at rural elections was especially low due to the law that required that the shortlist of candidates for various posts be restricted to the wealthiest tax-payers, who in the Rhineland were concentrated in the towns and cities. This provision in effect debarred rural cantonal assemblies from voting for favoured candidates with local ties. Absenteeism also afflicted the departmental and district electoral colleges.[95] The same was true of the departmental and district councils. Rarely more than seventy out of 200 councillors attended the Roër's departmental council when it convened in 1804. One reason was the considerable expense of travelling to and residing in the departmental or district *chefs-lieux*. One prefect's suggestion, that council members should receive a medal for every day they attended, was hardly likely to represent sufficient enticement.[96] Sickness was the usual excuse provided by absentee councillors. For at least some, higher principles were at stake, with one notable declining his seat on Cleves's district council because of his 'relationship with the Prussian state'.[97]

It might be supposed that low voter turnout and attendance reflected the regime's efforts to keep the colleges and councils on such a tight leash that free expression became impossible. Yet this does not appear to have been the case, or if it was, the government was singularly unsuccessful in achieving this aim. As noted, the councils occasionally submitted surprisingly blunt reports on the administration. As for the cantonal assemblies and electoral colleges, these arguably did afford opportunities for political participation, and the prevalence of factionalism, cabals, voter intimidation and coalitions in at least some of them suggests that Rhinelanders made use of these opportunities, though not necessarily in the way Napoleon had intended. The new structures and mechanisms institutionalised rivalries between the different *Länder* lumped together in the departments. This at least was the explanation proffered by the Roër's prefect in 1805 to account for the inability of the electoral colleges within his department to agree on the nomination of candidates for various posts.[98] The president of the Roër's electoral college made the same excuse in December 1809: failure to agree

[94] AN, F[IC]III Roër 2, no. 6.
[95] President of the cantonal assembly of Bracht to Méchin, 13 August 1804, AN, F[IC]III Roër 1, nos. 38, 42. For the departmental and district electoral colleges, *ibid.*, nos. 141–2; also, AN, F[IC]III Roër 2, nos. 15, 62–4, 66, 68.
[96] Méchin to the interior minister, 11 April 1804, AN, F[Ib]II Roër 2.
[97] Johann Adolf Kopstadt, *Ueber Kleve. In Briefen an einen Freund aus den Jahren 1811 und 1814* (Frankfurt a. M., 1822), p. 163.
[98] Laumond to the interior minister, 30 September 1805, AN, F[IC]III Roër 1, nos. 141–2.

on candidates arose 'because each district wishes to enjoy a preponderance of members'.[99]

Nor were Rhenish electors submissive in the face of Napoleonic bullying. The Roër's departmental electoral college spectacularly humiliated the government in 1804 when it refused to elect Marshal Bernadotte to the Senate, despite official entreaties. It instead elected Belderbusch, a former senior official of Max Franz who later became prefect of the Oise. Bernadotte, according to the college president, suffered from the '*circonstance fatale*' of having been stationed in the Rhineland in the 1790s and thus 'obliged' to impose 'terrible' requisitions on the region. The prefect, Laumond, complained that the electoral colleges simply refused to elect anyone other than locals and that the many Frenchmen living in the department who stood as candidates all failed.[100] Obviously, the *Indignatsprinzip* remained stronger than government pressure. This culture of stubborn defiance continued under one of Laumond's successors, Ladoucette, who in January 1810 complained to the interior minister that the departmental electoral college had just passed over seven government candidates for the departmental council, despite official 'instructions' to the college's president. Instead, according to a report from the police minister, Fouché, submitted to Napoleon, the college elected two judges previously sacked by the government.[101]

Examination of how the electoral colleges and consultative councils functioned *in practice* leads to the following conclusion: some Rhinelanders, for whatever reason, failed to engage with them, but a large number availed themselves of them for their own purposes. Foremost amongst these purposes was defence of the interests of the *Land* against threats such as the regime attempting to impose its favoured candidates at the expense of locals, and rival *Länder* gaining preponderance on this or that college or council. For the French government, the employment of its institutions for these ends represented an unintended outcome. It was extremely irritating that councils and colleges should serve as fora for 'useless debates and . . . idle discussions, which only hamper the administration without enlightening it', as one prefectoral circular characteristically put it.[102] Yet for Rhinelanders, the existence of participatory institutions was far from useless. Rather, it was something they were used to under the Reich. Napoleon, through his provision of such institutions unwittingly preserved a link between the

[99] Count Loë to the interior minister, 18 December 1809, AN, F^{IC}III Roër 2, no. 49.
[100] Laumond to the interior minister, 1 October 1805, AN, F^{IC}III Roër 1, nos. 141–2.
[101] Ladoucette to the interior minister, 21 January 1810, AN, F^{IC}III Roër 2, no. 47. Also, Hauterive, *Police secrète*, 5, p. 290 (report of 9 January 1810).
[102] Prefectoral circular of 5 January 1801, HStAD, Roër dept. 1520, no. 19.

practices of the Old Regime and the demands for participatory government that lay at the heart of nineteenth-century liberalism.

The reader may have approached this chapter with an image of Napoleonic government as centralised, efficient and authoritarian. This chapter has attempted to modify this image. The most important characteristic of Napoleonic government was less its centralisation and more its dependence upon local elites. Napoleon recognised the immutability of the 'notables', and designed his administrative structures accordingly. He hoped the notables would put aside the ideological differences of the past and 'rally'. In that sense, the Napoleonic system was politically relatively inclusive, though socially exclusive. For 'notability' depended chiefly upon wealth, with 'talent' playing a less significant though not unimportant role in defining status. Of course, wealth and talent as much as birth had, in practice, defined social status under the Old Regime to a greater extent than might be thought. We have seen how in old-regime Cologne, for example, civic institutions provided mechanisms whereby newcomers in possession of wealth and talent could rise to prominence within the city. Aachen had been less successful in this respect, in that a variety of institutional barriers prevented the perfect translation of wealth and talent into political power. Here, and in places where similar institutional barriers had previously existed, Napoleonic government resulted in significant modifications to the elite. Elsewhere, the new regime was marked by continuity.

Napoleonic rule was imposed upon the Rhineland from outside. However, it quickly gained a measure of local support. Rhinelanders, like their fellow Frenchmen, were weary of ideological conflict and welcomed Napoleon's 'depoliticisation' of public life. The new regime, in contrast to its revolutionary predecessors, showed outward respect for local traditions and sensibilities. For some ambitious Rhinelanders it even provided career opportunities. Certainly, these faced some discrimination, but as provincials and not as Germans. Furthermore, this discrimination diminished over time. However, the majority of Rhinelanders did not set their sights on careers that would transport them to the outer reaches of Napoleon's ever-expanding empire. The horizons of most remained confined to the city, town, 'Land' and, increasingly, the region; they wished to serve the new regime locally, and resented competition from Frenchmen. Similar tensions between centre and periphery would continue following the collapse of French rule, and persist for much of the nineteenth century.

Napoleonic rule gained acceptance not so much because it provided new opportunities to a large number of previously excluded wealthy and talented Rhinelanders, but because it restored law and order after a period characterised by arbitrariness. Napoleonic government has sometimes been seen as 'militarising' French society. One thinks of the uniforms for civilian officials, the rigid hierarchies and the prominence of the military in ceremonies and as recipients of patronage. However, it is possible to interpret things differently and indeed, documents relating to the Rhineland do tell another story. According to this, the 1790s were characterised by exploitation and arbitrary action by military commanders who acted independently of civilian control. After 1799, in contrast, military commanders found themselves constrained by an increasingly formidable *civilian* apparatus whose backbone was provided by the prefects. These wore uniforms, but this reflected not so much the 'militarisation' of the civilian administration but rather Napoleon's attempt to boost its status in the eyes of the population. Hence, the time and paperwork lavished on questions related to etiquette and precedence. The fruit of this effort was not the triumph of military values, but the re-establishment of ordered civilian administration.

Of course, this administration was not perfect. In practice, it failed to conform to the impressive blueprint drawn up in the various laws of Year VIII. Much of this chapter has been devoted to revealing the limitations of Napoleonic administration. These were especially glaring in rural areas, but also in larger towns and cities where the established elite remained intact. Overall, the Napoleonic state's ability to penetrate the peripheral departments – departments whose inhabitants spoke a foreign language – should not be overestimated. In practice, old ways survived, albeit within the new administrative framework. The Rhineland was not 'colonised' by the French Empire; rather, Rhinelanders 'colonised' certain French institutions. This was especially the case with the judiciary. The various consultative councils and colleges designed to allow the expression of 'confidence' from below must also be mentioned in this context. Evidence suggests these played a more important function than previously thought. As we saw in earlier chapters, Rhinelanders were used to institutions that allowed for a degree of popular participation in government and that placed restrictions on the exercise of power. It is therefore unsurprising that Rhinelanders quickly adopted the new Napoleonic judicial and consultative structures as their own, even though they then used them not to further the interests of the state as the French intended, but of the *Stadt* and *Land*. Ironically, French rule ultimately gained widespread acceptance in the Rhineland because of what Napoleon and his circle would have identified as its weaknesses.

CHAPTER 5

Identities and state formation

At Cologne they speak simply a coarse vulgar German, which degenerates in approaching the flats of Holland: but at A[a]chen, bad German, bad French, some Dutch and Flemish (bad or good I know not) and a mixture of the *Walloon* dialect, of which you hear more at Liège, conspire to form a Babel of harmonious diversity.[1]

An objection [against the reunion of the Rhenish departments with France] . . . is that a mixture of many peoples of differing language and character can destroy harmony, public opinion, internal peace.[2]

Few sights more disconcerting could have confronted a rationally minded Napoleonic bureaucrat than the heterogeneous Rhineland. He viewed cultural diversity 'not [as] the characteristic of the rational individual, but [as] evidence of the historical survival among groups and communities of beliefs and superstitions that belonged to earlier ages'.[3] It was not only that a Rhenish department like the Roër encompassed under the Old Regime thirty-two territorial entities. Territorial fragmentation was matched by confessional diversity and a plethora of local patois, or 'local dialects and ways of speech', as Braudel more accurately refers to them.[4]

Contemporaries experienced difficulty placing Rhinelanders within any single, culturally defined category. Dorsch, the former radical who became sub-prefect of Cleves, distinguished between Rhinelanders of Dutch origin, who spoke 'German gibberish', and 'Prussians'.[5] Many Germans from the

---

[1] C. E. Dodd, *An Autumn Near the Rhine; or, Sketches of Courts, Society, Scenery, & c. in Some of the German States Bordering the Rhine* (London, 1818), p. 523.
[2] Lakanal (French government commissioner of the Rhenish departments) to Cambacérès (minister of justice), 13 October 1799, Joseph Hansen, *Quellen zur Geschichte des Rheinlandes im Zeitalter der Französischen Revolution 1780–1801* (4 vols., Bonn, 1931–8), 4, p. 1197.
[3] Stuart Woolf, 'French Civilisation and Ethnicity in the Napoleonic Empire', *Past & Present*, 124 (1989), p. 107.
[4] Fernand Braudel, *The Identity of France* (2 vols., London, 1988–90), I, pp. 91–6.
[5] Dorsch to the justice minister, 16 March 1798, Archives Nationales (AN), F^{1c}44, dossier 'Correspondance relative à la division territoriale des quatre départements an VI–VIII'.

right bank believed Rhinelanders closer to the Dutch in character.[6] The episcopal authorities in Aachen counted a total of 120 Dutch-speaking parishes within the Roër, something reflected in the 'reunion addresses' submitted in 1798, which were made in French, German and Dutch.[7] The last French prefect in Aachen, Ladoucette, mistook the local dialect of Cleves as a mixture of Dutch and Walloon.[8] Albert Klebe, who travelled through the region during the Consulate, commented on the poor German he encountered everywhere, including in public announcements; these were so confusing that he relied upon the French translations. Even the lecture list for the central school in Cologne was written in this poor German.[9]

Cultural divisions in the Rhineland also divided socially, as was to be expected in a pre-industrial society.[10] Close to Belgium, for example, the majority spoke Walloon or a Liège patois but the elite Dutch.[11] A Prussian observer recorded that although the Rhenish elite did not speak particularly good high German, it could rarely speak the local patois of the majority either. Cologne's bicultural elite proved an exception, happily switching from high German, which it used to distinguish itself from the plebeians, to the local dialect (*Kölsch*), whose use marked its members out as long-term residents as opposed to recent immigrants.[12] In Aachen, the elite commonly spoke French and further to the north, along the Meuse, either French or Dutch, whilst everyone else employed 'Walloon'. The local Rhenish patois merged into Dutch the further north one travelled.[13]

---

[6] Johann Adam Boost, *Was waren die Rheinländer als Menschen und Bürger, und was ist aus ihnen geworden?* (Mainz, 1819), p. 202.

[7] The cantons of Geldern, Horst and Wankum were mainly Flemish speaking. Hauptstaatsarchiv Düsseldorf (HStAD), Roër dept., 1520. Klaus Friedrich, *Marc Antoine Berdolet (1740–1809), Bischof von Colmar, erster Bischof von Aachen. Sein Leben und Wirken unter besonderer Berücksichtigung seiner pastoralen Vorstellung* (Mönchengladbach, 1973), pp. 376, 380. For the reunion addresses, see AN, F^{IC} III Roër 3, nos. 162–6.

[8] Jean Charles François de Ladoucette, *Voyage fait en 1813 et 1814 dans le pays entre Meuse et Rhin, suivi de notes, avec une carte géographique* (Paris, 1818), p. 191.

[9] Albert Klebe, *Reise auf dem Rhein durch die teutschen und französischen Rheinländer nach Achen und Spaa* (2nd edn, Frankfurt a. M., 1806), pp. 557–8.

[10] Ernest Gellner, *Nations and Nationalism* (Oxford, 1983), p. 12.

[11] Heinrich Simon van Alpen, *Geschichte des fränkischen Rheinufers, was es war und was es jetzt ist* (2 vols., Cologne, 1802), I, p. 43.

[12] Johann Daniel Friedrich Neigebaur, *Statistik der Preußischen Rhein =Provinzen, in den drei Perioden ihrer Verwaltung: 1) Durch das General =Gouvernement vom Niederrheine; 2) Durch jenes vom Nieder= und Mittelrheine; 3) Nach Ihrer jetzigen Begränzung und wirklichen Vereinigung mit dem Preußischen Staate. Aus officiellen Quellen. Von einem Preußischen Staatsbeamten* (Cologne, 1817), p. 56. Elaine Glovka Spencer, 'Regimenting Revelry; Rhenish Carnival in the Early Nineteenth Century', *Central European History* 28 (1995), pp. 470–1. James M. Brophy, 'Mirth and Subversion: Carnival in Cologne', *History Today* 47, 7 (1997), p. 43.

[13] Ladoucette, *Voyage*, p. 60. Neigebaur, *Statistik*, p. 56.

The region's sixteenth- and seventeenth-century role as a receptacle for Catholic and Protestant refugees from France and the Netherlands, and for economic migrants, contributed to its cosmopolitanism. In the eighteenth century, these migrants were joined by frequenters of spa towns. An early nineteenth-century Prussian official noted the consequences of territorial fragmentation and contact with outsiders:

the large number of different sovereignties into which the country was formerly divided, and the resulting conflicting interests, is the sole reason why no particular national character ever appeared. This was even more blurred through the mass of foreigners, who were drawn here from all the neighbouring countries by the factories, and by trade and industry, and who subsequently settled down. Another contributory factor was the many foreign visitors who came for short periods either because of business or for the famous spas. Through this constant friction and contact with the most diverse peoples, the inhabitants . . . have gained an excellent style of cunning and shrewdness in all dealings of a bourgeois nature.[14]

State-building involves erecting clearly demarcated boundaries within which favoured, standardised, high cultures flourish.[15] The Rhineland lacked such boundaries prior to French rule; before then, its borders were bands pock-marked with enclaves and exclaves, not abrupt frontiers marked with a double line of customs posts.

Cultural diversity was acceptable in the eighteenth-century Rhineland. It was unwelcome to revolutionary state-builders. The French interior minister, visiting in 1798, was shocked by the numerous customs that confronted him, and which he blamed for obstructing 'the fusion of the various parts of these diverse countries into a completely republican single whole'.[16] The old territorial divisions were so great as to utterly confuse revolutionary commissioners posted to the region.[17] For them, the imposition of cultural and above all linguistic uniformity was not merely a question of administrative efficiency. Nor was it an example of cultural imperialism, for the revolutionaries evinced little interest in attempting to impose French beyond the Republic's 'natural frontiers'. 'A universal language', the Abbé Grégoire observed, 'is of the same order as the philosopher's stone in chemistry.' Rather, the question was political, as reflected in Grégoire's famous report to the National Convention of 4 June 1794. This condemned local patois – 'the gothic style' – within France as sustaining the 'divide and

---

[14] Neigebaur, *Statistik*, p. 48.   [15] Gellner, *Nations*, p. 62.
[16] François de Neufchâteau to the executive directory, 17 August 1798, AN, F^{Ie} 42, dossier 'Dénonciation des abus qui seront introduits dans l'administration de ces départemen[t]s'.
[17] Talleyrand (minister of foreign affairs) to Lambrechts (justice minister), 24 October 1798, AN, F^{Ie} 44, dossier 'Correspondance relative à la division territoriale des quatre départements an VI–VIII'.

rule' strategy of feudal forces. For Grégoire, the question revolved around popular participation in government:

If these places [official posts] are occupied by men incapable of expressing themselves and writing correctly in the national language, how will the rights of citizens be guaranteed in the laws whose wording will include inaccurate terms and a confusion of ideas? If, on the other hand, ignorance [those ignorant of the French language] is excluded from positions, soon there will be reborn that aristocracy which formerly employed patois in order to show its protecting affinity with those it insolently called *les petites gens*. Soon, society will be re-infected by the 'proper sort'. The liberty of suffrage will be restricted, cabals easily formed and more difficult to break, and in consequence a kind of hierarchy established between the two separated classes [officials and citizens]. Thus ignorance of the language will either compromise the social wellbeing or destroy equality.

Grégoire rejected the translation of official documents into local patois on grounds of cost, the slowing of the administrative process, and because the 'sense' of a law might be lost or undermined by counter-revolutionaries. This last concern was not unfounded: in the Napoleonic Rhineland, unpopular measures, especially those concerning the Church, were often moderated in tone when translated into German by local authorities.[18]

Grégoire's stance reversed the cultural liberalism of the early Revolution, when the Constituent Assembly had decreed (14 January 1790) the translation of legislation into local patois. Grégoire, in contrast, condemned patois as 'very degenerate' and recommended they be replaced by standard French through 'national festivals' and military service. Grégoire's Jacobin contemporaries proposed even more radical measures in exterminating such feudal leftovers as German in Alsace, a region where French was virtually unknown outside the major towns.[19] Under the Old Regime, Alsatians happily reconciled allegiance to the French crown with the preservation of German culture. Even after the Revolution, the elite continued to think in terms of a 'separate, inviolate Alsatian German "cultural sphere"' within the larger framework of French sovereignty'. Some Alsatians even viewed the region as a bridge between Germany and France. The revolutionaries in Paris initially welcomed these ideas. The outbreak of war in 1792, followed by the rise of the Jacobins, destroyed prospects for diversity. Two ideas now fused and justified 'Frenchification': the classification of all languages on

---

[18] For Grégoire's report, see *Archives Parlementaires de 1787 à 1860. Recueil complet des débats législatifs et politiques des chambres françaises. Imprimé... sous la direction de MM. I. Mavidal et E. Lurent, etc.* 1st series (1787–99), (Paris, 1868–), 91, pp. 318–27.

[19] The rest of the paragraph, on Alsace, is based on David Bell's excellent article, 'Nation-building and Cultural Particularism in Eighteenth-century France: the Case of Alsace', *Eighteenth-Century Studies* 21 (1987–8), pp. 472–90.

a scale from civilised to savage and the theory of the culturally defined nation.[20] The Jacobin Convention ordered the elimination of local languages and patois throughout France, and despatched Saint Just to Alsace to 'Gallicise' the province. He accused defenders of German of spreading '*poison royalistico-aristocratique*', and had them guillotined. Paris shut down Strasbourg university, whose professors had dared mount a Burkean defence of Alsace's historical development. For one visiting member of the Convention even this was insufficient: he recommended guillotining one-quarter of all Alsatians and the expulsion of the rest. Only the Jacobins' overthrow in July 1794 prevented 'Gallicanisation' of the Republic's peripheries through ethnic cleansing. Anti-German legislation in Alsace was subsequently repealed. The Lakanal Law on primary education (17 November 1794) did not insist that French be the exclusive language of instruction in areas where the population spoke German, Breton, Flemish or some other language.[21]

The Rhineland was fortunate that its permanent occupation came after the Jacobins' overthrow. The regimes that followed were distinguished by pragmatism, not cultural purity. On the Rhine, Paris was concerned with sustaining the war effort, not linguistic uniformity, and officials posted to the region made pragmatic concessions to gothic particularism. Grégoire, who had earlier denounced Alsatian German as the language of slaves, now justified the introduction of revolutionary government in the Rhineland on the grounds it conformed with ancient *Germanic* custom.

Plans to transform Rhinelanders into 'new Frenchmen' came only with the decision to integrate the region administratively with France. In January 1798, justice minister Lambrechts outlined French cultural policy in the occupied territories. Ignorance, he wrote, accompanies servitude and enlightenment must precede conferment of liberty, especially where crushed for centuries by 'fanaticism' and 'tyranny'. Liberation would come only with French, enabling communication between locals and Frenchmen which would result in the former being transformed into virtuous citizens. French instruction in schools, Lambrechts continued, was a necessity, though unfortunately one that would bear fruit only in the long term. Two months later, Rudler decreed French the official language of the new departments.[22] His successors spent the following sixteen years battling to

[20] Peter McPhee, 'A Case-study of Internal Colonization: the Francisation of Northern Catalonia', *Review* 3 (1980), p. 406.
[21] Isser Woloch, *The New Regime. Transformations of the French Civic Order, 1789–1820s* (London and New York, 1994), p. 183.
[22] For Lambrecht's memorandum, see Hansen, *Quellen*, 4, pp. 503–5. For Rudler's subsequent decree, Karl Theodor Friedrich Bormann and Alexander von Daniels (eds.), *Handbuch der für die königlich-preußischen Rheinprovinzen verkündigten Gesetze, Verordnungen und Regierungsbeschlüsse aus der Zeit der Fremdherrschaft* (8 vols., Cologne, 1833–45), 6, p. 635.

enforce this. Little had been achieved by June 1802, when another commissioner, Jeanbon Saint-André, reminded subalterns that all public acts
must be in French. 'This is the formal intention of the government,' he
admonished, 'and it is the duty of all officials who are placed amongst the
inhabitants of the four departments to employ their efforts to make them
accustomed to the idiom of their new *patrie*.' Even sub-prefectures were still
using German, he complained. He ordered the prefects to make monthly
progress reports on French usage and identify those ignoring his directive.[23]

State formation includes the imposition of standard cultural practices.
As in other areas, so with language, the French encountered huge obsta-
cles. In practice, they recognised that German would remain the majority
language for at least a generation. The state councillor, Dauchy, reporting
to the Consuls on his fact-finding mission of 1802, wrote that 'knowledge
of the German language will be indispensable for a long time for those
Frenchmen destined for administrative or judicial functions in our new
acquisitions; it will always be useful for those who wish to make progress in
a diplomatic or military career'.[24] The commissioners Jollivet and Jeanbon
Saint-André recommended the government appoint only bilingual prefects
in the Rhineland.[25] Paris considered it especially important that gendarmes,
who came into daily contact with ordinary people, understand German.
The same held for the judiciary, especially following complaints from state
procurators that Rhenish juries were reaching perverse verdicts because of
difficulties over the translation of German into French, difficulties smart
lawyers exploited.[26] Judges who understood only French were prejudicial
to fair proceedings, complained one procurator, as most defendants and
witnesses were Germans, and the translation of evidence proved extremely
difficult when the innocence or guilt of the accused depended upon the
sense, nuance and inflection of particular words and phrases in the local
jargon.[27] Paris therefore favoured bilingual Frenchmen, notably Alsatians,
in its appointments; the Alsatian objective of bridging French and German
culture thereby came true.

The government printed public pronouncements and laws in German
and French throughout the Napoleonic period. Napoleon took a pragmatic line on the propagation of French, which he himself had difficulty

---

[23] Jeanbon Saint-André (general commissioner of the Rhenish departments) to Jacobi (acting-prefect
of the Roër), 22 June 1802, HStAD, Roër dept. 1520, no. 254.
[24] AN, AFIV 1025, dossier 3, no. 2.
[25] The minister received this advice from Jollivet on 14 August 1801 and Jeanbon Saint-André on
8 March 1802, AN, F^{1b}II Roër 1, dossier 'Préfet- renseignements . . .'
[26] Landeshauptarchiv Koblenz (LHAK), Bestand 241, 1043, nos. 61–2, and Bestand 241ff., 2279,
nos. 1–12.
[27] LHAK, Bestand 241, 1029.

mastering. Though he despatched Senator Garat to the Rhineland in 1804 to 'investigate the condition of public education and to research the means to take for the propagation of the French language in these countries and accelerate the progress of the fusion of their spirit into the general spirit of the Empire', he allocated few resources to this end.[28] The comment: 'Let them speak their jargon, as long as they fight like Frenchmen,' summed up his priorities.[29] Prefects were judged on their success in mobilising conscripts and raising taxes, not their enforcement of French, the overzealous imposition of which created a plethora of administrative problems.

'Frenchification' was stepped up only in the final years of Napoleonic rule. In August 1810, an ordinance directed that all public and *private* announcements be made in French – 'the general language of the Empire' – though a German translation might be provided. It also changed street signs from German to French and ordered the closure of schools that did not teach French from 1 January 1811. At the same time, the government accorded higher pay to bilingual teachers and introduced French as the language of instruction in secondary schools.[30] When France annexed the strategically sensitive enclave of Wesel in 1811, Napoleon decreed that only 'Frenchmen originating from the old departments of the empire' might settle there so that the laws, language, 'customs' and 'usages of the Empire' might establish themselves; as from 15 March 1812, no teacher could occupy a post in Wesel unless he knew French, whilst the town's inhabitants were banned from sending their sons to foreign universities. The interior minister recognised these provisions infringed a citizen's basic right to settle in any part of France, but conceded that this 'right' could be overridden by a measure of '*haute police*'.[31]

'Frenchification's' effect is difficult to assess. Reports from the Consulate suggest that most Rhenish notables already had a knowledge of French: 'there is not a single house belonging to the decent bourgeoisie where one cannot speak and write it passably well', Aachen's mayor confidently stated.[32] Reports from elsewhere identified 'merchants and bourgeois families' as propagators of French; it was they who sent their children to France to learn French, whilst the 'old rich' – nobles and ex-officials – remained

[28] For Garat's mission, see Napoleon I, *Correspondance de Napoléon Ier publiée par ordre de l'empereur Napoléon III* (32 vols., Paris, 1858–69), 9, pp. 431–2.
[29] Bell, 'Nation-building', p. 489.
[30] *Recueil des actes de la préfecture du département de la Roër* (11 vols., Aachen, 1802/3–13), (1810), pp. 226–8.
[31] AN, F^{Ic}III Roër 4, nos. 145–7, 153.
[32] Stadtarchiv Aachen (StAA), Bestand RAII (Allgemeine Akten), 248, no. 40.

attached to the German universities.[33] A similar socio-cultural pattern emerged elsewhere, notably in the Pyrenean departments, where the nobility refused to adopt French whilst professionals, merchants and functionaries accepted it, thereby enhancing their social prestige.[34] French was hardly spoken by ordinary Rhinelanders, according to Dauchy. Whilst reports submitted to him estimated that about half the population was literate in German – including 98–9 per cent of Protestant and 80 per cent of Catholic men – only a twentieth knew French, which was only taught in a few towns.[35] Amongst the remedies put forward to rectify this was the suggestion that all priests learn French, that schoolteachers teach *in* it, and that both Germans and Frenchmen be employed in the administration.[36] The Sarre's prefect, who reported the 'inhabitants continue to reconcile their customs and mores to those of the old departments, without appreciating it themselves', identified the new tariff frontier along the Rhine, which shifted commercial relations towards France, as a potentially decisive factor. He hoped that the intermarriage of Germans and French speakers promised the 'intimate union of the two nations'.[37] By the end of French rule, Dormagen's chronicler recorded that many local children aged between ten and fourteen attended French lessons in nearby Zons.[38] The Roër's prefect, Ladoucette, claimed in 1813 that French was spreading even beyond administrative centres.[39] An Englishman travelling in the region shortly after Napoleon's fall noted that 'everybody' in Mainz could speak 'bad or good' French, whilst in Kassel, on the right bank, 'only here and there an individual'.[40] Yet even Ladoucette recognised that officials who came into contact with Rhinelanders needed to speak German, whilst Rhenish departments were still approving higher than average administrative budgets in the final year of Napoleonic rule to cover the additional costs of governing a non-French-speaking people.[41]

[33] LHAK, Bestand 276, 1967, 'Mémoir[e] statistique sur la situation du dept. de la Sarre, prendt. les ans 10, 11 et 12, adressé par le prefet de ce dept. à S. Ex. le Ministre de l'Intérieur, pour faire faite au Grand mémoire statistique', p. 26.

[34] McPhee, 'Northern Catalonia', p. 404.

[35] LHAK, Bestand 276, 1062 (nos. 17–31 (Sarrebruck), 32–51).

[36] *Ibid.* (nos. 52–61). See also p. 25 of the 'Mémoir[e] statistique sur la situation du dept. de la Sarre, prendt. les ans 10, 11 et 12, adressé par le prefet de ce dept. à S. Ex. le Ministre de l'Intérieur, pour faire faite au Grand mémoire statistique', in LHAK, Bestand 276, 1967.

[37] LHAK, Bestand 276, 1967, Mémoire statistique An XIV/1806 (pp. 24–5).

[38] Hermann Cardauns (ed.), *Die rheinische Dorfchronik des Johann Peter Delhoven aus Dormagen 1783–1823* (Neuss, 1926), p. 206.

[39] Ladoucette, *Voyage*, p. 62.   [40] Dodd, *Autumn*, pp. 12–13.

[41] Ladoucette to General Clarke (minister of war), 9 August 1809, Archives de l'Armée de Terre, Vincennes (AG), C¹⁰57, dossier '9 Août 1809' (no. 36). For the Rhin-et-Moselle's departmental budget, see LHAK, Bestand 256, 93, no. 79.

Recently, historians have generally dismissed nationalism as a force motivating German opposition to Napoleon.[42] Yet portrayals of Germans as
passive spectators of the Napoleonic wars are misleading. Certainly, this was
not an assessment made by the French themselves. Rhinelanders, like other
Europeans, possessed multiple identities. However, under French rule, culture and language increasingly entered the equation. Not that the territorial
status of the Rhineland engendered any political German nationalism on
either bank before 1813. Indeed, the initial lack of interest in Germany in
the Rhineland's fate contrasted starkly with the lively debate in France over
'natural frontiers'. To paraphrase Friedrich Meinecke, the Rhineland had already been lost by the time German philosophers took an interest in the real
world.[43] Certainly, lingering dynastic loyalties provided some immunity to
'Frenchification'. However, these were only strong in the former Prussian
duchies, where the cult of Frederick the Great permeated widely.[44] Rather,
it was the imperial Habsburg ideal that emerged as a substitute for the
immediate loyalties formerly focused on the electors, especially amongst
Catholics. Austria's struggle against Napoleon reaffirmed its prestige, and
provided a link between the old imperial patriotism and emerging German
nationalism.[45]

Pro-Habsburg sentiment manifested itself in the War of the Third
Coalition. Police reports reflected growing public agitation as the Grande

---

[42] For a recent deconstruction of the 'modernist' school of nationalism, as represented especially by
Eric Hobsbawm, John Breuilly, Ernest Gellner and Benedict Anderson, see Adrian Hastings, *The
Construction of Nationhood. Ethnicity, Religion and Nationalism* (Cambridge, 1997), pp. 1–34. T. C.
W. Blanning emphasises the importance of German 'national consciousness' as an ingredient of
Rhenish counter-revolutionary sentiment in the 1790s. T. C. W. Blanning, *The French Revolution
in Germany. Occupation and Resistance in the Rhineland 1792–1802* (Oxford, 1983), 247–54. Less
convincing, in this respect, is Michael Broers's otherwise stimulating survey of Napoleonic Europe,
which places the Rhineland firmly within the 'inner core' of Napoleon's possessions in terms of
attachment and loyalty. Michael Broers, *Europe under Napoleon 1799–1815* (London, 1996), passim.
James Sheehan similarly asserts that the mass of Germans was 'unmoved' by the struggle against
France. James J. Sheehan, 'State and Nationality in the Napoleonic period', in John Breuilly (ed.),
*The State of Germany. The National Idea in the Making, Unmaking and Remaking of a Modern
Nation-State* (London and New York, 1992), p. 57. As Sheehan writes, opposition and resistance in
Germany was a reaction against the unrestrained power of the abstract state as symbolised by the
power to tax, conscript and interfere with religious practices. However, for Rhinelanders at least,
these evils were inextricably associated with the French.

[43] Friedrich Meinecke, *The Age of German Liberation, 1795–1815* (Berkeley, Los Angeles and London,
1977), p. 19.

[44] Gustav Mücke, *Die geschichtliche Stellung des Arrondissements und seines Verwalters zur Zeit der
napoleonischen Herrschaft, dargestellt an dem Leben und Wirken Karl Ludwig von Keverbergs als
Unterpräfekt in Cleve* (Bonn, 1935), p. 6.

[45] Thomas Nipperdey, *Germany from Napoleon to Bismarck 1800–1866* (translated by Daniel Nolan,
Dublin, 1996), p. 14. Delhoven, in his chronicle, referred to the Emperor of Austria as the 'German
emperor' even after 1806. Cardauns, *Dorfchronik*, p. 201.

Armée moved through the Rhineland in September 1805 on its way to the Danube: throngs of people travelled daily across the Rhine to read prohibited newspapers; Austrian agents recruited Rhenish volunteers into the Habsburg army; a priest in Cologne cathedral preached 'in an equivocal sense'; conscripts were discouraged from doing their duty; rumours spread of the enemy's imminent appearance; an anonymous riposte to the Bishop of Aachen's pastoral letter urging prayers for Napoleon circulated anonymously; people wore Habsburg cockades; and so on.[46] A report from a commissioner general of police writing from Cologne was full of pessimism:

From my arrival in this country, I have especially devoted myself to knowing its public opinion, and unfortunately have acquired the certainty that the majority of its inhabitants detest France and Frenchmen, and desire ardently to pass under the domination of another.

I have endeavoured to find out, Monsieur le Conseiller d'État, the motives of this hatred, above all on the part of the inhabitants of Cologne, and I have learnt that they have always detested the French, being fanatical to excess, they will never forget that one has sold the property of the clergy, a matter of personal interest rather than religion, because there hardly exists a family in these lands one of whose members was not destined for a religious benefice; they abhor above all the customs administration, because it hampers their illicit speculations; but, up to the point of the declaration of war on Austria, if they had not distinguished themselves by their attachment to the government, at least they had not shown themselves to be enemies; this war, in giving them all hope, has rekindled all their hate; they have sought all the means to harm the government, as much as by obstructing the progress of conscription as in spreading here and in neighbouring departments the most alarming news concerning our armies and their invincible chief, our allies, and our finances. Above all, for several days now, Monsieur le Conseiller d'État, one publicly utters the worst of remarks, one announces the arrival of the Prussians, and one congratulates oneself on passing under their domination; in Cleves, above all, and in the entire district (a former Prussian province), the spirits there have risen to a point where one believes that one is already occupied by our enemies.

The report went on to complain that the local police failed to prevent the spread of seditious rumours, that the 'immense quantity of Catholic clergy' poisoned public opinion, and that people purchased 'journals & libels written by England'.[47] Dynastic loyalties rather than German nationalism remained the strongest ingredient. Police reports from former Hohenzollern territories were less unequivocally anti-French in content, whilst in former Wittelsbach territories rival pro-French and pro-Austrian factions emerged

---

[46] AN, F⁷3686⁹, 'Bulletin de Police', reports of 4–8, 10, 13 October 1805.
[47] Desputtniel (commissioner-general of police in Cologne) to Miot (councillor of state), 13 December 1805, AN, F⁷8390, dossier 'Situation'.

from a population that had formerly owed allegiance to a prince now allied to Napoleon.[48]

In contrast, reports from the Rhineland in October 1806, at the height of the Prussian campaign, were less alarming.[49] The only noteworthy incident occurred in Aachen, where someone smeared Napoleon's statue with what the authorities politely called 'oil' or 'the black'.[50] Jena might have spurred on Prussia to prepare for a rematch; in the Rhineland, it reaffirmed the solidity of French rule. This was again challenged by the Habsburgs in 1809. The overthrow of the Spanish Bourbons in 1808 and the resistance this provoked convinced the Habsburgs that Napoleon represented a mortal threat, but also that he might be defeated by a popular uprising. Inspired by this, the Austrians attempted to whip up German national sentiment as they declared war (9 April 1809).[51] Hopes of a Spanish-style rising proved optimistic: the one rising that did occur, in the Tyrol, was motivated by provincialism, not nationalism. Nationalist stirrings in French-occupied Berlin, where Fichte delivered his *Reden an die deutsche Nation*, had no echo west of the Elbe. It was Austrian irregulars who deserted, not the conscripts of Napoleon's German allies, who distinguished themselves alongside the French regiments.[52] This despite a number of small-scale 'freelance' raids, including the abortive attempt by an ex-Prussian lieutenant to seize Magdeburg on 2 April and an attempted coup in Kassel led by an officer in the Westphalian royal guard three weeks later. More serious was the Prussian Major Schill's unauthorised 'invasion' of Saxony and Westphalia at the head of 500 cavalry. This eventually came to grief at the hands of Danish and Dutch troops in Stralsund. The Duke of Brunswick-Oels's freelance expedition at the head of his 'Black Legion of Vengeance', which briefly occupied Dresden (11 June), similarly fizzled out.

None of these campaigns attracted *active* popular support. Reports from the Rhineland were mixed in their assessment of public opinion. The commander of the 25th military division reported that opinion remained tranquil throughout the crisis.[53] The prefectures were less confident, urging the

---

[48] AN, F⁷3686⁹, 'Bulletin de Police', reports of 18, 25–6, 29–30 October, 4–6 November 1805. See also Johann Adolf Kopstadt, *Über Cleve. In Briefen an einem Freund aus den Jahren 1811 und 1814* (Frankfurt a. M., 1822), pp. 175–6.

[49] Reports from the 25th and 26th military divisions, October 1806 in: AG, C¹⁰14 D2, no. 162; C¹⁰15 D1, nos. 53, 176; C¹⁰15 D2, no. 145.

[50] StAA Bestand RAII (Allgemeine Akten), 285, nos. 59–63. For contemporary confirmation of the relative tranquillity in the former Prussian duchies, see Kopstadt, *Kleve*, p. 180.

[51] Rainer Wohlfeil, *Spanien und die deutsche Erhebung 1808–1814* (Wiesbaden, 1965), passim.

[52] Gunther E. Rothenberg, *Napoleon's Great Adversary. Archduke Charles and the Austrian Army, 1792–1814* (London, 1982), pp. 155, 175, 177–9.

[53] AG, C¹⁰57, dossier '6 Aug.' (no. 23), '7 Aug.' (no. 21), and C¹⁰60, dossier '6 Nov.' (no. 21).

war minister not to denude the region of security forces and questioning the wisdom of convening the cantonal assemblies.[54] Police reports were even more alarmist, especially with respect to the 'emotion' caused by the execution of eleven of Schill's accomplices in Wesel.[55] The police blamed deteriorating opinion on the pamphlets and rumours circulated by 'partisans of Austria', and 'malcontents' who crossed the Rhine to read foreign newspapers, extracts from which formed the basis of subversive pamphlets.[56] The unlikely source of one of the most nuanced reports on public opinion emanated from a military engineer attached to the cartographical survey in the region. Dated 1 July 1809 (after Napoleon's defeat at Aspern-Essling, but before his victory at Wagram), it blamed old-regime officials and former monks living off modest state pensions for fostering the notion that the Rhineland would not remain part of France. People believed in rumours of Napoleon's defeat, the report concluded, because they hoped for it.[57] Yet, as the prefect Ladoucette observed in July 1809, public opinion might be bad, but at least the population fulfilled its obligations to the state:

One cannot deny that the language, mores and ancient customs of the imperial cities [and] Prussian, Palatine etc. countries... attaches them only to Germany; that notables unwillingly see themselves burdened by public duty or denied their petty sphere of power; that perhaps one does not count on the services of a native being provided with complete devotion; that indirect taxes cost an infinite amount; that one would like to be exempt from conscription and the National Guard; finally, that one would probably prefer, above all in the cities, to return to that which one knew previously. However, though one thinks and speaks indiscreetly in several households, the laws are nevertheless executed punctually; direct and indirect taxes are collected, and national properties sold; the conscripts are in the army, the National Guard in Wesel; whilst one shows interest in Prince Charles [Archduke Charles, Austria's military commander], the affairs in Rome [the excommunication of Napoleon by Pius VII on 11 June and the latter's arrest on 6 July] have not provoked any public rumours. I ask you, Monsieur le Comte, not to make me act

[54] Ladoucette to Clarke (minister of war), 12 August 1809, AG, C^{10}57, dossier '6 Aug.' (no. 23), and Ladoucette to Fouché (acting minister of the interior), 17 October 1809, AN, F^{1c}III Roër 2, no. 60.

[55] Duke of Conegliano (first inspector-general of the *gendarmerie*) to Fouché, 14 July 1809, AN, F^{7}8390, dossier 'Situation'.

[56] Fouché to Count Réal (councillor of state, and head of the 1st imperial police district), July 1809, AN, F^{7}8390, dossier 'Situation'. See also Fouché to Napoleon, 2 October 1809, Ernest d'Hauterive (ed.), *La Police Secrète du Premier Empire: Bulletins quotidiens adressés Par Fouché à l'Empereur, 1804–1810* (5 vols., Paris, 1908–64), 5, p. 203.

[57] AG, M^R 1124, 'Statistique et historique de la ville et canton de Cologne Département de la Roër', 1 July 1809. For the cartographical survey itself, see Peter Effertz, 'Die Kartenaufnahme der Rheinlande durch Tranchot', *Rheinische Vierteljahrsblätter* 54 (1990), pp. 211–39.

abruptly, but to allow me to conquer the public's esteem; that will enable me to guide opinions.[58]

The seeming invincibility of the French columns that bludgeoned the Austrians aside at Wagram assisted by confirming the permanency of French rule. This was made palatable by Napoleon's marriage to the Habsburg archduchess, Marie-Louise, in April 1810, an event whose impact was described as 'sensational' in a region one French official described as 'Austrian to the core'.[59]

The creation of 'new Frenchmen' along the Rhine necessitated the region's insulation from Germany. So, the French introduced the exclusive demands of nationality. They compelled Rhinelanders in public employ to swear an oath 'not to entertain any relations' with foreign sovereigns.[60] Nonetheless, Napoleonic police reports record that *'correspondances suspectes'* by individuals with *'opinions politiques'* and *'relations au dehors'* continued. Some Rhinelanders opted to remain in foreign service, though French law, framed in response to the *émigré* threat, stated this was incompatible with citizenship. Napoleon responded by issuing further laws, *avis* and decrees which together contributed to the development of modern nationality law.[61] He was especially worried about Rhinelanders in Habsburg service. These fears came to the fore during the 1809 war, when Vienna attempted to provoke an anti-French rising. Napoleon responded (decree of 6 April 1809) by threatening 'Frenchmen exercising political, administrative or judicial functions abroad' with civil death and the confiscation of their property should the power they served engage in war with France.[62] A few weeks after Wagram, Napoleon informed his foreign minister of the need to expel 'Frenchmen' from Habsburg service.[63] These instructions met with only partial success, necessitating their subsequent reinforcement

[58] Ladoucette to Count Réal, 12 July 1809, AN, F⁷8390, dossier 'Situation'.

[59] Georgeon (commander of gendarmerie in the Roër) to Count Réal, 15 March 1810, AN, F⁷8390, dossier 'Situation'. See, also, Ladoucette to Montalivet (minister of the interior), 1 November 1810, AN, F¹ᶜIII Roër 4, no. 25.

[60] For more on this, see Michael Rowe, 'Divided Loyalties: Sovereignty, Politics and Public Service in the Rhineland under French Occupation, 1792–1801', *European Review of History* 5 (1998), pp. 151–68.

[61] For more on nationality law in this period, see Hellmuth Hecker, *Staatsangehörigkeit im Code Napoléon als europäisches Recht. Die Rezeption des französischen Code Civil von 1804 in Deutschland und Italien in Beziehung zum Staatsangehörigkeit* (Hamburg, 1980), pp. 13–14.

[62] *Bulletin des lois de l'Empire Français*, 4th series (Paris, April/May 1804–March 1814), 10, pp. 131–8.

[63] Napoleon to Champagny (minister of foreign affairs), 24 July 1809, Napoleon I, *Correspondance*, 9, pp. 280–2. The bulky carton AN, F⁷6132 contains the names of those French citizens in Austrian service. Most served in a military rather than civilian capacity, and the majority were natives of the Belgian and Rhenish departments.

(decree of 26 August 1811 and *avis* of the Council of State of 21 January 1812). The French were more flexible when it came to foreigners in their service: when the police minister complained that native Prussians served as officials in the Rhineland, he was told by the justice minister that many non-Frenchmen were employed there, and that when they had obtained the 'confidence' of the government, 'one does not pay particular attention to their place of birth'.[64]

The French disrupted cultural links between the Rhineland and Germany. They imposed restrictions on the import of printed material.[65] This, combined with cultural arrogance, arguably reinforced Rhinelanders' sense of German identity. The derogatory comments by one Parisian journal on German literature – what could be translated from German was not worth translating, and what was worth translating was untranslatable – elicited an especially indignant response from the *Kölnische Zeitung*: 'If only the Parisians would cease finding fault with a language whose *Original-Genius* they cannot hope to reach, and whose tortured and diluted translation into their wretched idiom leaves no idea of the strength, meaning and national spirit of German.'[66] For though not at the centre of German intellectual developments, the Rhineland nonetheless participated in them. Rhinelanders visited German universities; they flocked across the frontier to read newspapers censored at home; they had in their midst Joseph Görres and Friedrich Schlegel, who maintained connections with leading thinkers across the Rhine. Görres's house in Koblenz became a meeting place for intellectuals, poets and playwrights from all Germany.[67]

However, despite these beacons and some lesser lights, tough restrictions on the freedom of expression were not conducive to the dissemination of new ideas. Napoleon stated that if he allowed press freedom, he would lose power within three months. Hence, he created a 'division for press liberty' within the police ministry to enforce censorship. A later decree (5 February 1810) forcing all printers and book-dealers to apply for new licences, aimed at restricting their number. Prefects provided a raft of reports and statistics not only on newspapers, printers, book clubs, book-dealers and bookbinders, but even on itinerant peddlers of publications. These reveal that subscriptions to newspapers were falling as the public lost interest

---

[64] Fouché (minister of police) to Abrial (minister of justice), 28 January, 3 February 1800, AN, F[ib]II Roër 1, dossier 'C[en] Ehrlich originaire de Prusse' (nos. 2, 3).
[65] Napoleon to Regnier (minister of justice), 4 April 1804, Napoleon I, *Correspondance*, 9, p. 314.
[66] *Kölnische Zeitung*, 11 October 1803.   [67] *Neue Deutsche Biographie* (Berlin, 1953–), 4, pp. 532–6.

in these over-censored and increasingly boring publications. Though a few cultured French officials showed an interest in German intellectual developments, the Napoleonic period overall was not the golden age of the printed word.[68]

Cultural differences occasionally gave rise to national hostility. As demonstrated previously, national differences were to an extent institutionalised within the administration. Commissioner Shée – himself of Irish ancestry – warned in 1800 to take precautions against local cabals seeking the total removal of native French judges and administrators.[69] Lawyers representing Frenchmen in Rhenish courts complained that juries were biased against their clients.[70] Senior French officials admitted the existence of national animosities, which they blamed on the *émigrés* and the corrupt hangers-on who had entered the region with the revolutionary army. They nonetheless hoped that the return of peace after Lunéville would improve 'national' relations.[71] Evidence that this was occurring came with the intermarriage of French speakers and Germans. There was a surprisingly large number of mixed marriages. Examination of 450 marriage certificates from Koblenz, spanning the period September 1798 to September 1802, reveals that one in seven marriages in the city was mixed, with 61 Frenchmen and two French women marrying Rhinelanders.[72]

Napoleon viewed such unions favourably and took steps to encourage them. One means were the military colonies he established in the Rhineland and Italy, which 'by alliances in departments newly reunified with the Republic, attach more and more their inhabitants to the *patrie*, and there introduce the French language and spirit'. The concept of veterans' colonies was mooted as early as the Directory, including by Cologne's police commissioner in a report in 1799. 'It is through their colonies that Athens, Rome, Tyre, Marseilles, Corinth etc. derived their power and their splendour,' he wrote.

---

[68] Hansgeorg Molitor, 'Zensur, Propaganda und Überwachung zwischen 1780 und 1815 im mittleren Rheinland', in *Vom alten Reich zu neuer Staatlichkeit. Alzeyer Kolloquium, 1979: Kontinuität und Wandel im Gefolge der Französischen Revolution am Mittelrhein* (Wiesbaden, 1982), p. 34; Jeremy Popkin, 'Buchhandel und Presse in napoleonischen Deutschland', *Archiv für Geschichte des Buchwesens* 26 (1986), pp. 288–90.

[69] Henri Shée, *Situation de l'administration civile dans les quatre nouveaux départemens sur la rive gauche du Rhin, à l'époque du premier Brumaire an 8* (Mainz, 1800), p. 33.

[70] President of the criminal tribunal of the Rhin-et-Moselle department to Jollivet (government commissioner of the four departments), 23 April 1801, LHAK, Bestand 241, 1043, nos. 77–9.

[71] LHAK, Bestand 276, 1062 (nos. 52–61).

[72] Etienne François, 'Die Volksbildung am Mittelrhein im ausgehenden 18. Jahrhundert. Eine Untersuchung über den vermeintlichen "Bildungs-Rückstand" der katholischen Bevölkerung Deutschlands im Ancien Régime', *Jahrbuch für westdeutsche Landesgeschichte* 2 (1976), pp. 281–2.

Could not France also procure for itself equally great advantages, in strengthening more and more the ties of union which connect all her children and in moderating the character of one through that of the others? What better means of achieving this aim than through the establishment of colonies, or rather, through the transplantation of the diverse peoples of the French Empire. Could we soon not have, stretching from the Rhine to the Pyrenees, only one spirit, one language, and one homogeneity of sentiments?[73]

Paris set aside 6 million francs of nationalised land for five veterans' camps in the Rhineland and north Italy (law of 1 Floréal XII (20 April 1804)), including two centred on the citadels of Jülich and Mainz. The veterans were required to farm their own land and form a home guard in times of crisis.[74] The government also encouraged them to marry local girls, thereby furthering the assimilation process. Eventually, only one camp was established in Jülich, though other veterans settled independently in the region. However, the overall numbers involved were too small for this policy to make any cultural impact or contribute to assimilation. Rather, it was the host culture that assimilated the veterans. In addition to the veterans' colony, the French planned to establish an orphanage in Max Franz's former summer residence in Brühl for the children of soldiers, something that can be viewed as another element of Napoleon's 'transplantation' policy.[75]

Ultimately, the Rhineland's assimilation into France depended upon time. Even within families, the passage of a generation was sometimes sufficient to change allegiances. Such was the case with the Gossens of Jülich-Berg. Franz Heinrich Gossen, son of a leading Wittelsbach official, entered French service in 1796 and subsequently rose to head the domains administration of Krefeld where he commanded a massive annual salary. His father, in contrast, lost his job with the arrival of the French and steadfastly refused any dealings with them.[76] The same pattern was followed amongst the von Keverbergs of Geldern. The young Karl Ludwig von Keverberg was captivated by Napoleon, whom he viewed a worthy successor of Frederick the Great. He entered French service, first as sub-prefect of Cleves and then as prefect of the Upper-Ems department. Following Napoleon's fall, he entered Dutch service and eventually rose to the Council of State. His father, in contrast, who had served the Prussian monarchy for a quarter of a

---

[73] AN F[1c] 42, 'Mémoire sur la situation des esprits dans les 4 nouveaux départements de la rive gauche du Rhin, par Commissionnaire Rostan, Cologne 13 Pluviôse VII [1 February 1799]'.
[74] Napoleon I, *Correspondance*, 8, pp. 40–1. For Jülich's camp, see HStAD, Roër dept. 2332, no. 77.
[75] Ladoucette, *Voyage*, p. 88.
[76] August Klein, *Die Personalpolitik der Hohenzollernmonarchie bei der Kölner Regierung. Ein Beitrag zur preußischen Personalpolitik am Rhein* (Düsseldorf, 1967), p. 36.

century before the invasion, refused all French offers of employment.[77] By the Napoleonic period's end, the prospect of a restoration of the old order was viewed unenthusiastically by the younger generation. 'The old are for the old constitution and the young generation tends towards the French', a Prussian official noted in 1815. This was unsurprising, he concluded, as the younger generation had not consciously experienced the French brutality of the 1790s.[78] More positively, French rule provided earlier than expected career opportunities for the next generation. Under the Old Regime, re-tired soldiers often monopolised official posts, especially in the Prussian territories. This explains the high average age of officials as recorded in the personnel lists on the eve of the French takeover. Those listed in Prussian Cleves, Geldern and Moers in 1797 averaged in the high fifties or low sixties, with a sprinkling of septuagenarians and even octogenarians.[79] The new French administration was youthful in comparison: the average age of the 251 officials listed in the Roër in 1800 was thirty-eight years. The average age of mayors was generally the mid-forties.[80] It was sometimes stated by the French that older officials were set in their ways and less capable of adapting. Hence their preferment of new blood. As one thirty-four-year-old commissioner confidently predicted, his chances of promotion were good, as the French no longer needed the older generation.[81]

Education was vital in shaping the next generation's allegiances. Whilst Napoleon cared little for the schooling of the masses, where he relied upon the cash-strapped municipalities and the imperial catechism, he took great interest in the education of the *'masses de granit'*. For them, he created or refounded several institutions, including specialised law and medical schools, and the *école polytechnique*. He encouraged and often bullied them into sending their sons to these institutions, the most important of which were the *lycées*.[82] Napoleon announced the foundation of the first thirty of these in November 1801: 'The youth of the reunified departments will be called to *lycées* in the interior', he stated, 'and will there learn our customs and manners, nourish themselves on our maxims and take back to their

---

[77] Mücke, *Stellung*, p. 193.   [78] Neigebaur, *Statistik*, p. 64. See also Kopstadt, *Kleve*, p. 206.

[79] HStAD, Kleve-Kammer, 3577, nos. 248–50, 253–60, 263–76, 279, 287–93, 311–36.

[80] HStAD, Microfilm A54, 'Etat des services des fonctionnaires du département de la Roër fourni au Commissaire du Gouvernement dans les nouveaux Départemen[t]s de la rive gauche du Rhin pendant le mois de Germinal an 8'. See also 'Liste des maires et adjoints à la nomination du Préfet, 1807', AN, F^{1b}II Roër 3.

[81] HStAD, Microfilm A54, no. 56.

[82] Jean Tulard, 'Ecoles', in idem (ed.), *Dictionnaire Napoléon* (Paris, 1987), pp. 640–1.

families a love of our institutions and our laws.'[83] Napoleon stressed the importance of teacher-training institutes in binding together the empire, and instilling in it 'not only uniform methods and the art of communicating instruction, but rather common impressions and habits, and the sentiments which must animate the entire teaching body'.[84]

The new *lycées* replaced the central schools set up under the Directory. They embodied Napoleonic concepts. They were centralised: the central government funded them, the head of state appointed their teachers and special inspectors from Paris supervised their teaching. They were militarised, with military exercises and uniforms for pupils. Their curriculum was conservative, providing a classical education centred on Latin, maths and literature. This contrasted with the radical mix of ethical philosophy, mathematics, science and 'legislation' (including natural law) provided by the central schools, where the emphasis was on the creation of useful *and active* citizens. Napoleon aimed at stability, not activity, and trusted old methods. The culmination of Napoleon's reaction against the pedagogical philosophy of the 'Ideologues' came in 1808 with the foundation of the imperial university. This functioned as an education ministry and was headed by Louis de Fontanes. Beneath him emerged the new educational hierarchy, headed by specialised institutes for training professionals, *lycées* and secondary schools, which emphasised practical training including, in the Rhineland, two-year courses in French. Fees for the secondary schools were modest – 24 francs for the two junior classes, and 48 francs for the two senior – as compared to the exclusive *lycées*. These remained the elite's preserve, though the government offered a small number of scholarships to gifted sons of soldiers and officials who lacked the necessary financial means.[85]

Napoleon's educational institutions failed to 'lock' in the Rhenish elite, which resented the destruction of the universities. More fundamental was the absence of 'professionalisation' within the Napoleonic bureaucracy. This lacked the standard examination requirements for entry and set, depersonalised, promotion paths as were then being introduced into the bureaucracies of the south German states, and which had been pioneered

[83] Napoleon's 'exposé de la situation de la République' of 22 November 1801, Napoleon I, *Correspondance*, 7, p. 327.
[84] AN, F^{IC}I, nos. 14–23, dossier 'Exposé de la situation de l'Empire. Fin de l'Année 1813', sub-file 'université' (no. 1).
[85] Wilhelm Leyhausen, *Das höhere Schulwesen in der Stadt Köln zur französischen Zeit [1794–1814]* (Bonn, 1913), pp. 44–5.

by eighteenth-century Prussia. A caste of bureaucrats bound together by *Bildung* and celebrated by Hegel as the universal estate never appeared in France, though the Napoleonic auditors came close. Professionalisation in the strict sense was unacceptable to Napoleon, who rejected limitations on his power to appoint or promote whom he liked when he liked. He relied upon 'old-regime' methods to control his officials, as with the creation of a new nobility.[86] Though the *baccalauréat* was revived in March 1808 and stands as a great Napoleonic legacy, it did not then enjoy the prestige it gained subsequently. The stipulation that those embarking upon higher education first acquire the '*bac*' was simply ignored. As there were no set educational requirements for state employment, Rhinelanders had less incentive to patronise either the *lycées* or *écoles spéciales*. Ultimately, this diminished their interest in the survival of French institutions as a whole after the collapse of Napoleonic rule, as they had little 'cultural capital' invested in them. In contrast, one of Berlin's first actions upon assuming control in 1815 was to found Bonn university as an institution where Rhinelanders might gain the stringent educational requirements necessary for entry into the Prussian bureaucracy.

The distrust many Rhinelanders felt for Napoleonic schools and academies was in part also a legacy of the Directory's anti-clericalism.[87] Rhinelanders had boycotted the central schools set up by this regime: whilst the university and *Gymnasien* in Cologne counted over 700 pupils annually in the final years of their existence, the French *école centrale* that replaced them averaged well under 300 pupils. One might surmise that those who did attend were attracted less by the radical new curriculum and more by the teaching staff of the new school, half of whom came from the old university.[88] Instead, Rhenish parents sent their sons to private boarding schools, where they received instruction in the classics and religion, and then to German universities. The fact that the language of instruction in the *lycées* and *écoles spéciales* was French, and that Rhenish applicants for the *école polytechnique* needed to sit preliminary examinations in Brussels, Mainz or Strasbourg in French grammar, may have served as a further

[86] Bernd Wunder, 'Rolle und Struktur staatlicher Bürokratie in Frankreich und Deutschland', in Helmut Berding, Etienne François and Hans-Peter Ullmann (eds.), *Deutschland und Frankreich im Zeitalter der Französischen Revolution* (Frankfurt a. M., 1989), pp. 166–71. See also Clive Church, *Revolution and Red Tape. The French Ministerial Bureaucracy* (Oxford, 1981), p. 263.

[87] For the Roër, see AN, F¹ᶜV Roër, no. 123. For similar problems in the Sarre, see LHAK, Bestand 276, 1967, 'Mémoir[e] statistique sur la situation du dept. de la Sarre, prendt. les ans 10, 11 et 12, adressé par le prefet de ce dept. à S. Ex. le Ministre de l'Intérieur, pour faire faite au Grand mémoire statistique', p. 22.

[88] Leyhausen, *Schulwesen*, pp. 31–2.

disincentive.[89] Nor can cost be discounted: the annual fee of the *école polytechnique* was 800 francs, excluding the uniform, books and writing materials required of each pupil.[90] In addition came the considerable costs of moving to and living in far-off cities. Both the Rhenish general councils and the state councillor Dauchy cited this as an important disincentive.[91] The only Rhenish *lycée* was in Mainz, at the region's southern extremity; the only other nearby academies or universities were in Brussels, Göttingen and Leiden. Ironically, Dauchy recommended the foundation of 'a grand institution for public education at Bonn', something that occurred only under the Prussians. Not that Napoleon was not tempted by the prospect of luring Germans to study in France. In November 1804, he even accorded Germans (from across the Rhine) studying in the *lycée* of Mainz permission to enter the imperial *écoles spéciales* of France, whilst the French law school in Koblenz attempted to attract German students by sending out prospectuses to Westphalia and Hamburg.[92] Yet, despite his ambitions, Napoleon, unlike the impoverished Prussians, refused to lavish money on the foundation of new universities.

His failure to do so reflected the divergence in German and French concepts of what higher education was for. Germany's universities reformed and revived under the Old Regime whilst their equivalents in France stagnated. Hence, the revolutionaries' willingness to abolish them, along with other privileged corporations.[93] Napoleon favoured not the recreation of the universities but rather specialised institutes designed to produce useful professionals. His ideal was expressed in comments on the *école polytechnique*: 'Its pupils,' he declared in 1806, 'subject to an almost military discipline, will there become used to order and devote all their time to the objects of their study.'[94] The German universities, in contrast, he treated as havens for indisciplined students when he encountered them on his campaigns. He was especially dismissive of non-vocational subjects. For example, he treated the idea of an academy for literature with scorn: no decent literature

[89] Prefectoral *avis* (Roër) of 27 July 1805 and 12 July 1806, *Recueil* (1805) and (1806), pp. 419–20 and p. 559 respectively.
[90] Prefectoral *avis* (Roër) of October 1805, *Recueil* (1806), p. 89. See also the *Recueil* (1803) and (1805), pp. 168–9 and pp. 62–3 respectively.
[91] District council of Aachen, 9 January 1809, HStAD, Roër dept. 199, no. 45. See also AN, F⁷8390, dossier 'Situation', 'Résumé des motifs que sait valoir la ville de Cologne pour obtenir une Académie'.
[92] Helmut Coing, 'Die Französische Rechtsschule zu Koblenz', in *Festschrift für Franz Wieacker zum 70. Geburtstag* (Göttingen, 1978), p. 204.
[93] Klaus Papst, 'Bildungs- und Kulturpolitik der Franzosen im Rheinland zwischen 1794 und 1814', in Peter Hüttenberger and Hansgeorg Molitor (eds.), *Franzosen und Deutsche am Rhein 1789–1918–1945* (Essen, 1989), p. 193.
[94] 'Exposé de la situation de l'Empire', 5 March 1806, Napoleon I, *Correspondance*, 12, p. 150.

had been produced since the Greeks and in any case, according to his own experience, one had learnt everything one needed to know about this subject by the age of fourteen.[95] Such views diametrically opposed the neo-humanistic concept of *Bildung* then taking hold in Germany and which underlay Humboldt's foundation of the University of Berlin in 1810. The kind of specialised, 'useful' training favoured by Napoleon, in contrast, underwent social devaluation in Germany.

As a result, many Rhinelanders dismissed the *lycées* as military training camps, 'where one trained future servants of the state according to the principles and forms used to train the Guard'.[96] The militarisation of education went beyond the uniforms and strict discipline. Napoleon increasingly tapped the *lycées* for army recruits. In October 1811, he decreed that at least four pupils from each of the Empire's sixty *lycées* be selected for service in the artillery.[97] This amounted to another form of conscription and provided an additional reason for Rhinelanders to send their sons to German universities. Johann Kopstadt, a native of Cleves, wrote in May 1811 that he planned to send his son to the new *lycée* in Bonn to teach him order and subordination in the militaristic French spirit and then to a German university to educate him in the liberal ideas of leading German thinkers. Only then would he send him to Paris or Brussels to gain experience in state service.[98] Other prominent families, like the von Grootes of Cologne, similarly sent their sons to German universities.[99] Only half of the twenty-four free places at the *lycée* in Metz reserved for pupils from the Sarre department were filled.[100] Of a sample of 1,500 applicants for the Ecole Spéciale Militaire of St Cyr in 1807–09, only eleven came from the four Rhenish departments. The nine Belgian departments did even worse, proportionately, supplying eighteen applicants out of a population of 3.3 million, the same number as the two Alsatian departments with their combined population of only 900,000 souls.[101] Nor was the despatch of a son to a French *lycée* or academy proof of attachment to the Napoleonic regime. The Count von Hompesch, a prominent personality in Jülich, sent his younger son to the military academy at La Flèche as a substitute for his

[95] Napoleon's 'observation' of 19 April 1807, *ibid.*, 14, pp. 103–10.

[96] Boost, *Rheinländer*, p. 63.

[97] Napoleon to General Clarke, 18 October 1811, Napoleon I, *Correspondance*, 12, pp. 508–9.

[98] Kopstadt, *Kleve*, pp. 6–7.

[99] Eberhard von Groote was sent to Heidelberg in 1809. Klein, *Personalpolitik*, p. 23.

[100] LHAK, Bestand 276, no. 1967, 'Mémoir[e] statistique sur la situation du dept. de la Sarre, prendt. les ans 10, 11 et 12, adressé par le prefet de ce dept. à S. Ex. le Ministre de l'Intérieur, pour faire faite au Grand mémoire statistique'.

[101] AG, 4YB 35, 'Contrôle des Elèves'.

eldest – who had been 'designated' by the Emperor – on the supposed grounds of the latter's weak constitution. The police subsequently reported Hompesch as having said that in reality he was reserving his eldest for 'a more meticulous and better education than one ordinarily receives in a *lycée*'.[102]

The only academy established in the Rhineland was the law school in Koblenz. It occupied Count Metternich's former house, which still stands. Though Napoleon distrusted lawyers, whom he blamed for the Revolution, he was sufficiently enlightened to recognise the importance of law and its administration by professionals. As a result, the judiciary was the only part of the administration to experience genuine professionalisation, and only jurists who had passed the relevant examinations could enter the profession. This in turn created a need for law schools. Koblenz's opened in November 1806. Napoleon was determined to limit the curriculum of the schools to the learning by rote of his codes, not theory ('metaphysics') or natural law ('political speculation'). Experienced jurists rejected this view, asking what a lawyer without theoretical knowledge would do if the relevant code provided no solution to a particular case. However, Napoleon, as was often the case, represented the opinion of France, which was tired of debates and theories. So, the new academies ignored natural and international law, and examined Roman law only in relation to the civil code. The greatest Prussian jurist of the period, Friedrich Karl von Savigny, provided the most damning criticism of this education when he observed that the lawyers emerging from the new French law schools would not themselves be able to produce a work comparable in scope to the Napoleonic codes they studied so meticulously. Potential German students shared this assessment, and the mainly Rhenish professors in Koblenz admitted as much when they offered additional classes in Roman law in order to compete with such German universities as Heidelberg and Würzburg. The prospect of being taught '*éloquence du barre*' by Görres should have served as an additional attraction for potential students. Yet, despite these efforts, Koblenz's law school remained the worst attended in the Empire.[103]

Whilst Germany's intellectual elite had transcended the culture of the Enlightenment before the Napoleonic period, the majority of Rhenish notables remained enthused by its ethos. The Enlightenment provided

---

[102] Georgéon (commander of the gendarmerie in the Roër) to Count Réal (head of the 1st imperial police district), 15 March 1810, AN, F⁷8390, dossier 'Situation'.

[103] Luitwin Mallmann, *Französische Juristenausbildung im Rheinland 1794–1814. Die Rechtsschule von Koblenz* (Cologne and Vienna, 1987), pp. 56–8, 107, 111–13, 120–1, 148–51.

the channel through which French cultural imperialism preceded the armed expansionism of the 1790s. Napoleon subsequently exploited the pan-European cosmopolitan ideology associated with it.[104] The Enlightenment represented 'sociological' propaganda, 'the penetration of an ideology by means of its sociological context'. It informed lifestyle rather than mere opinion. This life-style was subsequently built upon by 'direct' Napoleonic propaganda.[105] Through it, the Napoleonic administration associated itself with Rhenish notables in 'improvement'. Propaganda portrayed Napoleonic France as the sole repository of enlightenment, and its enemies as feudal or anarchic.[106] During the Consulate, government-sponsored *sociétés d'émulation* formed in the Rhineland and explicitly linked the spread of Enlightenment with the extension of French rule.[107]

These societies, like the official chambers of commerce and semi-official agricultural societies, co-operated with the new regime in the gathering of local statistics that satisfied the ministerial hunger for information. For the 'science' of enlightened administration was 'the knowledge of the facts', as Lucien Bonaparte commented when interior minister. The co-option of local notables encouraged them in their belief that they were engaged in some wider, progressive project, and indeed they did perform invaluable service in gathering the data which formed the basis of the great departmental topographical descriptions compiled during the Consulate.[108] Paris encouraged French officials to join unofficial local 'improvement' societies as a means of influencing notables in an apparently relaxed social atmosphere, a method regarded more subtle than the use of official bulletins. From October 1810 onwards the interior minister even sent prefects a weekly secret circular of what they should say at private gatherings, whilst reminding them to report any rumours they themselves heard during conversations.[109]

The official image of cosmopolitan, apolitical co-operation for the common good was blemished by not infrequent instances of political and

---

[104] Jean Tulard, *Le Grand Empire* (Paris, 1982), pp. 12–16.

[105] For the distinction between 'sociological' and 'direct' propaganda, see Jacques Ellul, *Propaganda. The Formation of Men's Attitudes* (translated from the French by Konrad Kellen and Jean Lerner; with an introduction by Konrad Kellen, New York, 1968), pp. 15, 30, 62–70.

[106] Robert B. Holtman, *Napoleonic Propaganda* (Baton Rouge, 1950), pp. 25–6, 30.

[107] Undated report presented by the *société d'émulation* of the Rhin-et-Moselle department to the minister of the interior, AN, AFIV 1025, dossier 3, no. 62. This report was included in Dauchy's presentation to the Consuls. See also, Alpen, *Geschichte*, I, pp. XIX–XX. Mücke, *Keverberg*, pp. 47–8, 122–3. Antoinette Joulia, 'Der Departementalverein Ober-Ems (1812). Ein Erbe der Aufklärung oder ein Produkt des napoleonischen Dirigismus?', *Osnabrücker Mitteilungen* 78 (1971), pp. 151–9.

[108] Those covering the Rhin-et-Moselle department can be found in LHAK, Bestand 276, fascicles 1063, 1065 and 1067.

[109] Ministerial circulars (interior) of October 1810 and 11 November 1811, AN, F^IcI, 25, nos. 448–9, 464.

national disharmony within Rhenish societies and clubs. Some contemporaries reported that such disharmony was a legacy of the 1790s. Albert Klebe, who travelled through the Rhineland during the Consulate, was struck by the complete absence of reading clubs, lending libraries and learned societies where anything other than politics was discussed; 'family societies' were scarce because political differences caused division everywhere.[110] In Cleves, national differences between the German, Dutch and French communities prevented the formation of common societies and clubs that encompassed the elites of all three.[111] In Aachen, the local elite reacted against French officials' domination of the city's salons by founding the 'German Society' ('Die Deutsche Gesellschaft') in 1805. Though its name was quickly changed to the less provocative 'Club Aachener Casino', none of its eventual 100 members included any French officials. Societal life in Bonn similarly divided along national lines.[112] The same was true of Cologne, where the elite associated itself closely with local culture from which the French were excluded. In 1805, the elite founded the Olympischen Gesellschaft with the aim of furthering the city's culture including the local dialect, *Kölsch*. Though the society dissolved in 1813, many of its members were prominent in the revival of the Cologne Carnival a decade later.[113] In addition, the city's innocuous sounding Société de la Charité maternelle was reportedly anti-French. No French families could expect aid from it unless French women were also appointed members, the local police commissioner warned.[114] Membership of similar charitable societies elsewhere declined by the end of French rule as people recognised that Paris treated their revenues as a form of voluntary taxation.[115]

Napoleonic manipulation followed by local disillusionment and declining membership similarly occurred with respect to Rhenish masonic lodges. Early on, Napoleon recognised the potential of freemasonry as a tool for binding the *masses du granit* to the regime. He organised all French lodges into a rigid, hierarchical structure with its apex, the Grand Orient, headed by his brother, Joseph, who assumed the title 'Grand Master'. Other members of the Bonaparte clan occupied high positions within

---

[110] Klebe, *Reise*, pp. 554–5.   [111] Kopstadt, *Kleve*, pp. 21–2, 180.
[112] For Aachen, see Thomas Kraus, *Auf dem Weg in die Moderne. Aachen in französischer Zeit 1792/93, 1794–1814. Handbuch-Katalog zur Ausstellung im "Krönungssaal" des Aachener Rathauses vom 14. Januar bis zum 5. März 1995* (Aachen, 1994), pp. 326–7. For Bonn, Molitor, *Untertan*, p. 155.
[113] Gisela Mettele, 'Kölner Bürgertum in der Umbruchszeit (1776–1815)', in Lothar Gall (ed.), *Vom alten zum neuen Bürgertum. Die mitteleuropäische Stadt im Umbruch 1780–1820* (Munich, 1991), pp. 269–72.
[114] Pauzle d'Ivoy (special police commissioner in Cologne) to Réal, 26 September 1811, AN, F⁷8390, dossier 'Situation'.
[115] Kopstadt, *Kleve*, pp. 50–1.

the hierarchy. Cambacérès, Napoleon's imperial arch-chancellor, became a kind of minister for masonic affairs, adopting the pompous title 'Grand Commander of the Supreme Council'. French masonic imperialism subsequently extended into the German satellites. Napoleon subordinated lodges in these states to the Grand Orient in Paris and cut existing ties with rival mother lodges located in enemy capitals. French officials who dominated the governments of Berg and Westphalia joined local lodges, where they rubbed shoulders with native elites. Their true function became apparent in 1811, when amid growing Franco-Prussian tension, German masons in Kassel appealed that they should continue to act in the interests of humanity as a whole. This was swept aside by the Grand Master, the Frenchman Siméon, who also happened to be Westphalia's chief minister, with the observation that politics was more important than masonic solidarity.[116] Association with the foreign invader would earn freemasonry the enmity of German nationalism.[117]

Of Germany's numerous lodges, the Rhenish had forged the closest links with Paris under the Old Regime. Lodges in both Aachen and Cologne had been affiliated to the Grand Orient of France and received their original constitutions from Paris.[118] In 1779, Aachen's freemasons even appealed to France for protection against persecution by the magistracy. In the 1780s, many of Aachen's freemasons joined the so-called 'New Party' attempting to reform the *Reichstadt*'s antiquated constitution. The following decade, they distinguished themselves in their espousal of the French cause. Their calls for 'reunion' with the mother lodge in Paris paralleled those for political 'reunion' with France.[119] In the ceremony marking masonic 'reunion' in 1799 – two whole years before the legal annexation of Aachen to France – the city's freemasons swore an oath 'to be obedient and attached to the laws of the Government of the Republic'. In a banquet a few days after Brumaire, Aachen's masons celebrated the renaissance of their lodge – Constance – under Napoleon's patronage and contrasted this with the trials and tribulations previously faced from 'prejudiced fanatics' and 'superstitious people' under 'monkish influence'. Aachen's other lodge, Concorde, founded in 1803, similarly flattered Napoleon as the restorer of 'interrupted masonic

[116] Heinz Gürtler, *Deutsche Freimaurer im Dienste napoleonischer Politik: die Freimaurer im Königreich Westfalen 1807–1813* (Struckum, 1988 reprint), pp. 20, 41.

[117] Ernst Moritz Arndt, *Noch ein Wort über die Franzosen* ([Leipzig], 1814), pp. 29, 33.

[118] Winfried Dotzauer, *Freimaurergesellschaften am Rhein. Aufgeklärte Sozietäten auf dem linken Rheinufer vom Ausgang des Ancien Régime bis zum Ende der napoleonischen Herrschaft* (Wiesbaden, 1977), p. 235.

[119] Bibliothèque Nationale, Paris (BN) (Manuscrits), FM²533, dossier 1, nos. 6–9.

harmony'.[120] Cologne's lodge, Secret des trois Rois, pointed proudly at its pro-French actions during the 1790s, notably the assistance it had accorded French POWs in 1793, when demanding 'reunion' with the Grand Orient in 1801 and in currying favour with Napoleon subsequently.[121] Significantly, the lodge's pre-Revolution representative in Paris, Riffé-Caubray – a defence-counsel in the *cour de cassation* who represented other Rhenish lodges – was subsequently reappointed, providing yet another example of the return to normality that was a theme of Napoleonic propaganda.[122]

Masonic lodges throughout the Rhineland initially flourished under the French. The revolutionary army founded lodges wherever it went and encouraged Rhinelanders to re-establish their own following the clampdown of the late 1780s; the language used by the French in official proclamations was often overtly 'masonic'.[123] Of the 2,566 known members of Napoleonic Rhenish lodges, 44 per cent were Rhinelanders, 28 per cent Frenchmen, 6 per cent Germans from the right bank of the Rhine, with 21 per cent of unrecorded origin.[124] The French presence was especially marked in administrative seats and garrison towns: Aachen registered a large number of Frenchmen in both its lodges, including the prefects Laumond, Lameth and Ladoucette; in contrast, the Secret des trois Rois in Cologne, a city that failed to attract important government offices, was dominated by the native elite.[125] The lodges were predominantly urban, with members from the countryside attending rarely and then only for the most solemn of ceremonies.[126] As for the 21 per cent for whom details are unavailable, it seems possible that a proportion were Germans who wished their membership kept secret for fear of reprisals from their own governments: the Secret des trois Rois, in a letter to Riffé-Caubray in July 1801, expressed concern that care be taken not to correspond with its Austrian members, and that their names not appear on official membership lists lest they fall into the hands of the Habsburg government.[127]

---

[120] *Ibid.*, nos. 10, 17, 24.
[121] Secret des trois Rois to the Grand Orient, 1 August 1801, and Dominikus Oestges (a Freemason in Cologne) to Napoleon, 8 September 1806, BN (Manuscrits), Microfilm 4589, nos. 78, 64 respectively.
[122] *Ibid.*, nos. 74, 78.   [123] Hansen, *Quellen*, 4, p. 1299.
[124] Dotzauer, *Freimaurergesellschaften*, pp. 106–9.
[125] Membership lists of 1 December 1803 and 23 August 1805, BN (Manuscripts), FM²534, dossier 1, no. 44, and dossier 2, nos. 21–2 respectively. See also Dotzauer, *Freimaurergesellschaften*, pp. 200, 206–15, 243.
[126] Concorde to the Grand Orient, 10 February 1810, BN (Manuscrits), FM²533, dossier 2, no. 52.
[127] BN (Manuscrits), Microfilm 4589, no. 64.

Freemasons stood isolated within society as a whole. Priests, despite government and episcopal warnings, denounced them in the confessional.[128] A few freemasons no doubt rejoiced in their status as an enlightened minority battling fanaticism and as favoured children under Napoleon's special protection. Yet association with the regime carried its own risks, including manipulation and subordination by the Napoleonic propaganda machine. Lodges within France came under the Grand Orient, with which they corresponded via a representative. These were appointed on the basis of their 'zeal for the public good' and 'attachment to the government'.[129] Lodges were required to celebrate Napoleonic victories and Bonapartist dynastic events, such as the baptism of the King of Rome. From 1805, Paris ordered that their meetings open and close with the triple cry: 'Vive Napoléon le Grand et son auguste famille.' Abandoning all pretence of acting for humanity's good, France's lodges were enlisted as part of a masonic struggle between the Grand Orient in Paris and its equivalent in London for supremacy.[130] Falling membership suggests increasing disillusionment amongst Rhenish masons. The reasons are unclear, though there appears to have been considerable bitterness, with former masons making 'indiscreet and injurious expressions' against their old lodges.[131] Politics seems to have played a role: despite the fact that the statutes of lodges expressly forbade political discussion, reports reached Riffé-Caubray of the blackballing of candidates deemed worthy by the government, a practice described as 'very common in a country where political opinions... are so conflicting'.[132] Established to further harmonious co-operation with an enlightened regime, Rhenish lodges ended the Napoleonic period tainted by association with a discredited government, internally divided, and with falling membership.

Masonic lodges, philanthropic societies, reading clubs – in short, the cosmopolitan sociability of the Enlightenment – attracted only the elite. An even smaller minority was engaged at the avant-garde of Germany's cultural development. Popular culture remained focused, as before, on locality and religion. Of the region's estimated 1.6 million souls, over

[128] Secret des trois Rois to the Grand Orient, 9 June 1808, BN (Manuscrits), Microfilm 4589, nos. 95–6.

[129] *Ibid.*, no. 53. Extract from *Concorde's* 'livre d'architecture', 3 July 1812.

[130] Dominikus Oestges to the Grand Orient, 10 February 1804, BN (Manuscrits), FM²533, dossier 2, nos. 1, 22–3. See also BN (Manuscrits), Microfilm 4589, no. 87, and AN, F¹ᶜIII Roër 4, nos. 33–4.

[131] Secret des trois Rois to Riffé-Caubray, 9 January 1810, BN (Manuscrits), Microfilm 4589, no. 105.

[132] Constance to Riffé-Caubray, 18 February 1800, BN (Manuscrits), FM2533, dossier 1, no. 75. The statutes of the Napoleonic Secret des trois Rois were published as *Réglemens de LAL∴ du secret des Trois Rois A L'O∴ de Cologne* (Cologne, 1811).

1 million were Catholic, 200,000 Calvinist, 200,000 Lutheran, 22,000 Jewish – representing nearly a third of the French Empire's Jews – and several thousand Mennonite. Non-Catholics made up about 40 per cent of the population of the southern Sarre and Mont-Tonnerre, 25 per cent of the Rhin-et-Moselle, and only 8 per cent of the Roër.[133]

The essence of Bonapartism was simple, according to Napoleon: it was to govern as the majority desired. Religion, which had motivated counter-revolution in the 1790s, remained the key to winning public consent. 'By turning Catholic I ended the war in the Vendée,' Napoleon wrote, 'by becoming a Moslem I established myself in Egypt, by becoming an ultramontane I won over the Italians. If I was governing a people of Jews, I would rebuild the Temple of Solomon.'[134] Napoleon especially respected the influence of Roman Catholicism, and declared the Pope equivalent in importance to an army of 200,000 men. His interest centred on the mystery of the social order, not that of the Incarnation. Catholicism, he believed, like other faiths, prevented the poor from turning into highway robbers by holding up the prospect of equality in the life to come. Only 're-establishment of the empire of religion over consciences' would restore social harmony, Napoleon and his officials argued.[135] Within months of Brumaire, the First Consul opened negotiations with Rome.

The outcome of these was the Concordat, published in May 1802. This provided the legal basis for the abolition of the ancient archdioceses of Cologne, Trier and Mainz. In their place, Napoleon established three new dioceses, under the archdiocese of Mechelen: Aachen, covering the Roër and Rhin-et-Moselle; Trier, covering the Sarre; and Mainz covering Mont-Tonnerre. The dioceses were sub-divided into larger parishes, based on the cantons, and smaller parishes, corresponding to the communes. This parish structure remains fundamentally intact today. Financially, the Church was completely dependent upon the government following the nationalisation of endowments. The exception was some of the smaller parishes, which were supported by the municipalities. Paris assumed responsibility for these too after 1807. Those few unsold goods and properties returned to the parishes were administered by boards composed of the parish priest, local mayor

---

[133] Hansgeorg Molitor, 'La Vie religieuse populaire en Rhénanie Française, 1794–1815', in Bernard Plongeron (ed.), *Pratiques religieuses dans l'Europe révolutionnaire (1770–1820). Actes du colloque, Chantilly 27–29 novembre 1986* (Paris, 1988), p. 59.

[134] Quoted from Martyn Lyons, *Napoleon Bonaparte and the Legacy of the French Revolution* (Basingstoke, 1994), p. 82.

[135] LHAK, Bestand 276, 1967, 'Mémoir[e] statistique sur la situation du dept. de la Sarre, prendt. les ans 10, 11 et 12, adressé par le prefet de ce dept. à S. Ex. le Ministre de l'Intérieur, pour faire faite au Grand mémoire statistique', p. 25.

and selected parishioners, under episcopal and sub-prefectoral supervision. Ironically, it now required French intervention to insure that municipalities provided adequate support for their priests. Apart from the dioceses and parishes, the most important Catholic institutions were the seminaries of Mainz and Cologne, institutions initially dominated by Alsatians. They subsequently became centres of ultramontanism, despite the Gallican tendencies of the Napoleonic church that had founded them.[136]

According to the Concordat, Napoleon had the authority to name archbishops and bishops within France, though the Pope retained the power of canonical investiture. For the people, the subordination of Church to state was symbolised by newly appointed bishops having to swear an oath of loyalty to the state between the hands of the prefect, and parish priests having to do the same between the hands of the mayor. Napoleon nominated an Alsatian, Marc Antoine Berdolet, as first bishop of the largest Rhenish diocese, Aachen, in April 1802. Berdolet owed his appointment partly to his knowledge of German and partly to his acquaintance with Josephine Beauharnais, which dated from the time of the Terror. These factors counted for more than the opposition of Pius VII, who opposed former 'Constitutionals' and who delayed Berdolet's canonical investiture until 1805.

Initially, Rhinelanders rejected Berdolet as a tool of French rule. Yet though obsequiously loyal to Napoleon, whom he credited with having saved religion, Berdolet took his pastoral duties very seriously, travelling throughout his diocese to areas never before visited by a bishop. He assisted in the return of stolen relics and used his connections with the Beauharnais clan to assert his position against the secular authorities.[137] Gradually, he won the trust of the public, for whom this modest bishop represented a completely new experience. For Berdolet marked the transition from the aristocratic Church of the Old Regime to the ultramontane of the nineteenth century: like his predecessors, he discouraged over-enthusiastic displays of baroque piety and was influenced by Jansenism; like his successors, he strictly followed the Papal line on such issues as mixed marriages.[138] Berdolet died in August 1809, and was succeeded by Jean-Denis-François Camus, who was appointed in October 1810, but never invested because of Napoleon's renewed conflict with Pius VII after 1808.

---

[136] Eduard Hegel, *Geschichte des Erzbistums Köln*, vol. 4: *Das Erzbistum Köln zwischen Barock und Aufklärung vom Pfälzischen Krieg bis zum Ende der französischen Zeit 1688–1814* (Cologne, 1979), pp. 523–6.

[137] Jakob Torsy, *Geschichte des Bistums Aachen während der französischen Zeit (1802–1814)* (Bonn, 1940), pp. 45–9, 59, 65.

[138] Hegel, *Köln*, pp. 514–15, 530–1.

Church–state relations were relatively harmonious in the diocese of Aachen, whose population was predominantly Catholic. By contrast, church–state conflict erupted in the diocese of Mainz (which, according to a statistical report of 1811, contained 182,000 Catholics, 107,000 Lutherans, 131,000 Calvinists, 12,400 Jews, 2,500 Mennonites and 1,000 Anabaptists and Quakers) over mixed marriages.[139] Matters were aggravated by the fact that the long-serving prefect of Mont-Tonnerre, Jeanbon Saint-André, was a former Huguenot pastor and ex-member of the Committee of Public Safety. Mainz's new bishop, Louis Colmar – like Berdolet, an Alsatian – stubbornly adhered to the Papal line on mixed marriages. The tension be-tween marriage's status as both a civil contract and holy sacrament was aggravated by the differing traditions that existed historically in France and Germany. Whilst in France mixed marriages had not been tolerated before the Revolution, in Germany the situation varied from territory to terri-tory, depending upon whether the Westphalian settlement had accorded minority faiths mere tolerance or the right to worship. Colmar ignored the German tradition and adopted the intolerant position subsequently con-firmed in Pius VII's circular of February 1809. Conflict ensued with Jeanbon Saint-André when Colmar refused to recognise the validity of mixed mar-riages approved by the civil authorities and when his priests insisted that mixed couples bring up their children as Catholics. The issue remained unresolved when Napoleonic rule collapsed.[140]

Cause for clerical opposition was also provided by the abolition of Rhenish religious communities in July 1802, with the exception of a tiny number deemed 'useful' for serving educational or health functions. The large-scale secularisation of monastic property that followed went against the spirit of the Concordat. There was no Papal protest, however, and lay Catholics proved as enthusiastic purchasers of the property as non-Catholics. Purchasers of *biens nationaux* were condemned as collaborators and immoral by German nationalists after 1814.[141] Urban elites, patricians and business leaders predominated amongst the purchasers, and such re-sentment as there was tended to be in the form of rural hostility to urban speculators rather than hostility to secularisation per se.[142] Paris took the purchase of secularised property as a measure of public opinion and the

[139] Georg May, *Seelsorge an Mischehen in der Diözese Mainz unter Bischof Ludwig Colmar. Ein Beitrag zum Kirchenrecht und Staatskirchenrecht im Rheinland unter französischer Herrschaft* (Amsterdam, 1974), p. 18.

[140] May, *Seelsorge*, pp. 29–31, 87.

[141] *Rheinischer Merkur*, 17 March 1815. See also Johann Gottlieb Koppe, *Die Stimme eines Preußischen Staatsbürgers in den wichtigsten Angelegenheiten dieser Zeit* (Cologne, 1815), p. 42.

[142] Cardauns, *Dorfchronik*, p. 197.

level of sales figured in prefectoral reports. It was only in the last months of 1813 that political uncertainty was reflected in the auction rooms.[143]

The regular clergy was mostly pensioned off, though several hundred received nothing, because they were not natives of the Rhenish departments. Even those entitled to pensions complained they were not being paid out on time. Many were reduced to begging. A whole pool of malcontents was thus created. Ex-regulars provided recruits for the illegal brotherhoods that celebrated abolished feast days in defiance of both hierarchy and state, often with the connivance of local authorities.[144] The government feared the ex-regulars as potential subversives and, with the worsening of France's international position after 1812, placed them under surveillance.[145] However, the image of fanatic monks and priests whipping up opposition to the French should not be exaggerated. Frequently, it was the clergy that was pressurised by lay persons into celebrating banned feasts or leading processions whilst the elite, formerly contemptuous of such manifestations, demonstrated its opposition to the new regime by participating in them. The French felt confident enough to employ large numbers of ex-regulars as priests, if only to avoid paying pensions. By 1805, 1,006 out of the 2,696 parish priests in the Roër department were ex-monks. They plugged a widening gap, for the clergy as a whole was ageing rapidly. The closure of the old theological faculties meant fewer young men entering the priesthood. By 1812 there were 360 unfilled vacancies in the Roër alone.[146]

For lay Catholics, Napoleon represented as much a culmination of the Old Regime as a new beginning. His prefects' attempts to stamp out baroque piety and enlist the Church as a development agency differed little from the electors'. If anything, Napoleon proved more sympathetic to popular religion, as he recognised its potential for propaganda purposes. For this reason, he relaxed former blanket restrictions on public religious displays imposed in 1798: from April 1803, such displays were allowed within Catholic areas and from February 1806 in areas without churches belonging to other confessions, though public flagellation remained illegal.[147] The government, through its return of looted relics, encouraged manifestations of popular piety that would have shocked the last generation of prince archbishop; over 45,000 pilgrims flocked to the exhibition of relics in Aachen's cathedral on the last day of their public display in 1804, whilst still larger numbers

[143] Ladoucette to the interior minister, 5 September 1813, AN, F^{Ic}III Roër 4, no. 204.
[144] Ladoucette to the police minister, 11 October and 29 November 1811, AN, F^{7}3686^{10}.
[145] Hegel, *Köln*, pp. 499–500. Torsy, *Aachen*, pp. 204–6.
[146] Torsy, *Aachen*, p. 188.   [147] *Ibid.*, pp. 223–5, 232.

converged on Trier for a glimpse of Christ's shroud.[148] Rather than ban processions and pilgrimages, Napoleon's government regulated them. Those crossing diocesan boundaries were forbidden outright, partly because it was suspected they acted as a cover for smuggling. Paris also regulated the ringing of church bells. In reality, such restrictions were often flouted. Even processions spanning the Rhine continued, as did the celebration of banned feast days.[149]

Education proved the most fruitful area of church–state co-operation. Napoleon always believed that religion should be taught in school and after 1802, secondary schools were legally required to provide such instruction if demanded by a majority of parents. For financial reasons, the government increasingly relied upon the clergy to run and inspect state schools. In rural areas, it was common for church sextons to be employed as schoolteachers. In 1807, Paris introduced episcopal visitations of schools to ensure that religion was being taught and by the following year, with the foundation of the imperial university, religion was firmly embedded in the education system. The Catholic hierarchy assisted in overcoming peasant superstition when preaching in favour of small-pox vaccinations; it used its influence to support conscription. Yet there were limits to what even Napoleon could get away with: the attempt in April 1806 to introduce the Imperial Catechism, which threatened those who opposed the Emperor with eternal damnation, met with determined resistance, and was largely abandoned, as it was in neighbouring Belgium.[150] The cult of St Napoleon similarly failed to recommend itself, and people remained seated or left church when the priest led prayers for the Emperor. Yet, despite setbacks, the relationship between the Catholic Church and state was close enough by November 1811 for Rhinelanders to request that the French complete Cologne cathedral.[151] In the century following Napoleonic rule, the Rhineland witnessed a resurgence in popular Catholic piety.

French rule marked a turning point for Rhenish Protestantism. Communities that had previously been merely tolerated were now allowed to worship freely. Elsewhere, completely new communities were founded. Not that the French were the first to foster tolerance. During the eighteenth century, neighbouring Protestant and Catholic Rhenish states tacitly agreed to treat their minorities decently. Electors defied popular opposition in encouraging Protestant settlement to stimulate economic development. At the elite level,

---

[148] Hegel, *Köln*, p. 529.
[149] Justus Hashagen, *Das Rheinland und die französische Herrschaft. Beiträge zur Charakteristik ihres Gegensatzes* (Bonn, 1908), pp. 140–7, 158.
[150] Hegel, *Köln*, p. 534. Torsy, *Aachen*, p. 279.   [151] Hashagen, *Rheinland*, p. 178.

inter-confessional relations remained harmonious under Napoleon, as reflected in some prominent mixed marriages.[152] The same could not be said
lower down society. The redrawing of territorial boundaries upset the delicate Westphalian balance. Territorial reordering gave rise to new conflicts
over such issues as the allocation of former Catholic churches for use by
Protestants, regulations over religious processions in mixed areas and the
confessional balance in the new consultative councils.[153] Napoleon's government, recognising the problems, generally appointed mayors sharing
the same confession as the communities they served, whilst in mixed areas
prefects appointed mayors, adjuncts and councillors from the various confessions so as to 'manage prejudices'.[154] However, in places like Aachen, the
newly dominant socio-economic and political position of the Protestant
minority (2 per cent of the population, but 28 per cent of the 100 top
tax-payers) could only breed resentment.

Napoleonic reforms affected relations within the Protestant community,
between Calvinists and Lutherans. These took the first steps towards union,
a pragmatic policy dictated by the need to co-operate in the establishment
of new communities in predominantly Catholic areas where Protestant
worship had previously been forbidden. In Aachen and Cologne, for example, the two communities held their services in common, with ministers
alternating every week.[155] Complete union was blocked by Napoleon, as it
conflicted with the structures he imposed on both communities in May
1802. These included consistories at the departmental level. These were
dominated by the highest tax-payers, and met annually to elect pastors –
whose appointment needed Napoleon's confirmation – and administer
Church property. Extraordinary consistorial meetings could only take place
with government authorisation. Pastors, upon their appointment, swore an
oath of loyalty to the state between the hands of the prefect. They too were
now paid by the state. They had to be French citizens, entertain no connections with foreign powers, and were required to lead public prayers
for the good of France and Napoleon. From 1804, they wore French-style
uniforms. At the higher level, Calvinist congregations were supervised by

[152] Thomas Mergel, *Zwischen Klasse und konfession: katholisches Bürgertum im Rheinland 1794–1914*
(Göttingen, 1994), pp. 5ff. Karl-Georg Faber, *Andreas van Recum 1765–1828. Ein rheinischer Kosmopolit* (Bonn, 1969), pp. 181ff. For mixed marriages amongst Aachen's elite, see Michael Sobania,
'Das Aachener Bürgertum am Vorabend der Industrialisierung', in Lothar Gall (ed.), *Vom alten
zum neuen Bürgertum. Die mitteleuropäische Stadt im Umbruch 1780–1820* (*Historische Zeitschrift*
Beiheft 14, Munich, 1991), p. 217.
[153] LHAK, Bestand 256, 93, no. 84.   [154] LHAK, Bestand 256, 172, nos. 1–4, 91–3.
[155] J. F. Gerhard Goeters, 'Neubegründung evangelischer Gemeinden in der Rheinprovinz während der
Franzosenzeit', *Monatshefte für evangelische Kirchengeschichte des Rheinlandes* 39 (1990), pp. 25–31.

a 'synod', and the Lutherans by an 'inspection'. Members of both were appointed for life by Napoleon.[156]

French officials generally concurred that Protestants were, on average, better educated and wealthier than Catholics, and consequently more interested in preserving social order.[157] Yet, despite signs that Protestants might be natural allies in the predominantly Catholic region, the Catholic flavour of the Napoleonic regime, especially in such areas as education, heightened fears amongst Protestant Rhinelanders that the Catholic Church would soon be restored to its old privileged state.[158]

The status of Rhenish Jews improved under French rule. Yet neither the Old Regime's moves towards greater tolerance nor Napoleon's treatment of Jews as less than equal citizens should be ignored. The French occupation provided both dangers and opportunities, and Jews themselves recognised the risk of being seen as Francophile. Nevertheless, they were twice as likely to sign the petitions in 1798 in favour of 'reunion' with the Republic than their Christian neighbours, even though the French continued to exploit 'feudal' impositions, including discriminatory taxes.[159] Many French commanders, including Hoche, were ill-disposed towards Jews, whilst pragmatic Napoleonic bureaucrats recognised that being perceived as pro-Jewish was not the best way of winning over public opinion. No general measure sweeping away anti-Jewish discrimination appeared before 1800, though the ghettos were closed and Jews allowed to settle in places where they had previously been excluded. Less could be done to expurgate popular anti-Semitism, which remained a fact of life, especially in rural backwaters like the Eifel and Hunsrück. There, anti-Semitism came to the fore with the activities of the most infamous bandit of the period, Schinderhannes, who won some popular support because he mainly robbed Jews. Jews were subject to harassment and recipients of hate mail.[160]

One problem facing Jews was the legacy of the so-called 'Jew tax' – a form of protection money – which they had paid under the Old Regime. This had been levied upon the Jewish community as a whole and covered by loans taken out by the community collectively, which enjoyed a greater

[156] Graumann, *Verwaltung*, pp. 212–21.
[157] LHAK, Bestand 276, 1967, 'Mémoir[e] statistique sur la situation du dept. de la Sarre, prendt. les ans 10, 11 et 12, adressé par le prefet de ce dept. à S. Ex. le Ministre de l'Intérieur, pour faire faite au Grand mémoire statistique', p. 23.
[158] Boucqueau de Villeraie (prefect of the Rhin-et-Moselle) to Fouché, 18 February 1802, LHAK, Bestand 276, nos. 3–10.
[159] Hansgeorg Molitor, 'Die Juden im französischen Rheinland', in Jutta Bohnke-Kollwitz *et al.* (eds.), *Köln und das rheinische Judentum. Festschrift Germania Judaica 1959–1984* (Cologne, 1984), pp. 87–94.
[160] LHAK, Bestand 241, 1029, nos. 11–14.

reputation for credit-worthiness than individual Jewish borrowers. The community sub-divided the debt burden between its members. Under the new regime, many Jews viewed themselves as equal citizens, and refused to acknowledge their outstanding debts. Following appeals from creditors and a precedent set in Metz, Paris ruled that Jews were still liable for the debts, and set up a special commission in Bonn – composed of non-Jewish notables and, with a consultative voice only, representatives of the Jewish community – with the authority to compel individuals to pay.[161]

Subsequently, Paris further restricted the equality supposedly enjoyed by Jews. Following a meeting with Jewish leaders in 1806, Napoleon discounted the possibility of ever integrating the Jews. Instead, he viewed them as a foreign body within the Empire, and signed a series of restrictive decrees aimed especially at the sizeable minorities in the Rhineland and Alsace. These limited the right of Jews to sign contracts and culminated in the so-called 'infamous decree' of 1808, which restricted where Jews might settle and what trades they might enter. This decree governed the status of Rhenish Jews until 1848. Jews were also barred from hiring replacements for conscription, though in 1812 this was relaxed to the extent that they might hire fellow Jews.[162] At the same time (1808), the Jewish community was reorganised into its own hierarchical, national structure. Rabbis, like priests and pastors, became civil servants.

Despite restrictions, the French period generally proved positive for the Jewish community. Composed mainly of small craftsmen and petty-traders, the community's socio-economic position gradually improved in the early nineteenth century; and, despite Napoleon's scepticism, wealthy Jews began integrating into elite culture.[163] For example, they rubbed shoulders with Gentiles in Napoleonic Cologne's elitist Casino-Gesellschaft, founded in 1809, which dominated societal life in the city.[164] It was not unknown for Jews to be nominated as adjuncts or even mayors during the Napoleonic period.[165] In some towns, an attempt was made to select municipal council-lors from every confession, including Jews. Such was the case in Kreuznach, for example, whose Jews unsuccessfully petitioned the Allied authorities in 1814 to continue this practice. Significantly, they enjoyed the Christian mayor's support in their request.[166] Overall, the experience of Rhenish

[161] LHAK, Bestand 241, 1079.   [162] Molitor, 'Juden', p. 91.

[163] Alwin Müller, 'Die sozialprofil der Juden in Köln (1808–1850)', in Bohnke-Kollwitz, *Köln*, pp. 103–4, 107–13.

[164] Mettele, 'Kölner Bürgertum', pp. 269–72.

[165] LHAK, Bestand 256, 172, nos. 51, 67, 107–8.   [166] LHAK, Bestand 371, 1.

Jews during the Consulate and Empire reflected the tensions between Napoleonic pragmatism and the principles of 1789.

Napoleon's pragmatism distinguished efforts to forge a new identity by superimposing his own personality cult onto existing traditions. The revolutionaries, in contrast, had attempted to forge a completely new republican identity from scratch. To this end, they introduced fest-cycles to fill the void created by the abolition of exuberant displays of baroque religiosity. However, it quickly became obvious that the imposition of the revolutionary calendar on the Rhineland would founder and Paris abandoned the attempt soon after the outbreak of the War of the Second Coalition.[167] It was Napoleon who discovered the winning formula of grafting new propaganda onto existing popular culture. Whilst the revolutionaries condemned the past, he quarried its seams for material to construct an image for the new regime.[168]

The Consulate tolerated a measure of nostalgia for the Old Regime in a way its predecessors could not. Immediately after Brumaire, Paris toned down the revolutionary rhetoric that had previously embellished public pronouncements, abolished divisive republican festivities and removed liberty trees from towns where they caused most offence.[169] Instead, Napoleonic interior ministers instructed prefects to organise celebrations that were in keeping with the customs of each *pays* and to 'renew old customs, dear to the peoples of the countries in our possession'.[170] Napoleon tolerated 'only those festivals...which belonged to periods when public opinion was unanimous'.[171] Revolutionary festivals, which served only to illustrate ideological divisions, contradicted the essence of Bonapartism, namely the depoliticisation of society and neutralisation of factionalism.[172] Napoleonic propaganda set itself the modest aim of pacification rather than mobilisation. Nonetheless, a degree of popular participation was required to justify the second part of the dictum that authority emanates from above and confidence from below.[173] To encourage participation and avoid damaging boycotts, the regime transformed national festivities into free entertainment

---

[167] T. C. W. Blanning, *The French Revolution in Germany. Occupation and Resistance in the Rhineland 1792–1802* (Oxford, 1983), pp. 225–6.

[168] Molitor, *Untertan*, pp. 176–7.   [169] Hansen, *Quellen*, 4, p. 1260 n. 3.

[170] Prefectoral circular to the sub-prefects, mayors and adjuncts of the Roër, 8 April 1811, AN, F^{Ic}III Roër 4, 1, no. 13.

[171] Holtman, *Propaganda*, p. 106.

[172] Michael Rowe, 'Forging "New-Frenchmen": state propaganda in the Rhineland, 1794–1814', in Bertrand Taithe and Tim Thornton (eds.), *Propaganda* (Stroud, 1999), pp. 115–30.

[173] Jean-Denis Bredin, *Sieyès. La clé de la Révolution française* (Paris, 1988), p. 469.

in which the population was demoted to a passive spectator. The Catholic Church, which enjoyed over a millennium's experience in the field, was now co-opted and the revolutionary calendar finally abolished (1 January 1806). Instead, a new festive cycle was instituted and grafted onto the Church calendar: the feast of the Assumption (15 August) became St Napoleon day and, together with the first Sunday of December (commemorating Napoleon's coronation and the Battle of Austerlitz), served as the most important national holiday. By merging his personality cult with the religious fest-cycle, Napoleon succeeded in creating something all-encompassing, in contrast to revolutionary festivities, which stood isolated in space and time.

Napoleonic festivities, whether commemorating 15 August, 2 December or the baptism of the King of Rome, followed a fixed pattern. At the centre of the day's activities was the marriage of a French veteran to a local girl 'of spotless character', with the newly weds receiving an endowment from the local municipality. In practice, municipalities often failed to find suitable brides, provoking suspicions in Paris less as to the virtue of local women than of a reluctance to squander money on endowments. A religious service followed the civil wedding, attended by officials in full dress uniform. In mixed communities, officials attended services in the churches of both confessions. There, they would hear an appropriately obsequious sermon, the best of which were subsequently reprinted in departmental newspapers. They generally included the assertion that Napoleon was 'fighting for peace', followed by an appeal to conscripts to do their duty. Following the service, bread and meat were distributed to needy families.[174] In summer, outdoor activities might follow, including processions of honour guards and officials in resplendent uniforms, the distribution of free wine, horse races, shooting competitions, aerostatics, the distribution of prizes to enterprising farmers and entrepreneurs, and athletic events. One mayor even organised athletic events for young women, who were normally excluded from such activities, provoking official concern at the 'amazonisation' of his municipality.[175]

Napoleon sought to win local opinion by praising old institutions. Cologne's ancient university, previously condemned as 'fanatic', was thus rehabilitated.[176] The French played on local pride and civic rivalries that had only increased as cities competed for the location of criminal courts, prefectures and bishoprics to compensate for the loss of the old universities, electoral courts and archbishoprics. Market towns similarly competed for

---

[174] LHAK, Bestand 276, 314, nos. 139–40, 155–66.   [175] LHAK, Bestand 276, no. 315.
[176] Ladoucette's *compte moral* to the departmental council of 15 February 1810, HStAD, Roër dept., 199, no. 35.

sub-prefectures and civil courts, and smaller towns for the location of a cantonal seat. Such competition was given an additional edge when communities formerly belonging to different principalities found themselves lumped together in the new administrative sub-divisions. Napoleon exploited such rivalries to pose as a benefactor for which the Rhineland, with its historical associations, offered an especially appropriate setting. The new regime contrasted its plans for poplar-lined avenues, canals, harbours, prisons, barracks and schools with revolutionary vandalism. During Napoleon's two official visits, in 1804 and 1811, cities bombarded him with petitions for the relocation of this or that *lycée*, foundation of a new bishopric or seminary, or creation of an additional sub-prefecture.[177] Amongst the two most important infrastructure projects planned were a canal connecting the Meuse and Rhine – something Charlemagne first thought of, according to the Roër's prefect – and a new port in Cologne, 'a city already rendered famous by Caesar, Agrippa, Clovis and Charlemagne'.[178] Civic pride and imperial propaganda combined in a more bellicose form in 1804, when the Rhenish departmental councils agreed to finance the construction of gunboats for the invasion of Britain, though only on condition that they were named after local towns and rivers.[179]

Napoleonic rule coincided with the first stirrings of romanticism, a movement that emerged in part as a reaction against the despoliation of the Church. In response to this cultural tragedy, a small number of private enthusiasts agitated for the cataloguing, protection and restoration of ancient monuments and historical artefacts. The beginnings of some famous collections of medieval church art, notably that housed within Cologne's Wallraf-Richardtz Museum, date from this period. The French, for propaganda purposes, associated themselves with this cultural development. Officials, such as the Rhin-et-Moselle's prefect, Lezay-Marnesia, enthusiastically co-operated in the preservation effort. They founded *sociétés d'émulation* as a means of furthering integration between Rhinelanders and Frenchmen, and associating the government with local history and culture. Some of these societies survived Napoleonic rule and a few are still in existence.[180] Local authorities subsequently saved many fine monastic churches by declaring them parish churches and substituting them for less significant structures. The new regime made good some of the cultural vandalism inflicted by the revolutionaries, returning items hauled off to Paris

---

[177] StAA, Bestand RAII (Allgemeine Akten), 248, nos. 50–55, 59–60.
[178] Ladoucette's *compte moral* to the departmental council, 15 February 1810, HStAD, Roër dept., 199, nos. 41–2.
[179] Hashagen, *Rheinland*, p. 126.   [180] Pabst, 'Bildungs- und Kulturpolitik', p. 195.

or elsewhere, including the relics of the Magi and Christ's Robe, restored to Cologne and Trier respectively.[181] The French initiated the restoration of a number of important monuments damaged not by revolutionaries but by centuries of neglect. In 1804, for example, during his visit to Trier, Napoleon symbolically ordered the removal of medieval accretions from the Roman Porta Nigra.[182] Official inscriptions on other monuments – Clovis's tomb in Zulpich, the cathedral and restored baths in Aachen – now proudly proclaimed the beneficence of the 'Imperator Neapolio'.[183] In a similar vein, Napoleon allowed Rhenish cities to celebrate their annual Carnival festivities again from 1801 onwards and restored market days to their original dates.[184]

Napoleonic heraldry, introduced in March 1808, symbolised the new regime's association with the old. Cities, headed by the *bonnes villes*, received new coats of arms to replace those destroyed by the revolutionaries. The new heraldic devices were a curious mixture of old emblems embellished with Bonapartist bees and eagles.[185] Mayors of *bonne villes* enjoyed the right to attend great imperial dynastic events, including coronations, weddings and baptisms. Aachen and Cologne's mayors led delegations from their cities at the baptism of the King of Rome in Paris on 2 June 1811. The government instructed their accompanying servants to wear a livery composed of the ancient coats of arms of their cities, lending them the appearance of feudal retainers.[186] The metamorphosis of revolutionary, national, republican propaganda into a supra-national, monarchical, pseudo-Carolingian personality cult was now complete.

Aachen, Charlemagne's former capital, stood at the heart of this transformation. A month before his visit in 1804, Napoleon restored the feast of Charlemagne in Aachen. During the visit he pointedly meditated in front of the Carolingian emperor's throne. In 1805, he presented Aachen with a painting of Charlemagne in commemoration of his own coronation as

---

[181] HASK, FV 2058, no. 18. See also Hegel, *Köln*, p. 513, and Elisabeth Wagner, 'Revolution, Religiosität und Kirchen im Rheinland um 1800', in Peter Hüttenberger and Hansgeorg Molitor (eds.), *Franzosen und Deutsche am Rhein 1789–1918–1945* (Essen, 1989), p. 284.

[182] Eva Brües, *Die Rheinlande. Unter Verwendung des von Ehler W. Grashoff gesammelten Materials* (Munich, 1968), p. 412.

[183] Ladoucette (*'Ruranae Praefectus'*) to the departmental council, August 1811, *Recueil* (1811), pp. 255–72.

[184] Hashagen, *Rheinland*, pp. 28–9. The prefectoral (Roër) circular of 12 October 1805 includes a table with the dates of fairs in the recently restored Gregorian calendar. Municipal councils were allowed to request that these dates be changed. *Recueil* (1806), pp. 39–40. These were then subsequently changed by imperial decree.

[185] Heiko Steuer, *Das Wappen der Stadt Köln* (Cologne, 1981), pp. 119–22. For Aachen, see Kraus, *Handbuch-Katalog*, pp. 485–7.

[186] Ladoucette to the mayors of Cologne and Aachen, 25 April 1811, AN, F¹ᶜIII Roër 4, 1, no. 9.

King of Italy. In 1809, Napoleon's portrait was unveiled in the hall where medieval emperors had received loyal oaths after their coronation. Not surprisingly, Aachen's first hope upon learning of the fall of Vienna that same year (in a war French propaganda compared to the Saxon's treason against Charlemagne) was to get back the German imperial insignia, evacuated by the Austrians during the 1790s.[187] Celebrations marking the baptism of the King of Rome in Aachen in 1811 included the parading around the city of an effigy of Charlemagne, on which was inscribed (in French and German), 'I am only surpassed by Napoleon'.[188]

The cult of Charlemagne superseded revolutionary propaganda that had dwelt on the Franks as the first Germanic tribe that had (in 1789) regained its ancient liberties.[189] References to liberty fell out of fashion under Napoleon. Instead, the theme of reversing the Treaty of Verdun (843) came to the fore.[190] The imperial cult reached a climax with Napoleon's marriage to the Habsburg archduchess, Marie-Louise, in 1810. Thereafter, official ceremonies became less specifically French, and more Napoleonic interpretations of Roman, Carolingian and even Germanic traditions.[191] Denationalisation reflected the changing nature of the expanding empire. The centre of power, Napoleon's court itself, took on a more 'European' or 'imperial' flavour, much to the chagrin of the 'national' party: between 1809 and 1815, 34 per cent of those presented at court were non-French, as were 26 per cent of senior household officials; an increasingly large number of imperial chamberlains now originated from noble families from Lorraine, who were traditionally pro-Habsburg rather than pro-Bourbon.[192] 'The present epoch carries us back to the time of Charlemagne,' Napoleon declared in March 1811. 'All the kingdoms, principalities and duchies which formed themselves out of the debris of the Empire have been rejuvenated under our laws. The Church of my Empire is the Church of the Occident and of almost the whole of Christendom.' Rome was declared 'the second city of the Empire', the heir to the throne entitled 'King of Rome', a decree issued stipulating that Napoleon's successors should be crowned in Rome within ten years of their coronation in Paris and plans laid for an imperial palace

---

[187] AN, F¹ᶜIII Roër 4, 2, nos. 461–2. *Recueil* (1804), p. 37. Ladoucette to the minister of the interior, 26 May 1809, AN, F⁷6528, dossier N°.1619, Sᵗⁱᵉ2. See also AN, F¹ᶜIII Roër 4, nos. 16–19.

[188] Ladoucette's report on the celebrations, 9 May 1811, AN, F¹ᶜIII Roër 4, nos. 33–4.

[189] For references to 'Frankish liberties', see the 'reunion' addresses of early 1798, AN, F¹ᶜIII Roër 3, nos. 108, 160, 173, 177, 205.

[190] AN, F¹ᶜIII Roër 3, no. 32.   [191] Hashagen, *Rheinland*, pp. 191–5. AN, F¹ᶜIII Roër 4, no. 41.

[192] Philip Mansel, *The Court of France 1789–1830* (Cambridge, 1988), pp. 57–69. The historical connection between the Habsburgs and Lorraine had been reinforced by the marriage of Francis of Lorraine to Maria Theresa in 1736. Lorraine itself only fell to France in 1766, following the death of Francis's successor as duke, Stanislas Lesczinski.

on the Capitol.[193] Rhinelanders, rather than finding themselves within a narrowly defined nation state, appeared again to be reverting to their old status as subjects of an empire with universalistic pretensions.

Modern state formation has been marked not only by the development of government institutions, but also by attempts at the imposition of uniform 'standard high cultures'. The French Republic of the early 1790s might be cited as the first attempt to forge a nation state through the marriage of culture and power. The implications of this for the Rhineland, a culturally diverse frontier region, were obviously great. However, the Jacobins' fall in 1794 on the eve of the Rhineland's occupation heralded a more pragmatic French policy that took greater account of local conditions. 'Frenchification' was not exactly put on hold under the Directory and Napoleon; however, it moved down the priority list. There it remained until the final years of French rule, by which time the officially approved culture appeared more 'imperial', 'European' or 'Bonapartist' than 'French'.

To what extent did the culture and identity of Rhinelanders evolve under French rule? Certainly, Rhinelanders, be they businessmen or peasants, were not transformed into Frenchmen. Whether they were in the process of making this transition is hard to say. Fragmentary evidence suggests that the usage of the French language was spreading slowly; there is also evidence of a surprisingly high level of intermarriage between Rhinelanders and Frenchmen and French women. However, societal life seems to have fractured partly along national lines, at least in some cities. There is also evidence of national friction in the law courts. So it is difficult to arrive at a conclusion. More generally, it has been argued that French imperialism in the Napoleonic era built upon cultural imperialism of the preceding century. Whilst accepting the argument that the Enlightenment cannot be viewed as purely 'French', it is nonetheless true that Napoleon could build upon some shared eighteenth-century cultural foundations that bound France with other regions of Continental Europe. Napoleon's somewhat crude exploitation of freemasonry for his own ends is an example. However, it is ironic that just as France and Germany moved together politically, so new cultural divisions opened up between them. These partly revolved around the purpose of education and the value attached socially and culturally to specialised, vocational knowledge as opposed to what Germans called '*Bildung*'. This divergence had serious implications for the long-term

---

[193] Hans Kohn, *Prelude to Nation-States. The French and German Experience, 1789–1815* (Princeton, 1969), pp. 94–6, 102–5.

establishment of French rule, which depended upon the cultural integration of the local elite. The Rhenish elite found little incentive to invest its cultural capital in Napoleonic France.

Clearly, Rhinelanders were far from becoming Frenchmen in 1813/14. Were they any closer to becoming 'Germans'? This question is of some import given the centrality of francophobia and conflict over the Rhine in defining German nationalism in the nineteenth century. Certainly, the Rhineland's cultural elite maintained close links with the rest of Germany throughout the Napoleonic period. They formed part of a wider German, not French, cultural elite. As for the bulk of the population, conclusions remain tentative. There is substantial evidence of surviving '*Reichspatriotismus*' and loyalty directed towards the person of the Habsburg Emperor. Indeed, a significant number of native Rhinelanders remained in Austrian service throughout the Napoleonic wars. Apprentices from the left bank continued to leave the region to work in other parts of Germany as part of their professional training, whilst students were more attracted by universities across the Rhine than by Napoleon's special schools. However, there is little evidence that Rhinelanders were becoming any more 'German' in terms of their political outlook in this period. Loyalties to locality and confession remained paramount for the majority: territorial consolidation if anything reinforced local loyalties, at least in the short term, whilst religious loyalties (and divisions) were on the point of experiencing a revival as a consequence of the destruction of the delicate confessional balance established by the Peace of Westphalia.

CHAPTER 6

War and society

The Grande Empire's multi-national character was reflected in early 1812, when Napoleon massed 650,000 troops for the invasion of Russia. It was the largest force concentrated in history up to that point, representing the armed might of Continental Europe. French regiments comprised a third of this host: of the eleven infantry corps, five were composed entirely of foreign contingents – Polish, Bavarian, Saxon, Westphalian and Prussian – while another four contained non-French units. The Austrians provided their own semi-autonomous expeditionary corps. Overall, Germans outnumbered Frenchmen as the largest 'national' contingent, a contribution that included the German-speaking 'new Frenchmen' of the Rhine serving in the regular French regiments.

The Russian invasion marked the culmination of the revolutionary and Napoleonic wars, a generation of conflict unparalleled in scale. Eighteenth-century armies were measured in the tens of thousands; under Napoleon they frequently exceeded 100,000. This expansion not only affected the battlefield, but European society as a whole. Not only was conflict large scale, but also of long duration, something ascribable to Napoleon himself. Despite the rapidity and decisiveness of his campaigns, his policy towards his neighbours precluded any possibility of the French Empire successfully integrating itself into a stable international framework.[1] Consequently, Europe suffered successively the wars of the second, third and fourth coalitions (1799–1801, 1805 and 1806–7 respectively), the Franco-Austrian war (1809), the Russian campaign (1812), Wars of Liberation (1813), and invasion of France (1814), not to mention protracted guerrilla warfare in Spain (1808–14). Peace only followed Napoleon's defeat in the Hundred Days campaign (1815). France was continually at war with at least one of the Great Powers from 1792 to 1814, with the exception of a fourteen-month interlude following the Peace of Amiens (1802).

[1] Paul Schroeder, *The Transformation of European Politics, 1763–1848* (Oxford, 1994), pp. 391–5.

158

The most tragic consequence of warfare was death. An estimated 5 million Europeans died as a result of the Napoleonic wars, equalling the proportion lost in the First World War. Yet only recently has historical appreciation of the Napoleonic wars extended beyond the campaign narratives that provided the foci of older studies.[2] For underpinning the great deeds of commanders was a system of resource mobilisation that required ever greater penetration of society by the state. This was especially true of Napoleonic France, a state that approximated the old description of Prussia as not a state with an army, but an army with a state.[3] If anything, Napoleonic France, with its revolutionary inheritance of equal citizenship and universal conscription, went beyond Frederick the Great's Prussia, an entity based upon functional estates that mediated the individual's relationship with the state. Rather, France represented the forerunner of the modern state whose governing principles were extended into Germany by the tribute system Napoleon imposed upon the Confederation of the Rhine, and by defensive modernisation in Prussia and Austria.[4] The result was 'state-building' on a continental scale, including fiscal consolidation, modern debt management, administrative reform, and the strengthening of coercive instruments.

The Rhineland, located on France's frontier with Germany, experienced militarisation that, in terms of contrast with the Old Regime, was greater than other parts of Europe.[5] For though traditionally a receptacle for Europe's warring armies, the region had no prior experience of conscription.

---

[2] Isser Woloch, 'Napoleonic Conscription: State Power and Civil Society', *Past & Present* 111 (1986). Idem, *The New Regime: Transformations of the French Civic Order, 1789–1820s* (New York and London, 1994), pp. 380–426. Geoffrey Best, *War and Society in Revolutionary Europe, 1770–1870* (London, 1982), pp. 108–21. Alan Forrest, *Conscripts and Deserters. The Army and French Society during the Revolution and Empire* (Oxford, 1989).

[3] Best, *War*, pp. 111–12.

[4] Robert Holtmann, *The Napoleonic Revolution* (Baton Rouge and London, 1981), p. 85. For military reform in Prussia, which went furthest in implementing the 'revolutionary' policy of universal service, see Peter Paret, *Yorck and the Era of Prussian Reform* (Princeton, 1966). For military matters in the Habsburg Empire, see G. E. Rothenberg, *Napoleon's Great Adversaries. The Archduke Charles and the Austrian Army, 1792–1814* (London, 1982). For the smaller states, see John H. Gill, *With Eagles to Glory. Napoleon and his German Allies in the 1809 Campaign* (London, 1993 reprint). For Italy, Alexander Grab, 'Army, State, and Society: Conscription and Desertion in Napoleonic Italy (1802–1814)', *The Journal of Modern History* 67 (1995), pp. 25–54, and Frederick C. Schneid, *Soldiers of Napoleon's Kingdom of Italy. Army, State and Society, 1800–1815* (Boulder, Colo., 1995).

[5] Given this, the paucity of literature on conscription in the Rhineland, is surprising. The lacuna is only partially filled by Roger Dufraisse, 'Les Populations de la rive gauche du Rhin et le service militaire à la fin de l'Ancien Régime et à l'Époque Révolutionnaire', *Revue Historique* 231 (1964), pp. 103–40; Calixte Hudemann-Simon, 'Réfractaires et déserteurs de la Grande Armée en Sarre (1802–1813)', *Revue Historique* 277 (1987), pp. 11–45; and Josef Smets, 'Von der "Dorfidylle" zur preußischen Nation. Sozialdisziplinierung der linksrheinischen Bevölkerung durch die Franzosen am Beispiel der allgemeinen Wehrpflicht (1802–1814)', *Historische Zeitschrift* 262 (1996), pp. 695–738.

The recruitment by foreign powers of Rhenish troops throughout the eighteenth century represented an economic transaction rather than an act of compulsion. Arguably such recruitment, far from being socially disruptive, smoothed social tension by removing young men living on the fringe of an over-populated region.[6] Military service was revolutionised under Napoleon. Though his wars were conducted well away from the Rhine, their impact was felt everywhere in the form of conscription; and despite the stereotype of German suitability for military service shared even at the time, conscription proved as alien for Rhinelanders as for Vendéens or Neapolitans. Alan Forrest's observation that conscription 'created an open clash between the archaic and the modern, and though in the long term the modern undoubtedly triumphed in the short term it antagonised public opinion, and put the governability of the state at risk', is equally applicable to the Rhenish departments.[7]

Old-regime military institutions reflected the Holy Roman Empire's complexity. Two tiers, imperial defence and territorial armies maintained by the states, existed side by side. The imperial structure centred on the ten circles (*Kreise*) created in 1512 and reformed in 1681. Three covered parts of the Rhineland: the Burgundian, electoral Rhenish and Lower-Rhenish Westphalian. The strength of the imperial army was set at 40,000 (12,000 cavalry and 28,000 infantry), though with provision for 'multiplication' when required. Each circle furnished a contingent of fixed strength: the electoral Rhenish's was 600 cavalry and 2,707 infantry, and the Lower-Rhenish Westphalian and Burgundian 1,321 cavalry and 2,708 infantry each.[8] The effectiveness of imperial defence was generally low, especially in circles that covered part of one of the larger states, whose military effort was concentrated in their own armies. It was more effective in the fragmented German south-west, whose states were too small to maintain their own forces.[9] The Rhenish circles lay somewhere in between.

[6] For recruitment of foreign contingents and mercenaries in old-regime Germany, see Peter H. Wilson, *War, State and Society in Württemberg, 1677–1793* (Cambridge, 1995), pp. 74–96. Also, Charles W. Ingrao, *The Hessian Mercenary State. Ideas, Institutions, and Reform under Frederick II, 1760–1785* (Cambridge, 1987); Peter Keir Taylor, *Indentured to Liberty. Peasant life and the Hessian Military State* (Ithaca, N.Y. and London, 1994).

[7] Forrest, *Conscripts*, p. viii.

[8] Gerhard Papke, *Von der Miliz zum Stehenden Heer. Wehrwesen im Absolutismus [1648–1789]* (Munich, 1979), p. 241.

[9] Karl Otmar Freiherr von Aretin, *Heiliges Römisches Reich 1776–1806* (2 vols., Wiesbaden, 1967), I, pp. 218–29. Peter H. Wilson, *German Armies. War and German Politics 1648–1806* (London, 1998), passim. The Swabian district, as a result of its comparative effectiveness, has received more attention than the others. J. A. Vann, *The Swabian Kreis. Institutional Growth in the Holy Roman Empire, 1648–1715* (Brussels, 1975). H. G. Borck, *Der schwäbische Reichskreis im Zeitalter*

By 1789, significant German military might was vested only in the Austrian and Prussian armies. The former maintained over 300,000 and the latter in excess of 190,000 troops.[10] The gap between Austria and Prussia and those occupying the next rung – Bavaria, Saxony, Hanover, Hessen – widened during the eighteenth century. Yet even the forces of these medium-sized states appeared formidable compared to the 3,000 soldiers of electoral Mainz, 1,200 men of electoral Cologne, and the seventy-seven grenadiers and 129 fusiliers maintained by the imperial city of Aachen.[11] Well might the Prussians sneer that these 'armies' were good only for escorting Corpus Christi processions. They quickly dissolved under the French revolutionary onslaught. Half-hearted attempts at the introduction of conscription, both in the Seven Years War (1756–63) and in the 1790s, foundered against determined opposition. For corporate privilege, imperial law and, above all, territorial fragmentation, shielded from the recruiting sergeant even those living under the sceptre of the militaristic kings of Prussia. When Frederick William I – under whose reign Prussia's army expanded from 38,000 to close to 80,000 – attempted to enforce compulsory quotas on Cleves, large numbers of locals simply emigrated. Between 1722 and 1734, the population of the duchy declined by 10,000, whilst nearby Duisburg lost 8 per cent of its population. Frederick William's successor, Frederick the Great, recognised the inevitable and, in 1748, accepted monetary payments in lieu of conscripts. Krefeld was completely exempt because of its economic importance, whilst the estates of the duchies of Cleves and Geldern paid 2,500 *Reichsthaler* per head in lieu of their quotas. Conscription in the western duchies was finally abolished in 1789. In the eastern part of the Monarchy, in contrast, one in six males of military age could expect to be conscripted under the cantonal system of 1733. This system was unenforceable in the west because of the absence of a landowning nobility enjoying that bundle of non-economic rights known as *Herrschaft* over a subject peasantry. Of course, only half the army Frederick led in the Seven Years' War were cantonists. The other half consisted of mercenaries,

---

der französischen Revolutionskriege (1792–1806) (Stuttgart, 1970). The rosy picture painted in these two accounts is questioned by R. Graf von Neipperg, *Kaiser und schwäbischer Kreis (1714–1733). Ein Beitrag zu Reichsverfassung. Kreisgeschichte und kaiserlicher Reichspolitik am Anfang des 18. Jahrhunderts* (Stuttgart, 1991).

[10] Wilson, *German Armies*, p. 283.

[11] For Aachen, see Archives de l'Armée de Terre, Vincennes (AG), M^R 1124, 'Mémoire descriptif et historique de la ville d'Aix-la-Chapelle et ses environs', an undated report drawn up by a French officer attached to the Tranchot cartographical survey. For electoral Cologne, see Herbert Müller-Hengstenberg, 'Werbung, Rekrutierung und Desertion beim kurkölnischen Militär im 18. Jahrhundert', *Annalen des historischen Vereins für den Niederrhein* 195 (1992), pp. 167–75. For Mainz, T. C. W. Blanning, *Reform and Revolution in Mainz 1743–1803* (Cambridge, 1974), pp. 58–9.

adventurers, criminals, dregs, and those naive enough to be scooped up by recruiting officers. Cleves, Geldern and Moers, though spared conscription, were not spared the attention of these officers, whose methods were often indistinguishable from Royal Navy press-gangs.[12]

The other Rhenish states entertained no military ambitions. This left the field open for recruiters from foreign powers, notably the maritime powers, who drew military manpower from the region despite the opposition of local governments. Illegal foreign recruitment – notably by the Dutch – remained a problem even during the Napoleonic period. The Habsburgs, as emperors, enjoyed legal recruiting rights in the region which they viewed as an important source of manpower. Non-Austrian Germans were considered better officer material than their own subjects. Close to half of Austria's soldiers and an even higher proportion of her non-commissioned officers were recruited from the non-Austrian part of the *Reich*, notably the Catholic south and west.[13] The tradition of service to Austria in these regions survived the Napoleonic period.

France occupied the entire Rhineland, bar Mainz, at the end of 1794. Except for a few regiments from electoral Cologne that fought on with the Austrians and individuals serving in the Coalition forces, Rhinelanders submitted to their fate. Whilst the French requisitioned everything imaginable, including people – officials to run local government, drivers to support logistics, workers to build fortifications – they stopped short of compelling the 'liberated' to fight for their freedom. The revolutionary concept of military service extended only to free citizens, not foreigners. Only volunteers were accepted. A few Rhinelanders did come forward, though sources on this are scanty, anecdotal and contradictory. Whilst pro-French publications boasted of many volunteers, anti-French sources reported that young men were crossing the Rhine for fear of being conscripted and that the few volunteers who had joined did so because of generous bounties.[14] Overall, volunteers were small in number, with the majority emanating from the

[12] Otto Büsch, *Militärsystem und Sozialleben im Alten Preussen 1713–1807. Die Anfänge der sozialen Militarisierung der preußisch-deutschen Gesellschaft* (Berlin, 1962), pp. 27–30, 36–7. Heinrich Holthausen, *Verwaltung und Stände des Herzogtums Geldern preußischen Anteils im 18. Jahrhundert* (Geldern, 1916), pp. 69–72.

[13] Kaunitz to Maria-Theresa, 26 November 1779. Reprinted in Karl Otmar Freiherr von Aretin, *Heiliges Römisches Reich 1776–1806. Reichsverfassung und Staatssouveränität* (2 vols., Wiesbaden, 1967), 2, pp. 24–8. More generally, C. A. Macartney, *The Habsburg Empire 1790–1918* (London, 1969), pp. 18, 99, 172–3.

[14] Joseph Hansen, *Quellen zur Geschichte des Rheinlandes im Zeitalter der französischen Revolution 1780–1801* (4 vols., Bonn, 1938), 4, pp. 490, 940, 1092 n. 1.

illiterate margin of society, as indicated by their signature of their enlistment papers with a cross.[15] The French authorities – amongst themselves – admitted the failure of voluntary enlistment, which they variously blamed on counter-revolutionary tavern owners, madmen and fanatics who discouraged locals from joining. The possibility of retribution from vengeful princes, who banned their subjects from joining the revolutionary army, together with the 'vexations' Germans encountered in the French forces, were two further disincentives. Whilst voluntarily enlistment under the Old Regime was viewed as an economic transaction, enlistment in the French army was interpreted by the majority of Rhinelanders as denoting ideological affiliation with the Revolution. Only the Clubbists and *Cisrhénans* pressed their compatriots to volunteer, so as to strengthen their campaign for a sister-republic or annexation. For Paris had made it clear that 'reunion' would only be achieved if Rhinelanders themselves fought alongside their 'Frankish' brothers.[16]

Military over-stretch in the early stages of the War of the Second Coalition forced Paris to reconsider its enlistment policy. The trickle of Rhenish volunteers – Mont-Tonnerre, with over 400,000 inhabitants, produced a mere fifty-seven in the first half of 1799 – remained negligible. One possible means of tapping the region's tempting manpower reserves was the formation of an independent Rhenish army, where Germans might serve together. The idea was first mooted by the *Cisrhénans* in 1798, but rejected by the French war minister.[17] Military necessity dispelled scepticism. In July 1799, the war minister presented a report supporting the creation of a Rhenish division within the French army. This would contribute both to the military strength of the Republic, and attach the new departments to the common cause. Both French chambers approved the proposal.[18] The result was the 'Legion of North Franks' (Légion des Francs du Nord), a name that in itself is revealing. It proved one of the least successful formations in French military history. Its planned strength was four infantry battalions, four cavalry squadrons and a company of artillery, totalling 5,600 men.[19] Rudolf Eickemeyer, a former lieutenant-colonel in Mainz's army, was eventually appointed commander of the Legion after a brief audience

[15] Stadtarchiv Aachen (StAA), Handschriften: Französische Zeit (no. 682).

[16] Hansen, *Quellen*, 4, pp. 1018–19.   [17] *Ibid.*, pp. 1092–4.

[18] Report from the minister of war to the executive Directory, 7 Thermidor VII (25 July 1799), Archives Nationales, Paris (AN), C586, no. 175. For the parliamentary approval, AN, C462, no. 35, 'Extrait du Registre des délibérations du Directoire exécutif', 7 Thermidor VII (25 July 1799).

[19] Hansen, *Quellen*, 4, pp. 1180–1. A report to the minister of war in Prairial IX (May/June 1801) suggested the force might eventually attain the strength of 10,000. AG, X^k41.

with Napoleon – now First Consul – in December 1799.[20] The choice was inauspicious: Eickemeyer was viewed as a traitor by his compatriots for having prematurely surrendered Mainz to Custine in 1792.

Equally inauspicious was the political context surrounding the Legion's formation. Organisation occurred in the charged atmosphere following the coup of Prairial VII (18 June 1799), which brought to power extremists whose policies alienated Rhinelanders further. In addition, enemy triumphs in the opening phase of the War of the Second Coalition emboldened counter-revolutionaries and intimidated potential supporters of the French. Volunteers for the Legion were consequently slow to come forward, to the glee of counter-revolutionaries who questioned why radicals refused to add their names to the enlistment rolls.[21] Numerous scandals befell the Legion in the following months. Paris never accorded it priority in the allocation of supplies and uniforms, and instead used it as a dumping ground for foreign deserters, including Irish volunteers whom it no longer needed following the failure of anti-British uprisings, and French officer rejects with dubious backgrounds.[22] Discipline broke down to an extent that shocked even the regular French army: General Chambarlhac, commander of the Mainz garrison, complained to the war minister of the Legion's brigandage, and enclosed a list of murders and thefts committed by its soldiers. The force was viewed with 'horror' by the entire population, he complained, whilst severe punishment failed to overcome its endemic indiscipline which renewed itself like a 'Hydra'.[23]

The Legion was never tested in combat, but instead deployed along the Rhine to counter smuggling. There it became riddled with corruption, its soldiers protecting smugglers in return for a cut of their profits.[24] It never came close to attaining the strength of 30,000 men predicted by its supporters. Eickemeyer claimed its strength peaked at 3,500, whilst war ministry reports suggest a more modest 2,000 men. The degree of Rhenish participation is lost in the global figures which record the recruitment of non-Rhinelanders, especially Belgians, to make up the Legion's strength.[25] An interesting legal problem was posed in the occupied Hohenzollern duchies

---

[20] Eickemeyer's memoirs were subsequently published in Heinrich König (ed.), *Denkwürdigkeiten des Generals Eickemeyer* (Frankfurt a. M., 1845). They, together with the relevant carton in the war ministry archives in Paris (AG, X^{k}41), constitute the chief source for the Legion.

[21] Hansen, *Quellen*, 4, p. 1207 n. 7.

[22] Dorsch to the minister of justice, 26 April 1800, AN, F^{1c}III Roër 3, no. 12. Adjutant-General Junker to the minister of war, 26 June 1800, AG, X^{k}41.

[23] General Chambarlhac to the minister of war, 7 March 1801, AG, X^{k}41.

[24] H. Cardauns and R. Müller (eds.), *Die rheinische Dorfchronik des Johann Peter Delhoven aus Dormagen, 1783–1823* (Cologne, 1926), p. 173.

[25] Eickemeyer to the minister of war, 3 February 1801, AG, X^{k}41.

which, according to the Treaty of Basel, remained *de jure* Prussian. The French eventually decided to risk recruiting there.[26] Such attempts at casting the net wider achieved little, and complaints about the Legion and the incompetence of its commander flooded into the war ministry. The Legion experienced nearly 1,800 desertions, something blamed on the recruitment of 'professional' deserters and the force's deployment close to the homes of those serving in it. At the end of the war, the ministry recommended its dissolution or deployment to the interior.[27] Napoleon, never one to tolerate military inefficiency, dissolved it soon after Lunéville and ordered the arrest of its commander, whose accounts were investigated. Though eventually acquitted, Eickemeyer never again held a military command. He later claimed Napoleon's vindictiveness was due to his earlier association with the First Consul's rivals, Pichegru and Moreau. Eickemeyer's colleagues proved less fortunate: the commander of the Legion's cavalry was transferred to Guiana, where he died after a few months, whilst the infantry commander ended his days in Batavia (Java), and the inspector of recruitment was posted to Saint-Domingo (Haiti). The rank and file were incorporated into the 55th demi-brigade.[28]

The dearth of volunteers for the North Frankish Legion encouraged calls for conscription. Eickemeyer suggested this, in a vain attempt to preserve his command. Paris, for political reasons, resisted the tempting prospect of the untapped reserves of the region's 1.6 millions, which could support an estimated 30,000 troops rising to 50,000 in time of war.[29] Napoleon's commissioner in the region, Henri Shée, said it would set 'brother against brother, thereby giving the war for liberty the odious character of a civil war'.[30] A lengthy report covering every aspect of the governance of the four Rhenish departments, produced by the justice ministry in October 1800, made no mention of conscription.[31] Official reticence was understandable given the rebellion provoked by conscription's introduction in the Belgian departments in 1798, itself an echo of the Vendée. Even

---

[26] Lakanal to the minister of justice, 13 October 1799, Hansen, *Quellen*, 4, p. 1197.

[27] König, *Denkwürdigkeiten*, p. 352. See also the reports to the minister of war of 22 April and June 1801, AG, X^{k}41.

[28] Consular arrêt of 7 Messidor IX (25 June 1801), AG, X^{k}41. See also König, *Denkwürdigkeiten*, pp. 353–9.

[29] Eickemeyer's report of 2 April 1800, AN, F^{1e}40, dossier 2 (no. 34). Also, Eickemeyer to Hargenvilliers (chef du bureau de recrutement), 2 September 1800, AG, X^{k}41.

[30] Shée to the minister of justice, 29 April 1800, AN, F^{1e}43, no. 370.

[31] AN, F^{1e}44, dossier 'Expedition sur compte pour le M. de l'Interieur' (no. 3) ('Rapport général sur l'administration et la situation actuelle des quatre départements situés sur la rive gauche du Rhin', dated October 1800).

Eickemeyer predicted that the extension of conscription to the Rhineland might provoke violence.[32]

Lunéville, followed by annexation, legally paved the way for the introduction of conscription in the Rhineland. Yet Napoleon delayed promulgating the relevant legislation. Paris waited a full year (until 5 July 1802) before extending the law of 19 Fructidor VI (5 September 1798) – the famous Loi Jourdan-Debrel – to the new departments.[33] This law was so well framed that it formed the basis of conscription in France until 1872. Its preamble and first article reflected the revolutionary principle that underlay the state's right to call upon all citizens for defence: 'Every Frenchman is a soldier and must devote himself to the defence of the *patrie*.'[34] The following articles, which were slightly modified by Napoleon, put these principles into practice. The law classified all single men aged between twenty and twenty-five years as 'conscripts', liable for mobilisation. It divided these into five 'classes' according to age, and mobilised the youngest first. Those reaching twenty-five years without mobilisation were automatically discharged from further commitments. The proportion of conscripts mobilised depended upon military requirements, so that the burden placed on individual classes varied. Initially, mobilisation was authorised by the Corps Législatif, which also fixed each department's contribution. From September 1805 onwards, contingents were mobilised by *senatus consultum*, a device that allowed Napoleon to bypass the legislature.

Victory depended upon the rapid mobilisation of resources, and the conscription process that emerged was quintessentially 'Napoleonic': strategic decision-making was centralised, representative bodies by-passed, and the exercise dependent upon the administration functioning like clockwork. How the system was supposed to work even when Napoleon was campaigning at the other end of Europe – in this case, Poland – is illustrated in the director-general of conscription's report of April 1807. One hundred days elapsed from the presentation of a relevant law in Napoleon's privy council to the conscripts' departure for their units: day 1: presentation of the draft law to the privy council; day 2: presentation to the senate; day 4: adoption by the senate; day 5: presentation to the council of state dividing the contingent between the departments; prefects ordered to form lists of conscripts; day 6:

[32] Eickemeyer to the minister of war, undated (1801), AG, X^k 41.
[33] Karl Theodor Friedrich Bormann and Alexander von Daniels (eds.), *Handbuch der für die königlich-preußischen Rheinprovinzen verkündigte Gesetze, Verordnungen und Regierungsbeschlüsse aus der Zeit der Fremdherrschaft* (8 vols., Cologne, 1833–45), 7, pp. 486–7.
[34] C. M. Galisset, *Corps du droit français ou recueil complet des lois, décrets, ordonnances, sénatus-consultes, règlements, avis du conseil d'état, rapports au roi, instructions ministérielles, etc., publiés depuis 1789 jusqu'à nos jours* (11 vols., Paris, 1833–52), 1, pp. 1828–31.

draft sent to general headquarters in East Prussia for imperial ratification; day 18: decree ratified; day 30: ratified decree reaches Paris; day 35: ratified decree sent to prefectures; day 45: decree reaches prefectures; day 53: decree arrives in sub-prefectures after sub-partition of contingents by prefects; day 58: decree arrives in communes after sub-partition by sub-prefects; day 63: lists of eligible conscripts posted up in communes; day 74: lists verified, conscripts summoned to cantonal *chefs-lieux*; day 89: recruitment councils convene; day 99: conscripts depart for their units.[35]

Rhinelanders were first introduced to this process in 1802. The burden was not particularly heavy, for France now found herself at peace. The overall levee demanded of the nation was only 30,000, drawn from the classes IX – that is, those reaching twenty in Year IX (September 1800 to September 1801) – and X. The quota demanded of the Rhenish departments was kept proportionally much lower (closer to 0.03 per cent of the population, as opposed to 0.1 per cent) than the rest of France. The Roër department, for example, with almost 600,000 inhabitants, furnished a mere 150 conscripts. As its prefect stated, the government viewed the mobilisation as a trial run to familiarise the new departments with conscription.[36] Napoleon had learnt the lessons of the Vendée and Belgium, and his cautious approach proved successful. Even his opponents admitted as much.[37] Napoleon was also fortunate in that conscription was introduced to the Rhineland at a time when his standing was never higher, thanks to the peace treaties of Lunéville and Amiens, and the Concordat.

Conscription remained disproportionately low until 1804–5, as shown in table 1, which illustrates the relative burden in the Rhineland up to 1810, as compared with the French Empire and the German-speaking Alsatian departments to the south.

In Year XIII (1804–5), the Rhenish figure surpassed the national rate by about 8 per cent, and rose steadily thereafter until it exceeded the French average by 42 per cent in 1810. Significantly, the population figures for the Rhineland employed by the director-general of conscription, Hargenvilliers, as the base for his calculations were at least 20 per cent lower than most other estimates: the Roër's was given as 516,287, despite the fact that the military cartographers came up with 629,182; 342,316 was the estimate for Mont-Tonnerre, though the real figure was closer to 425,000;

---

[35] Lacuée (directeur des revues et de la conscription) to Napoleon, 2 April 1807, AN, AFIV 1123, no. 59.
[36] Prefectoral circular, 26 Vendémiaire XI (17 October 1802), *Recueil des actes de la préfecture du département de la Roër* (11 vols., Aachen, 1802/3–13), I (1802/3), pp. 31–7.
[37] Kopstadt, *Kleve*, p. 173.

Table 1. *Number of conscripts mobilised, Year IX (1800/1) to 1810*

	Rhineland[a]	Alsace[b]	French Empire[c]
Population	1,280,942	839,549	35,613,473
Years IX and X (1800/1 and 1801/2)	2,400 (52)*	3,200 (106)	128,000 (100)
XI and XII (1802/3 and 1803/4)	4,355 (96)	3,123 (105)	125,616 (100)
Year XIII (1804/5)	2,326 (108)	1,598 (113)	60,000 (100)
1806	4,429 (114)	2,845 (111)	108,254 (100)
1807	4,680 (124)	2,560 (103)	104,911 (100)
1808	4,576 (122)	2,583 (114)	104,211 (100)
1809	4,947 (132)	2,804 (114)	104,291 (100)
1810	5,554 (142)	3,141 (123)	108,552 (100)

[a] Roër, Mont-Tonnerre, Rhin-et-Moselle and Sarre departments.
[b] Bas-Rhin and Haut-Rhin departments.
[c] Excluding the Italian departments of Arno, Méditerranée, Ombrone and Vicariats de Pontrenoli.
* The numbers in brackets represent the proportionate burden of conscription in the Rhineland and Alsace as a percentage of the burden on the population of the French Empire as a whole.
Source: Gustav Vallée, *Le Compte général de la conscription de A. A. Hargenvilliers* (Paris, 1937), pp. 8, 16–23, 38–41, and AN, AFIV 1124.

the Rhin-et-Moselle's 203,290, as opposed to 250,000; the Sarre's 219,049 instead of 280,000.[38] This was significant, for up until at least 1810 the war ministry based the division between the departments solely on the size of population, according other possible factors, such as the economic state of each department and the physique of local youth, little or no weight. In practice, Hargenvilliers's survey of 1808 revealed massive regional inequalities in the burden of conscription, with 1 in 97 inhabitants of the Yonne department mobilised from the five previous classes as compared to the national average of 1 in 138, or the 1 in 212 of the Rhône department that lay at the other extreme.[39] By then, the Rhineland too bore a disproportionately high burden. Overall, 80,000 Rhenish conscripts served in Napoleon's army, representing about 30 per cent of the age groups eligible for service. In 1813, the rate was running closer to 60 per cent, a desperate situation that was reflected, as elsewhere in France, by the dramatic rise in the price for replacements.[40]

[38] For the calculations and policy of the directorship-general of conscription, see Vallée, *Compte général*, p. 8.
[39] Vallée, *Compte général*, pp. xxv–xxvii. See also Forrest, *Conscripts*, pp. 40–5.
[40] Smets, 'Dorfidylle', pp. 712–16.

The bare figures recording the *impôt de sang* hardly do justice to the administrative achievement they represented. Initially, this achievement was based upon devolution. This was greatest in the early years of the Jourdan Law. However, the government soon discovered that delegation to the localities resulted in inequalities, injustice and the paying-off of old scores.[41] The government responded by centralising the process, yet even then local notables remained crucial for the success or failure of conscription. They, like the prefects, were reminded that their preferment depended upon their management of the draft. 'It is in this part of your duties,' the Roër's prefect reminded his mayors in 1805, 'that you must give proof of your firmness and devotion...it is the most certain evidence you can give him [Napoleon] of your attachment to his person, and at the same time the surest way of assuring yourselves of his benevolence.'[42] The special handbook prepared for officials in the Rhenish departments devoted 200 out of its over 1,000 pages to conscription, a duty given priority over all others.[43] Significantly, the Loi Jourdan entrusted mayors and sub-prefects with preparing the lists of young men that formed the basis for the entire operation. These lists recorded their name, date of birth, height, profession and domicile. The government compelled mayors who missed the deadlines for preparing these lists to pay special commissioners appointed 'to stimulate their activity'. It held sub-prefects responsible for delays if they failed to employ all the means at their disposal. Every year the government sacked a number of mayors and hauled them before the courts for failing to fulfil their duties, publicising their fate in local newspapers as a warning. Yet, as one contemporary with access to departmental records in the Rhineland noted, local officials continued to present deliberately deflated population estimates. Furthermore, even when compiled, communal lists needed to be preserved from destruction through accident or arson – perhaps with the connivance of local officials – something difficult to guarantee in isolated rural areas lacking proper archives.[44]

A fundamental principle of the Jourdan Law was that each tier – department, district, canton, commune – was held collectively responsible

[41] Forrest, *Conscripts*, pp. 27–31.
[42] Hauptstaatsarchiv Düsseldorf (HStAD), Roër dept., 2332, no. 80.
[43] Anton Keil, *Handbuch für Maire und Adjuncten, für Polizey-Commissare, Gemeinde-Räthe, Einnehmer und Vertheiler der Steuern, Spital- und Armenverwalter, Pfarrer, Kirchen-Räthe und Kirchenmeister, Feld- und Forsthüter und Geschäftsmänner. Zweyte ganz umgearbeitete und vermehrte Auflage* (2 vols., Cologne, 1811–13).
[44] Sylvain Meinrad Xavier de Golbery, *Considérations sur le département de la Roër, suivies de la notice d'Aix-la-Chapelle et de Borcette. Ouvrage composé d'après les recherches de l'Auteur et les documents réunis dans les archives de la préfecture* (Aachen, 1811), pp. 501–7.

for its quota. Whilst conscription furthered centralisation and penetration by the state through the strengthening of an entire range of compulsive instruments, it also crystallised community solidarity. Resistance to the draft was always a matter of local solidarity and cohesion rather than individual choice.[45] Prefects, sub-prefects and mayors, though representatives of the state, in practice also presented the interests of their *administrés* to the tier above. To an extent, they acted as a buffer, being familiar both with the state of local opinion and versed in the arguments that would impress their superiors. Capable prefects, such as Jeanbon Saint-André of Mont-Tonnerre, Laumond, Lameth and Ladoucette of the Roër and Lezay-Marnesia of Rhin-et-Moselle, frequently petitioned Paris for an alleviation of the burden on their departments and attempted to ward off punitive methods by providing glowing reports of loyalty and devotion. Those with powerful connections in Paris, such as Lezay-Marnesia, a client of the Josephine clan in whose 'pocket' the Rhin-et-Moselle lay, stood some chance of receiving a favourable response.[46] Sub-prefects and mayors in turn petitioned prefects in an attempt to reconcile the requirements of the state with local opinion. Failure to strike a balance between the two might result in popular resistance or government repression. Fear, obduracy, humanitarianism, economic self-interest and the wish to shield clients, provoked notables into repelling, or rather, deflecting onto those at the margins, the burden of conscription. And despite its formidability, the Napoleonic state tolerated a certain degree of local interpretation of the law so long as the flow of taxes and conscripts continued. Over time the regime, in its desperation for ever more troops, increasingly ignored legality, fairness and social justice.[47]

One weakness in the law exploited by notables to protect clients was the provisions concerning exemptions. These expanded as the egalitarian principles of the Loi Jourdan-Debrel were progressively relaxed. Married men were exempt from the beginning, but were subsequently joined by the eldest sons of widows, brothers of those in uniform, and ecclesiastics.[48] Inconsistencies in the definition of this last group allowed local officials to

---

[45] Woloch, *New Regime*, pp. 412ff.

[46] Director-general of conscription to Lezay-Marnesia, 30 October 1807, HASK, Bestand 256, 6227, [nos. 11–12]. See also Ladoucette to Montalivet, 24 December 1810, AN, F^{IC}I, dossier 25, no. 335, and Ladoucette to Savary, 14 May 1813, AN, F^{7}3609, 'Roër 1806–1813', [no. 21].

[47] Forrest, *Conscripts*, pp. 36, 40–1.

[48] Married men needed to prove they had wed at least one day before the law mobilising their class arrived in their department. For the extension of exempt categories in general, see François Monnier, 'Conscription', in Jean Tulard (ed.), *Dictionnaire Napoléon* (Paris, 1987), p. 470. Also, Forrest, *Conscripts*, pp. 53–6.

arrive at a definition broader than that intended by the government, whilst the provision concerning married men led to the emergence of an entire industry built up to exploit this loophole, replete with professional wives and marriage brokers.[49] Scope for skulduggery was also provided by the system through which the physically unfit were weeded out. Hargenvilliers described the medical examination process as the most important element of conscription – and the most abused.[50] The director-general estimated that only one in six conscripts should be discharged for medical reasons, though this proportion might vary regionally depending on the physique of the local population. In Brittany, for example, 50 per cent of young men failed to meet the height requirements. According to statistics relating to the years IX to XIII (1800–1805), the average discharge rate for France as a whole was 32 per cent, with the Rhineland managing a creditable 26 per cent. Far from declining, this rate increased over time, both in France as a whole, which averaged 36 per cent between 1806 and 1810, and in the Rhineland, where exemptions spiralled to 40 per cent.[51] Military surgeons contended with the most ingenious attempts at faking ill-health. Removal of the front teeth – used for biting open paper cartridges containing the musket ball and powder – and of the right index finger – for pulling the trigger – were only the most common forms of self-mutilation.[52] Within the Rhineland, the majority of exemptions were granted for failure to meet the statutory height requirements, whilst many others were discharged for the somewhat vague reason of having a 'weak constitution'.[53]

The government progressively centralised conscription to stamp out abuses, transferring responsibilities from locals to more reliable bureaucrats and army officers. In August 1802, it removed responsibility for sub-dividing quotas between the districts and cantons from the departmental and district councils to the prefects and sub-prefects. Paris also established departmental recruitment councils made up of the prefect and army officers but no local representatives. These could reverse exemptions granted by the municipalities, a responsibility formerly exercised by local councils composed

[49] Prefectoral (Roër) circular of 13 Pluviôse XI (1 February 1803), *Recueil* (1802/3), part 2, p. 86. For the 'marriage industry', see Forrest, *Conscripts*, p. 51.

[50] Vallée, *Compte général*, p. 25.

[51] *Ibid.*, pp. 28–31. AN, AFIV 1124, 'Compte général sur la conscription depuis l'établissement de la Direction, jusqu'au 1er Janvier 1811'.

[52] For a fascinating early-nineteenth-century account of ingenuity in faking illness, and the challenge this represented to the military surgeon, see Henry Marshall, *Hints to young Medical Officers of the Army on the Examination of Recruits; . . . with official documents and the regulations for the inspection of Conscripts for the French and Prussian Armies* (London, 1828).

[53] For a list of exemptions from the Roër's *chef-lieu* see, STAA, RA II no. 391.

of fathers of serving conscripts assisted by a government representative and doctor.[54]

Yet bribery, clientage, exploitation of legislation on exemptions, falsification of medical examinations and inter-departmental rivalry undermined conscription even in later years. In 1813, the general in charge of recruitment in the Gironde reported that sons of rich Bordeaux families were still able to secure bogus medical exemptions, whilst the local prefect complained that if medical notes were to be believed, the entire population must be hospitalised.[55] One scandal, exposed in Cologne in 1812 by the special police commissioner, serves as an example for many other cases that could be related on account of its inclusion of all the most popular methods of draft evasion. The scandal centred around a certain Müller, whose tutor attempted to 'purchase' his discharge with the co-operation of officials in the sub-prefecture. These placed Müller in the category least likely to be called up on the spurious grounds that he was the eldest brother of orphans. This falsity was discovered and Müller compelled to participate in the draw. When he drew an unlucky number, the officials resorted to bribing the recruitment council, whilst a doctor named Kruse helped Müller fake various deformities in return for 1,500 francs. Kruse, according to Cologne's special police commissioner, enjoyed 'great influence' with the departmental recruitment council and exploited this 'for affairs of the same nature, which have earned for him considerable sums'. The commissioner, who reported directly to the police ministry, warned against involving the local sub-prefecture in his investigation, as it had covered up the affair and could not be trusted. Instead, he interrogated Müller in person, as the suspect possessed a fortune of 9,000 francs and might 'make use of [this as a] means of seduction, [something] he appears accustomed to employ and which the Germans [*sic*] have great difficulty in resisting'. Far from supporting the commissioner, the prefect, Ladoucette, was enraged when he discovered the secret investigation and the accusations levelled at the recruitment council chaired by himself. Ruffled feathers were hardly smoothed when the commissioner tersely informed the prefecture that he was acting under the direct authority of the police ministry. The matter now progressed beyond the fate of Müller and revolved around the responsibilities of the special police commissioners appointed by Napoleon in major cities in 1811. The relationship between the commissioners and the prefects was never clearly delineated, resulting in endless conflict. Ladoucette eventually won the tussle, and Müller was discharged. Any other decision would

---

[54] Forrest, *Conscripts*, pp. 35–47.   [55] *Ibid*., pp. 46, 48.

have impugned the prefect's authority, something Napoleon was not prepared to countenance. The distinct impression of a cover-up is reinforced
by the subsequent failure of two independent military surgeons to find
anything wrong with Müller.[56]

Müller, given his fortune, might have done better to hire a replacement,
for Napoleonic legislation became increasingly flexible with respect to this
and the related practice of substitution. Replacement represented a legal contract that included the payment of a 100-franc tax and involved
an individual agreeing to replace somebody who was definitely mobilised.
Substitution was simply a private arrangement between individuals whereby
conscripts from the same class and locality undertook to swap their numbers before it had been decided how many would be mobilised. Revolutionary governments in the 1790s viewed replacement with ambivalence.
The *right* of replacement was conceded in the law of 28 Floréal X (18 May
1802), and so preceded the extension of conscription to the Rhineland. This
right was originally restricted, but subsequently extended until a free market for replacements existed at a national level by the end of the Empire.[57]
Criticised as one more Napoleonic retreat from revolutionary principle, the
practice drew on traditions of communal self-help in the Rhineland and
provided an opening for notables not only to avoid conscription themselves, but also extend protection to clients and thereby retrieve some lost
autonomy.

Under the Old Regime, Rhinelanders had avoided military service by offering their princes monetary compensation. This practice continued during the revolutionary wars, when localities struck deals with both the princes
and French invaders to avoid military conscription or compulsory labour
service. When electoral Cologne ordered Worringen to supply nine men
for its army in 1794, for example, the local authorities paid an indemnity
instead. Other towns in electoral Cologne collected voluntary donations

---

[56] The account of this scandal is based on the correspondence between Cologne's special police commissioner (Pauzle d'Ivoy) and Réal (head of the 1st police district) from August to October 1812,
contained in AN, F⁷3609, dossier 'Roër 1806–1813'.

[57] The law of 28 Floréal X (18 May 1802) allowed a conscript who drew an unlucky number to pay
a serving soldier with at least one year's service to remain in the army for a further five years.
Subsequent laws (18 Thermidor X (6 Aug. 1802) and 16 Floréal XI (26 April 1803)) allowed draftees
to hire substitutes from outside the army corps to which they had been assigned. The original
stipulation that only individuals from the same *arrondissement* might be hired was first tightened
by the imperial decree of 18 Nivôse XIII (7 January 1805), which limited the selection to the smaller
canton, and shortly thereafter liberalised by the decree of 8 Fructidor XIII (25 August 1805), which
allowed substitutes to be hired from anywhere in the department. Eventually, even this restriction
was lifted. Monnier, 'Conscription', pp. 466, 471. See also Forrest, *Conscripts*, pp. 58–61.

from their citizens which were then spent in neighbouring territories to 'purchase' substitutes.[58] Such practices were followed at the highest levels, with representatives of the Lower Rhenish and Westphalian military circle and the imperial city of Cologne spending most of 1793 haggling over the price they should pay in lieu of meeting their quotas. The other smaller states, lacking sufficient economies of scale to maintain their own forces, similarly provided monetary contributions.[59]

Napoleonic replacement represented, to an extent, a continuation of such practices. Legally, the provision of a replacement was a transaction between two individuals and the state, with no room for 'brokers' or corporate dealings. In practice, the French authorities proved more flexible. In the Rhin-et-Moselle department, Lezay-Marnesia openly encouraged citizens to come to arrangements amongst themselves when meeting their National Guard quotas. The drawing of lots should only take place as a last resort. Communal agreements, whereby the municipality as a whole pooled its resources to 'purchase' conscripts were more humane, he argued, because they guaranteed support for the dependants of those mobilised, thus spreading the burden evenly rather than exposing an unlucky few to complete ruin. Such a system also saved the administration much bother by eliminating appeals and requests for exemption.[60] Notarial records reveal that a veritable service industry subsequently sprang up in response to demand for insurance against the lottery of the recruitment councils' urns. This industry, with its brokers, bloomed by the end of the Napoleonic period. It flourished especially in the Lower Rhine, where wealthy manufacturers encouraged replacement as a means of retaining skilled workers possessing trade secrets. By August 1810, the activities of 'traders in replacements' reached sufficient proportions for Ladoucette, who was less tolerant than Lezay-Marnesia, to order their detention for the duration of the call-up.[61] Even this drastic measure failed to end the trade, for in 1812 we learn of speculators travelling around the countryside buying replacements in order to sell them at a higher price in the towns. The prefectoral authorities were still ordering the arrest of such fraudsters in the final weeks of French rule.[62]

---

[58] Cardauns, *Dorfchronik*, pp. 89–90, 92–108.

[59] Hansen, *Quellen*, 2, pp. 768, 823–37, 843–8, 879–84. For electoral Cologne specifically, see Karl Essers, *Zur Geschichte der kurkölnischen Landtage im Zeitalter der französischen Revolution (1790–1797)* (Gotha, 1909), p. 76.

[60] Landeshauptarchiv Koblenz (LHAK), Bestand 256, 6229.

[61] Ladoucette to Dumas (director-general of conscription), 20 August 1810, AN, F⁷3609, dossier 'Roër 1806–1813', [no. 43].

[62] *Ibid.*, [nos. 151, 243].

Notables, including local officials, were involved in replacement. Amongst those exposed at a relatively early stage were the mayors of Hörstgen, Suchtelen and Viersen (Roër), all involved in scandals that came to light in 1806. Mayors were well positioned to act as contractors by providing young men with fraudulent certificates enabling them to offer themselves as replacements and then 'selling' them to clients. Hörstgen's mayor accepted 593 francs for such a contract, recorded for posterity in the careful hand of a notarial clerk as if it were legal. In Suchtelen, the municipal administration contracted an entrepreneur to furnish ten replacements for local conscripts at the price of 400 *écus* per head. The dealer recruited Austrian and Prussian deserters. The mayor provided them with fake certificates which made out they were conscripts who had fulfilled their obligations and could therefore act as substitutes. The prefect Lameth ordered the arrest of the replacements, middle man and mayor, and urged Paris that an example be made on the grounds that a very large number of mayors were engaged in similar activities.[63] Other mayors set up insurance schemes to which families contributed to finance the purchase of replacements. Viersen's scheme collapsed after those outside the scheme all drew lucky numbers, with the result that the fund was insufficient to purchase enough replacements for all those called up. These, believing themselves exempt, failed to respond when mobilised and were condemned as 'draft dodgers'. The mayor, for his efforts, was fined 500 francs plus costs, sentenced to six months imprisonment and appeared prominently in one of Fouché's police reports presented to Napoleon. Lameth circulated printed extracts of the trial and sentence to all communes as a warning.[64] Yet despite the risk, officials continued to involve themselves in shady dealings. A list of twenty suspected dealers in replacements arrested in the Roër in 1811 included a serving JP, former mayor, and former municipal secretary.[65]

Replacements fluctuated widely in price over time, reflecting the burden of conscription and its relative unattractiveness. Possibly, such fluctuations stimulated wider awareness in international affairs.[66] Examination of 100

[63] For Hörstgen, HStAD, Schloß Kalkum, Notarial Akten, Rep. 326,3 (Notary Houben of Xanten), no. 485. For Suchtelen, Lameth to Fouché, 6 October 1806, AN, F⁷3609, dossier 'Roër 1806–1813', [no. 10].

[64] Extract from the minutes of the imperial secretariat of state, 23 September 1806, AN, F¹ᵇII Roër 2. An extract of this trial, in the form of a broad-sheet printed in German and French, survives in HASK, FV 3103, 2. For Fouché's report to Napoleon on the affair, see Ernest d'Hauterive (ed.), *La Police secrète du Premier Empire: Bulletins quotidiens adressés par Fouché à l'Empereur, 1804–1810* (5 vols., Paris, 1908–64), 3, no. 43.

[65] Réal to Ladoucette, 1 April 1811, AN, F⁷3609, dossier 'Roër 1806–1813', [no. 62].

[66] Eugen Weber, *Peasants into Frenchmen. The Modernization of Rural France 1870–1914* (London, 1977), p. 294.

Table 2. *Average price, in francs, of substitutes in the Roër, 1806–1813*

Year	Average Price	Highest Price	Lowest Price	No. of contracts
1806	1,067	1,480	592	9
1807	1,767	2,547	889	15
1808	1,854	2,573	1,500	14
1809	1,714	3,600	592	12
1810	1,277	1,650	870	4
1811	2,902	4,214	2,073	10
1812	2,381	3,900	1,200	22
1813	3,192	7,540	1,270	14

Source: HStAD, Schloß Kalkum, Notarial Akten, Reps. 326 (Notary Houben of Xanten), 2873–5 (Notar Hoven of Cologne), 287–8 (Notar Hopmann of Cleves) and 2685 (Notar Rüttgers of Düren).

contracts from notarial records in the Roër department (table 2) indicates that the fluctuations followed the same pattern as those provided by Alain Maureau for Avignon.[67]

The number of contracts peaked in 1807 before falling back to a low in 1810, and then rising to a new high in 1812 before falling back slightly. The average price of replacements followed a similar pattern: relatively high in 1807–8, low in 1809–10, and very high in 1811–13. The high average price in 1813 coupled with the decline of contracts indicates a fall in the supply of replacements rather than any decrease in demand for their services. The final year of Napoleonic rule witnessed the collapse of replacement as a safety valve. To put the prices in perspective, an agricultural worker earned about fifty centimes a day, an urban artisan one franc, and an adult cotton weaver one franc fifty centimes.[68] However, until 1813 at least, even Rhinelanders with relatively modest means – notarial records reveal labourers, farmers, boatmen and clog-makers – insured themselves against the lottery of the draft by forming syndicates.[69] The contracts between the syndicates and replacements were often quite complicated, reflecting the macabre calculations made of the likelihood of injury or death in Napoleon's army. Some contracts included the provision for annual pensions in the case of a replacement returning wounded.[70] In 1813, replacements increasingly demanded

---

[67] Alain Maureau's figures for Avignon are quoted in Forrest, *Conscripts*, p. 59.
[68] H. Milz, *Das Kölner Großgewerbe von 1750–1835* (Cologne, 1962), p. 92.
[69] HStAD, Schloß Kalkum, Notarial Akten, Rep. 287 (Notary Hopmann of Cleves), nos. 498, 514.
[70] *Ibid.*, no. 182.

payment in foreign currency, reflecting the perilous position the Napoleonic Empire found itself in.[71] Such subtleties reflected the complexities of the replacement market and the commercial acumen of Rhinelanders.[72]

Many contracts concerning the provision of replacements by officials acting as intermediaries were witnessed by notaries, indicating they were considered perfectly legal.[73] A conclusive account of the scale of this practice in the Rhineland awaits detailed analysis of all the relevant notarial records. The general view for France as a whole is that about 5 per cent of those conscripted were replacements. The practice was more common in the Rhineland, where the price of a replacement was significantly lower than in 'old France'. The colonel of the 9th Cuirassiers, stationed in the region, complained to the war minister in 1804 that most conscripts from the area were replacements whose only motivation was to receive their money and then desert. Indeed, many were professional deserters, including from foreign armies. The colonel requested that no more conscripts from the recently annexed departments be sent to his regiment, as a seventh of the last batch had deserted in a few months.[74] The general direction of conscription informed Napoleon in January 1811 that 8 per cent of Rhenish conscripts called up between 1806 and 1810 were in fact replacements, with the wealthy Roër department averaging close to 9 per cent, double the rate for France as a whole.[75] This suggests the existence of a commercialised market in replacements, as would emerge in France under the Restoration and July Monarchy. Whilst in the interior departments, substitution and replacement met with resentment from those lacking the means to escape service, there is little evidence of such hostility in the Rhineland. The tradition of purchasing replacements in lieu of performing military duty, plus the commercial acumen of the region, are explanations of why this was the case. Against this context, the victory of the Napoleonic state in

---

[71] *Ibid.*, Rep.160,13 (Notary Efferz of Cleves), no. 114.

[72] Following the collapse of French rule, the question arose as to the validity of replacement contracts. The Austro-Bavarian occupation authorities issued an ordinance on 21 February 1815 which ruled that those substituted could not demand any money back that had already been paid out, whilst those replacements discharged on account of their wounds, or the families of those killed, must be paid the full amount agreed. In other cases, the amount due would be calculated according to the proportion of the expected five-year term the replacements actually spent with their regiments before the 30 May 1814 (First Treaty of Paris). LHAK, Bestand 371, 549.

[73] For examples, see HStAD, Schloß Kalkum, Notarial Akten, Rep. 287 (Notary Hopmann of Cleves), nos. 4 and 246 respectively, and Rep. 2874 (Notar Hoven of Cologne), no. 7420.

[74] Colonel of the 9th Cuirassiers to Berthier (minister of war), 6 June 1802, AG, C^{10} 1, D1, no. 124.

[75] AN, AFIV 1124, 'Compte général sur la conscription depuis l'établissement de la Direction, jusqu'au 1er Janvier 1810'. The figure of 8.2 per cent for the two Alsatian departments was also comparatively high.

imposing its will must be qualified. Certainly, the state got its conscripts, but the management of their supply was partly on Rhenish terms.[76] Replacement smoothed the conscription process. Significantly, its incidence was highest in those departments that made the greatest contribution to the Napoleonic war effort: the departments of the north and east, with their tradition of soldiering. In contrast, departments with the highest incidence of draft evasion and desertion were also those with the lowest level of replacement. In the Rhineland at least, dealers in replacements 'purchased' young men in the countryside in order to 'sell' them in the towns where they commanded a higher price. Whilst the Rhineland can hardly be said to have enjoyed an especially strong military tradition – its small states maintained only tiny armies in the eighteenth century, geared towards policing and representational duties – it was nonetheless a centre of the soldier trade, with the British, Dutch, Prussians and Austrians all recruiting in the region. The Dutch extended their activities even into the Napoleonic period. A ready supply of potential replacements existed on the right bank and, as already shown, Rhenish mayors collaborated with dealers by the provision of bogus certificates in tapping this supply. Overall, the structure of the replacement industry reinforces the sociological thesis that the Napoleonic Empire functioned best in commercial, urbanised regions, such as the Rhenish departments.

Despite replacement, desertion and draft dodging remained the only means of escaping military service for the majority.[77] The two *comptes généraux sur la conscription*, drawn up by the directorate for conscription in 1808 and 1810, and covering the periods 1798 to 1805 and 1806 to 1810 respectively, include detailed statistics on desertion and draft dodging. They are broken down by department, allowing for comparison between regions of the French empire over time.

Draft dodging rather than desertion posed the greater problem in the Rhineland, accounting for about a third of those mobilised, compared to the national average of 21 per cent (1800/1–1804/5) and 31 per cent (1806–10). The vast majority of these, perhaps 90 per cent, simply failed to present themselves for medical examination and the drawing of lots in the cantonal *chefs-lieux*. Desertion, on the other hand, was less of a problem, averaging only 13 per cent of those mobilised from years 1800/1

---

[76] For substitution in France as a whole, including the prices of replacements in other departments, consult Woloch, *New Regime*, pp. 397–404, 411–26.

[77] A deserter was a soldier who illegally left his unit. A draft dodger was someone who failed to present himself for conscription.

Table 3. *Draft dodgers and deserters, Year IX (1800/1) to 1810*

	Rhenish departments[a]	Alsatian departments[b]	French Empire[c]
Mobilised, Years IX–XIII (1800/1–1804/5)	9,081	7,921	313,616
Mobilised, 1806–1810	24,186	13,933	530,219
Draft dodgers, Years IX–XIII (1800/1–1804/5)	2,763 (30%)	615 (8%)	65,220 (21%)
Draft dodgers, 1806–10	8,138 (34%)	2,386 (17%)	162,831 (31%)
% of draft dodgers arrested, IX–XIII (1800/1–1804/5)	6	13	11
% of draft dodgers arrested, 1806–10	8	17	20
Deserters, Years IX–XIII (1800/1–1804/5)	1,203 (13%)	1,813 (23%)	87,288 (28%)
Deserters, 1806–1810	725 (3%)	1,843 (13%)	64,100 (12%)

[a] Roër, Mont-Tonnerre, Rhin-et-Moselle and Sarre departments.
[b] Bas-Rhin and Haut-Rhin departments.
[c] Excluding the Italian departments of Arno, Méditerranée, Ombrone and Vicariats de Pontrenoli.
Source: Vallée, *Compte général*, pp. 38–41, 72–9, and AN, AFIV 1124.

to 1804/5 and an impressive 3 per cent for 1806 to 1810. This compared favourably both with the Alsatian departments and France as a whole. Research on the Napoleonic Kingdom of Italy suggests that deserters generally abandoned their units within the first fourteen to eighteen months, but rarely afterwards.[78] Most Rhinelanders who strongly opposed conscription dodged the draft rather than deserted and, it appears, stood a good chance of evading arrest.

The proximity of the Rhine frontier was probably crucial in accounting for the relatively high incidence of draft dodging, a hypothesis reinforced by the fact that the Sarre – poor, hilly and sparsely populated, that is, ideal bandit country, yet also the one Rhenish department not bordering the Rhine – had the best record. The border offered a unique opportunity for evasion thanks to the lack of co-ordination between the French authorities and those of neighbouring states. Newly established frontiers failed to eliminate seasonal migration, be it in the Pyrenees, or along the Rhine, across which large numbers of apprentices continued to travel as part of

[78] For the example of Italy, see Schneid, *Soldiers*, pp. 90–103, 126–30. Also, Josef Smets, 'De la coutume à la loi. Le pays de Gueldres de 1713 à 1848' (Montpellier III Doctorat d'Etat, 1994), pp. 646–9.

their training. For the Napoleonic state such movement was unwelcome in creating additional administrative problems.[79] On average, only one gendarme covered every league of frontier. Regimental commanders warned repeatedly that Rhenish conscripts stationed for prolonged periods near the river fled into Germany and found employment, whilst Paris complained that local police in riverain communities connived with deserters crossing the Rhine, or at least demonstrated gross incompetence.[80] Evidence suggests that at least some deserters and draft dodgers made a living through smuggling, in return for protection. Smuggling proved an ideal means of survival, as it was a socially acceptable form of criminal activity; alternatives risked alienating the wider population, upon whom deserters and draft dodgers were ultimately dependent. On occasion, local authorities and even *douaniers* were involved in illegally harbouring fugitives.[81]

The French employed greater repression to prevent evasion. They restricted freedom of movement through a system of internal checks and frontier controls. Rhinelanders wishing to cross into Germany required passports issued by the prefecture – documents prepared by mayors were invalid – stating they had met their military obligations. Bulging files in police archives attest to the frequent harassment of young men at the frontier. In particular, such restrictions disrupted the traditional ties that Rhenish apprentices maintained with Germany.[82] Within the departments, draft dodgers and deserters needed to defeat a multi-tiered security apparatus. At the lowest level, they encountered the village mayors, and in the larger towns professional police inspectors. In addition, the prefects disposed of special budgets for the employment of secret police. The entire security establishment was tightened up in 1804 with the re-establishment of the police ministry, under Fouché, and division of France into four police districts. The Rhineland was assigned to the 1st, under the councillor of state Pierre François Réal. Prefects reported to Fouché on all matters relating to security, often on a daily basis. The system was further reinforced in 1811 with the appointment of about thirty *commissaires spéciaux de police* to strategic points throughout the empire, including one each in Mainz

---

[79] Hudemann-Simon, 'Réfractaires', pp.12–13, 39–41; Forrest, *Conscripts*, pp. 84–9. On the other hand, the level of draft dodging in the riverain Alsatian departments averaged less than a third of the Rhenish in the Years IX–XIII and under one half from 1806 to 1810.

[80] Klespe (sub-prefect of Cologne) to Wittgenstein (mayor of Cologne), 17 May 1804, HASK, FV 3051, no. 2. For the Rhin-et-Moselle department, see LHAK, Bestand 256, 88, no. 157.

[81] AG, C¹⁰ 1, D1, no. 124. AN, F⁷3609, dossier 'Roër 1806–1813', [nos. 45–6]. HASK, Bestand 256, 6227, [nos. 5–7].

[82] For apprentices arrested by Cologne's police whilst attempting to cross the Rhine, see HASK, FV 3020.

and Cologne. They reported directly to the police ministry and, as noted earlier, often found themselves in conflict with the prefects.[83]

Statistically, deserters and draft dodgers stood the greatest chance of arrest by the gendarmerie. Garrisoned separately from the population, it totalled 15,500 men in the empire in 1809, with 527 stationed in the Rhineland after its introduction in 1798. Most gendarmes were mounted, and grouped into 'brigades' of five men commanded by a junior officer. These in turn formed companies, covering single departments, and squadrons, two of which patrolled the four Rhenish departments, which formed the 25th gendarmerie 'legion'. About a quarter of the gendarmes stationed in the Rhineland were locals, and even native Frenchmen serving were supposed to have a knowledge of German.[84] Mayors, as well as sub-prefects and prefects, could summons the gendarmes if they feared a breakdown of order. As part of the struggle against draft dodging and desertion, the gendarmerie carried out regular sweeps of the countryside, and searches of private homes and manufacturing establishments. Manufacturers harbouring such fugitives received heavy fines. Yet, despite their efforts and those of other security forces, only 7 per cent of draft evaders were arrested in the Rhineland, as compared with 16 per cent for France as a whole.[85]

As we shall see in chapter 8, the security apparatus was reinforced in 1813, as Coalition forces advanced through Germany. Even then, the government succeeded only in containing evasion rather than preventing it completely. The government therefore fell back on a carrot-and-stick policy of offering amnesties followed by the deployment of dreaded mobile columns to collectively bully communities into surrendering the intransigent. Mobile columns consisted of soldiers and gendarmes who swept through the departments, flushing out deserters, draft dodgers, and any other social flotsam they might net. They were garrisoned at the expense of communities being administered punishment and where possible, on the relatives of deserters and draft dodgers. In practice, these were usually too poor to meet the expense of forced billeting, or pay other fines imposed upon them. Of the twenty-nine families of condemned draft dodgers in Cologne in 1807, for example, only five owned any property which could

---

[83] The best account of policing in the Napoleonic Rhineland is provided by Hansgeorg Molitor, *Vom Untertan zum administré. Studien zur französischen Herrschaft und zum Verhalten der Bevölkerung im Rhein-Mosel-Raum von den Revolutionskriegen bis zum Ende der Napoleonischen Zeit* (Wiesbaden, 1980), p. 118–29.

[84] Hansen, *Quellen*, 4, pp. 521 n. 2, 959 n. 3. For later gendarmerie strengths, see AG, C¹⁰60, dossier '15 Novembre', n. 6 (unpaginated).

[85] AN, AFIV 1124, 'Compte général sur la conscription depuis l'établissement de la Direction, jusqu'au 1ᵉʳ Janvier 1810'.

be confiscated.[86] Those with means generally purchased replacements, as the alternative was probably long-term economic disaster and the loss of security parents hoped for in old age. Even forced billeting and fines were worth enduring to prevent this.

The French twice deployed mobile columns in the Rhineland on a large scale, first in 1811, following the expiry of the amnesty decreed on 25 March 1810 and as part of the mobilisation for the Russian invasion, and in 1813, to make good the losses suffered during the invasion. Their use was interpreted as a threat to both the population and local authorities, who usually pleaded against their employment. The weeks before their scheduled arrival were marked by frantic efforts to round up deserters and draft dodgers, including the imposition of forced billeting and other measures of *haute police* to forestall worse.[87] Collective punishment, Napoleon believed, stimulated popular pressure on recalcitrant parents to reveal their sons' whereabouts. Dormagen's chronicler recorded how in June 1811 a column, comprising thirty-four gendarmes, were billeted on his town at local expense. The cost was 235 francs every five days, in addition to the cost of the gendarmes' provisions and wages. The mayor responded swiftly (and illegally), imprisoning the parents of the deserters until they betrayed the whereabouts of their sons. This they eventually did and the mobile column evacuated.[88] In nearby Cologne, the municipality responded to similar pressure by circulating inflammatory fly-sheets, which included details of the costs that would be imposed on the community, and encouraged citizens to provide information by guaranteeing confidentiality and offering rewards. A list of the draft dodgers and their parents was included, whose popular victimisation the general tone of the fly-sheets did much to encourage. The likelihood of draft dodgers being denounced depended largely on the community's cohesion.[89] The deployment of mobile columns achieved considerable success. The column deployed to the Roër in 1813, for example, reduced the number of deserters and draft dodgers in the department from 2,000 to 670 in a few weeks.[90]

Captured deserters and draft evaders were marched back to one of eleven specially created military depots under heavy guard, their escorts under strict orders to shoot those attempting to escape. Not even those confined

[86] HASK, FV 3023, no. 10.
[87] For the operation of mobile columns in the Sarre in 1811, see LHAK, Bestand 276, 1983. For the district of Cologne, HASK, FV 3044.
[88] Cardauns, *Dorfchronik*, p. 208.   [89] HASK, FV 3042.
[90] Report from the ministry of war, 15 August 1813, and General d'Hastrel (director-general of conscription) to General Clarke (minister of war), 12 October 1813, AG, C¹º136.

to hospital beds were allowed to remain behind, but were transported to the interior in requisitioned carts.[91] The penalties they faced depended upon the precise circumstances of their crime; draft dodgers, who were tried before civilian courts, could expect a 1,500-franc fine and a five-year sentence in a depot. The penalty for desertion, which was tried before special *conseils de guerre*, varied from two years' hard labour for simple desertion to ten years in the hulks for those deserting on foreign soil or with their equipment. Capital punishment was prescribed for those deserting to the enemy.[92]

Mobile columns proved relatively successful. The great drive implemented in 1811 came close to grinding down opposition to conscription. On one level, this marked another advance in the onward march of the state, though another possible explanation for success might be the economic crisis of that year that made military service more attractive. On another level, the use of collective punishment revealed the continued reliance of the state on local elites and the inability of the state to establish a direct relationship between itself and the individual citizen. One can thus agree with Alan Forrest's final observation with regards to conscription, namely that it revived village archaisms and jeopardised the new civic order that Napoleon attempted to construct.[93]

This conclusion appears more convincing following recent research into compulsory military service elsewhere in Europe. Even in eighteenth-century Prussia, conscription was not simply about brutal state power as represented by the corporal's stick. Rather, compulsion was the last resort, employed only if the acceptance of volunteers and those deemed burdensome on the community failed to raise sufficient numbers. The Prussian authorities too demonstrated a preference for the devolution of the process. Nor can the scope for legal redress in the Prussian courts be entirely dismissed. The image of the 'socially disciplined' or 'socially militarised' Prussian peasant, brutalised into submission, as is provided in the older literature, is thus overturned. The attempt to apply the same concept – 'social disciplining' – to Napoleonic France must be treated with similar reservation. Bureaucratic routine over generations, not the dramatic appearance of a mobile column for a few weeks, alone could achieve such a fundamental social transformation.[94]

---

[91] General de Bon to the commander of gendarmerie in the Sarre, 22 May 1811, LHAK, Bestand 256, 6227, [no. 121].
[92] Forrest, *Conscripts*, p. 188.   [93] *Ibid.*, p. 237.
[94] Peter H. Wilson, 'Social Militarization in Eighteenth-Century Germany', *German History* 18 (2000), pp. 1–39, 117–18.

Napoleon's regular army was recruited nationally. However, it was not the only military establishment in France, though it has received almost all the attention. Mention must be made of the National Guard, a territorially organised paramilitary force mobilised to reinforce internal security and augment the regulars in time of crisis.[95] On active service, it was subject to military discipline. Public officials were exempt from service in its ranks. Napoleon was suspicious of the National Guard, a force steeped in the revolutionary tradition and tied to the localities. Its introduction in the Rhineland was delayed until 1805, when war created a need for additional manpower. Napoleon decreed (29 September 1805) all citizens aged between twenty and sixty as eligible for National Guard duty.[96]

Paris's plans for the National Guard's introduction at a time of war with Austria caused more consternation in the Rhineland than the earlier imposition of conscription. The Rhin-et-Moselle's prefect, Lameth, questioned whether it was 'politic', whilst a police report from Aachen stated Napoleon's decree created considerable public disquiet. A report from Cologne stated that burghers in the city intended to renounce their French citizenship and emigrate so as to avoid mobilisation.[97] The authorities, to dispel public fears, forced priests to read out appeals that stressed the National Guard would be used for home defence only, that the duty of the rich was to assist in preserving order, and that the Great Terror had occurred when they had forgotten this duty.[98] Rhinelanders remained sceptical, and saw the National Guard as a device for recruiting cannon-fodder. Mayors hesitated in supplying parish registers listing those eligible for duty, fearing reprisals. Some received death threats, others were assaulted or saw their houses attacked by armed bands numbering as many as fifty, and at least one was assassinated.[99] A police report reaching Fouché from the Roër explained the reasons for the upsurge in opposition:

---

[95] The duties of the National Guard were laid out in the report from the section of the interior of the Council of State, 26 Fructidor IX (12 September 1801), AN, 29 AP 75, no. 182. This reiterated, in its essentials, article 48 of the constitution of year VIII (13 December 1799).

[96] The report from the interior minister to the Consuls of 10 June 1802 expressed concurrence with the decision to postpone the mobilisation of the National Guard in the Rhenish departments, though no specific reason was given. AN, F^{1c}43, no. 98.

[97] Lameth to Champagny, 17 November 1805, LHAK, Bestand 256, 6229. Also, AN, F^{7}3686^9, 'Bulletin de Police', 13 October 1805 and 25 October 1805. With respect to Cologne's prospective emigrants, the police minister recognised their theoretical right to change their residence, but noted that 'current circumstances' and their motives necessitated a ruling from the Council of State. Fouché to the Council of State, 29 October 1805, AN, F^{7}3617.

[98] *Recueil* (1806), pp. 81–4.

[99] Police bulletins and reports from the inspector general of gendarmerie to the police minister, 2 December 1805 to 3 April 1806, AN, F^{7}3686^9.

These lands were formerly either under the control of Prussia, the ecclesiastical authorities [or] imperial regencies, and everywhere voluntary contributions and replacements recruited from abroad substituted compulsory service. Everywhere, one gave money instead of soldiers, so that the military spirit is absolutely zero and the inhabitants do not even hide their aversion to the dangers of war…in these conditions the organisation of the National Guard would be extremely difficult even in ordinary times.[100]

In the former Hohenzollern duchies, there were fears that Prussia would join Austria, and that those serving in the National Guard would be treated as rebels. Lameth reported to Marshal Lefebvre, commander of the National Guard contingents, that a large number of communes in the Rhin-et-Moselle department formally opposed the mobilisation. He had been compelled to deploy troops to re-establish order, 'the resistance and spirit of disobedience having spread with extreme rapidity.' He doubted the deadline for the supply of the Rhin-et-Moselle's contingent could be met.[101] Only Napoleon's decisive victory at Austerlitz, which came just before the Rhenish National Guards were fully mobilised, relieved some of the pressure.

Opposition to the National Guard re-emerged with the outbreak of the Prussian war in 1806, but subsided following rapid French victories.[102] Even more widespread resistance, representing one of the biggest overt manifestations of defiance Napoleon faced within French borders, occurred during the Franco-Austrian war of 1809. During that conflict, the British attempted to assist their Habsburg allies by landing 40,000 men on Walcheren island off the Netherlands. With Napoleon and the army engaged on the Danube, Fouché – as police and acting interior minister – activated the National Guard in a display of Jacobin initiative. The mobilisation passed off smoothly in Mont-Tonnerre, the Roër and Rhin-et-Moselle. In the Sarre, it provoked large-scale disturbances in early September in three – Birkenfeld, Prüm and Trier – out of four *arrondissements*, with bands of several hundred converging on the cantonal *chefs-lieux* to sack official buildings and mishandle officials. The troubles lasted twenty-four hours, and were provoked as much by local circumstances as wider events.[103] The prefect, Keppler, ordered the gendarmerie to make many arrests, and circulated a paternalistic warning in which he blamed the rebellion on enemies who

---

[100] Report from 2nd imperial police district to Fouché, 12 November 1805. AN, F⁷3617.
[101] Lameth to Lefebvre, 17 November 1805, LHAK, Bestand 256, 6229.
[102] Lameth to Réal, 4 November 1806, AN, F⁷3617, dossier 'Roër'.
[103] Roger Dufraisse, 'Une Rébellion en pays annexé: le «soulèvement» des gardes nationales de la Sarre en 1809', *Bulletin de la Société d'Histoire Moderne* 14th series, no. 10, 68th year (1969), pp. 1–6.

had misled citizens into believing that the mobilisation was illegal because it had not been authorised by an imperial decree.

Keppler subsequently inspected the affected areas, as local reports remained vague, and ordered further arrests in October and November.[104] An infuriated Napoleon ordered Réal to investigate the disturbances. He was especially interested in the conduct of local officials and clergymen during the disturbances. Both Keppler and the sub-prefects reported that priests were not in a position to oppose their parishioners on whom they were financially dependent. As for local officials, only two distinguished themselves, including one who completed the draft barricaded inside a church brandishing two pistols against the insurgents. Overall, mayors and JPs had not dared resist the insurgents, Keppler reported. The prefect nonetheless opposed draconian retribution as unnecessarily provocative.[105]

Napoleon ignored the advice and established (on 5 December) a special military commission under General Henry, commander of the imperial headquarters guard, to conduct an investigation. The preamble to the decree reflected Napoleon's fury at the 'many communes of the Sarre... communes [that] uniquely amongst those of our vast empire have been agitated by evil doers who have compromised public tranquillity and therefore given hope to our external enemies...'[106] Investigation revealed that several mayors from the canton of Daun had a hand in the disturbances. These were arrested and interrogated by the president of the tribunal of first instance in Prüm, who rejected the accusations and ordered the mayors' release. It then emerged that most of the suspects were linked to the president of the tribunal himself, and that several judges and policemen in his pay were assisting in a cover up.[107] Further investigation ordered by the local sub-prefect concluded that the ringleaders of the original rebellion – who had circulated pieces condemning the mobilisation of the National Guard and advising young men to resist – had been protected by the local authorities. The president, together with other judges and officials were arrested, and interrogated by one of Henry's subordinates. The sub-prefect informed Keppler that the tribunal in Prüm had always shown hostility to the government in its judgements.[108]

Surprisingly, Napoleon did not act on these allegations. No officials were amongst the 300 individuals arrested. Of those arrested, fifty-seven were

---

[104] Prefecture (Sarre) to Réal, 9 October 1809, LHAK Bestand 276, 1883.
[105] Keppler to Réal, 16 November 1809, *ibid.*   [106] *Ibid.*
[107] Prudhomme (sub-prefect of Prüm) to Keppler, 22 December 1809, *ibid.*
[108] Gerhards (prefectoral councillor and acting prefect in Trier during Keppler's tour of the troubled areas) to Réal, December 1809, *ibid.*

tried before the special military commission. Sixteen were sentenced to death, twenty-eight to between eight and twelve years in irons, eleven to four months detention, and two were acquitted. Ten were subsequently executed in the *chefs-lieux* of their respective districts.[109] Keppler suggested that the other 200 prisoners, who were languishing in custody, should be conscripted and counted against the Sarre's quota. Details provided for forty-five held in Prüm reveal that most insurgents were unmarried young farm labourers, with a sprinkling of millers, shepherds, servants, charcoal burners and thatchers. They represented the rural poor. Most were subsequently released, following a petition from their parents to the new Empress, Marie-Louise, to intercede on their behalf. Keppler supported the request, playing down the rebellion as a 'momentary aberration', and implicitly blamed Fouché – who was sacked in June 1810 – for mobilising the National Guard through a ministerial ordinance, though legally it required an imperial decree.[110]

Napoleon reorganised the National Guard after 1809, transforming it into a more effective army reserve. He was concerned lest the new departments be pressed too hard and expressly ordered that their quotas be light. In July 1810, Napoleon set the basic strength of the National Guard at about 800,000 men, divided into 'armies' of 60,000 recruited from districts each containing 3 million inhabitants. As an example, Napoleon listed the individual departmental contributions to the Armée d'Anvers, which grouped together contingents from Deux-Nèthes, Escaut, Dyle, Lys, Sambre-et-Meuse, Ourthe, Meuse Inférieure and the Roër, with the latter's contribution to the 63,000-man force set at 12,000. In Napoleon's projected reorganisation, one-tenth of all National Guards would be classified 'elite', and ready for immediate mobilisation in time of crisis.[111] Part of this force was mobilised on 13 March 1812, to protect the coasts against British amphibious operations and garrison inland fortresses during the Russian invasion. These forces were raised from those remaining from the classes 1807–12. Most of the Rhenish contingents were employed in garrisoning Mainz, which they did loyally. Nonetheless, Napoleon remained suspicious of the Rhenish National Guard, which he refused to mobilise in 1813 to confront the advancing Coalition forces.

The regular army and National Guard were conscript forces, theoretically composed of a cross-section of society. In reality, most of the rich provided

[109] Keppler to Fouché, Montalivet and Réal, 26 January 1810, *ibid*.

[110] Keppler to Regnier (minister of justice), 18 May 1810, and Réal to Keppler, 25 July 1810, *ibid*.

[111] Napoleon to Montalivet (minister of the interior), 21 July 1810, Napoleon I, *Correspondance de Napoléon 1er publiée par ordre de l'empereur Napoléon III* (32 vols., Paris, 1858–69), 20, pp. 518–22.

their sons with substitutes. Napoleon responded to this by establishing units aimed at binding the wealthy to the regime. These included the Guards of Honour, which sprang up spontaneously during the Consulate and were regulated by the government in the early Empire.[112] Young men from better families joined them to dissociate themselves from the meaner orders in the National Guard and to participate in a heroic age by wearing fantastic uniforms. Napoleon always expected to be welcomed by Guards of Honour during his departmental tours and was displeased should he spot any inferior social elements among them. Rhenish notables, unlike their French counterparts, demonstrated little enthusiasm in joining: when, in 1803, the French authorities in Cologne raised Guards for Napoleon's expected visit, twenty-three of those invited to join refused on grounds of ill-health, business commitments, absence (including one in a German university), lack of money for a uniform, general circumstances, or family affairs. When Napoleon postponed his visit until 1804, a twenty-fourth candidate pulled out, claiming he had volunteered only for 1803.[113]

Most Rhinelanders neither dodged the draft nor deserted. Their experience within the most successful war machine of the age can be gleaned from their correspondence and published memoirs. Periods of boredom, consisting of garrison duty interspersed by marching, rather than glorious or gory combat, were the norm. Indeed, one can detect a certain longing for action on the part of conscripts after months of monotony. Even then, their chances of falling in combat were relatively small compared to the danger posed by disease, hunger and the elements.[114]

In all, France mobilised 2 million troops between 1800 and 1814, or 7 per cent of the population. Half never returned. The concept of 'national service' represented a novelty in the Rhineland, whose own contribution to the *impôt de sang* stood at 80,000, or one in twenty of the population.[115] The transformation was not completed overnight. Many Rhinelanders remained in foreign service, for example, despite laws forbidding this. Napoleon's own brother, Louis, as King of Holland, despatched his recruiting agents into the four departments.[116] In February 1810 Napoleon expressed his displeasure over foreign service to a Rhenish deputation in Paris paying him homage:

---

[112] Georges Carrot, 'Gardes d'Honneur', in Tulard, *Dictionnaire*, p. 778.
[113] Justus Hashagen, *Das Rheinland und die französische Herrschaft. Beiträge zur Characteristik ihres Gegensatzes* (Bonn, 1908), pp. 281–2, 284–5.
[114] Rory Muir, *Tactics and the Experience of Battle in the Age of Napoleon* (New Haven and London, 1998), pp. 4–11.
[115] J. Houdaille, 'Le Problème des pertes de la guerre', *Revue d'histoire moderne et contemporaine* 17 (1970), pp. 411–23. Smets, 'Dorfidylle', pp. 711–12.
[116] HSAK, Bestand 276, 1583.

'I desire,' he commanded, 'that those amongst your fellow citizens with children in foreign service recall them to France. A Frenchman must shed his blood only for his prince and for his *patrie*.'[117] He estimated that 10,000 'Frenchmen' remained in Austrian service and offered them an amnesty if they returned by the end of the year. Even this measure was not a complete success. In the following year, families in Cologne were still being subjected to forced billeting because their sons were serving in the Habsburg army.[118]

'Nationalisation' of military service occurred throughout Europe. In Italy, conscripts were subjected to a sustained policy of eliminating local identities in favour of a supra-regional consciousness.[119] A similar attempt at identity formation occurred in Bavaria, which introduced conscription in 1804, Württemberg (conscription introduced in 1806), and Baden (1808/9). In Württemberg, for example, the recruitment of foreigners was discouraged, foreign recruiters expelled, new national decorations introduced, subjects from the old and new territories mixed in the same units, and subjects serving abroad recalled under threat of seeing their property confiscated. At least one unfortunate Württemberger serving with the Austrians in 1809 was captured, tried by court martial for treason, and presumably shot. As in the Rhineland, the Habsburg connection remained strong: in Baden, many officers resigned their commissions in 1805 rather than fight against *their* emperor, Francis II. Yet, overall, the south German armies served loyally and effectively alongside regular French units in both the 1809 and 1812 campaigns. Conscription, though unpopular, appears to have met with little resistance, despite the fact that the south German princes not only met their treaty requirements with respect to their contingents, but exceeded them (in Württemberg's case by 50 per cent in 1809), placing a greater burden on their peoples than Napoleon on France. Further north, Westphalia – a totally new creation – similarly experienced few problems in raising an army in excess of what was required, thanks in part to a reliable gendarmerie composed almost entirely of German-speaking Frenchmen. Again, an attempt was made to forge a truly 'national' army. To an extent, this succeeded, with most of the army remaining loyal during the abortive risings of Katte, Dörnberg (an ex-Prussian officer serving in the Westphalian guard) and Schill in 1809. Less rosy was the situation in Berg. Not only was conscription hated in the grand duchy – that was hardly unique in Napoleonic Europe – but was especially hard to administer, particularly in former Prussian districts that remained loyal to the Hohenzollerns. French officials who administered Berg warned against the employment of its troops within

[117] Napoleon I, *Correspondance*, 20, pp. 174–6. See also *ibid*., 21, pp. 54–6, 285–6.
[118] HASK, FV 3042, no. 143.   [119] Schneid, *Soldiers*, pp. 90–103, 126–30.

Germany, despite the fact that German-speaking Frenchmen – mainly Alsatians – made up a significant proportion of the officer corps.[120]

States no longer regarded military service in terms of individual choice or economic transactions, but as a national affair. Yet military service in itself contributed little to the forging of a 'national' identity in this period, either in the French army or in those of its opponents. Instead, soldiers were bound to each other through an unspoken, moral code that was ruthlessly enforced.[121] Conscription transformed peasants into Frenchmen only much later, after the introduction of the 1889 conscription law which called up a larger number for a shorter period. Before then, the minority conscripted under the Loi Jourdan for five or more years who returned to their villages invariably discovered they were alienated from the rest of the community.[122] An English traveller to the Rhineland after 1815, Charles Dodd, encountered two such Napoleonic veterans in Mainz: 'raw, unhinged-looking fellows', he wrote, who appeared 'fairly denationalised, and resemble neither Frenchmen nor Germans'.[123]

Napoleon's army was never strictly 'national', even without counting the allied contingents. Germans had served in the revolutionary army, despite republican aversion for 'mercenaries'. Dormagen's chronicler observed large numbers of 'Germans' amongst the occupying French forces in 1795. These included not only Alsatians, but also foreign deserters and soldiers from the former Bourbon German regiments.[124] The disproportionately large number of Alsatian officers in the French army ensured that Rhinelanders stood a good chance of encountering German-speakers amongst their superiors and comrades. Whilst the Napoleonic army was recruited nationally rather than territorially, conscripts tended to be assigned to units whose depots were relatively close to their native departments with the result that conscripts from particular regions tended to be concentrated in certain regiments. In part, this was to diminish the physical and psychological problem of *mal du pays* – melancholy associated with acute homesickness – that had been known to decimate entire units.[125] The national element was further diluted with the incorporation of more Germans, Italians and Swiss, not to mention entire Dutch-speaking regiments, as Napoleon's empire expanded. The Napoleonic army reversed the revolutionary concept of a 'Nation in Arms'.

[120] John H. Gill, *With Eagles to Glory. Napoleon and his German Allies in the 1809 Campaign* (London, 1993 reprint), pp. 64–70, 127–34, 178–87, 217–23, 248–75, 321ff., 385–6, 411ff., 465–87.
[121] For the British army, see Muir, *Tactics*, p. 199.   [122] Weber, *Peasants*, pp. 294, 297.
[123] Charles Edward Dodd, *An Autumn Near the Rhine; or Sketches of Courts, Society, Scenery, &c. in Some of the German States Bordering on the Rhine* (London, 1818), p. 330.
[124] Cardauns, *Dorfchronik*, p. 117.   [125] Forrest, *Conscripts*, pp. 96–7.

Rhinelanders in French service were more likely to be 'praetorianised' than nationalised. During the Directory, soldiers' allegiances shifted from the nation state, which neglected them, to their commanders, who supplied them with loot. Napoleon monopolised this form of control after Brumaire. The loyalty instilled in soldiers by Napoleon as a charismatic leader remained personal and transcended national differences even after he became head of the French state. Equally significant, no doubt, was the fact that French officers led from the front, as reflected in the disproportionately high casualties they suffered.[126] The intensity of loyalty felt by Rhenish soldiers was often extreme, judging from surviving memoirs and letters. Often, this ran counter to the sentiments shared by their parents at home. Karl Schehl from Krefeld, for example, though he had experienced the rigours of the Russian campaign, reminisced years later that whilst he had wept at the news of Napoleon's downfall, his parents rejoiced. He had shared in the legendary esprit du corps of the imperial army: 'we loved all our officers,' he wrote, 'from sergeant to field-marshal; the emperor, however, we viewed as a superior being'.[127]

Such enthusiasm provided an ingredient for the later Napoleonic cult, which was preserved in the numerous Rhenish veterans' associations that sprang up from the 1830s onwards, to the Prussians' annoyance. The longevity of this legacy can be gauged from the fact that the last recorded veteran died in 1883.[128] The memory of these veterans lives on in the monuments to Napoleon's soldiers in the region's cemeteries. One, erected in the 1850s, can still be seen in Melaten in Cologne, where it sits in uncomfortable proximity to a suitably martial-looking tomb of a Prussian General von Seydlitz and to a memorial commemorating those Rhenish soldiers who defeated Napoleon's nephew in 1870.

Military conscription represented the area where the interests of state and society diverged most widely. This was especially the case in the Rhineland, where military service had previously been viewed almost as a voluntary commercial transaction, and where even during the revolutionary wars communities offered monetary payments in lieu of contingents. The absence of a martial tradition encompassed even the Hohenzollern duchies

---

[126] An estimated 60,000 French officers were killed or wounded between 1805 and 1815. Muir, *Tactics*, p. 189.

[127] Karl Schehl, *Mit der großen Armee 1812 von Krefeld nach Moskau. Erlebnisse des niederrheinischen Veteranen Karl Schehl, Krefeld* (Düsseldorf, 1912), pp. 54, 126. In addition, a small number of letters of Rhinelanders serving in Napoleon's forces survive in HASK, Bestand 256, 6225.

[128] For the Rhenish veterans' societies, see Walther Klein, *Der Napoleonkult in der Pfalz* (Munich and Berlin, 1934).

of the Lower Rhine. Napoleon eventually extended the Loi Jourdan to the
Rhenish departments in 1802. The context of its introduction seemed propi-
tious enough; Napoleon's popularity was riding high. Thanks to peace, the
contingents demanded were low as a proportion of the population. Unlike
in the Vendée and Belgium, the introduction of conscription passed off
smoothly. Nor was there any significant problem over the following years,
despite the ever-increasing burden. Indeed, by the end of the Napoleonic
period, the Rhenish departments were contributing significantly more than
their fair share.

On one level, the successful enforcement of conscription might be viewed
as the triumphant imposition of state power. However, this is heavily qualified by the observation that the Napoleonic state, even through the mechanism of conscription, never established an unmediated relationship between
itself and the individual citizen that must surely represent the hallmark of
modern government. Rather, collective responsibility was reinforced, not
undermined, by conscription. For though the conscription process was progressively centralised, the local element could not be eliminated entirely.
It remained crucial. This element provided the opportunity for local elites
to deflect the burden of military service onto those on the margins, and
away from themselves and their clients. Loopholes with respect to exemptions, weaknesses in the system of medical examination and, above all, the
replacement industry were fully exploited to these ends. Draft dodging,
which remained high in the Rhenish departments throughout, attested
to the survival of communal solidarity; the proportion of draft dodgers
arrested was always dismally low, apart from those brief periods when the
French deployed mobile columns. Of course, Napoleon received his levees.
He did not break social cohesion, however. Arguably, the various weaknesses
listed above – replacement, fraud, draft dodging – represented the necessary
pressure-valves that made conscription sustainable until the system began to
unravel in the final months of 1813. Napoleon could get away with creaming
off up to about 30 per cent of males within eligible age-groups. Anything
more than that, including supplementary levees for the National Guard,
created problems. Within bounds, Napoleonic conscription proved less socially disruptive than might have been thought. That is not to diminish
the disaster it represented for the many individuals who collectively made
up the statistical raw material so valuable for the historian.

CHAPTER 7

The Rhineland and the Continental System

The Rhineland's military contribution to Napoleon's war effort, though impressive, made up but a small fraction of the total combined effort of the Grande Empire. The region's place within the so-called Continental System, the economic component of Napoleon's struggle for hegemony, was in contrast central. First, the region was one of the most industrialised within the French Empire. It thus made an important contribution to Napoleon's attempts to establish autarchy within the Empire's frontiers and French economic dominance beyond them. Second, the Rhineland's geographical location placed it on the frontline in the war against smuggling, which posed the greatest threat against the System. However, before examining this, it is necessary to look at the Rhenish economy more generally. Despite the dramatic expansion of manufacturing in parts of the Lower Rhine in the late eighteenth century, agriculture remained the most important sector within the region as a whole. Here, French rule brought three important developments: the abolition of 'feudalism' (26 March 1798), the sale of secularised lands and 'privatisation' of common rights.

The abolition of 'feudalism' in the Rhineland was less favourable to the peasantry than in France proper, but more generous than elsewhere in German-speaking Europe. The French abolished tithes, the corvée, noble administrative and judicial privileges, as well as exclusive hunting and fishing rights. They did this without requiring the payment of compensation to landlords. In addition, they granted peasants enjoying hereditary tenure full property rights over their land. However, they required that peasants compensate their landlords for dues defined as 'commercial' at the rate of twenty times (twenty-five times if paid in kind) their annual value. The government, as the greatest landowner, had a vested interest in defining 'commercial' as broadly as possible and thereby maximising the compensation payments flowing into the treasury. The result was a '*réaction seigneuriale*', with even seemingly personal obligations requiring compensation.[1]

The provisions concerning the redemption of 'feudal dues' made little difference to the overall economy. This was especially the case in the Lower Rhine, where tenants and landlords had long been bound by purely commercial obligations. Of greater significance was the secularisation of the vast holdings of the Catholic Church and their auction from 1803 onwards. Unlike in 'old France' and other parts of Germany, the authorities in the Rhineland sold these properties – *biens nationaux* – without first dividing them into smaller plots. Napoleon's aim in selling these was to maximise returns, not to engage in any social engineering. The government's decision to fix the minimum price for individual lots at twenty times their average annual revenue, which was higher than in the French interior, was further evidence of the primacy of fiscal considerations. The totals subsequently offered for sale were vast. In the Roër department alone, they amounted to 33,614,220 francs' worth of land. In all, the authorities presented 16,521 individual lots at auction in the four departments and of these 13,824 were sold.[2] This represented a total of 92,000 hectares, or 8.1 per cent of all cultivatable land. The volume of sales peaked in 1807. In addition to land, the government also auctioned off numerous ecclesiastical buildings. Many of these were deliberately sold at knock-down prices to businessmen to serve as manufactories. Finally, Napoleon also transferred a considerable amount of secularised property to the Domaine extraordinaire de la Couronne to endow the imperial nobility, Légion d'honneur, Senate and veterans. Much of this land was also subsequently auctioned off to third parties.[3]

One effect of secularisation was the destruction of the social relief provision of the Catholic Church. This brought hardship, for the state, despite some initiatives, never proved able to fill the gap in provision it had created. As for agriculture, the effects of secularisation were rather limited. The size of holdings remained largely as before, though associations of speculators (who played a large role in the initial purchase of *biens nationaux*) occasionally divided or consolidated lots to maximise their value before selling them on at a profit. As for the final purchasers, any conclusions remain somewhat imprecise, as the notarial records only provide details on

[1] Roger Dufraisse, 'De quelques conséquences économiques et sociales de la domination française sur les régions du Rhin inférieur 1794–1814', in Peter Hüttenberger and Hansgeorg Molitor (eds.), *Franzosen und Deutsche am Rhein 1789–1918–1945* (Essen, 1989), pp. 129–41.
[2] Wolfgang Schieder (ed.), *Säkularisation und Mediatisierung in den vier rheinischen Departementen 1803–1813: Edition des Datenmaterials der zur veräussernden Nationalgüter* (5 vols., Boppard am Rhein, 1991), I, p. 44.
[3] *Ibid.*

the first buyers. It seems that the most prolific purchasers of secularised properties in the Lower Rhine were members of the well-established urban elites who sat upon generations of accumulated capital. They enjoyed an additional advantage in that auctions occurred in the departmental capitals and not in the countryside. Nonetheless, wealthier farmers also purchased neighbouring plots, shoved off tenants and rounded out their holdings. The proportion of land farmed by owner-occupiers relative to tenants increased. This did not amount to a social revolution, but rather reinforced existing socio-economic conditions. Possibly the most important consequence of the sale of the *biens nationaux* was that it further blurred the distinction between town and country. Urban purchasers of secularised lots now possessed a vested interest in the countryside, something that accounts for their support for the elimination of legal and administrative distinctions between rural and urban communes under the Napoleonic system. Prussian attempts to reintroduce such distinctions after 1815 aroused widespread opposition. A slightly different though broadly comparable pattern emerged in the Middle Rhine region south of Bonn. Here, where smaller farming units (under 15 hectares) accounted for two-thirds of the total cultivated area, secularisation tended to reinforce established patterns of land-ownership rather than benefit the urban elite. In the Palatinate, for example, only one-fifth of purchasers of national property came from outside the region, and half originated from the area in which the property was located. Whilst it might be thought that secularisation diverted capital away from potentially more fruitful sectors such as trade and industry, it should be remembered that land represented security on which to take out future loans for investment elsewhere. So, on balance, it indirectly assisted developments in the non-agricultural sector.[4]

As for the privatisation of common lands, the French government proved more circumspect. Indeed, in 1798 the government passed a law forbidding indebted Rhenish communes from selling their common lands without higher authority. This policy was only reversed in the final desperate months of French rule in 1813, when Napoleon in effect confiscated and sold all communal holdings to finance the war. A related area, namely forestry policy, experienced more dramatic change. Not surprisingly, the Rhineland's forests

---

[4] Gabriele Clemens, *Immobilienhändler und Spekulanten: die sozial- und wirtschaftsgeschichtliche Bedeutung der Grosskäufer bei den Nationalgüterversteigerungen in den rheinischen Departements (1803–1813)* (Boppard am Rhein, 1995), passim. For secularisation in the Palatinate, Roger Dufraisse, 'L'Influence de la domination française sur l'économie du Palatinat', in idem, *L'Allemagne à l'époque napoléonienne. Questions d'histoire politique, économique et sociale* (Bonn and Berlin, 1992), pp. 141–3. For the Lower Rhine, Dufraisse, 'Rhin inférieur', pp. 142–4, 148–52, 154.

suffered terribly from over-exploitation during the 1790s. This was caused not only by the French army, but also by Rhenish communities that exploited the upheaval to reassert 'ancient rights'. The Napoleonic regime finally brought order to forestry administration through the establishment in 1801 of the Administration des Eaux et Fôrets and along with it the strict French forestry code that essentially dated back to Colbert. This placed severe restrictions on common usages. Less positively, the Napoleonic administration failed to undertake any grand replantings of forests to make good earlier deprivations. The lack of access to cheap wood subsequently became an increasingly serious social issue, as will be discussed in chapter 9.

Nonetheless, overall Rhenish agriculture recovered during the Napoleonic period. Encouragement of enterprise, especially agriculture, was one area where individual prefects could demonstrate initiative. Lezay-Marnesia in particular distinguished himself in encouragement of agricultural improvement.[5] Amongst various government initiatives that succeeded in boosting the sector was the introduction of clover in the highlands of the Eifel and Hunsrück, a measure that encouraged animal husbandry in these poor areas. Previously, such innovations had been hindered by legal restrictions and patterns of property ownership. Now, the replacement of the variable tithe with a fixed property tax encouraged productivity improvements. Slowly, the area under cultivation increased. In Speyer district (Mont-Tonnerre), for example, the increase was from 58 per cent of the surface area in 1800 to 67 per cent in 1813. The wider implementation of innovations initiated in the eighteenth century – new crops, stall feeding, mineral fertilisation – boosted productivity. The only area, apart from forestry, that took longer to recover was livestock farming. This too suffered immensely in the 1790s and, despite the ban on livestock exports introduced in 1800, never fully regained its pre-1792 levels even by the end of Napoleonic rule. Viticulture, in contrast, recovered quickly and even expanded in the area of cultivation. Wine remained an important export commodity from the region, with Mont-Tonnerre alone accounting for 120,000 hectolitres in an average year.[6]

More dramatic was the spread of other commercial crops, including madder, oil-seed rape and tobacco. Napoleon particularly encouraged crops that substituted for colonial produce. In September 1811, his government reserved vast tracts of land throughout the Empire for sugar beet production, including 1,000 hectares in the Rhin-et-Moselle department, 6,000

[5] Egon Graf von Westerholt, *Lezay Marnesia. Sohn der Aufklärung und Präfekt Napoleons (1769–1814)* (Meisenheim am Glan, 1958), passim.
[6] Dufraisse, 'Palatinat', pp. 105–92.

in Mont-Tonnerre and 750 in the Sarre. By 1812, Mont-Tonnerre alone counted two officially recognised experimental establishments for manufacturing sugar beet, plus thirteen private enterprises. However, as with other similar initiatives – notably, the attempted introduction of Merino sheep – the experiment in sugar beet quickly collapsed amidst bureaucratic error and ignorance of local conditions.[7]

Cereals, of which the Rhineland produced substantial surpluses, remained the most important crop. Rising prices in the eighteenth century encouraged commercialisation. Generally, the cereal harvest exceeded domestic consumption by two-thirds in an average year; the Roër's surplus alone in 1809 amounted to 2 million hectolitres (worth 25 million francs); 1813's surplus came close to 5 million. Cereal prices in the region were amongst the lowest in France. In Mont-Tonnerre, the price of a hectolitre of grain only breached the 24-franc threshold that triggered state intervention in the first six months of 1812. Improvements in cereal output were qualitative as well as quantitative, with a shift towards high-quality cereals for the production of white bread, and away from rye. However, Paris prevented the region from fully exploiting its comparative advantage: the French banned the export of cereals in 1798, though between 1804 and 1810 they allowed a limited resumption of exports to friendly countries. As transport links with the French interior were relatively under-developed, there was no alternative to traditional markets in Germany and the Netherlands.[8] Nor should one ignore the limitations of French reforms in the agricultural sector. Napoleon never completed the rural code and the agricultural landscape, with its scattered holdings and collectively determined methods and usages ('*Flurzwang*'), remained fundamentally unchanged.[9]

Restrictions on agricultural exports was one element in a trade policy dominated by the 'Continental System'. Whilst Paris extended the free market within France with measures such as the Le Chapelier Law abolishing guilds (extended to the Rhineland on 26 March 1798) and elimination of internal tolls, this policy did not extend to French-controlled Europe. With the move of the French tariff barrier eastwards to the Rhine on 1 July 1798, the river became the frontline in the economic struggle with Britain

---

[7] Jean Charles François Baron de Ladoucette, *Voyage fait en 1813 et 1814 dans le pays entre Meuse et Rhin. Suivi de notes, avec une carte géographique* (Paris, 1818), pp. 77ff. Dufraisse, 'Palatinat', pp. 167–9. Manfred Koltes, *Das Rheinland zwischen Frankreich und Preußen. Studien zu Kontinuität und Wandel am Beginn der preußischen Herrschaft (1814–1822)* (Cologne, 1992), pp. 311–13, 327–9.

[8] Johann Joseph Eichhoff, *Mémoire sur les quatre départements réunis de la rive gauche du Rhin, sur le commerce et les douanes de ce fleuve* (Paris, 1802/3), pp. 24–8.

[9] Marie-Luise Schultheis-Friebe, 'Die französische Wirtschaftspolitik im Roër-Departement 1792–1814' (Bonn D.Phil., 1969), p. 109. Koltes, *Rheinland*, p. 309.

for economic supremacy. Under Napoleon this struggle, initiated by the Directory, blossomed into the 'Continental System'. Officially instituted with the Berlin and Milan decrees (1806–7), the 'System' aimed at keeping the British out and establishing the economic supremacy of France at the expense of other Continental states. These the System treated as economic colonies whose function was to supply France with cheap raw materials and a captive market for French manufactures. To this end, the French ban on imported manufactured goods extended to all states and not just the British.[10]

Assessment of the Continental System's impact divides economic historians, though the Rhineland is generally held up as the one region which benefited most.[11] Certainly, the System could draw upon a modicum of support from some Rhinelanders, who believed Britain had grown fat on the stolen wealth of the Continent.[12] However, sectors dependent upon international commerce suffered from both the Continental System, the British blockade and the various wars in Germany. These collectively depressed trade along (though not across) the Rhine. This is revealed in statistics

[10] For French economic policy, see Geoffrey Ellis, *Napoleon's Continental Blockade: the Case of Alsace* (Oxford, 1981), pp. 104–48.

[11] A mass of literature has been lavished on the Continental Blockade and Continental System. Interpretations have been bound up with the debate between proponents of free trade and protectionists. Eli F. Heckscher, *The Continental System. An Economic Interpretation* (Oxford, 1922), remains a classic critique of the Blockade from the perspective of the former. The counter argument, that *moderate* protection was a precondition for industrial development, is posed (amongst others) in François Crouzet, 'Wars, Blockade, and Economic Change in Europe, 1792–1815', *Journal of Economic History* 24 (1964), pp. 567–88. With respect to Germany and French departments bordering Germany, it makes sense to distinguish between the Blockade (which eliminated British competition) and the System (which favoured French manufactures). Such is the approach of Marcel Dunan, *Napoléon et l'Allemagne. Le système continental et les débuts du royaume de Bavière 1806–1810* (Paris, 1942), and also Ellis, *Continental Blockade*, studies which illustrate the short-term benefits that accrued to Continental manufacturers through the elimination of British competition, but which also reveal the additional boost given to French manufacturers at the expense of their Continental rivals. Taken together, according to Crouzet and Ellis, the System and Blockade had the effect of shifting the economic centre of gravity in Continental Europe away from the Atlantic seaboard and towards the Rhine. Amongst those who stress the benefits of these developments to the Rhineland in detail is Herbert Kisch, in 'The Impact of the French Revolution on the Lower Rhine Textile Districts. Some Comments on Economic Development and Social Change', *Economic History Review* 2nd series, 15 (1962–3), pp. 304–27. Less positive in their assessment of the Napoleonic contribution are F. Schulte, *Die Entwicklung der gewerblichen Wirtschaft in Rheinland-Westfalen im 18. Jahrhundert* (Cologne, 1959), and Max Barkhausen, 'Government Control and Free Enterprise in Western Germany and the Low Countries in the Eighteenth Century', in Peter Earle (ed.), *Essays in European Economic History 1500–1800* (Oxford, 1974), pp. 212–73, both of which give due consideration to economic development achieved in the pre-French period. More recently, Koltes, *Rheinland*, reaffirms the critique that much of the growth achieved during French rule proved ephemeral and withered after 1815. This view in itself, however, does not contradict Kisch or Jeffry M. Diefendorf, *Businessmen and Politics in the Rhineland, 1789–1834* (Princeton, 1980) in their positive assessment of the wider contribution made by French institutions.

[12] Heckscher, *Continental System*, p. 53.

gathered by Johann Joseph Eichhoff, the director-general of the Rhenish Octroi. This body was established in 1805 to manage commerce on the Rhine, including the ancient trans-shipment rights of Mainz and Cologne. Its statistics show that trade was greatly undermined by war in 1805–7 and fell back further in 1809. The volume of imports into the port of Mainz, for example, declined by 42 per cent (from 1,231,200 *Zentner*, or metric hundredweight, to 711,178) between 1807 and 1809, whilst exports leaving the port dropped 44 per cent (1,490,154 to 833,462 *Zentner*) over the same period; Cologne, meanwhile, registered falls of 38 per cent (2,798,450 to 1,737,609 *Zentner*) for imports and a staggering 63 per cent (2,421,522 to 891,639 *Zentner*) for exports.[13]

Eichhoff's statistics reveal an especially dramatic decline in long-distance trade. Already in 1806/7, trade between Rhenish cities and Holland experienced a complete breakdown, the director-general wrote. According to his figures, it declined further over the following three years. The volume of goods imported into Cologne from Holland declined by 87 per cent between 1807 and 1809, and the volume of exports fell by 71 per cent, for example. Nor can this decline be blamed solely on the war of 1809 and British expedition to Walcheren, as figures for 1808 already indicate a dramatic downward trend. Imports (or more precisely, legal imports) of colonial products – coffee, cotton, tobacco, sugar – all but dried up, whilst Rhenish manufactures were hit hard by the closure of the Dutch ports. At the same time, east–west overland trade assumed a new significance, to the extent that by 1811, 19 per cent of French foreign trade passed through the Rhenish departments. Eichhoff claimed that products from a third of France passed across the river for markets in Germany – silks from Lyon, luxury goods from Paris, and wines from Burgundy, Lorraine and Champagne. A proportion of these products came along the Moselle to the Rhine, and statistics recording the movement from one river to the other suggest that this trade held up relatively well. However, this did not make up for the decline in commerce overall, something that posed a serious threat to the owners and crews of the estimated 1,300 boats engaged in trade on the Rhine.[14]

---

[13] Johann Joseph Eichhoff, *Topographisch-statistische Darstellung des Rheins, mit vorzüglicher Rücksicht auf dessen Schifffahrt und Handlung, bisherigen Zustand seiner polizeilichen Verfassung, deren mögliche Verbesserung und Ausdehnung auf die Übrigen grossen Ströme, womit ertheils schon in Verbindung steht, theils noch gebracht werden könnte* (Cologne, 1814), pp. 29, 58, 60.

[14] Apart from Eichhoff, *Darstellung*, see also Eichhoff, *Mémoire*, p. 49, and (for a list of goods imported into/exported from the port of Cologne) Ladoucette, *Voyage*, pp. 313–14. On Rhenish trade from the perspective of the Alsatian departments, see Ellis, *Continental Blockade*, pp. 129–31, 134–43, 155ff., 170–6, 192, 199–200.

Manufacturers reliant upon imported raw materials suffered. The disruption of supplies of raw material figured prominently in petitions from businessmen for a reduction or elimination of customs duties. The most important such material was raw cotton. Initially, this attracted only a modest duty, but from February 1806 Paris increased this to 60 francs per two-hundredweight, and from February 1810 to 120 francs. The government imposed still greater restrictions on spun cotton, which it banned outright from December 1809. Such restrictions placed Rhenish industry at a disadvantage to its counterparts in Germany, where the Blockade was less strenuously enforced and raw materials correspondingly cheaper. For example, in 1812 raw Louisiana cotton cost 14 francs per kilogram on the left bank, but only 6 francs per kilogram on the right bank of the Rhine. The tobacco industry, which had represented the largest industrial sector in Cologne measured by capital invested and value of output, suffered from the ban on manufactured tobacco and tobacco leaves emanating from British sources, and the restriction on the importation of leaves from elsewhere to designated entry points against payment of an ever-increasing duty. Due to this, the industry was already in decay before the *coup de grâce* was delivered with the introduction of a state monopoly in December 1810.[15]

The French blockade was never watertight. The British managed to mitigate its effects through their seizure of Heligoland in 1807, which became a huge warehouse for English manufactures destined for Germany. Only after July 1810, with the French annexation of Holland and the Hanseatic cities, and the Fontainebleau decree (18 October 1810), did the blockade become effective, and then only briefly. Smuggling and fraud, which appeared in the Rhineland with the extension of the tariff barrier, undermined the Continental System.[16] Court records and official reports suggest that it occurred on a grand scale, with at least 5,000 smugglers active between Mainz and Antwerp. The public's acceptance of smuggling is revealed by the involvement of a whole cross-section of society, from wealthy merchants and bankers to humble boaters, porters and peasants, who might earn in one night's smuggling the equivalent of a week's wages. Even lawyers and the future rector of the academy of Mainz were caught smuggling. Mayors and tavern owners often played a key role: whilst the former provided

---

[15] Roger Dufraisse, 'La Contrebande dans les départements réunis de la rive gauche du Rhin à l'époque napoléonienne', *Francia* 1 (1973), pp. 511, 514.

[16] French law distinguished between fraud and smuggling. The former was tried by 'correctional' courts and carried a maximum sentence of six months' imprisonment followed by five years' special police surveillance plus a fine equivalent to triple the value of the property seized; the latter came under the purview of the criminal courts. These imposed long prison sentences with forced labour and branding, or, in extreme cases, capital punishment.

fraudulent paperwork, the latter supplied the premises on which operations were planned and illicit wares stored. Even the army was involved, with several generals implicated. Amongst these was General Georgeon, commander of the gendarmerie in the Rhineland until his removal in 1802. On one occasion at least, troops provided military support, firing upon intruding *douaniers*. The regular courts, for their part, lost no opportunity in exploiting legal technicalities to win acquittals.[17] Smuggling eventually developed into a sophisticated industry, centred on Cologne, Mainz and Strasbourg. The great smugglers, who were rarely caught, managed operations that covered a vast area. They maintained relations with British suppliers, established great networks of warehouses outside the Empire and distribution networks within France itself. To spread risk, a special insurance company was founded in Cologne in 1808 to guard against injury and death for those involved in smuggling, and against loss of merchandise.[18]

Grain was the most common commodity illicitly exported until the relaxation of restrictions in 1804. Colonial products, especially cotton and later tobacco, made up the bulk of goods smuggled in the opposite direction. Fiscally, smuggling, or more accurately, customs fraud, deprived the French state of many millions; the authorities in Cologne estimated that the smuggling of tobacco alone cost the exchequer 3 million francs annually.[19] Economically, smuggling arguably placed smaller businesses at a disadvantage, as they were less able to finance illicit operations. The 'moral' effect of smuggling, especially with respect to popular attitudes towards law and authority, was an additional cause of concern for the government, though it is impossible to quantify. Arguably, co-operation in a common enterprise that pitted the entire social spectrum against the state reinforced social cohesion.[20]

Apart from the *douanier*, the tax-collector, in his various guises, represented the most unpopular figure in Napoleonic officialdom. Whether French or Prussian taxes were higher sparked fierce debate after 1815.[21] Certainly, the fiscal burden under the Old Regime was lighter than either. A French memoir of 1803 recorded that the Roër paid 11,138,406 francs in taxes in that year, compared to an estimated 6,250,000 under the Old Regime. However, though taxes were substantially higher under French

[17] Dufraisse, 'Contrebande', pp. 519–25. Jean Bourdon, 'La Contrebande à la frontière de l'Est en 1811, 1812, 1813', *Annales de l'Est* 5th series, 2nd year, no. 4 (1951), pp. 273–305.
[18] Dufraisse, 'Contrebande', pp. 519–20.   [19] *Ibid.*, p. 530.   [20] *Ibid.*, pp. 513, 529–32.
[21] Notably, with the publication of David Hansemann, *Preussen und Frankreich: Staatwirtschaftlich und politisch, unter vorzüglicher Berücksichtigung der Rheinprovinz* (Leipzig, 1833). This debate is discussed below, in chapter 9.

rule, they were at least distributed more equitably. This observation holds true despite the fact that property taxes fell disproportionately on land as opposed to manufacturing. Overall, property taxes remained relatively stable in the Napoleonic period, whilst indirect taxes and the *centimes additionels* steadily increased. As to the wider economic effects of fiscal policy, the key consideration is whether there was a net inflow or outflow of tax revenues into/out of the region. For this, no figures exist, though government expenditure on major infrastructure projects as well as on the entire apparatus of the French state in this strategically important frontier region would suggest an inflow.[22]

Growth in agriculture and manufacturing depended upon access to capital as well as raw materials and markets. However, the Rhineland's financial sector, which was centred on Cologne, remained undeveloped and made only a modest contribution to economic development. In the eighteenth century, Cologne's merchant-shippers started lending their accumulated capital as a side activity and it was they (not the court bankers) who represented the antecedents of nineteenth-century banking. The most important Napoleonic contribution to this sector came indirectly, through the auctioning of secularised lands. Real estate auctions led to the formation of speculative groups and the newly emerging banks supplied the capital for their operations; indeed, one of the largest of these speculative groups was headed by two prominent Cologne bankers, Herstatt and Schaaffhausen. They purchased large blocks of land which they then resold in smaller lots to clients to whom they also offered mortgages. The profits from this business – plus those from supplying the French military and lucrative smuggling operations – more than compensated for the losses incurred during the Revolutionary Wars. Herstatt's capital grew from 100,000 to 260,000 *Thalers* between 1796 and 1810, whilst Schaaffhausen's increased from 80,000 *Thalers* in 1800 to 170,000 in 1810 and 250,000 in 1818. Similar growth was recorded by other proto-banks in Cologne. Nonetheless, the role of banks in financing Rhenish industrial development in this period was negligible. Rhenish banking lagged far behind Britain's financial infrastructure. The transition to specialised banking occurred only in the 1830s and 1840s, along with the railway construction boom. Before then, manufacturers relied upon reinvestment of profits.[23] The absence of well-developed

[22] Schultheis-Friebe, 'Wirtschaftspolitik', pp. 53–77.
[23] Richard Tilly, *Financial Institutions and Industrialization in the Rhineland 1815–1870* (Madison and London, 1966), pp. 46–57. For contemporary references, T. C. Banfield, *Industry of the Rhine* (2 vols., London, 1846–8), 2: *Manufactures: Embracing a View of the Social Condition of the Manufacturing Population of their District*, pp. 192, 213–15. J. J. Eichhoff, *Mémoire sur les quatre départemens réunis de la rive gauche du Rhin sur le commerce et les douanes de ce fleuve* (Paris, 1802/3), pp. 16–25.

financial markets resulted in cash shortages throughout the French period. Smaller denominations, required to pay workers, were especially scarce so that wages were often paid in kind or else in larger denominations to groups of employees who were then forced to exchange them into smaller units at disadvantageous rates. Furthermore, a range of currencies – German, pre-revolutionary French, Dutch – remained in circulation, and would do so until the 1860s. These fluctuated against each other, with real exchange rates varying from locality to locality, depending upon trade flows and irrespective of official rates. The franc was simply one of many currencies, though after 1808 it became the only one in which taxes could be paid.[24]

Coins were not only of economic importance, but provided a visible sign of the state's presence. The same was true of infrastructure projects. Napoleon embarked upon an ambitious road construction programme throughout France. Roads fell into several categories: 'classified' roads – first- and second-class imperial routes and third-class departmental roads – funded from national and departmental funds, and non-classified routes funded locally. A decree even laid down the height of poplars to line each category and another specified that prefects and sub-prefects make annual and quarterly inspections of roads within their jurisdictions. Amongst the more important imperial routes were the Paris–Mainz and Metz–Mannheim connections, completed and managed, like the entire network, by the famed Administration des ponts et chaussées. This body was also responsible for bridges, canals and rivers as well as the introduction of new weights and measures. At the local level, prefects in effect reimposed the old *corvée* (compulsory labour service) on municipalities in order to maintain local roads. Apart from roads, the most spectacular projects included the 12 million-franc 53 kilometre-long Meuse–Rhine canal started in 1808 but abandoned following the annexation of the Netherlands, and a new all-weather harbour for Cologne to replace one destroyed in 1784.[25] Of course, superb infrastructure is no guarantor of economic vitality: as Arthur Young observed during his visit before the Revolution, France might have superb roads, but they were devoid of commercial traffic.[26] If anything, they represented a misallocation of scarce resources. However, it can be conceded that in the long term, the *absence* of decent infrastructure might hinder further development.[27]

Apart from infrastructure, the French established institutions to support trade and industry. In the 1790s, Rhenish businessmen came to prominence

[24] Tilly, *Financial Institutions*, pp. 19–29.   [25] Ladoucette, *Voyage*, pp. 82–4.
[26] Arthur Young, *Travels in France during the Years 1787, 1788 and 1789* (edited with an introduction by Jeffry Kaplow, Gloucester, Mass., 1976), p. 13.
[27] Sidney Pollard, *Peaceful Conquest. The Industrialization of Europe 1760–1970* (Oxford, 1981), pp. 125ff.

as suppliers of the army, using unofficial channels in their dealings with the invader. During the Consulate, chambers of commerce established in Cologne and Mainz (both in 1803) provided businessmen with direct access to the interior minister. They were subsequently complemented by Chambres consultatives pour les manufactures, fabriques, arts et métiers. At a national level, the Société d'encouragement pour l'industrie nationale (of which such leading Rhenish businessmen as Friedrich Heinrich von der Leyen were members) was consulted by the government on matters like the drafting of the commercial code. In addition, Napoleon established a system of commercial courts, labour arbitration boards and workers' passports, which were welcomed by manufacturers as a means of controlling a workforce that now enjoyed greater freedom in changing employer and possibly stealing trade secrets in the process.[28] The French also established a special fund to encourage deserving enterprises – Aachen cloth manufacturer Charles Nellesen was one beneficiary, receiving 10,000 francs to rebuild his plant after a fire – and industrial exhibitions where they distributed prizes for the best products.[29]

Economic expansion picked up, though it is important to remember that the Rhineland encompassed a range of economic zones that enjoyed varying experiences. The Lower Rhine blossomed. The Roër department, according to a contemporary survey, boasted a thriving non-agricultural sector employing 125,000 workers in 1,200 to 1,300 new enterprises. The department's forty-six leading manufacturers between them employed 17,000 workers, and of these a fifth were concentrated in 'special establishments' with an average of nearly eighty workers each and accounting for 23 million francs output.[30] However, despite these dramatic symbols of progress, the putting-out system remained dominant.[31] The beginnings of industrial concentration nonetheless encouraged mechanisation, which was no longer restricted by the guilds. The first power loom appeared in Aachen in 1812,

---

[28] For more on the commercial courts and labour arbitration boards, see Diefendorf, *Businessmen*, pp. 159–65; and Sabine Graumann, *Französische Verwaltung am Niederrhein. Das Roërdepartement 1798–1814* (Essen, 1990), pp. 162, 189–91.

[29] Details of Aachen's industrial competitions can be found in Ladoucette, *Voyage*, pp. 268–95. The autarchic flavour of Napoleonic policies is well illustrated in the reports submitted on the winning competitors.

[30] Sylv.-Meinrad Xavier de Golbery, *Considérations sur le département de la Roër, suivies de la notice d'Aix-la-Chapelle et de Borcette. Ouvrage composé d'après les recherches de l'Auteur et les documents réunis dans les archives de la préfecture* (Aachen, 1811), pp. 157, 363–4. J. A. Demian, *Geographisch-statistische Darstellung der deutschen Rheinlande, nach dem Bestande vom 1. August 1820* (Koblenz, 1820), p. 56. Ladoucette, *Voyage*, pp. 30–2, 233–6. Kisch, 'Textile Districts', pp. 312, 314.

[31] Michael Sobania, 'Das Aachener Bürgertum am Vorabend der Industrialisierung', in Lothar Gall (ed.), *Vom alten zum neuen Bürgertum. Die mitteleuropäische Stadt im Umbruch 1780–1820 (Historische Zeitschrift* Beiheft 14, Munich, 1991), pp. 215–16. Diefendorf, *Businessmen*, p. 156.

and the first English-type spinning mills followed, served by skilled English mechanics. Aachen, which belonged to a wider dynamic region extending to Liège and the Sambre valley, experienced dramatic growth in its metallurgical and textile industries from the late 1790s to 1810/11 – growth with 'no precedent in the history of continental Europe', according to one economic historian.[32] The output of the city's woollen industry mushroomed from 5 to 11 million francs between 1786 and 1811. Needle manufactures recorded a similar increase made possible by the introduction of new machinery. Prussian statistics from after 1814 indicated a trebling of the number of manufactories in the region around Aachen under French rule. Similar expansion occurred elsewhere in the region, notably in the vicinity of Düren.[33] The von der Leyen's textile business centred on Krefeld, the largest in the region, slowly recovered, using privileged access to the Italian market after 1806 and protection from competitors from Britain and Berg to offset the loss of other markets. By 1810, the business employed 3,000, producing 3 million francs, a figure all the more impressive when considering that the von der Leyens had lost their monopoly within Krefeld and faced competition from new textile manufacturers within the city.[34] Economic dynamism supported a burgeoning urban population in Krefeld and elsewhere. Cologne's population, which hovered around the 40,000 mark for centuries, resumed its ascent in the Napoleonic period, rising to over 56,000 by 1822. Aachen's population rose from 24,000 in 1799 to 32,000 in 1814; just over half were employed in textiles.

Economic recovery was dented by the downturn in 1810–13. Roger Dufraisse casts doubt on the traditional explanation of the crisis of these years as essentially a financial and commercial collapse brought about by a strengthening of the Continental Blockade in 1810. Rather, a series of poor harvests resulted in spiralling cereal prices from the autumn of 1809 onwards, and this depressed demand for other products. Large-scale speculation in cereals, as well as substantial purchases by the state, resulted in the export of substantial quantities from the left bank to the French interior, where basic commodities were in even shorter supply and hence commanded a higher price. This contributed further to additional inflationary pressures in the Rhenish economy and depressed the purchasing power of consumers over several years. Cereal prices remained abnormally high in the region until the end of French rule, despite satisfactory harvests

---

[32] Joel Mokyr, *Industrialization in the Low Countries, 1795–1850* (New Haven, 1976), p. 26.
[33] Koltes, *Rheinland*, p. 326.
[34] Wilhelm Kurschat, *Das Haus Friedrich & Heinrich von der Leyen in Krefeld. Zur Geschichte der Rheinlande in der Zeit der Fremdherrschaft 1794–1814* (Frankfurt a. M., 1933), pp. 44–5, 57–60, 72–4.

in 1810 and 1812, and a very good harvest in 1813. This, combined with the wider financial crisis throughout Europe, made its impact on Rhenish industry from about 1811 onwards. The crisis hit different sectors to varying degrees and at different times. Metallurgy was hardly affected. The picture was less rosy with respect to textiles, and in particular, cotton. Whilst in previous years, cotton weaving and spinning registered spectacular gains in output, so now it experienced a collapse. In Cologne, for example, the volume of cotton spun and woven fell to a mere fifth of its 1810 level in the last four months of 1813. Unemployment spiralled.[35] Attitudes amongst Rhenish businessmen towards the regime started to sour. At a banquet in Cologne in January 1811, attended by representatives of the economic elite, few responded to a toast to Napoleon and one even dared call out, 'We do not drink the health of the man who ruins us.'[36] Given that the economic downturn coincided with Napoleon's Fontainebleau decree (18 October 1810) instituting the so-called 'customs terror', with its burning pyres of confiscated contraband, it was hardly surprising that the government should be blamed for the economic crisis.

The downturn of 1810–13 might be dismissed as a traditional subsistence crisis that represented but a temporary dip on an upward curve. A more fundamental criticism of the Napoleonic economic achievement is that the manufacturing that developed within the hothouse climate of the Continental System proved too fragile to withstand British competition after 1815. That Rhenish industry faced painful readjustment after 1815 is conceded even by those sympathetic to the French achievement.[37] Prussian reports compiled after Napoleon's defeat suggest that the apparent spurt of growth under the French was deceptive and that in reality the Rhenish economic landscape of c.1815 was dominated by under-capitalised enterprises, employing out-of-date machines and badly trained workers under inefficient management, sitting on large stocks for which there was now no market. Only larger, better-established firms, producing top-quality manufactures and with at least half-a-year's credit, were able to survive the postwar transition and find alternative markets. Thirty major bankruptcies were reported in the region during the first nine years of Prussian rule. Even the von der Leyens' silk manufactory in Krefeld closed soon after French rule.[38]

---

[35] Roger Dufraisse, 'La Crise économique de 1810–1812 en pays annexé: l'exemple de la rive gauche du Rhin', *Francia* 6 (1978), pp. 407–40.

[36] Ladoucette to Klespe, 17 January 1811, Hauptstaatsarchiv Düsseldorf (HStAD), Roër dept., 3009, nos. 56–7.

[37] Kisch, 'Textile districts', pp. 325–6.

[38] Koltes, *Rheinland*, pp. 299–300, 330, 333–4, 344–8. For the fortunes of the von der Leyens' enterprise after 1815, see Kurschat, *Haus*, pp. 92ff.

Economic theory tends to support the Prussians in their appraisal of the French economic legacy in the Rhineland, a legacy determined above all by Napoleon's Continental System. In the short term, inclusion within the protected French market brought benefits. This was recognised by those excluded such as the manufacturers of Berg who, in 1811, petitioned Napoleon for annexation to France to stave off ruin.[39] However, access to a large market in itself cannot guarantee industrial growth. Such an assumption erroneously implies that economies of scale exist only at the level of the entire economy, not the individual firm, and that 100 manufactories serving 50 millions are inevitably more efficient than four serving 2 millions. Nor does inclusion within a large market appear crucial for capital investment when it is remembered that in Britain capital was generally invested locally, not nationally, during the earliest phases of industrialisation. More fundamentally, the same critique might be applied to the Continental System as has recently been applied to the Prussian *Zollverein*, namely that it did not create but divert trade. It simply substituted trade with areas beyond the customs area for trade within the area. As a result, comparative advantages were no longer fully exploited and resources misallocated.[40] In any case, of greater significance than the overall extent of markets is their stability. Only this allows for sustained specialisation which lies at the heart of modern economic development. And here, Napoleon's Continental System scored badly.[41]

Specialisation benefits from new technology. Arguably, the Continental System discouraged this by hindering 'technology transfer' from the leading manufacturing power, Britain. Such transfer involved far more than smuggling out blue-prints or disassembled machines, but required a painstaking process of dispersal, diffusion and assimilation, and this occurred only with economic incentives. These incentives could only be supplied by exposure to British competition, something that ended with the Continental System. This provided short-term protection, but removed a stimulus for technological advance; and, the further the Continent fell behind, the greater the costs of catching up. These conclusions hold true, despite such dramatic examples of technology transfer as the tanner Lieven Bauwens's smuggling of a spinning mule out of Britain in 1798 and the creation, based on this,

---

[39] Berg's annexation was opposed by Cologne's Chamber of Commerce, which demonstrated *Schadenfreude* at Berg's plight and welcomed the prospect of the 'return' of manufacturers from the grand duchy 'to their mother country', thereby reversing the emigration of the eighteenth century. Heckscher, *Continental System*, p. 314.

[40] Hans-Joachim Voth, 'The Prussian Zollverein and the Bid for Economic Superiority', in Philip G. Dwyer (ed.), *Modern Prussian History 1830–1947* (Harlow, 2001), pp. 109–25.

[41] Mokyr, *Industrialization*, pp. 208–15. Pollard, *Conquest*, pp. 36–7, 118.

of a cotton spinning industry in his native Ghent; or the activities of the British entrepreneur William Cockerill, who revolutionised the woollen industry in the Walloon provinces using technology also smuggled over in 1798. His son, James, subsequently built upon his success by settling in Verviers (Ourthe department) and starting the manufacture of jennies copied from smuggled originals. By 1810, Verviers boasted eighty-six cloth manufacturers, employing 25,000 workers. Leading Rhenish manufacturers were amongst Cockerill's customers. Indeed, James and his brother John married the two daughters of one of these, Philipp Heinrich Pastor, the owner of wool spinning mills in Aachen and Burtscheid. James Cockerill subsequently settled near Aachen and contributed to the transformation of its industry in the Prussian period. Yet, such cases, though individually significant, proved the exception rather than the rule. For despite Napoleon's encouragement of technology transfer – Bauwens, for example, received the Légion d'Honneur plus some cheap monastic buildings – the economic fundamentals of the Continental System diminished the incentives to invest in cutting-edge technology. This assessment is supported by statistics recording the export of Boulton and Watt steam engines to Continental Europe. Exports stagnated during the Napoleonic period, but multiplied with the collapse of the Continental System: orders from the Continent for the three years 1816, 1817 and 1818 equalled those for the entire previous decade. By the end of the Napoleonic period, France boasted a mere 200 steam engines, compared to 5,000 in Britain.[42]

The key to economic development is specialisation rather than industrialisation *per se* – in certain cases, specialisation might result in deindustrialisation. Specialisation depends upon trade connecting *complementary* areas. These existed in the Rhineland, which encompassed areas of commercialised agriculture producing surpluses, poor upland regions with few resources but an ample supply of cheap labour, and ancient commercial centres like Cologne, with generations of accumulated capital and connections to wider markets. French territorial consolidation encouraged interaction between these areas though, as has been argued, the barriers to region-wide commercial activity under the Old Regime should not be exaggerated. However, specialisation on an even grander scale was hampered by Napoleon's Continental System and instead awaited the arrival of railways. The French contribution to economic development nonetheless

---

[42] Banfield, *Industry*, 2, p. 236. Jennifer Tann and M. J. Breckin, 'The International Diffusion of the Watt Engine, 1775–1825', *Economic History Review* 31 (1978), pp. 542–7, 550, 552, 554–5; Pollard, *Conquest*, pp. 40, 146–8, 183–4; Henderson, *Britain*, pp. 25–6, 46, 59, 106–13; Mokyr, *Industrialization*, pp. 27–51; Heckscher, *Continental System*, pp. 281, 285.

extended beyond territorial consolidation into less tangible areas. Institutional reforms, especially with respect to law, established greater uniformity, simplicity and certainty. The abolition of the guilds removed a barrier to innovation. Reforms further strengthened the entrepreneurial spirit in the Rhineland. Wealth, including non-landed wealth, acquired an unparalleled degree of institutionalised social prestige. It determined membership of juries, electoral colleges, consultative councils, honour guards, and 'society'. Never had the socio-political as well as economic rewards of successful entrepreneurial activity been greater.

The Rhineland was economically stronger at the end of the Napoleonic period than at the beginning. That said, the beginning of Napoleonic rule came at a low point in the region's economic fortunes, following five years of ruthless exploitation. A far harder question is the counterfactual: would the Rhineland have been better off had the French Revolution, the Revolutionary Wars and the Napoleonic episode never happened, and instead the region continued on the steady upward trajectory sustained for most of the eighteenth century? Certainly, agricultural improvement would have continued, with the introduction of new crops and methods. More land would have been brought under cultivation, and the sector become increasingly commercialised. The secularisation of ecclesiastical lands would not have taken place. However, despite the vast amount of land concerned, the overall effects of secularisation appear to have been marginal, simply reinforcing existing structures and trends. As for trade and industry, the absence of economic warfare with Britain and the ever-growing flood of cheap textiles from that country would no doubt have stifled the kind of hothouse developments that characterised the Napoleonic years. Instead, only industries that could respond to competition with new techniques and technologies would have survived. Hence, the likelihood of faster technology transfer within a smaller but more efficient sector. Of course, the absence of the Continental Blockade would also have meant the absence of smuggling, a business that accounted for some very large fortunes that were subsequently invested in other sectors. Smuggling arguably encouraged the concentration of trade in a few hands whilst placing smaller commercial and industrial operations at a disadvantage. The absence of smuggling in favour of free, legal trade might have been disadvantageous to a wealthy few, but would have benefited a larger number of small and medium-sized enterprises. Some of the great infrastructure projects planned and carried through under Napoleon's auspices, such as the long-distance roads and all-weather port in Cologne, would have been beyond the small states into which the Rhineland had been divided previously. They would not have occurred, or at least would have been completed later once sufficient capital had accumulated within the region. What is hardest to quantify is the wider economic impact of the lack of any institutional reform, but instead the survival of a confused, fragmented system of overlapping jurisdictions. Certainly, it is hard to imagine the economic progress of the middle and later decades of the nineteenth century having occurred within such a framework. The question is whether the pressure of economic progress would have eventually forced institutional change, even without Napoleon. The evidence for the years preceding French rule suggests it would have done.

PART III

1813–1830: Transition, reform, reaction

CHAPTER 8

The end of the French Rhineland, 1813–1815

Napoleon lost 570,000 men in Russia in 1812.[1] Such unparalleled losses upset the balance of power and jeopardised the French position in central Europe. Napoleon abandoned the remnants of his army in early December 1812, passed through Mainz incognito, and arrived in Paris, which only two months previously had witnessed the attempted coup by General Malet. Having expelled the invader, Tsar Alexander followed the prompting of the Freiherr vom Stein and other Germans in his entourage who urged that the Russian army continue westwards. As it did so, the Prussian contingent in the Grande Armée defected. Its commander, General Yorck, signed a convention with the Russians at Tauroggen on 30 December 1812, an action disowned by Frederick William III. The Austrian corps managed to extricate itself from Russia intact. Vienna declared its neutrality, a position it maintained even after Prussia signed the Treaty of Kalisch with Russia (26 February 1813) and declared war on France (17 March). Napoleon ordered new levees and rebuilt his forces, which led to victory at Lützen (2 May) and Bautzen (20–1 May). These engagements proved indecisive, not least because the French lacked cavalry to exploit them. There followed the Armistice of Pleschwitz (4 June), which both sides welcomed as a breathing space. Metternich, Austria's foreign minister, now entered centre stage. He had no intention of seeing French hegemony replaced by Russia's, and hoped for the preservation of Napoleonic rule in the Rhineland. Napoleon, however, refused to make concessions, and a reluctant Austria entered the Coalition.[2] War resumed on 10 August. The Allies exploited their numerical superiority by adopting the 'Trachenberg Plan', according to which any army facing a force led by Napoleon in person fell back, whilst the others advanced, threatening the enemy's flanks. This strategy proved effective.

---

[1] David Gates, *The Napoleonic Wars 1803–1815* (London, 1997), p. 221.
[2] Paul W. Schroeder, *The Transformation of European Politics 1763–1848* (Oxford, 1994), pp. 459–76.

The climax of the German campaign came at Leipzig. There, from 16 to 18 October, the fate of central Europe was settled by 365,000 Austrians, Prussians, Russians and Swedes confronting 200,000 French. Crushed by the weight in numbers, Napoleon fled westwards, his German allies deserting him. The Bavarians even attempted to bar his retreat. On 1 November, Napoleon entered Mainz along with the typhus-ridden remnants of his army. He could do nothing to stem the inexorable enemy advance. By the beginning of December the Allies felt strong enough to mount large-scale raids across the Rhine. These were a prelude to invasion, which began on New Year's Eve, when General Blücher crossed the Middle Rhine at Caub, Lahnstein and Mannheim, whilst a northern thrust projected other contingents across the Lower Rhine a few days later.[3] The heavily outnumbered French pulled back into the interior, so that with the exception of a few besieged fortresses, the entire left bank was in Allied hands by late January 1814. The Allies continued their advance, whilst Napoleon traded space for time before launching a brilliantly conducted campaign that salvaged his reputation as the greatest military commander of the age. This only succeeded in delaying the Allied steamroller, which finally reached Paris at the end of March.

The Rhineland's future remained unresolved politically, despite decisive military victory. The first step in its resolution was the Treaty of Chaumont (9 March 1814), where the Allies sketched the outlines of the European settlement, including the reduction of France to her 1792 borders. This France accepted in the First Treaty of Paris (31 May 1814).[4] The question as to whom the Rhineland would be ceded remained, and dominated diplomacy for the next two years. Only the British took a consistent position. The Netherlands and northern Rhineland featured at the centre of London's strategic thinking after the collapse of Habsburg power in Belgium in the 1790s. According to the younger Pitt's plan of January 1805, Prussia would replace Austria as 'sentinel' guarding the North Sea coast, a function that could only be performed with a large wedge of Rhenish hinterland. This idea was adopted by Foreign Secretary Castlereagh in 1813, and confirmed in its essentials by the Cabinet on 26 December of that year.[5]

Berlin declined its allotted role. Instead, the Prussians sought gains in central Europe at Saxony's expense. The Rhineland's future thereby became entwined with the Poland-Saxony crisis which almost sparked war

---

[3] David Chandler, *The Campaigns of Napoleon* (London, 1993 edn), pp. 945–51.
[4] Alexandre de Clercq (ed.), *Recueil des traités de la France* (23 vols., Paris, 1861–1919), 2, p. 415.
[5] Inge Schlieper, 'Die Diskussion um die territoriale Neuordnung des Rheinlandes 1813–1815' (Cologne D.Phil., 1971), pp. 6–7, 16–17, 41–3, 74–85, 101–3, 157–60, 179–82.

in December 1814. Not that the Prussians were alone in not wanting the Rhineland, with its vulnerable location next to France. Other German powers, notably Austria and Bavaria, also schemed to consolidate their own position through acquiring conterminous territories that were easier to defend and to integrate with their existing states. Amongst the many ideas floated during 1814 was Austrian annexation of Alsace-Lorraine (suggested by the Russians, who wanted Galicia in return), a partition of the Rhineland between Prussia and Austria (proposed by the Prussian chancellor, Hardenberg, in August 1814), and the formation of a Rhenish state to compensate King Frederick Augustus for the cession of Saxony to Prussia (put forward by Hardenberg in December 1814). Only on 11 February 1815 were the essentials of the final settlement agreed, with Prussia receiving two-fifths of Saxony and the left bank of the Rhine north of the Moselle.[6] This represented a British triumph. For most Rhinelanders the future was settled: on 5 April 1815 King Frederick William III reluctantly took possession of his new western territories.

The Rhineland's future south of the Moselle remained unresolved and a matter of dispute between Bavaria and Austria. Vienna agreed in principle in the Treaty of Ried (October 1813) that Bavaria should receive compensation in exchange for ceding Salzburg to Austria. Where this compensation lay remained undetermined. Conflict also centred on Mainz, which the Bavarians claimed, but the Prussians refused to see under a traditional French ally. As no agreement was reached in time for the First Treaty of Paris, the Allies decided that the southern Rhineland (except Mainz) be provisionally administered jointly by the Austrians and Bavarians. Mainz was occupied by an Austro-Prussian garrison. Bavaria wished to acquire areas conterminous to itself, and the Rhineland lay too far to the west, separated from the core by Baden, Württemberg and Hessen-Darmstadt, states with similarly ambitious territorial appetites. Instead, Munich wished to keep Salzburg, which it had taken from Austria in 1809. Metternich, himself a Rhinelander, was happy to sacrifice Salzburg in return for the Rhineland-Palatinate, but was overruled by the army leadership, which maintained the area was militarily indefensible against the French.[7] To add to the uncertainty, the Prussian zone's extension to the south of the Moselle in May 1815 led to renewed conflict over the demarcation-line separating this area from the Austro-Bavarian area. Final agreement between Munich and

---

[6] Harold Nicolson, *The Congress of Vienna: a Study in Allied Unity 1812–22* (London, 1989 edn), pp. 69, 124, 175, 177–80.

[7] Friedrich Schmitt, *Die provisorische Verwaltung des Gebietes zwischen Rhein, Mosel und französischer Grenze durch Österreich und Bayern in den Jahren 1814–1816* (Meisenheim, 1962), p. 25.

Vienna was only reached in April 1816, after the appearance of Austrian troop concentrations near the Bavarian border. Bavaria accepted most of the Rhineland-Palatinate in return for areas ceded to Austria, whilst Hessen-Darmstadt was similarly bullied into accepting a small pocket on the left bank instead of various Westphalian territories she coveted.[8]

For Rhinelanders, the Napoleonic collapse in 1813 threatened a repeat of the horrors of war visited in the 1790s. Those associated with French rule faced the threat of retribution from fellow citizens and Allied troops, a prospect brought home by the sight of officials from the Hanseatic departments, Berg and Westphalia fleeing across the Rhine with their families.[9] Meanwhile, Napoleon demanded ever greater sacrifices. Extraordinary levees of horses were ordered throughout the Empire to replenish the depleted cavalry and logistical units. The Roër alone supplied 800 horses and mules in the first eight months of 1813.[10] Worse, Paris decreed (20 March 1813) the nationalisation of all communal property, a measure that carried to its conclusion the Napoleonic practice of deflecting burdens onto the localities. Rhenish departmental councils courageously complained about this in bitter terms, though without effect.[11]

Like most authoritarian regimes, Napoleon's demanded effusive public displays of loyalty as its foundations collapsed. It forced even masonic lodges to demonstrate their support, and instructed mayors to present 'spontaneous' addresses from their municipalities which it then published in the *Moniteur*.[12] Mainz, Cologne and Aachen were amongst those cities selected in October – just days before the Battle of Leipzig – to present such declarations. This provoked resistance: Cologne's council voted the address, including compromising references to former marshal Bernadotte, now Crown Prince of Sweden, but refused to send a deputation to Paris on the grounds of its members' important business commitments or ill-health. Cologne's mayor temporarily left the city to escape the prefect's bullying on the issue, claiming his vines needed urgent attention. Aachen proved similarly obdurate.[13] The prefect, suspecting the prevarication was motivated by 'sinister rumours' from Germany, eventually chaired extraordinary council

---

[8] Apart from Schlieper, see also Schmitt, *Verwaltung*, pp. 12–28.

[9] Report from the special police commissioner in the Roër to Réal (head of the 1st imperial police district), 11 March 1813. Archives Nationales, Paris (AN), F⁷3609, dossier 'Roër 1806–1813', [no. 211].

[10] AN, F¹ᶜI, nos. 14–23, 'exposé de la situation de l'Empire. Fin de l'Année 1813 . . . note sur les levées de chevaux et sur la statistique équestre'.

[11] Landeshauptarchiv Koblenz (LHAK), Bestand 256, 93, no. 84.

[12] Ladoucette to Montalivet (minister of the interior), 15 February 1813, AN, F⁹88. See also AN, AFIV 1947ᴮ, 'Roër'. The loyal address from Cleves was published in the *Moniteur*, 27 October 1813.

[13] Historisches Archiv der Stadt Köln (HASK), FV 3013, nos. 1, 3–4, 7, 12. For Aachen, see AN, F¹ᶜI, 25, no. 188.

meetings in both cities, and simply ordered the municipalities to send the delegations. Even then there was last-minute hesitation, provoking the prefect to enquire whether he was authorised to employ physical force against the councils. This proved unnecessary, with the Rhenish delegations setting out for Saint Cloud at the beginning of November amidst now justified rumours of the destruction of Napoleon's army.[14]

Most burdensome of all was conscription, which Napoleon increased to make good the losses incurred in Russia. The regime prematurely called up 'classes' of young recruits and roped in those previously passed over. The relevant *senatus consulta* authorising levees illustrate the sacrifices the Empire was called upon to make: that of 1 September 1812 mobilised 120,000 men from the class 1813, plus an additional 17,000 as reserves; that of 11 January 1813 conscripted 150,000 from the class 1814, and an additional 100,000 from the classes 1809–12; that of 3 April mobilised 80,000 national guardsmen, who were incorporated into the regular forces; another (9 October) mobilised an additional 120,000 from the classes 1808 to 1814. Finally, the *senatus consultum* of 15 November 1813 ordered the mobilisation of 300,000 eighteen-year-olds from the class 1815, though the Rhenish departments were eventually exempted from this. Amongst those young Rhinelanders called up in 1813 was the future Prussian finance minister, David Hansemann, whose father spent his entire fortune on purchasing a replacement.[15] The spiralling cost of replacements reflected the desperate situation: previously, they cost about 2,000 francs; by 1813 the average price was over 3,000 francs; Hansemann senior paid 4,080 francs.

Those able to afford such sums faced recruitment into the 'guards of honour', four regiments of which were raised after April 1813. Unlike their predecessors, these were frontline units, equipped like hussars. Officially, the government allowed only notables to join and required that they cover the cost of a mount, equipment and uniform, amounting in total to over 1,000 francs. Few if any Rhenish notables volunteered. Instead, they – through the municipalities – bribed more humble souls into joining, providing them with uniforms and (usually unfit) horses. The prefectures felt obliged to make enquiries into the 'moral qualities' of the tailor's apprentices, sons of tobacco salesmen, municipal employees and textile workers who subsequently presented themselves.[16] Throughout the region, rumours

---

[14] Ladoucette to Montalivet, 30, 31 October 1813, AN, F^{Ic}III Roër 4, nos. 207, 214.
[15] Alexander Bergengrün, *David Hansemann* (Berlin, 1901), pp. 19–21.
[16] LHAK, Bestand 256, 6233. For Aachen, Stadtarchiv Aachen (StAA), RR710. Biographical details for Aachen's guards were gleaned from the *Recensement de la Population de la Mairie d'Aix-la-Chapelle dressé en conformité de l'ârrêté de Monsieur le Préfet du Département Chevalier de la Légion d'Honneur, Baron de l'Empire en dâte du 16 Juin mille huit cent douze* (Aachen, 1812), held in the Stadtarchiv.

circulated of scandals involving the traffic in exemptions from service in the guards, and the police reported the widespread bribery of recruitment officers. Aachen's 'volunteers' failed to present themselves following news of French defeats.[17]

The strain of war began to tell in late autumn 1813. In November, a young man, possibly belonging to the 120,000 mobilised the previous month, shot himself in the head on Cologne's main square.[18] Other young men corresponded on how they might escape conscription, and whether they should join friends who had fled to Switzerland despite the difficulties of obtaining a passport.[19] The French imposed draconian restrictions on the freedom of movement across the Rhine, both to prevent such emigration, and to stop the import of German nationalist publications.[20] Increasingly, the region's prefects added their voices to those calling for peace. In Aachen, even the obsequiously loyal Ladoucette opposed the deployment of mobile columns on account of delicate public opinion following the Allied occupation of the right bank, and successfully argued for the postponement of the mobilisation of the 'children' belonging to the class 1815.[21]

Following Leipzig, many Rhinelanders serving in Napoleon's army deserted. Some simply disappeared, were separated from their units, or remained in Germany and found work whilst the rest of the army retreated. In such cases, little could be gained from victimising parents through forced billeting. Nonetheless, Napoleon ordered additional deployments of mobile columns to the Rhineland in December 1813. Attached to these formations, which were also responsible for requisitioning supplies, were fearsome special military tribunals to try cases of rebellion.[22] Especially worrying were reports that Rhenish conscripts were deserting to the enemy; one prefect estimated that over a fifth had in fact joined enemy forces.[23] Amongst a batch of thirty-eight Prussian prisoners captured in December 1813 were

---

[17] For Aachen's volunteers, StAA, RR710, nos. 24, 26–7, 29. For the Rhenish departments as a whole, special police commissioner in Mainz to Count Réal, 2 October 1813, AN, F⁷3609, dossier 'Roër 1806–1813', [no. 217].

[18] Ladoucette to Savary (minister of police), 8 November 1813, AN, F⁷3686¹⁰.

[19] Sulpiz to Melchior Boisserée, December 1813, HASK, Bestand 1018, no. 34.

[20] Prefectoral (Roër) *arrêt*, 26 October 1813, *Recueil des actes de la préfecture du département de la Roër* (11 vols., Aachen, 1802/3–13), (1813), pp. 257–9.

[21] Ladoucette to Savary (minister of police), 14 May 1813, and to Réal, 15 July 1813, AN, F⁷3609, 'Roër 1806–1813', [nos. 221, 225]. Also, Ladoucette to Montalivet, 30 September, 6, 12 October, 20 November 1813, AN, F¹ᶜIII Roër 3, nos. 74, 77, 78, 87.

[22] General Gerard to Clarke (minister of war), 29 November 1813, and Napoleon's order of 7 December, Archives de l'Armée de Terre, Vincennes (AG), C¹⁰136.

[23] General d'Hastrel to Clarke, 12 October 1813, AG, C¹⁰136. For a list of deserters from the Roër, dated 13 July 1813, see AN, F⁷3609, 'Roër 1806–1813', [no. 251].

seven Rhinelanders, all of whom had been taken during the Russian campaign and given the unappealing choice of entering Prussian service or being transported to Siberia.[24]

Natives of the former Hohenzollern duchies, where old dynastic loyalties proved durable, were especially unreliable. Many feared that to take up arms against Frederick William III would be viewed as treason.[25] Significantly, French propaganda in the duchies condemned the defection of General Yorck as an outrage to Frederick William, who disowned the act, rather than to Napoleon.[26] This deceit became ineffective following the Prussian declaration of war, whilst the traditionally pro-Habsburg sentiment of Catholic Rhinelanders gave Austria's entry into the Coalition in August 1813 an added, disquieting significance. Many in the region, including some senior officials, had relatives fighting with the Allies.[27] French unease as to their loyalty only increased following the defection of the *Rheinbund* contingents at Leipzig. In Mainz in early November, Napoleon wrote that he 'did not judge it appropriate to entrust the defence of the frontier to new Frenchmen'.[28] He avoided mobilising the national guard in the four departments. Napoleon similarly took precautions against other 'new Frenchmen': Belgian and Dutch conscripts, for example, were disarmed and interned. He also avoided appointing 'new Frenchmen' as officials in strategically sensitive prefectures located near the frontier.[29] Clearly, the Napoleonic regime itself sensed the limited degree to which non-native French elites had been integrated.

---

[24] Ladoucette to Montalivet, 21 December 1813, AN, F^{IC}III Roër 4, no. 286. Evidence suggests that German-speaking Rhinelanders captured by the Russians during the 1812 campaign received better treatment than their French comrades, though the fate of most was pretty grim. Thomas R. Kraus, *Auf dem Weg in die Moderne. Aachen in französischer Zeit 1792/93, 1794–1814. Handbuch-Katalog zur Ausstellung im 'Krönungssaal' des Aachener Rathauses vom 14. Januar bis zum 5. März 1995* (Aachen, 1994), pp. 338–41. Especially interesting are the published reminiscences of the Rhenish veteran, Karl Schehl, *Mit der großen Armee 1812 von Krefeld nach Moskau. Erlebnisse des niederrheinischen Veteranen Karl Schehl, Krefeld* (Düsseldorf, 1912).

[25] Ladoucette to Réal, 15 July 1813, AN, F^{7}3609, dossier 'Roër 1806–1813', [no. 225]. See also Johann Adolf Kopstadt, *Über Cleve. In Briefen an einem Freund aus den Jahren 1811 und 1814* (Frankfurt a. M., 1822), p. 7.

[26] Ladoucette wrote to Montalivet on 18 January 1813: 'La trahison du Général d'Yorck a rempli d'indignation les habitans loyaux et fidèles du département de la Roër, surtout ceux de la partie autrefois Prussienne.' AN, F^{9}119.

[27] Jean Charles François de Ladoucette, *Voyage fait en 1813 et 1814 dans le pays entre Meuse et Rhin, suivi de notes, avec une carte géographique* (Paris and Aachen, 1818), p. 357.

[28] Napoleon I, *Correspondance de Napoléon Ier publiée par ordre de l'Empereur Napoléon III* (32 vols., Paris, 1858–69), 27, pp. 405–6. See also Johann Adam Boost, *Was waren die Rheinländer als Menschen und Bürger, und was ist aus ihnen geworden?* (Mainz, 1819), p. 184.

[29] AN, AFIV 1068, no. 28. For the Belgiums, see AG, C^{10}128, dossier '13 Janvier' [1814], [no. 9]. For the Dutch, AG, C^{10}127, dossier '20 Décembre' [1813], [no. 18]. For the regiments of the grand duchy of Berg, *ibid.*, dossier '18 Décembre' [1813].

Concurrently, 'new Frenchmen' in Napoleonic service faced charges of 'collaboration' from fellow citizens. Isolated acts of insolence and even violence against officials in the Rhineland started soon after December 1812, when the public became aware of Napoleon's crushing defeat in Russia.[30] Seditious posters and threatening graffiti appeared on town halls and officials' houses. However, overall such incidents were sporadic.[31] Most mayors followed the ebbs and flows of public opinion, kept a low profile and sabotaged French attempts to mobilise local resources.[32] Unlike the Hanseatic departments and Berg, no major disturbances or insurrections occurred in the Rhineland before the Allies' appearance.

This changed once the Allies started raiding across the Rhine in November 1813. The hated (and mainly French) *douaniers* and tax-collectors now became objects of public retribution. When, on 2 December, a Prussian force of 1,500 troops raided Neuss and overwhelmed its garrison, locals assisted as guides, pointing out the houses of French officers whilst others pillaged the homes of tax-collectors. Inhabitants from surrounding villages demolished customs posts along the Rhine.[33] Prussian forces further south were accompanied by large numbers of local peasants hunting customs men, whilst mobs assaulted tax-collectors in at least three towns. French troops pillaged Neuss as punishment following the Prussians' withdrawal.[34] The town's mayor, according to reports, was too afraid of popular retribution to arrest the rebellion's ringleaders; officials had more to fear from their neighbours than from enemy troops, one administrator complained.[35] Given popular hostility, many native Frenchmen followed the example of their compatriots from Westphalia and Berg, and fled before the army's evacuation.[36]

Random violence against the age-old bogey, the forestry guard, was motivated by deeply ingrained hatreds over common rights and usages rather than nationalist literature trickling across the Rhine. It was committed

---

[30] The Russian disaster was first made public in the *Bulletin de la Grande Armée* (29) of 3 December 1812. It ended, famously, with the words: 'The health of His Majesty has never been better.'

[31] Ladoucette to Réal, 27 January 1813, AN, F⁷8390, no. 228. Ladoucette to Réal, 4 May 1813, AN, F¹ᶜIII Roër 3, no. 249. Ladoucette to Montalivet, 3 October 1813, *ibid.*, no. 75.

[32] First inspector general of gendarmerie to Savary, 15 December 1813, AN, F⁷8390, no. 354.

[33] Report forwarded by Pauzle d'Ivoy (special police commissioner in the Roër) to Réal, 13 December 1813, AN, F⁷8390, no. 379.

[34] Ladoucette to Montalivet, 8 December 1813, AN, F¹ᶜIII Roër 4, nos. 254–5.

[35] Statement of Hermen (an official from Wevelinghoven) to the gendarmerie, 4 December 1813, AN, F⁷8390, no. 358.

[36] A contemporary, Leonard von Beckerath of Krefeld, reported that all French officials and their families had fled the Rhine by the end of 1813. Gottfried Buschbell, 'Aus der Franzosenzeit in Krefeld', *Annalen des historischen Vereins für den Niederrhein* 115 (1929), p. 364.

almost exclusively by the rural poor, those least likely to be influenced by smuggled publications.[37] The French nevertheless believed in a nationalist threat. Ladoucette warned Paris in November 1813 that 'the German writers do everything they can to revitalise the spirit of the nation, make it forget its hatreds and divisions, and arm it with a single spirit', and in December that the Allies were attempting 'to revolutionise the left bank of the Rhine'.[38] 'If we had only had the English or Russians to fight,' he subsequently reported, 'then the entire department would have mobilised... We would have been able to arm that part [formerly] belonging to the electorate of Cologne, the duchy of Jülich, or the duchy of Cleves, depending on whether we were in conflict with the Prussians, Austrians or Bavarians. As we were at war with all Germany, we had to fear the commonality of language and custom, and familial ties.'[39] Paris was particularly concerned with the propaganda activities of Justus Gruner, the Allied governor-general in occupied Berg, who despatched agents to the former Hohenzollern duchies in order to en-courage local co-operation with the planned invasion.[40] Yet, Rhinelanders contributed little militarily to the overthrow of Napoleonic rule, something subsequently recognised by the Prussians themselves.[41]

More threatening to order was social tension, which increased with the Europe-wide economic depression caused by the Continental System and war. The estimated 100,000 under-employed workers in the industrially advanced Lower Rhine were especially dangerous, and the French urged manufacturers to provide relief so as to prevent trouble.[42] Bureaucratic dread of social disorder – of 'the unrestrained fury of the crowd... the dis-solution of the rule of law and the suspension of taxation... the poor man [grabbing] greedily at the affluence of the rich, the criminal [promoting] himself to judge, the repressed [seeking] to avenge himself through repres-sion' – similarly gripped the southern Rhineland.[43] General Henry, com-mander of Napoleon's headquarters guard, concluded that social tension might be exploited to overcome national division following his tour of the Rhineland in 1813. Whilst dismissing the old nobility as socially isolated,

---

[37] Report forwarded by Pauzle d'Ivoy to Réal, 13 December 1813, AN, F⁷8390, no. 379.

[38] Ladoucette to Montalivet, 29 November 1813, 11 December 1813, AN, F¹ᶜIII Roër 4, nos. 258, 265.

[39] Ladoucette to Savary, 3 February 1814, AN, F⁷8390, no. 412.

[40] Ladoucette to Montalivet, 27 November 1813, 10 December 1813, AN, F¹ᶜIII Roër 4, nos. 236, 261.

[41] Johann Daniel Ferdinand Neigebaur, *Darstellung der provisorischen Verwaltung am Rhein von Jahr 1813 bis 1819* (Cologne, 1821), p. 276.

[42] Ladoucette to Savary, 3 February 1814, AN, F⁷8390, no. 412.

[43] P. A. Müller, *Statistisches Jahrbuch für die deutschen Länder zwischen dem Rhein, der Mosel und der französischen Grenze auf das Jahr 1815* (Mainz, 1815), p. viii.

Henry argued that fear of the 'rabble' gripped 'decent people', defined as landowners, tradesmen, master craftsmen of all types, the purchasers of nationalised property and those in public service. This the government might exploit within the framework of the National Guard. This force would bind the elite to the regime, stimulate patriotism, and encourage co-operation between Frenchmen and Germans so that 'in future [they] represent only one nation, something which till now has not been the case'.[44] The hope that social conflict might push the *masses de granit* into the arms of the regime proved illusory. The Rhenish elite did spontaneously form its own civic guards as Napoleonic rule collapsed to maintain order, but these offered no military support and willingly co-operated with the Allies following the invasion.[45]

The invasion, when it came, was swift and largely unopposed by weak French defences, thereby avoiding a repetition of the 1790s. Only a thin cordon of 70,000 French troops, including substantial concentrations in Mainz and Wesel, guarded the frontier between Strasbourg and the North Sea against at least 300,000 Allies.[46] Napoleon, facing such odds, never contemplated defending the Rhine, and withdrew as Blücher's 'Army of Silesia' crossed the Middle Rhine on New Year's Day 1814, and elements of Bernadotte's 'Army of the North' crossed several days later. The invasion prevented the execution in the Rhineland of Napoleon's decree of 4 January 1814, ordering a *levée en masse* in all departments threatened by invasion.[47]

As the French army evacuated, 'collaborators' faced the choice of fleeing or serving the Allies. According to government instructions, senior officials were supposed to withdraw to fortified points and hold out as long as possible. The government placed them under notice that their actions would determine their future opportunities should Napoleonic rule be restored.[48] In practice, the prefects abandoned their departments, with the exception of Jeanbon Saint-André, who days before the invasion succumbed to the typhus epidemic raging in Mainz. Ladoucette intended to withdraw to the citadel of Jülich, but was forced to flee into the interior along with his colleagues from the Sarre and Rhin-et-Moselle because of

[44] General Henry to Clarke, 7 November 1813, AG, C^{10}136.
[45] J. Böcker to Sulpiz Boisserée, 28 January 1814, HASK, Bestand 1018, no. 31. Ladoucette to Montalivet, 4 March 1814, AN, F^{1c}III Roër 4, no. 325.
[46] General Merle to General Clarke, 19 December 1813, AG, C^{10}127, dossier '19 Décembre', [no. 1]. See also Chandler, *Campaigns*, pp. 945–51. F. Loraine Petre, *Napoleon at Bay 1814* (London, 1977 edn), pp. 2, 10, 13. Napoleon I, *Correspondance*, 27, pp. 26–31, 318–19.
[47] AG, C^{10}128, dossier '5 Janvier', [no. 1].
[48] Ladoucette's circular to *fonctionnaires civils* of 3 January 1814, AN, F^{1c}III Roër 4, no. 316.

the swift advance of Allied cavalry.[49] Over half the sub-prefects also with-drew. Others proved less loyal: the sub-prefect of Aachen – a Frenchman – disappeared when ordered to prepare Jülich for siege, only to re-emerge after the invasion as head of a '*commission administrative*' under Allied oc-cupation. His counterpart in Cologne – a German – emerged as leader of a similar commission in that city.[50] Others, including prefectoral councillors, were dispensed from having to evacuate but compelled to swear a special oath of loyalty to Napoleon.[51] Mayors, who were over-whelmingly local men, remained in their towns and villages, but tax-collectors, as common targets of popular hatred, fled in large numbers.[52] The mainly French *douaniers* and gendarmes, who were militarised in times of emergency, retreated into the interior with the army, whilst *gardes forestières*, who were generally locals, remained but were victimised when they attempted to oppose forestry infractions, which emerged as the most common popular response to collapsing authority. Peasants commit-ting such infractions – which were often directed at notables associated with French rule – justified themselves with crudely applied nationalistic rhetoric.[53]

The Allies took prompt action to re-establish order following the oc-cupation. Blücher, in his first proclamation, directed that local authori-ties request military aid where they feared a breakdown of order, and this support was proffered irrespective of officials' prior relationships with the Napoleonic regime. 'One ignored previous conduct,' observed one con-temporary, 'and above all one ignored previous political opinions, which are easily misinterpreted. It is thanks to this wise policy that the left bank remained generally calm, despite the efforts of a few isolated hotheads.'[54] Dormagen's chronicler recorded that on the day the Allies arrived, peasants assaulted the local JP and looted his house, justifying their crime by claim-ing he was a French agent. The mayor was also threatened with physical violence. The JP responded by travelling to Cologne and complaining to the Allied authorities. These promptly despatched a contingent to arrest the troublemakers, who subsequently received lengthy prison sentences.[55]

[49] Ladoucette, *Voyage*, pp. 247–8.
[50] Ladoucette to Montalivet, 20 December 1813, 4 February 1814, AN, F¹ᶜIII Roër 4, nos. 285, 325.
[51] Ladoucette to Savary, 3 February 1814, AN, F⁷8390, no. 412.
[52] LHAK, Bestand 353, 5, nos. 19, 53–4.
[53] Karl-Georg Faber, *Andreas van Recum 1765–1828. Ein rheinischer Kosmopolit* (Bonn, 1969), pp. 115–16; LHAK, Bestand 371, 549, no. 55.
[54] Müller, *Jahrbuch*, p. viii.
[55] H. Cardauns and R. Müller (eds.), *Die rheinische Dorfchronik des Johann Peter Delhoven aus Dormagen, 1783–1823* (Cologne, 1926), pp. 221–6.

Overall, the transition to Allied rule proceeded relatively smoothly.[56] Inevitably, soldiers committed isolated outrages, though on a considerably smaller scale than in the 1790s. Prussian volunteer units, notably Lutzow's Freikorps, earned a nasty reputation for treating the population as enemies rather than as liberated Germans, and the Russians left a trail of wreckage and emptied wine-cellars wherever they went.[57] Allied troops paid scant respect to the local civic guards established to maintain order.[58] In the Allied command there were initial misgivings as to the trustworthiness of locals, with reports warning that mayors and adjuncts included 'tools of the secret police employed by the French government, who are still not to be trusted'. The Allies drew up secret personnel reports and replaced 'dangerous' suspects with individuals who owned substantial assets which could be seized in case of treachery.[59] Overall, however, the military authorities made few changes to personnel, preoccupied as they were with fighting their way to Paris.

The exception to the smooth transition was Mainz, an important French fortress guarding the Rhine. It was surrounded by Allied forces and declared in a state of siege on 3 January. In addition, the city had a typhus epidemic to contend with, introduced by the remnants of Napoleon's army retreating after Leipzig. The epidemic carried off 18,000 soldiers before the garrison finally surrendered, and thousands of civilians including the prefect, Jeanbon Saint-André. The mayor of Mainz recollected in later years the difficulty of disposing of numerous rotting corpses once the burial pits were cut off, and how bodies were subsequently dumped into the Rhine. As during the three sieges of the 1790s, Mainz's civilians were bled white by the military garrison, which subjected them to an initial forced loan of 300,000 francs followed by monthly payments of 200,000 francs, in addition to the provision of supplies in kind. The death of Jeanbon Saint-André, who had long confronted the army's pretensions, weakened the civilians. The agony of Mainz lasted until after Napoleon's unconditional abdication, with the French garrison evacuating only on 4 May after having forced the city to swear an oath of allegiance to Louis XVIII.[60]

---

[56] An account of the intimidation faced by 'collaborators' in neighbouring Westphalia is provided by Hoffmann von Fallersleben, *Mein Leben* (Hannover, 1868), pp. 53–5. Hoffmann's father served as a mayor in the Kingdom.

[57] Sack to Frederick William III, 15 November 1815, Geheimes Staatsarchiv, Berlin (GStA), rep. 89, 13607, 'Acta betr. Zustand der Rheinprovinz 1814–19', nos. 11–12.

[58] LHAK, Bestand 354, dossiers 492, no. 557; Cardauns, *Dorfchronik*, p. 221.

[59] Allied military headquarters, Saint Avold, 14 January 1814, to Athenstedt (Allied Intendant of the Sarre department), LHAK, Bestand 353, 5, nos. 47–8.

[60] K. G. Bockenheimer, *Franz Konrad Macke. Bürgermeister von Mainz (1756–1844)* (Mainz, 1904), pp. 79–86.

On 12 January 1814 the Allies set up a provisional civilian authority in the liberated Rhineland subordinate to the Inter-Allied Central Administration. This body was headed by Prussia's former first minister, Karl Freiherr vom Stein, and was responsible for German territories 'vacated' by their sovereigns and whose future would be determined at the peace settlement. The Central Administration's remit was subsequently extended to occupied French departments. Its supreme executive organ, though established by the Allied powers, was not subordinate to any one of them individually. Composed of Austrian, Prussian and Russian officials, the blandly named Central Administration developed into a power base to further Stein's political agenda of providing Germany with robust, federal institutions, at the expense of the states of the Confederation of the Rhine. In the words of Stein's secretary, the nationalist Ernst Moritz Arndt, it provided the tool to reawaken the *Volk* and the *Reich* after 500 years of sleep.[61] The Central Administration quickly developed as a focal point for those who hoped that Napoleon's defeat had cleared the ground for radical political reform. Metternich suspected that Stein had placed himself at the head of the 'revolutionary' party in Germany and subsequently blamed the Central Administration's 'direct influence' for the revolutionary upsurge in later years. Significantly, Metternich's pre-emption of the Central Administration in most of Germany through the conclusion of separate agreements with the princes proved impossible in the 'vacated' territory to the west of the Rhine.[62]

The Allies grouped the Rhenish departments into two general-governments subordinate to Stein: the Lower Rhine, administered from Aachen by the Prussian privy-councillor Johann August Sack, and the Middle Rhine, under Justus Gruner, based in Trier. The Middle Rhine included the Rhin-et-Moselle, Sarre and Mont-Tonnerre, and the Lower Rhine the Roër together with the Belgian departments of Ourthe and Meuse Inférieure.[63] This arrangement continued until 31 May 1814, when the Allies dissolved the Central Administration and responsibility for the Rhineland devolved to the individual powers pending the final settlement. Prussia took over the region between the Maas, Rhine and Mosel, which became the general government of the Lower and Middle Rhine, and the Austrians and Bavarians established a joint commission (*k. k. österreichische und*

---

[61] Peter Graf von Kielmansegg, *Stein und die Zentralverwaltung 1813/14* (Stuttgart, 1964), p. 60.

[62] *Ibid.*, pp. 19–25, 60.

[63] Johann Daniel Ferdinand Neigebaur, *Statistik der preußischen Rhein = provinzen in den drei Perioden ihrer Verwaltung: 1) Durch das General = Gouvernment vom Niederrheine; 2) Durch jenes vom Nieder = und Mittelrheine; 3) Nach ihrer jetzigen Begränzung und wirklichen Vereinigung mit den Preußischen Staate. Aus offiziellen Quellen. Von einem preußischen Staatsbeamten* (Cologne, 1817), pp. 2ff.

k. bayerische gemeinschaftliche Landesadministrationskommission, or LAK)
south of the Mosel.[64]

Importantly for the Rhineland's long-term development, both Gruner
and Sack were men of stature who had played prominent roles in the
Prussian reform movement. Gruner, a native of Osnabrück and godson of
the thinker Justus Möser, entered Prussian service in 1802 and forged contacts with Stein, Hardenberg and other reformers after 1806. He served as
police-president of Berlin from 1809 and as head of the police for all Prussia
from 1811. His activities included whipping up anti-French sentiment and
counter-espionage. Disgusted by the Franco-Prussian alliance of 5 March
1812, Gruner joined the exiled Stein in Prague, and was drawn into schemes
to provoke a Spanish-style German rising once the French invaded Russia.
He assumed responsibility for these plans following Stein's departure for
St Petersburg, but was discovered by the French, who were on the point
of demanding his extradition when he was arrested by the Austrians and
imprisoned – for his own safety – in Peterwardein. He was released following
Vienna's declaration of war in August 1813, joined Stein's Central Administration and was appointed to the Middle Rhine following recommendations
from Blücher and Gneisenau. Gruner's subsequent agitation for reform and
association with individuals such as Görres added to his conservative enemies in Berlin, who eventually succeeded in neutralising him by awarding
him successive embassies to minor courts until his death in 1820.[65]

Gruner's counterpart in Aachen, Sack, was a native of Cleves and an
old friend of Stein's, under whom he had served during the 1790s. Of
non-noble birth, Sack remained throughout his life a critic of old Prussian
military values, his contempt for which only increased after 1806. Following
Jena, Sack was appointed governor of Berlin, and then head of the special
commission responsible for parts of Prussia under French occupation. He
supported Stein's reforms, assisted in drafting the *Städteordnung* and collaborated with Gneisenau and Scharnhorst over the militia ordinance. He
was a bitter enemy of the conservatives. In 1813, Sack organised the mobilisation of military forces against the French as governor of Prussia between
the Elbe and Oder. His appointment as governor-general of the Lower
Rhine in 1814 was made 'in recognition of his professional zeal and local
knowledge'.[66]

[64] Schmitt, *Verwaltung*, pp. 12–28.
[65] *Allgemeine Deutsche Biographie* (56 vols., Leipzig, 1875–1912), 10, pp. 42–8. *Neue Deutsche Biographie*
(Berlin, 1953–), 7, pp. 227–9.
[66] *Allgemeine Deutsche Biographie*, 30, pp. 152–3. *Deutsches biographisches Archiv microform: eine Kumulation aus 254 der wichtigsten biographischen Nachschlagewerke für den deutschen Bereich bis zum*

The Central Administration's first responsibility was to support the Allied forces.[67] This was not easy. The poorer Rhenish departments, the Rhin-et-Moselle and Sarre, lacked abundant resources and were badly affected by large-scale troop movements. The requisitioning of draught animals along the major supply routes was so burdensome that people sold their horses to avoid it, further exacerbating the logistical problem. The Sarre suffered especially at the hands of the Russians. Military movements were particularly large-scale immediately following the First Treaty of Paris: in June 1814 Sack's general-government alone accommodated and supplied 120,000 troops and 20,000 horses. Contingents were still returning from France throughout the winter of 1814/15, and just as these movements had been completed Napoleon's return from Elba provoked new deployments in the opposite direction, followed by a second passage of troops returning from France in November and December 1815.[68] Overall, the Central Administration ensured orderly supply through the prevention of excesses against civilians. Stein ceaselessly corresponded with the military commanders to this effect, and even authorised the establishment of civic guards so that civilians could defend themselves against disorderly soldiers in transit.[69]

Stein recognised above all the importance of involving local notables in public affairs, something consistent with the political proposals outlined in his famous *Nassauer Denkschrift* of 1807. In March 1814, Stein advised Gruner: 'It encourages the confidence of the inhabitants and greatly serves to reassure them when they see natives participating in the administration.'[70] At the same time, Stein condemned previous collaboration with the French. 'Believe me,' he wrote, 'all who served the enemy in such a fashion, and all without exception, can be used but not trusted... years spent in these filthy circumstances besmirch ones character, and cloud... ones judgement.'[71] He ordered that collaborators be barred from senior and sensitive posts, which instead should be entrusted to 'completely reliable German[s], or official[s] from one of the Allied Powers', or

Ausgang des neunzehnten Jahrhunderts (Munich, 1982), microfiche 1,073, nos. 363–9 (extract from the *Neuer Nekrolog der Deutschen*, 9, 1831 (1833)). See also Wilhelm Steffens, *Briefwechsel Sacks mit Stein und Gneisenau (1807/17)* (Stettin, 1931), part I, passim.

67 'Denkschrift Steins über die Bildung der Verwaltungs-Behörden für die französischen Provinzen', Basel, 11 January 1814. Reproduced in Walther Hubatsch (ed.), *Heinrich Friedrich Karl Freiherr vom und zum Stein, Briefe und amtliche Schriften* (10 vols., Stuttgart, 1957–74), 4, pp. 446–9.

68 GStA, rep. 89, 13607, 'Acta betr. Zustand der Rheinprovinz 1814–19', nos. 27–34.

69 Stein to Blücher, 14 February 1814 and Stein to Sack, 2 March 1814, Stein, *Briefe*, 4, pp. 528–9, 572–3. Johann August Sack, *Reglement über die Einrichtung einer Bürger-Militz im Gouvernement des Nieder-Rheins* (Cologne, 1814), p. 3. See also Kielmansegg, *Stein*, pp. 117, 140.

70 Stein to Gruner, 23 March 1814, Stein, *Briefe*, 4, p. 653.

71 Stein to Vincke (general-commissioner in the Westphalian provinces), 16 January 1814. *Ibid.*, p. 463.

native Rhinelanders selected 'with special reference to [their] attitude to the present French regime', to quote the official guidelines. The secret police in particular must include only '*Deutschgesinnten*' (men with a 'German attitude'), though gendarmes could 'on the whole be kept on, whilst higher officials must first be used and then discarded'.[72] Native sub-prefects were retained on condition they swore an oath of loyalty to the Allies, and mayors generally kept in place. In practice, the Allied administration encountered difficulties in finding notables willing to assume public responsibilities. With memories of the 1790s still fresh, few cherished the prospect of shouldering official burdens in turbulent times.[73]

Officially encouraged nationalist rhetoric undermined the credibility of the administration inherited from Napoleon. In Cologne, the mayor – who was forced by popular pressure not to wear the Légion d'Honneur – experienced a co-ordinated campaign of denunciation which employed German nationalist rhetoric in the mistaken hope that this would appeal to the new authorities.[74] When Tsar Alexander I visited Cologne in July 1814, elements controlling the civic guard humiliated and marginalised the mayor during the official celebrations, whilst posters appeared throughout the city denouncing him for 'consistently [showing] himself a friend and supporter of the hereditary enemy of Germans and of all that is sacred', and calling on 'the old courage and strength of the people of Cologne' to protect the ancient liberties of the Imperial City by petitioning 'the great Reichstag in Vienna'. Whilst the Allies attempted to persuade Cologne's mayor to resign, they stubbornly avoided the appearance of giving in to public pressure.[75]

More controversial was the position of native Frenchmen, whose dismissal from public office Stein ordered. Only this, he argued, would preserve 'the unique German common spirit' from 'corrupting, paralysing, interference', whilst the new Bourbon government's expulsion of 'new Frenchmen' from office provided further justification.[76] Gruner refused to implement Stein's order, arguing that Frenchmen settled in the Rhineland should be treated like Germans so long as they were not Bonapartists. Stein's order

---

[72] *Ibid.*, pp. 446–9.
[73] The Allies experienced difficulty in finding Rhinelanders willing to shoulder public responsibility even in the larger towns and cities, including Krefeld, Monschau and Aachen. Bölling to Sack, 28 October 1814, 4 February 1815, HStAD, Gen. Gouv. Nieder- und Mittel Rhein, 27.
[74] Ladoucette to Montalivet, AN, F¹ᶜIII Roër 4, no. 326. Ladoucette reported that Wittgenstein wished to retire but was prevented from doing so by the Allied authorities. See also HASK, Bestand 890, 387, nos. 1–4, 7–8.
[75] HASK, Bestand 890, 387, nos. 9–10, 17–20, 25–6, 29–30, 37–8, 41–2.
[76] Stein, *Briefe*, 4, p. 771.

provoked a flood of appeals, both from the Frenchmen concerned and their Rhenish colleagues, who reminded the Allies that many Frenchmen had in practice been naturalised and even taken German wives and learnt the German language.[77] Gruner argued that naturalisation was an accepted principle in most countries, that many Frenchmen were more loyal than some Germans, and that Stein's instruction appeared 'hard and contrary to the good cause' and detrimental 'to the principles which will preserve the old, honest reputation won by our German Fatherland'. Gruner, it transpired, was personally interested through his recent marriage to the daughter of one of the threatened French officials. The dissolution of the Central Administration prevented Stein from taking further action, and enquiries made the following year, during the One Hundred Days campaign, revealed that many Frenchmen remained in their posts.[78]

Of greater long-term significance was the positive assessment made by Gruner and Sack of many Napoleonic institutions. Gruner praised the departmental councils for their work in apportioning fiscal and requisitioning burdens, as it conformed with his notion of involving notables in government. Sack was similarly impressed by the prefectoral councils, which he preserved as '*provisorischer Landes Direktorial Räthe*'.[79] In several memoranda sent to Frederick William III, Sack argued that the provisioning of troops was greatly facilitated by the involvement of local notables in public affairs, especially the appointment of property-owners as local commissioners to sub-divide Allied fiscal and military burdens. He also stressed the importance of allowing individual municipalities wide autonomy in such matters.[80]

Above all, Sack praised the Napoleonic judicial organisation, especially juries. In June 1814, he wrote to Gneisenau that he wished to see such judicial procedures extended to the rest of Prussia, though he feared he would stand little chance of success against the 'prejudiced gentlemen' in Berlin without the general's support.[81] Both Sack and Gruner relied heavily upon Rhenish jurists in their general-governments, as they were best qualified, enjoyed public confidence, and were accepted as having tempered the worst aspects of Napoleonic despotism.[82] Sack counted them

---

[77] LHAK, Bestand 355, 38, [nos. 3–4, 14–15, 21–3].
[78] Gruner to Stein, 12 June 1814, Stein, *Briefe*, pp. 849–53. See also LHAK, Bestand 355, 38, [nos. 1–2].
[79] LHAK, Bestand 355, nos. 41–2.
[80] Sack to Frederick William III, 10 August 1814, 15 November 1815, GStA, rep. 89, 13607, 'Acta betr. Zustand der Rheinprovinz 1814–19', nos. 1–2, 27–8.
[81] Sack to Gneisenau, 21 June 1814, Steffens, *Briefwechsel*, part 2, pp. 81–2.
[82] LHAK, Bestand 353, 5, nos. 9, 15, 37, 39, 41.

as allies in his struggle against militarism.[83] It was fortuitous that Stein, whose extreme Francophobia led him to dismiss institutions that in many respects encapsulated his own ideas, was kept safely away by his wider political ambitions. These required his presence close to Allied headquarters, which moved into France in early 1814. This, coupled with the relative lack of interest of the Prussian government in the region – Berlin hoped to acquire Saxony, not the Rhineland – allowed Gruner and Sack considerable leeway in running their general governments according to their own principles. Thus were facts established on the ground before annexation to Prussia.

Sack and Gruner, despite their admiration for certain Napoleonic institutions, agreed on the need to enlist nationalist intellectuals to 're-Germanise' the Rhineland. This provoked conflict with the other Allies, notably Bernadotte, commander of the Army of the North and Crown Prince of Sweden, who was ingratiating himself with the French people in his quest for the throne vacated by Napoleon. Bernadotte supported French retention of her 'natural' frontiers.[84] This contradicted the vision of Stein, Gruner, Sack, and nationalists led by Arndt and Görres, who argued that Germany's frontier should extend as far as the German tongue. These tensions surfaced in December 1813, when Gruner smuggled nationalist proclamations across the Rhine promising the left bank's reunification with Germany, and was immediately contradicted by Bernadotte, who publicly insisted on the territorial integrity of France.[85] Relations between the Prussian and Swedish high commands deteriorated further following the Allied occupation of the Rhineland, hampering day-to-day administration.[86] Bernadotte's first act upon entering Cologne in early February 1814 was to proclaim that: 'Enlightened men everywhere cherish the hope of seeing France preserved'. When a Prussian officer started organising a militia in the former Hohenzollern duchies, Bernadotte intervened, complaining, ironically, of the evil of forcing Frenchmen to fight fellow Frenchmen. Bernadotte also interfered with Sack's weekly newsletter published

---

[83] For civil–military 'collisions' in the Lower Rhine before Sack's arrival, see LHAK Bestand 349, 86, nos. 1, 3–5. See also Frederick William III to Sack, 26 June 1814, GStA, rep. 77, tit. 50, nr. 1, bd. 1, no. 80, and Sack's reply to Frederick William III, dated 10 August 1814, GStA, rep. 89, 13607, 'Acta betr. Zustand der Rheinprovinz 1814–19', nos. 1–2.

[84] Alan Palmer, *Bernadotte. Napoleon's Marshal, Sweden's King* (London, 1990), pp. 196, 203, 208–12.

[85] Ladoucette to Montalivet, 11 December 1813, AN, F^{1C}III Roër 4, no. 265.

[86] See, for example, mayor Wittgenstein's complaints in February 1814 over the contradictory instructions he received from Bernadotte and the Prussians. HASK, Bestand 10 (81/1), no. 2, and Bestand 10 (81/2), no. 6.

in Aachen because it contained too much German in an area that was French. Sack complained to Gneisenau, accusing the Swedes of enriching themselves, not fighting Napoleon. Gneisenau replied that Prussian headquarters knew of Bernadotte's 'treachery', that they had even more evidence of it than he, but that nobody had the courage to confront him with his 'trickery'. Sack, Gneisenau urged, should make public Bernadotte's outrages to turn public opinion against him and so further the 'good cause'.[87]

Allied disunity confused Rhinelanders over their future status and confirmed the lack of dynastic bonds attaching them to the rest of Germany. Indeed, a secret article of the First Treaty of Paris implied that most of the region would aggrandise Holland, not some German state. As German nationalists never tired of pointing out, the threat from France remained omnipresent, even under Louis XVIII: 'In those [Bourbon] lillies,' Görres wrote, 'with which it decorates itself, remain hidden the old [Bonaparte] bees and wasps, still on the lookout for honey.'[88] Rumours abounded. In April 1814, Cologne's mayor listed those circulating in the city. Many predicted – and feared – Prussian rule, whilst others spoke of the Powers uniting the four departments into a single 'Kingdom of Austrasia', ruled over by the Austrian Archduke Ferdinand.[89] The possibility of Habsburg rule was lent greater credence by the Austrians regaining recruiting rights in the region.[90] The press and pamphlets stimulated public speculation of an imminent restoration of French rule in the form of hordes of customs officials.[91] Given the uncertainty, one can understand the exasperation of one Rhinelander, who despaired that 'only the gods know whether and when our souls in this land shall be badenised, darmstadtised, prussianised or austrianised'.[92]

Such uncertainty was unwelcome to Gruner and Sack, who supported the expulsion of the French and stronger German federal structures

---

[87] Sack to Gneisenau, 17 March 1814, and Gneisenau's reply of 23 April. Steffens, *Briefwechsel*, part 2, pp. 77; Kielmansegg, *Stein*, p. 119.

[88] *Rheinischer Merkur*, 19 May 1814.

[89] Wittgenstein to Fritz von Coels (Wittgenstein's stepson), 24 April 1814, HASK, Bestand 1123, Kastennr. 22, dossier 'Johann Jakob von Wittgenstein (Briefe); Abschriften aus dem Archiv v. Coels-Aachen, 1814'.

[90] The Austrian Baron von Luninck recruited Rhinelanders for the *Legion des Nieder-Rheins*, and Count Bentheim for the Austro-German Legion. For the former see the printed broad-sheet dated 14 April 1814 in StAA, Bestand RAII (Allgemeine Akten), 1231, no. 3. For the latter, see Stein's letters to Gruner and Sack of 10 March 1814. Stein, *Briefe*, 4, p. 621.

[91] *Rheinische Merkur*, 27 April 1814.

[92] 'Übrigens, wissen die Götter, wenn und wann unsre Seelen hier zu Lande gebadet, gedarmt, gepreußt oder geösterreichert werden.' Schmitt, *Verwaltung*, p. 24 n. 58.

reinforced by Austro-Prussian dualism. They rejected the pretensions of Napoleon's south German allies, and saw it as their mission to renationalise Rhinelanders, something undermined by speculation that the French might return. In their re-education campaign, the governors-general relied on leaders of the national movement, especially the writer Ernst Moritz Arndt. Arndt had joined Stein in St Petersburg in 1812 as his private secretary and subsequently launched a propaganda campaign to rouse German resistance against Napoleon. Especially influential was his *Kurze Katechismus für deutsche Soldaten*, which was aimed at German soldiers captured during the 1812 campaign and incorporated into the Russo-German Legion. In 1813 he published one of the most important German nationalist pamphlets of the Napoleonic Wars, *Der Rhein: Deutschlands Strom, nicht Deutschlands Grenze* (*The Rhine: Germany's River, not Germany's Border*). This rejected 'natural' borders, marked by geography, and favoured the coincidence of political and cultural frontiers. Language defined the nation: 'Was ist das Deutschen Vaterland? So weit die deutsche Zunge klingt.' Arndt considered it his task to promote German culture in the Rhineland, where it had been suppressed by a generation of French rule.[93]

Germany's cosmopolitan elite had paid little attention to the Rhineland's separation in the 1790s.[94] After 1813, in contrast, the region became the focus of the romantic-national revival, with the incomplete hulk of Cologne's gothic cathedral in particular serving as a place of pilgrimage. Rhinelanders were now somewhat condescendingly portrayed as long-lost prodigal brothers, in need of rehabilitation to remove foreign cultural contamination. Arndt, following his visit in early 1814, was especially conscious of the challenge: the Rhineland's urban elites, he reported, were 'depraved and poisoned', its youth 'on the whole feeble', and fifteen out of sixteen of its officials Francophile.[95] To rectify this, Gruner employed the printed word and patriotic ceremonies. Within days of his arrival, he ordered religious festivities and thanksgiving services for recent Allied victories. In recognition of their 'loyal, German character' and to encourage civic patriotism, he also allowed Rhenish cities to display their old coats-of-arms.[96] He issued the first of several patriotic appeals:

---

[93] Gruner to Stein, 3 June 1814, Stein, *Briefe*, 4, p. 836. For Arndt more generally, see Hans Kohn, *Prelude to Nation-States. The French and German Experience, 1789–1815* (Princeton, 1967), pp. 252–66.

[94] Friedrich Meinecke, *The Age of German Liberation, 1795–1815* (Berkeley and London, 1977), pp. 18–19.

[95] Karl-Georg Faber, *Die Rheinlande zwischen Restauration und Revolution. Probleme der Rheinischen Geschichte von 1814 bis 1848 im Spiegel der zeitgenössischen Publizistik* (Wiesbaden, 1966), p. 27.

[96] LHAK, Bestand 371, 549, nos. 67, 73.

Peoples of these long-oppressed, German lands! As a German I come amongst you, long-lost brothers who have been won back at great cost! To return you freedom, independence, honour and happiness in the name of generously hearted monarchs. Prove yourselves worthy of such great gifts. Earn the blood that has flowed on your behalf. Make willing and immediate sacrifice to secure an honourable, happy future. Seek to earn and preserve what the victorious Allied armies have given you. Remember the noble German princes, whose rule was happy and who remained worthy in good times and bad. Think of the great imperial union and the common language, which binds you with us in perpetuity. Prove yourselves worthy of being German, and you will remain so.[97]

Gruner subsequently called upon Rhenish youth to take up arms for the Fatherland, dwelling on the debt it owed for liberation. Freedom was being reintroduced from the east, and in recompense, Rhinelanders were expected to contribute to the national cause.[98]

The place to make this contribution was the militia, or *Landwehr*. This was both a military formation and school to nationalise youth. Stein organised the *Landwehr* in other areas under his control from autumn 1813 onwards, and structured it so as to undermine territorial state boundaries. Metternich opposed this by negotiating separate bilateral agreements with the princes regulating their military contributions to the coalition.[99] The *Landwehr*'s prospects were rosier in the Rhineland, where there were no sovereigns to contend with. By the end of February, Gruner had taken measures for its organisation in the region, setting the force level at 1 per cent of the population and distributing 10,000 copies of Arndt's patriotic *Landwehrkatechismus*.[100] Sack subsequently started organising the *Landwehr* in his zone. Mobilisation soon encountered difficulties. There was a shortage of suitably qualified officers and a lack of weapons despite shipments from Britain.[101] Above all, ordinary Rhinelanders demonstrated little enthusiasm for joining, something the *Rheinischer Merkur* blamed on former collaborators.[102] Amongst the minority who heeded the patriotic call was the young David Hansemann, to the fury of his father, who had just spent a fortune buying him out of French service.[103] Despite setbacks, Gruner could inform Stein in April that he was a

---

[97] *Ibid.*, no. 59.   [98] LHAK, Bestand 349, no. 85.
[99] Kielmansegg, *Stein*, pp. 26, 51–5.
[100] Stein to Ernst, Duke of Saxony-Coburg, 14 January 1814, Gruner to Stein, 28 February 1814, Stein to Gruner, 5 March 1814 and Gruner to Stein, 11 March 1814, Stein, *Briefe*, 4, pp. 457–8, 560, 590, 624 respectively. See also Kielmansegg, *Stein*, p. 120.
[101] Wilhelm Just, *Verwaltung und Bewaffnung im westlichen Deutschland nach der Leipziger Schlacht 1813 und 1814* (Göttingen, 1911), p. 11.
[102] *Rheinischer Merkur*, 29 March 1814, 13 April 1814.   [103] Bergengrün, *Hansemann*, p. 21.

fortnight away from mobilising over 10,000 men. Napoleon's unconditional abdication made this unnecessary.[104] Gruner, employing the language of Friedrich Ludwig Jahn's patriotic gymnastic societies, nevertheless lauded the Rhenish *Landwehr* for fulfilling a vital 'moral-physical' function. The Austro-Bavarian authorities were less enthusiastic, and immediately dissolved the *Landwehr* upon assuming responsibility for the Middle Rhine.[105]

Even more influential than Arndt as a nationalist activist was Joseph Görres. Politically disillusioned following Brumaire, the former *Cisrhénan* worked as a physics teacher in Koblenz under Napoleonic rule, but remained in touch with German cultural developments. Under the pseudonym 'Orion', he published articles in which he deplored the tragedy of a people that forgot its own character and instead aped foreign ways. Initially, following Napoleon's defeat in Russia, Görres doubted French rule could be overthrown. Following Leipzig he changed his mind, and devoted all his journalistic and literary talents to what he interpreted as an ethical crusade. Gruner appointed Görres director of education in the Middle Rhine in early 1814.[106]

Görres's greatest contribution came as editor of the *Rheinischer Merkur*, one of the most influential German newspapers during the period of its publication from January 1814 to January 1816.[107] In its editions, German nationalism evolved from optimism to bitter disillusionment. Initially, the emphasis was on hatred of France, expressed in the most uncompromising of terms. Following Napoleon's defeat, the focus shifted to the future settlement in Germany, though Francophobia remained a strong ingredient. Görres, like other nationalists, expressed great disappointment that Alsace-Lorraine was not returned to Germany. After April 1814, the *Merkur* increasingly focused on the German states formerly allied with Napoleon within the Confederation of the Rhine, a body it denounced as a 'betrayal of its own people'.[108] In particular, the *Merkur* condemned Bavaria as 'Napoleon's sweat in Germany', as 'un-German' and of being governed by

---

[104] Gruner to Stein, 24 March 1814, 13 April 1814 and Stein to Sack, 12 May 1814, Stein, *Briefe*, 4, pp. 658, 699–700, 785–6 respectively.

[105] LHAK, Bestand 371, 549, no. 33.

[106] *Neue Deutsche Biographie*, 6, pp. 532–6. For Görres more generally, see Kohn, *Nation-States*, pp. 289–300, and Jon Vanden Heuvel, *A German Life in the Age of Revolution: Joseph Görres, 1776–1848* (Washington, D.C., 2000).

[107] Published in Koblenz, the *Merkur* enjoyed a circulation of about 3,000. Alfred Herrmann, 'Die Stimmung der Rheinländer gegenüber Preußen 1814/16', *Annalen des historischen Vereins für den Niederrhein* 115 (1929), p. 385.

[108] *Rheinischer Merkur*, 13 March 1814, 29 December 1814.

Illuminati.[109] The south German governments responded by banning the *Merkur* in the summer of 1814.[110] To Berlin's embarrassment, the *Merkur*'s attacks continued during the One Hundred Days, when the south German states were allied with Prussia.[111] As for the Congress of Vienna, the *Merkur* supported Stein's vision of robust federal structures, including a German (Habsburg) emperor within the framework of Austro-Prussian dualism. It favoured Berlin playing the leading role in the Rhineland. Significantly, it supported the re-establishment of the old representative estates as the only means of countering 'Napoleonic' bureaucracy.[112]

The *Merkur* consistently condemned the survival of Napoleonic bureaucracy in Germany. Its malignant roots had been shaken, but not dislodged. The tyrannical 'machine-state', with its thousands of pumps and levers sucking the life-blood out of society, still reigned all-powerful, and would do so whilst 'collaborators' remained in positions of power.[113] Like other romantics, Görres refused to compartmentalise, rejecting not only French politics and institutions, but also French lifestyle and culture. The *Merkur* differed from many of the Prussian reformers in its indiscriminate rejection of 'liberal' French institutions, such as the judiciary and quasi-representational bodies, which arguably tempered Napoleonic despotism. Such institutions, the *Merkur* argued, were superficial, and served only to cloak authoritarianism.[114] It condemned other Rhenish publications for employing French words and phrases – 'disgusting German-French mishmash' – and demanded the purification of the German language in the region.[115] Concessions on the cultural front would benefit the French politically, it argued.[116] At the same time, liberal elements remained important in early romanticism, and the *Merkur* consistently condemned all forms of censorship as 'the stinking leftovers of the Napoleonic period', and secret police as the 'twig that first shot forth from the poisonous tree of the French police'.[117]

Increasingly, the *Merkur* employed 'France' as convenient patriotic shorthand for the ills identified within Germany, including Prussia. The liberal rather than nationalist-conservative ingredient of its critique of Napoleonic forms is apparent in the contributions of Johann Friedrich Benzenberg.

---

[109] *Ibid.*, 9 July 1814, 13 July 1814, 21 September 1814, 21 March 1815.
[110] Wolfgang Piereth, *Bayerns Pressepolitik und die Neuordnung Deutschlands nach den Befreiungskriegen* (Munich, 1999), pp. 66–75.
[111] *Rheinischer Merkur*, 9 April 1815.   [112] *Ibid.*, 5 October 1814, 9 October 1814, 22 January 1815.
[113] *Ibid.*, 13 July 1814, 19 July 1814, 29 July 1814, 31 July 1814, 15 September 1814, 9 October 1814, 7 April 1815.
[114] *Ibid.*, 26 August 1814.   [115] *Ibid.*, 17 July 1814, 2 August 1814.
[116] *Ibid.*, 23 June 1815.   [117] *Ibid.*, 29 July 1814, 20 August 1814.

Described as the first Rhenish liberal, Benzenberg had initially admired Napoleon, but in 1813 was won over to the patriotic cause. After the Allied occupation of the Rhineland, he joined the cluster of reformers gathered around Gneisenau in Koblenz.[118] He too condemned bureaucratic centralisation and despaired of the individual's defencelessness against the state. Significantly, he employed the historicist argument that the 'constitution' for each province in Germany must conform to social reality to press the case of the *'Mittelstand'* (bourgeoisie) as alone representing an alternative to bureaucracy in the Rhineland.[119] This, in its essentials, was the argument employed by Rhenish liberals until the middle of the century.

Those opposed to the Prussophile Francophobia of the *Merkur* found a mouthpiece in the Bavarian-sponsored press in the southern Rhineland. Bavaria, as the leading state of the former Confederation of the Rhine and Napoleon's chief German ally, represented the greatest impediment to those hoping for greater national unity. In addition, Munich was engaged in a dogged dispute with Sack's general government over the border between its zone and the Prussian zone in the Rhineland, and over the future of Mainz. The kingdom emerged as champion of those favourable to the Napoleonic order in Germany.[120] Munich responded to the insults of the *Merkur* and other nationalist publications by sponsoring Rhenish writers hostile to Prussia and more sympathetic to French institutions.

Georg Friedrich Rebmann emerged as the leading figure in this press, and Görres's most noteworthy opponent. Rebmann, like Görres, had initially welcomed the French Revolution and joined radical circles in the 1790s. Unlike Görres, he served under Napoleon, as an appeals court judge in Mont-Tonnerre. As noted earlier, he exploited this office to temper the worst abuses of the increasingly despotic regime. Rebmann was drawn into the Prusso-Bavarian dispute in 1814, and over the following years published several pamphlets and articles directed against the *Rheinischer Merkur*. This was not out of hostility to German nationalism per se; indeed, whilst in Napoleonic service, Rebmann published a piece emphasising the German character of the Rhineland. Rather, he recognised the illiberal potential of the nationalism spouted by Görres. He rejected north German accusations that south Germans and Rhinelanders had besmirched themselves through collaboration, and defended the French legacy against those who sought to 'de-Napoleonise' everything. In a balanced way he listed the pros and

[118] *Neue Deutsche Biographie*, 12, p. 60.
[119] Johann Friedrich Benzenberg, *Wünsche und Hoffnungen eines Rheinländers* (Paris, 1815), pp. 14, 34.
[120] Piereth, *Pressepolitik*, pp. 106ff.

cons of Napoleonic rule. Amongst the former he included the principle of representation, abolition of feudal impositions, tithes and tax privileges, the respect accorded private property, conscription as the basis for a national army, state encouragement of agriculture, and the civil and commercial codes (though not the criminal code, which he rejected as tyrannical). The Napoleonic era, he observed, had allowed the south German states to modernise antiquated institutions in the spirit of the eighteenth-century Enlightenment, in which his own liberalism was firmly rooted; in Prussia, he conceded, it had been marked by brutal occupation and exploitation. He completely rejected and ridiculed the unhistorical romantic glorification of the Middle Ages.[121]

Rebmann and Görres represented the political press that formed in Germany in the years between the collapse of Napoleonic censorship and repression following the Karlsbad Decrees of 1819.[122] This press polemically elaborated and disputed fundamental political questions and concepts that would dominate German discourse for almost half a century. The French legacy in Germany, and especially in the Rhineland, lay at the heart of this. The press's actual impact on the wider population is harder to discern. We know that 10,000 copies of Arndt's *Landwehrkatechismus* were circulated in the Rhineland in early 1814, and that the circulation of the *Rheinischer Merkur* peaked at about 3,000 later that year. Such figures reveal little on how this material was received, or the role of mediators in disseminating and interpreting it to third parties. We have already seen that the literacy rate in the Rhineland was one of the highest in Europe. Charles Dodd, an English traveller in the region shortly after Napoleon's defeat, noted with surprise that even most peasants could read and write well. Rhinelanders evinced an insatiable appetite for news. During Napoleonic rule they had crowded across the Rhine in droves in order to read material censored at home. Dodd described how this appetite was in part met after 1814 by the 'casinos' that existed in almost every town, the best of which subscribed to a profusion of both French and German journals.[123] The same traveller might condescendingly criticise German journals for being somewhat abstract. Yet seemingly abstract debates about the French legacy had very tangible implications for those formerly employed in the Napoleonic administration, purchasers of *biens nationaux* and businessmen who faced

---

[121] Faber, *Rheinlande*, pp. 46–55.

[122] Karl Heinz Schäfer, *Ernst Moritz Arndt als politischer Publizist. Studien zur Publizistik, Pressepolitik und kollektivem Bewußtsein im frühen 19. Jahrhundert* (Bonn, 1974), pp. 217–25.

[123] Charles Edward Dodd, *An Autumn Near the Rhine; or Sketches of Courts, Society, Scenery, & c. in Some of the German States Bordering on the Rhine* (London, 1818), pp. 485–8, 493.

exclusion from lucrative markets and British competition following the Continental System's collapse.

Nationalist efforts to instil a sense of patriotism in Rhinelanders were tested sooner than anyone would have predicted. On 26 February 1815, Napoleon escaped from Elba where he had been exiled following his first abdication. Within a month he was in Paris. The news of his escape broke in Vienna on the morning of 7 March. The assembled Allied monarchs and ministers reacted decisively: within a week they issued a public declaration indicting 'Napoleon Bonaparte' as an outlaw, by which time instructions had been sent to the armies placing them on alert. On 25 March, Austria, Britain, Prussia and Russia each pledged 150,000 troops to defend the European settlement. Napoleon decided to strike before his opponents concentrated their forces. In mid-June he advanced into Belgium at the head of 120,000 men. The only troops opposing him were a motley force under Wellington's and Blücher's army, which had moved into eastern Belgium in order to cover the British. At this critical point Bavarian propaganda scored its first success. The previous December had witnessed the culmination of the Poland-Saxony crisis. Bavaria opposed Prussian aggrandisement at the expense of a fellow medium-sized former member of the Confederation of the Rhine. As part of its campaign, the Bavarian authorities in the Rhineland sponsored the publication of an anti-Prussian piece entitled *Sachsen und Preußen*, which they then circulated amongst the sizeable Saxon contingents stationed near Koblenz which had been forcibly assimilated into the Prussian army. The piece called on the Saxons to fight only under their lawful king. This subversion bore fruit in Belgium in April and May, when the Saxon units subordinate to Blücher's command mutinied. Order was only restored after severe repression.[124]

Of greater concern to Sack in Aachen, which lay within walking distance of the Belgian frontier, was the presence of an estimated 20,000 Rhenish veterans of the Napoleonic army. Almost immediately after his return, Napoleon ordered the distribution of pamphlets in Belgium and the Rhineland calling on veterans to return to the eagles.[125] Sack, fearing for the veterans' loyalty – their 'continued devotion to Napoleon was only too well known' – took decisive measures to neutralise the threat. On 24 March – four days after Napoleon's arrival in Paris – he decreed that all veterans must join the Prussian forces within twenty-four hours, thereby

[124] Schmitt, *Verwaltung*, pp. 61–2, 141. Piereth, *Bayerns Pressepolitik*, pp. 112–13.
[125] Napoleon to Marshal Davout, 10 April 1815, Napoleon, *Correspondance*, 28, pp. 99–100.

bringing Blücher's regiments up to strength. Sack later estimated that 13,000 Napoleonic veterans were thus called up, representing a significant proportion of the 80,000 Prussian troops engaged in the Waterloo campaign, though there is some evidence that these soldiers performed badly.[126]

Fighting in Belgium heightened fears of a possible French invasion of the Rhineland, and the Prussian authorities moved quickly to assert their authority. They compelled Rhenish public servants to take an oath of allegiance in Aachen on 15 May. As one Prussian official noted: 'In the newly won provinces, where public opinion remained volatile, and where faith in Napoleon's genius remained alive, not the least doubt could be expressed as to the successful conclusion of the new campaign.'[127] Görres's propaganda activities were therefore supplemented by Arndt, who received official approval for the publication of a patriotic newspaper, *Der Wächter*.[128] At the same time, the Prussians took precautionary measures against potential fifth-columnists. They made enquiries into the number of native Frenchmen still serving in the administration.[129] Those suspected of maintaining correspondence with French acquaintants were placed under surveillance, their letters intercepted, and some deported to the right bank.

A few native officials, including Cologne's mayor, Wittgenstein, were removed. Wittgenstein had maintained contacts with France during the previous months. In January 1815 he even received notification that Louis XVIII had awarded him the Fleur de Lys. He also received a letter from a member of the Garde du corps du Roi, one of the elite units in the Bourbon household troops, thanking him for services rendered during the French retreat the previous year. 'Many respected generals and officials here remember you with affection,' the letter stated, 'and regret that you and the city of Cologne no longer enjoy the protection of the French flag.'[130] Whether or not the Prussian authorities were aware of this correspondence, they now decided to act. On 6 May 1815, Sack dismissed Wittgenstein, together with a number of his subordinates, on the grounds that Cologne's administration was 'neither conducted with enthusiasm for the sacred cause, nor with the energy and order one would hope to see at any time, but which

---

[126] Many were concentrated in the 25th infantry regiment, a unit that was deemed to have disgraced itself at the Battle of Ligny, though details remain scanty. GStA, rep. 89, 13607, 'Acta betr. Zustand der Rheinprovinz 1814–19', nos. 20–43. For the reference to the disgraced 25th infantry regiment, see Rory Muir, *Tactics and the Experience of Battle in the Age of Napoleon* (New Haven and London, 1998), pp. 210–11.

[127] Neigebaur, *Statistik*, p. 101. [128] Steffens, *Briefwechsel*, part 2, p. 90.

[129] For the Sarre department, see LHAK, Bestand 354, 352. Unfortunately, the promised comprehensive lists are not included.

[130] Morass to Wittgenstein, 18 January 1815, HASK, Bestand 1123, carton 22, dossier 'Entlassungs und Pensions-Versuch des Bürgermeister Joh. Jacob von Wittgenstein betreffend'.

is even more vital in the current critical situation threatening the city'.[131] As the One Hundred Days campaign reached it climax the following month, Sack issued confidential instructions to his subordinates on evacuation procedures in case of an invasion.[132]

Waterloo, followed by Napoleon's second abdication on 22 June, removed the threat and closed a two-year period of uncertainty. Rhinelanders had witnessed dramatic events in that period. Large armies moved through their region, their territorial status changed, and they found themselves at the heart of a debate over Germany's future. The Napoleonic order's destruction in 1814/15, like the Third Reich's collapse, appeared to many contemporaries to return the clock to *Stunde Null*. Germany might now be reordered at will, and a new blue-print imposed upon an apparently clean slate.[133] In the brief interlude following the collapse of Napoleonic censorship and the political clampdown instituted by the Karlsbad Decrees, these alternatives were presented quite openly to a wider public. Within the Rhineland itself, a set of almost fortuitous circumstances in the years 1813–15, starting with the collapse of the least popular and most authoritarian elements of Napoleonic governance, followed by the arrival of Gruner and Sack and their relative freedom of action, resulted in the appearance of a new blue-print. It was based upon principles already well ingrained in the region: participation in governance, a degree of representation and, above all, the limitation of executive power by law. This settlement subsequently proved difficult to modify, as we shall see.

Continuity rather than change distinguished life in the village and small town in these turbulent years. Two-thirds of the sixty-seven mayors, for example, in the former *arrondissement* of Cologne in 1816 had been inherited from the French. Over a quarter had served for at least a decade.[134] The degree of continuity was even greater in the southern Rhineland, administered by the Austro-Bavarian LAK after June 1814. The LAK favoured officials who had formerly served under the French not least because both the Austrians and Bavarians were most concerned with the fiscal exploitation of the Palatinate to fill their own empty coffers. A disruptive personnel policy would hinder this. Additionally, the Austrians and Bavarians were more suspicious of Prussophiles than Napoleonic collaborators. The LAK re-employed many officials, including native Frenchmen, formerly removed

---

[131] HASK, Bestand 890, 214, no. 53.   [132] LHAK, Bestand 354, 354.

[133] This sense of possibility is well brought out in Piereth, *Pressepolitik*.

[134] This is extrapolated from the *Annuaire du département de la Roër* (Aachen 1809–13), the *Kalender für den Kreis und die Stadt Köln auf das Schaltjahr nach der Geburt unseres Herrn Jesu Christi 1816* (Cologne, 1816) and the *Handbuch über den Königlich-Preussischen Hof und Staat für das Jahr 1818* (Berlin, 1818).

during the limited 'de-Napoleonising' exercise conducted under Stein's prompting. Individuals closely associated with Gruner and the German patriotic movement, on the other hand, experienced great difficulty in finding employment under the LAK. Overall, 84 per cent (136 out of 162) of the officials confirmed in their posts by the Bavarians after they formally annexed the Rhineland-Palatinate in 1816 had previously served the French.[135] The French legacy therefore lived on, with implications not only for the Bavarian Rhineland-Palatinate and the Prussian *Rheinprovinz*, but for Germany as a whole.

Napoleonic rule collapsed in 1813. Its unravelling exposed a lack of any deep-seated popular commitment to French rule. Certainly, conscripts marched off, taxes were paid and supplies provided, but only reluctantly and under compulsion. There was no hint of enthusiasm or urgency in defence of the Napoleonic regime. Rather, in the climate of uncertainty, social tensions came to the fore. For many ordinary Rhinelanders, the collapse of legitimate authority provided an opportunity to attack such age-old bogeys as the forestry guard, tax-collector and customs man. These were often native Frenchmen, which gave an opportunity subsequently to justify actions as being patriotic. For its part, the Rhenish elite feared social upheaval, but not to the extent of rallying around the crumbling Napoleonic regime. German nationalism, though it loomed large amongst French fears, in reality played hardly any role in the events of 1813 and 1814. Rhinelanders remained wedded to sub-national identities. German nationalists such as Arndt, who flocked to the Rhine following its liberation, interpreted this lack of national commitment as a sign of depravity resulting from a generation of alien rule.

The actual transition from French to Allied rule came relatively quickly and proceeded surprisingly smoothly. That was in no small part due to the professionalism and calibre of those serving within the Inter-Allied Central Administration. This body was dominated by some leading lights of the Prussian reform movement, notably Stein, Sack and Gruner. Significantly, none of these three were 'old Prussians', though they had long served the Hohenzollerns. Instead, they originated from the west: from Nassau, Cleves and Osnabrück respectively. They did not share the same emotional attachment to the old Prussian values that could be found east of the Elbe. Instead, they hoped to carry forward their reforms and extend them to

[135] Heiner Haan, 'Kontinuität und Diskontinuität in der pfälzischen Beamtenschaft im Übergang von der französischen zur bayerischen Herrschaft (1814–1818)', *Jahrbuch für westdeutsche Landesgeschichte* 2 (1976), 285–309.

Germany as a whole. In this, they faced opposition not only from Prussian conservatives, but also from Metternich and the princes of the Confederation of the Rhine states. Prussian reformers and German nationalists hated the princes on account of their collaboration with Napoleon and their introduction of 'bureaucratic absolutism' as the governing principle of their states. For their part the princes, with some exceptions, managed to escape the clutches of the Central Administration by striking timely deals with Metternich and defecting from the Napoleonic camp before it was too late. However, in the Rhineland, which was classified as vacated enemy territory, the Central Administration enjoyed a relatively free hand. This was partly because none of the German powers had any interest in acquiring this strategically exposed region, and were thus willing to consign its administration to the Inter-Allied body. With Stein away at Allied headquarters, Sack and Gruner and their subordinates were left to manage affairs. They faced a huge challenge in meeting the requirements of the Coalition armies. In rising to this challenge, they quickly came to appreciate some of the strengths of French institutions. Not only should these be preserved, but they should be extended eastwards, where they would contribute to Germany's renewal.

CHAPTER 9

The Rhineland and the development of Germany, 1815–1830

On 5 April 1815, Frederick William III proclaimed the incorporation of the two Rhenish provinces – the grand duchy of the Lower Rhine, and the duchies of Cleves, Berg and Geldern – into Prussia. Two million souls, including 1.5 million Catholics, were thereby added to his kingdom.[1] Frederick William undertook to protect property, safeguard religious beliefs and ensure justice. Significantly, he promised the creation of a representative body.[2] The vast majority of Rhinelanders became aware of the transfer of sovereignty with the appearance of Hohenzollern eagles in their towns instead of French symbols. On 30 April, Berlin decreed the future administrative structure for the enlarged Monarchy, and the King promised 'respect for the constitution, uniformity of action, liberality and impartiality', and the protection of 'all advantages gained through the free employment of personal talent'. Prussia was divided into ten provinces, each headed by a governor (*Oberpräsident*), and twenty-five districts, administered by district governors (*Regierungspräsidenten*). The two Rhenish provinces were Jülich-Cleves-Berg, administered from Cologne, and the grand duchy of the Lower Rhine, governed from Koblenz. Each was sub-divided into three districts.[3] At the local level, the French structure remained intact and, like other Napoleonic institutions, became the focus of dispute between reformers and conservatives. To complement the administrative reforms, Frederick William issued his fateful edict of 22 May, promising 'representation of

---

[1] J. A. Demian, *Geographisch-statistische Darstellung der deutschen Rheinlande, nach dem Bestande vom 1. August 1820* (Koblenz, 1820), pp. 30, 39, 41.
[2] Geheimes Staatsarchiv Preußischer Kulturbesitz, Berlin-Dahlem (GStA), rep. 74, HII 'Organisation Niederrhein', no. 2ᵃ Bd. 1, nos. 10–11, 14–15. The government published the two patents of annexation – one for each province – in the special supplement of the *Journal des Nieder- und Mittel-Rheins* of 16 April 1815.
[3] The grand duchy of the Lower Rhine included the districts of Koblenz, Trier and Aachen, whilst the province Jülich-Cleves-Berg grouped together the districts of Cologne, Düsseldorf and Cleves. GStA, rep. 74, HII 'Organisation Niederrhein', no. 2ᵃ Bd. 1, nos. 29–34 ('*Verordnung wegen verbesserte Einrichtung der Provinzial-Behörden*'). See also Max Bär, *Die Behördenverfassung der Rheinprovinz seit 1815* (Bonn, 1919), pp. 124–34.

the people' through an 'assembly of representatives of the land', a vague formulation that implied representation through estates. Nevertheless, the edict raised Rhenish expectations.

Prussia's expansion occurred at a decisive moment in the struggle between reformers and conservatives. In Bavaria, in contrast, a broad consensus emerged favourably disposed towards the French legacy in its new western province, the Rhineland-Palatinate. Indeed, Montgelas's government wished to see Napoleonic institutions extended throughout Bavaria as a whole.[4] Bavaria underwent 'state-building from the periphery' whilst Prussia experienced centre–periphery conflict. That reformers should dominate Prussia's western provinces whilst the political pendulum in Berlin was swinging towards reaction was in part fortuitous, as we have seen.[5] Their conservative opponents were led by interior minister Friedrich von Schuckmann and police minister Wilhelm Ludwig von Wittgenstein, together with privy councillor Karl Albert von Kamptz. Kamptz remained a bugbear amongst Rhenish liberals into the 1830s. The balance between reformers and conservatives was held by state chancellor Karl August von Hardenberg, the statesman next to Stein most associated with Prussia's regeneration. He was sympathetic to reformers in the Rhineland and favoured aspects of the Napoleonic legacy, but was also sensitive to conservative tendencies at court. Hardenberg, more than Stein, represented those ambiguities in the reform movement that caution against viewing the political alignments in Prussia in terms of homogeneous blocs of 'reformers' and 'conservatives'.[6]

Following annexation, Berlin intended to appoint Sack governor of Jülich-Cleves-Berg, and Friedrich zu Solms-Laubach governor of the Lower Rhine. By late 1815, Sack's position looked increasingly tenuous. His outspokenness against the 'obscurantist' 'Hatzfeldt-Schuckmann-Wittgenstein clique' gained him enemies, as did his tolerance of Görres. In the *Rheinischer Merkur*, Görres bluntly reminded Frederick William of his promise to grant the Rhineland 'an appropriate constitution', whilst criticising various government policies and shortcomings. His portrayal of the *Merkur* as an arena for the free expression of political opinion incensed Frederick William. When Sack refused to suppress the newspaper, the King pressurised

---

[4] Heiner Haan, 'Die bayerische Personalpolitik in der Pfalz von 1816/18 bis 1849', *Jahrbuch für westdeutsche Landesgeschichte* 3 (1977), pp. 351–94.

[5] Graf Peter von Kielmansegg, *Stein und die Zentralverwaltung 1813/14* (Stuttgart, 1964), pp. 23, 75, 100, 111–12, 138, 140–1, 144.

[6] For the complexities of Hardenberg's position, see Matthew Levinger's article, 'Hardenberg, Wittgenstein, and the Constitutional Question in Prussia 1815–22', *German History* 8 (1990), pp. 257–77.

Hardenberg into by-passing Sack and banning the paper outright (Cabinet order of 3 January 1816).[7] A few days later Sack complained bitterly to the reform-minded Gneisenau, now commanding general in the west: 'I leave it for you to judge whether it be good for this region to introduce obscurantism instead of open-mindedness, and despicable, secretive slyness instead of open, honest administration.'[8] Sack's friendship with Gneisenau, whose headquarters in Koblenz conservatives dubbed 'Wallenstein's camp on the Rhine', hardly improved his prospects; nor did accusations of nepotism, in the form of the appointment of numerous 'Sacks and Sacks-in-law' from the close-knit clique of families that had dominated eighteenth-century Cleves.[9] In March 1816 Berlin finally acted, transferring Sack to Stettin as governor of Pomerania. He was replaced by Karl von Ingersleben, who served first as governor of the Lower Rhine and then as governor of the unified *Rheinprovinz* following Solms-Laubach's death in 1822. Ingersleben remained in post until his own death in 1831. Sack served out his remaining days in Stettin, the only Prussian provincial governor before 1866 not to be ennobled.

Sack's abrupt transfer from the Rhineland, where he enjoyed popularity, further depressed public opinion. This could best be described as one of sullen resignation in the face of requisitioning burdens and isolated but well-publicised outrages committed by soldiers. Grumbling about taxes continued following Napoleon's defeat, when people expected a return to the fiscal policies of the prince-bishops.[10] Prussian prestige grew after Frederick William's constitutional promises and Waterloo – the authorities circulated hundreds of patriotic prints immediately following the victory – but then evaporated with the concomitant increase in the arrogance of

---

[7] Andrea Hofmeister-Hunger, *Pressepolitik und Staatsreform. Die Institutionalisierung staatlicher Öffentlichkeitsarbeit bei Karl August von Hardenberg (1792–1822)* (Göttingen, 1994), pp. 268, 303–4, 308–9.

[8] Sack to Gneisenau, 8 January 1816, Wilhelm Steffens (ed.), *Briefwechsel Sacks mit Stein und Gneisenau (1807/17)* (Stettin, 1931), part 2, p. 114.

[9] Amongst the numerous and in part conflicting interpretations of Sack's removal, see: Manfred Koltes, *Das Rheinland zwischen Frankreich und Preussen: Studien zu Kontinuität und Wandel am Beginn der preussischen Herrschaft (1814–1822)* (Cologne, 1992), pp. 111–14; Steffens, *Briefwechsel*, part 1, pp. 39–41, 52 and part 2, pp. 88–9, 111; Fritz Vollheim, *Die provisorische Verwaltung am Nieder- und Mittelrhein während der Jahre 1814–1816* (Bonn, 1912), pp. 29, 48–9; *Allgemeine Deutsche Biographie* (56 vols., Leipzig, 1875–1912), 30, pp. 152–3; Adolf Klein and Justus Bockemühl (eds.), *1770–1815. Weltgeschichte am Rhein erlebt. Erinnerungen des Rheinländers Christoph Wilhelm Sethe aus der Zeit des europäischen Umbruchs* (Cologne, 1973), passim; Bär, *Behordenverfassung*, pp. 128–9.

[10] Sack to Stein, 10 March 1814 and 31 May 1815, Steffens, *Briefwechsel*, part 2, pp. 67–9 and 94–5 respectively. See also H. Cardauns and R. Müller (eds.), *Die rheinische Dorfchronik des Johann Peter Delhoven aus Dormagen, 1783–1823* (Cologne, 1926), p. 226.

Prussian soldiers on Rhenish streets, which reawakened deep-seated fears of East-Elbian militarism.[11] Friction was aggravated by the size of military forces Prussia maintained in the region even after Napoleon's defeat. Cologne, for example, contained 4,000 troops and just over 4,000 private houses on which they could be billeted.[12]

Rhinelanders might accept rule from Berlin in order to remain German, but refused to become Prussian, in Benzenberg's neat formulation.[13] Historically, the predominantly Catholic Rhineland manifested pro-Habsburg sentiment, and during the Congress of Vienna, hopes were expressed that the German imperial dignity might be re-established with a Habsburg incumbent.[14] Three years later, during the Congress of Aachen, the Austrian Emperor, Francis I, was received enthusiastically by the inhabitants of the city – unlike Frederick William III – whilst Metternich's carriage, passing through Cologne, was mobbed by an enthusiastic crowd who mistook it for his sovereign's.[15] Similar pro-Habsburg manifestations would occur during the 1848–9 revolutions.[16]

Above all, Catholicism remained an important alternative focus for most Rhinelanders. This despite the fact that institutionally the Church emerged from the Napoleonic period in disarray. Plans for a German-wide concordat to reorder things never came to fruition. The individual states favoured bilateral agreements with Rome as more in keeping with their sovereignty, and the Papacy feared an all-German primate might dilute its influence. It too favoured bilateral agreements, concluding the first with Bavaria in October 1817. For the *Rheinprovinz*, the 1822 agreement with Berlin finally superseded the Napoleonic settlement and created a new province of the Lower Rhine. This comprised the dioceses of Trier, Cologne, Münster and Paderborn, with the Archbishop of Cologne as Metropolitan.

The Prussians fully supported the reconstruction of diocesan structures, whilst maintaining various controls more or less annoying for laity and

---

[11] Charles E. Dodd, *An Autumn Near the Rhine; or, Sketches of Courts, Society, Scenery, & c. in Some of the German States Bordering the Rhine* (London, 1818), pp. 503–4.

[12] For Prussian military deployments, see *Rang- und Quartier-Liste der Königlich Preußischen Armee für das Jahr 1819* (Berlin, 1819), pp. 18–19. See also Demian, *Darstellung*, pp. 86–7, and Walter Gerschler, *Das preußische Oberpräsidium der Provinz Jülich-Kleve-Berg in Köln 1816–1822* (Cologne, 1967), pp. 139, 143.

[13] Franz Petri, 'Preußen und das Rheinland', in Walter Först (ed.), *Das Rheinland in Preussischer Zeit* (Cologne and Berlin, 1965), p. 42.

[14] *Kölnische Zeitung*, 3 January 1815.

[15] Heyderhoff, *Benzenberg*, p. 105; Alan Palmer, *Metternich. Councillor of Europe* (London, 1997 pbk edn), p. 175.

[16] Jonathan Sperber, *Rhineland Radicals. The Democratic Movement and the Revolution of 1848–1849* (Princeton, 1993 pbk edn), pp. 281–3, 306–7, 312–13, 329.

clergy. Jesuits remained barred. Religious orders, with a few exceptions, were only readmitted in the 1850s. Restrictions on pilgrimages continued. Correspondence between the hierarchy and Vatican needed to pass through the Ministry of Ecclesiastical Affairs. This had been set up to administer the Protestant churches and contained no special department for Catholic affairs. Yet despite these irritants, relations between Berlin and Cologne's new archbishop, Ferdinand August von Spiegel (installed in 1825), were initially good. With government co-operation, he stamped his authority on the new province. Crucial to this were the forty-four deacons appointed in 1827 to act as an intermediate tier between himself and the 689 parishes, and it is their reports that provide the best insight into the state of the Church at local level.

Ordinary Catholics, the reports concurred, were generally apolitical, respectful of authority and even grateful to the Prussians for restoring order. Frederick William III, together with the Pope and bishops, were remembered in prayers. Subordinate Prussian officials, in contrast, were generally disliked because they were usually Protestant and considered prejudiced. Relations between them and priests were often strained. As for religious life, the reports suggested that ordinary people were devout, at least outwardly: their lives were governed by the Church calendar, they regularly received the sacraments and ostracised deviants. Even reports from the cities were generally optimistic in this respect, despite references to immorality blamed on French rule. There, religious brotherhoods survived Napoleon, escaping suppression with the connivance of local authorities. New foundations appeared after 1815, but increasingly resembled secular mutual benefit societies, preserving only tenuous religious connections.[17] Reports from majority Protestant areas were less optimistic, complaining that Catholics tended to be neglectful of their spiritual duties. The young also gave cause for concern. Overall, whilst most deacons were satisfied with outward displays of piety, they were less sanguine in their estimation of genuine piety. In particular, they complained about various popular practices, though they noted approvingly that the Prussians, unlike the French, were as hostile as themselves to these. As for the bourgeoisie, much of this was infected by secularising tendencies, viewed religion chiefly as a form of 'police' over the lower orders, participated in religious festivities simply to display its prestige, and undermined popular devotion through criticism and ridicule. Through Catholicism, it preserved its civic status under foreign rule. Nor

---

[17] Jonathan Sperber, *Popular Catholicism in Nineteenth-century Germany* (Princeton, 1984), pp. 33–4. Also, T. C. Banfield, *Industry of the Rhine* (2 vols., London, 1846–8), 2: *Manufactures: Embracing a View of the Social Condition of the Manufacturing Population of Their District*, pp. 46–7.

was it especially generous when it came to material support for the Church, as demonstrated by Cologne city council's stinginess in allocating funds for the unfinished cathedral (Frederick William III, in contrast, gave generously). The numerically small Catholic nobility, unlike the bourgeoisie, remained devout.[18]

Before focusing on the laity, Spiegel needed to improve the clergy. This emerged from Napoleonic rule divided into three ideological strands. Many older priests educated in pre-revolutionary Bonn retained sympathy for the Enlightenment and even Febronianism. Another group of older clerics remained attached to old-church scholasticism, which had been ingrained in them in pre-revolutionary Cologne. A third group of younger priests, finally, had received inadequate training in the deficient seminaries established by Napoleon.[19] Spiegel's hope for improvement lay in the theological faculty of the newly established university of Bonn, where the famous Georg Hermes occupied the chair in Catholic theology from 1820 until his death in 1831. Though subsequently condemned by Rome for his radical theology of reconciliation between religion and science, Hermes successfully filled his lecture theatres and contributed to the flowering of the faculty that by 1829 numbered 340 students.[20]

Focus on Church–state tension risks diminishing conflict within the Church itself. Relations between Spiegel and Rome were by no means free of discord. Conflict occurred when the Vatican, determined to bypass Berlin, opened an unofficial correspondence with a small group of trusted clerics in the Rhineland via the nunciature in Munich. Rome, to Spiegel's annoyance, employed this parallel information network to gather reports, and both he and the government agreed that this practice must cease. Within the archdiocese itself, many parish priests and parishioners resented the quarterly visitations by the deacons, and proved uncooperative. On this issue too, Berlin supported Spiegel's efforts to reinforce control. In 1829, the government acceded to Spiegel's request for an increase in the number of religious holidays from the Napoleonic four to fourteen, thereby bringing the *Rheinprovinz* into line with the rest of Prussia. As to moral issues relating to marriage, Spiegel found himself in harmony with Prussian

---

[18] Wilfried Evertz, *Seelsorge im Erzbistum Köln zwischen Aufklärung und Restauration 1825–1835* (Cologne, Weimar and Vienna, 1993), pp. 66–84. For Cologne cathedral, see Eberhard Gothein, 'Verfassungs- und Wirtschaftsgeschichte der Stadt Cöln vom Untergange der Reichsfreiheit bis zur Errichtung des Deutschen Reiches', in City of Cologne, *Die Stadt Cöln im ersten Jahrhundert unter Preußischer Herrschaft. 1815 bis 1915* (Cologne, 1915), p. 193.

[19] Evertz, *Seelsorge*, pp. 7–9.

[20] Walter Lipgens, *Ferdinand August Graf Spiegel und das Verhältnis von Kirche and Staat, 1789–1835. Die Wende vom Staatskirchentum zur Kirchenfreiheit* (2 vols., Münster, 1965), 1, pp. 349–50, 445–60.

conservatives, who favoured the extension westwards of stricter legislation, and in conflict with reformers and liberals fighting for the preservation of the French codes. On primary education, Prussian officials co-operated with the clergy in the reconstruction process necessitated by French neglect. The government founded Catholic as well as Protestant teacher training colleges, and accorded the deacons an important role as school inspectors. Ironically, this increase in Church influence over education contributed to the subsequent Catholic revival that would later cause Berlin so much trouble.[21]

There were some points of conflict between Church and state, even in the 1820s. Clerical jurisdiction, which had been eliminated by the French but existed elsewhere in Prussia, became a bone of contention; on this issue at least, even conservative ministers in Berlin argued the virtues of Napoleonic legislation. Yet it was only in the 1830s that a dramatic deterioration occurred. One reason was the death in 1831 of Ingersleben, with whom Spiegel had enjoyed excellent relations. More serious was increasing anti-Catholicism amongst court circles in Berlin. It was against this background that the issue of mixed marriages became important. Numerically, their number was minute, accounting for barely 3 per cent of the total in the archdiocese, a figure that is an interesting measure of inter-confessional relations. Differing practices in the eastern provinces, where the Catholic clergy took a lax view, led Frederick William to conclude that fundamental tenets of Catholic belief were not at stake. Instead, he favoured mixed marriages as a tool for Protestant proselytisation. This objective lay behind the 1803 law stating that where parents in a mixed marriage were in disagreement, all the children would be brought up according to the father's wishes. As the majority of Prussia's population was Protestant, and as men were more mobile than women, the majority of fathers in mixed marriages in the Rhineland tended to be Protestant.

Problems arose when Berlin extended the 1803 law to the *Rheinprovinz* in the cabinet orders of 6 April 1819 and 17 August 1825, the second of which threatened to remove priests who solicited promises from couples to raise their children as Catholics. Spiegel, who followed the strict Papal line on mixed marriages, failed to oppose Berlin directly but prevaricated and, to gain time, focused on the state's right to suspend clergy. As to the main issue, he recommended that Berlin should approach Rome whilst avoiding precipitous action against clerics. This advice was followed and, soon thereafter (in 1827), the Monarchy's resident in Rome optimistically reported that

[21] *Ibid.*, 1, pp. 430–5.

Pope Leo XII had accepted the Prussian legislation. This proved grossly inaccurate, but defused things until Clement August von Droste-Vischering succeeded Spiegel as archbishop in 1835. Droste-Vischering refused to believe Berlin's interpretation of negotiations with the Vatican and vigorously enforced conditions for the solemnisation of mixed marriages. The government responded by arresting Droste-Vischering in November 1837, an act that attracted Europe-wide attention. The most important consequence of the resulting struggle, which only ended in 1840 with Frederick William IV's accession, was the 'confessionalisation' of provincial politics and the emergence of a distinct Catholic 'party'.[22] Thereafter, the Rhenish Catholic liberal bourgeoisie, though not especially devout, demonstrated markedly less hostility to the Church than its counterpart in southern Germany, where Church and conservative forces within the states remained closely associated. The Rhenish bourgeoisie happily reconciled economic liberalism with its faith until at least the 1850s, and even thereafter its identity was never solely defined by class.[23]

The Cologne *Wirren*, as the conflict sparked by mixed marriages became known, aggravated relations between Catholic periphery and Protestant centre, and obscured tensions between laity and hierarchy. During riots in Cologne in 1830, Spiegel was lumped together with the Prussian authorities as an object of popular vitriol; seven years later, his successor became the focal point of opposition to the Prussians. As for popular religiosity, the real turning point came in the 1850s and 1860s. Until then, both Catholic hierarchy and Prussian state suspected, discouraged and controlled displays of popular piety, thus continuing the policy of the archbishop electors and the French. Pilgrimages all but died out in the 1840s, and their resurgence some twenty years later marked something new that was a direct consequence of the hierarchy which now, for the first time since the early eighteenth century, systematically encouraged and institutionalised popular religious sensibilities.[24]

Though the degree of Prussophobia should not be exaggerated before the late 1830s, Catholic Rhinelanders never doubted that the Monarchy was essentially Protestant.[25] Prussia was not *their* state, but that of their confessional rivals. Protestants, after all, dominated the court and highest

---

[22] *Ibid.*, 1, pp. 415–30. For the electoral consequences of the conflict see Herbert Obenaus, *Anfänge des Parlamentarismus in Preußen bis 1848* (Düsseldorf, 1984), p. 269.

[23] Thomas Mergel, *Zwischen Klasse und Konfession: Katholisches Bürgertum im Rheinland 1794–1914* (Göttingen, 1994), passim.

[24] Sperber, *Popular Catholicism*, pp. 30, 56.

[25] In the Bavarian Palatinate the confessional position was reversed, with a Protestant periphery battling against a Catholic core. An interesting contemporary French assessment of the nature of this conflict

echelons of the bureaucracy and army. A disproportionate amount of state funds was allocated to Protestant institutions. The Protestant theology faculty in Bonn, for example, received over twice as much government funding as the Catholic, despite the fact that it took a far smaller number of students. The Protestant flavour of the state was symbolically illustrated for all in public ceremonies. Only Protestant services were held to mark the opening of the provincial Rhenish *Landtag*, made up of a majority (though a disproportionately small one) of Catholic deputies.[26]

Yet, just as Catholic hostility should not be exaggerated, nor should differences between Protestants and the state be overlooked. Certainly, Rhenish Protestants traditionally favoured the Hohenzollerns, to whom they looked for protection. In 1814, they even requested that Berlin guarantee their rights should the Rhineland be ceded to a Catholic dynasty.[27] Rhenish Protestants found themselves incorporated into Prussia at a time when the Monarchy was forging ahead with the union of Calvinism and Lutheranism. This was a long-term project of the Hohenzollerns, a Calvinist dynasty ruling over predominantly Lutheran subjects. It was made feasible by the diminution of dogmatic differences between the two churches in the eighteenth century. Frederick William III was a firm believer in union, and the disaster of 1806/7 provided an opportunity to lay the institutional foundations. These foundations were completed in 1815/16, with the setting up of provincial consistories (*Provinzial-Konsistorien*) for the Protestant churches presided over by the provincial governors, and presbyteries and synods at the local level.

Frederick William was determined to extend the union to embrace matters of belief which he, despite his *jus in sacra*, had the duty to defend but not the authority to change. He nonetheless pressed ahead, exploiting the tricentenary of 1517 (the year Luther nailed his theses to Wittenberg cathedral) to announce the union. Not that Prussia was alone in following this path:

is located in Archives Nationales, Paris (AN), F⁷6821, dossier 2402. The relevant report is dated 2 July 1816. Paris took a keen interest in the Rhineland in the years following the end of Napoleonic rule.

[26] The confessional mix of the Rhenish *Landtag* was as follows:

	Catholics	Protestants
1826/7	46	34
1841	52	28
1846	44	31

Obenaus, *Parlamentarismus*, p. 304.

[27] Benzenberg to Hardenberg, 1 December 1816, Heyderhoff, *Benzenberg*, p. 50. See also J. A. Kopstadt, *Über Kleve. In Briefen an einen Freund aus den Jahren 1811 und 1814* (Frankfurt a. M., 1822), pp. xi, 54–7, and Johann Adam Boost, *Was waren die Rheinländer als Menschen und Bürger, und was ist aus ihnen geworden?* (Mainz, 1819), pp. 57–8.

Calvinists and Lutherans in the Rhineland Palatinate united in August 1818, as did their counterparts in Baden and Hessen several years later. As we have already seen, the Rhenish Protestant churches were already taking practical steps towards union during the Napoleonic period. In Prussia, Frederick William, a keen student of the liturgical practices of early Protestantism, proceeded to draw up a new liturgy for the united Church. This was published as *Der Entwurf einer preußischen Agende*, and was introduced in the army in 1821 with the civilian version following the next year. Though its adoption was technically voluntary, in practice official pressure was placed on congregations to employ it. This provoked resistance from some, both on the grounds that the new liturgy was too ceremonial and because of the principle that it represented an infringement of individual conscience. Frederick William responded by compromising, and allowing greater flexibility, something that encouraged acceptance. By 1830, only a minority in the eastern provinces rejected the *Agende*. In the *Rheinprovinz*, Lutherans and Calvinists generally welcomed the union, though there was some resistance in Jülich and Berg. The original *Agende*, however, was badly received in the west, because of its perceived Romanist tendencies: one parishioner in Elberfeld went so far as to ask a young pastor whether he would soon be sacrificing calves and rams! The revised *Agende* was accepted in the western provinces (in 1834), in return for a less hierarchical Church structure of local congregations, circuit synods and provincial synod. This was introduced in 1835, finally replacing the structure inherited from the French, and providing a model that was eventually extended elsewhere in Prussia and Germany.[28]

The Prussians confronted the challenge of improving public opinion amongst Rhinelanders of all confessions. Like the French, they sought to associate themselves with Rhenish culture. For example, they timed the return of looted artistic treasures to coincide with celebrations marking Prussian victories and Hohenzollern dynastic anniversaries.[29] They printed their official circulars on paper headed with old Rhenish symbols and authorised towns to restore their old coats of arms.[30] Their refoundation of Bonn university in 1818 provided an especially good opportunity to

---

[28] Ernst Rudolf Huber, *Deutsche Verfassungsgeschichte seit 1789* (3 vols., Stuttgart, Berlin, Cologne and Mainz, 1957–63), 2, pp. 458–70. Also, Christopher M. Clark, *The Politics of Conversion. Missionary Protestantism and the Jews in Prussia 1728–1941* (Oxford, 1995), pp. 213–17.

[29] Sack's circular of 21 July 1815, *Journal des Nieder- und Mittel-Rheins* (22 July 1815), pp. 739–40. Sack to Frederich William III, 15 November 1815, GStA, rep. 89, 13607, 'Acta betr. Zustand der Rheinprovinz 1814–19', no. 12. Also, *Kölnische Zeitung* 3 August 1815.

[30] R. A. von Kamptz (ed.), *Annalen der preussischen inneren Staats-Verwaltung* (23 vols., Berlin, 1817–39), 1, part 4, p. 117. *Kölnische Zeitung*, 15 March 1814.

contrast the neglect of higher education by the French, whilst also holding out the prospect of providing natives with the qualifications needed for state employment.[31] Above all, Berlin exploited the romantic fascination for the medieval. Official propaganda even claimed that Prussians were the descendants of Rhenish settlers who had migrated eastwards in the Middle Ages.[32] The architect, Karl Friedrich Schinkel, who visited Cologne and was impressed by its incomplete gothic cathedral, in 1816 proposed its completion 'as perhaps the only possible means of producing a positive opinion on the current state of affairs amongst the inhabitants of Cologne and the Rhine province'. Wilhelm von Humboldt proposed the same on similar grounds.[33] Schinkel also recommended the foundation of a Rhenish museum, and sought to preserve the medieval clutter of the region's cities against alien classicism. Hohenzollern princes, including the future Frederick William IV, converted romantic castles along the Rhine into cosy, Biedermeier retreats.[34]

Despite Prussian interest in their culture, Rhinelanders hardly warmed to their new rulers.[35] Benzenberg observed in July 1816 that a 'formal opposition' existed between locals and 'Lithuanians' (as Prussians were contemptuously called), who remained socially isolated, whilst Prince William, the king's brother, was struck by the poor state of public opinion during his inspection tour in 1819.[36] The Europe-wide economic downturn was partly to blame. Rhenish industry was especially vulnerable, given its integration into Napoleon's Continental System, and suffered greatly when the Dutch and French governments erected tariff barriers. British goods, meanwhile, inundated the region because Berlin pursued a free-trade policy best suited for the grain-exporting East Elbian landowners. In addition, flooding along the Rhine and generally unsettled weather conditions – in part a consequence of Mount Tomboro's cataclysmic eruption in the East Indies in 1815 – resulted in an especially poor harvest in 1816, high food prices and depressed consumption. The Prussians responded as best they

---

[31] Solms-Laubach to Bülow (Minister of Finance) and Schuckmann, 31 May 1816, GStA, rep. 77, tit. 50, nr. 50, nos. 4–12.

[32] *Journal des Nieder- und Mittel-Rheins* (25 July 1815), pp. 748–9.

[33] Eva Brües, *Die Rheinlande. Unter Verwendung des von Ehler W. Grashoff gesammelten Materials* (Berlin, 1968), pp. 4–17, 103, 107–8, 306–7. For Cologne cathedral, see also the *Rheinischer Merkur*, 20 November 1814, and *Kölnische Zeitung*, 24 November 1814.

[34] Brües, *Rheinlande*, pp. 4, 107–8, 128ff.

[35] See, for example, the particularly detailed report (of 10 June 1817) on public opinion from the district administration of Cologne, addressed to Frederick William III, in GStA, rep. 89, 13607, 'Acta betr. Zustand der Rheinprovinz 1814–19', nos. 71–84.

[36] Heyderhoff, *Benzenberg*, p. 40. Prince William to Frederick William III, 7 December 1819, GStA, rep. 89, 13607, 'Acta betr. Zustand der Rheinprovinz 1814–19', no. 122.

could, tightening export restrictions, releasing military supplies, banning the use of scarce grain for the production of spirits and purchasing 2 million *Reichsthaler* worth of rye in the Baltic ports that they then sold at below market prices in the western provinces. However, much of this arrived too late. In addition, the export ban proved difficult to enforce, and further supplies left the region legally to provision troops stationed in France. The inadequate poverty relief institutions were overwhelmed, whilst the multi-tiered collegiate administrative system appeared both excessively expensive – it accounted for a quarter of the government's budget – and ponderous in responding to the crisis when compared to its streamlined Napoleonic predecessor. Many notables decided self-help was more effective, and founded so-called 'Grain Associations' resembling joint stock companies that eventually purchased 1 million *Reichsthaler* of rye that they then sold at below market price. Civic initiative rather than the reputation of the Prussian state emerged strengthened from this immediate postwar crisis.[37]

Instead, economic difficulties fuelled Rhenish fears of exploitation by poor easterners, a perception best expressed by the wealthy banker Abraham Schaaffhausen, who, upon first hearing of the Rhineland's cession to Prussia in 1815, supposedly exclaimed: 'Jesus, Mary and Joseph! We are marrying into a poor family!' Such fears were reinforced by accusations that the Prussians, like the French, monopolised lucrative positions. The question of the balance between natives and outsiders in the administration remained controversial for most of the nineteenth century.[38] Certainly, initial official reports revealed grave misgivings on Berlin's part over the ability of Rhinelanders to govern themselves, because of Napoleonic contamination.[39] In part, this sense derived from the fiction maintained by the French that mayors should perform their duties unremunerated though, as noted earlier, they had in practice rewarded themselves with generous

---

[37] Hans-Heinrich Bass, 'Hungerkrisen in Posen und im Rheinland 1816/17 und 1847', in Manfred Gailus and Heinrich Volkmann (eds.), *Der Kampf um das tägliche Brot. Nahrungsmangel, Versorgungspolitik und Protest 1770–1990* (Opladen, 1994), pp. 150–75. Volcanologists consider the eruption of Tomboro as the greatest such event since 1500, with the volume of ash ejected into the atmosphere estimated at up to 1,000 cubic kilometres. The ejection of this mass of particles created a reverse greenhouse effect, reducing incoming solar radiation whilst allowing reflected radiation back out to space. The result was a global decrease in temperature in 1816, amounting to a 2.1 degree Fahrenheit drop below the average (for the years 1768–1819) in northern Germany. John D. Post, 'A Study in Meteorological and Trade Cycle History: The Economic Crisis Following the Napoleonic Wars', *The Journal of Economic History* 34, 2 (1974), pp. 315–49.

[38] A memorandum of 21 June 1831 sent to the ministry of the interior stated that the perception that natives were discriminated against, though not necessarily justified, had become deeply embedded. GStA, rep. 77, tit. 50, nr. 50, nos. 21–4.

[39] Bölling to Sack, 24 December 1814, Hauptstaatsarchiv Düsseldorf (HStAD), Gen. Gouv. Nieder- und Mittel Rhein, 27, [no. 18].

allowances. The French generally tolerated this, but not the Prussians.[40] Furthermore, many Prussians, notably provincial governor Solms-Laubach, remained distrustful of former 'collaborators'.[41] A detailed list of Rhenish candidates for government posts drawn up for Solms-Laubach in 1815 graded individuals according to their relationship with the Napoleonic regime: those who had remained 'German' in their self-perception during French rule were first class; those who, though professionally competent, had besmirched themselves through receipt of a French honour were second class; unreformed Bonapartists, like Cologne's 'completely French' former mayor, Wittgenstein, were third class.[42] Those who had fought in the Wars of Liberation – on the Coalition side – could expect favourable treatment.[43] Above all, Prussian conservatives, including Schuckmann, favoured the employment of 'old Prussians', condemning the Rhenish bourgeoisie as morally corrupt on account of its speculation in *biens nationaux* which had destroyed 'German' industriousness.[44] Senior Prussian civil servants, unlike their Napoleonic counterparts, faced a tough apprenticeship and exams before employment, and this posed an additional barrier to Rhinelanders educated under the French system.[45]

In practice, Berlin continued to rely upon natives, especially in the judiciary. Nonetheless, in the higher echelons of provincial government, the balance favoured 'old Prussians'. Provincial governors, like Napoleonic prefects, were generally drawn from outside. Significantly, no Catholic was appointed governor of the *Rheinprovinz* during the entire nineteenth century. Berlin also selected most district governors from outside the region, and these too were overwhelmingly Protestant. A report commissioned in 1817 by Hardenberg revealed that only about a quarter of the most senior posts were occupied by natives.[46] By the early 1820s, the native element had strengthened: in 1823, half of the superior officials in the provincial capital, Koblenz, were Rhinelanders.[47] The judiciary remained overwhelmingly Rhenish, despite allegations over the introduction of incompetent trainees from the east.[48] Nor is there much evidence that Catholics were discriminated against on account of their religion before the 1850s: Protestants did

---

[40] Boost, *Rheinländer*, pp. 147–8.   [41] *Allgemeine Deutsche Biographie*, 54, pp. 383–91.
[42] HStAD, Oberpräsidium Köln, 1534.   [43] Kamptz, *Annalen* 1 (1817), part 3, pp. 14–20.
[44] Klein, *Personalpolitik*, pp. 14, 52–3.
[45] For professional education in Prussia, see R. Steven Turner, 'The "Bildungsbürgertum" and the Learned Professions in Prussia, 1770–1830: The Origins of a Class', *Histoire Sociale* 13 (1980), pp. 121–3.
[46] Hardenberg to Solms-Laubach, 22 August 1817, HStAD, Oberpräsidium Köln 1147 xl, no. 66. See also Klein, *Personalpolitik*, pp. 16, 23, 76ff.
[47] Koltes, *Rheinland*, pp. 161, 164–5, 167.   [48] GStA, rep. 77, tit. 50, nr. 50, nos. 21–4.

disproportionately well because they were over-represented amongst university graduates, from whom civil servants were recruited. It was from the 1850s, with the rise of political Catholicism and politicisation of appointments following the 1848 revolution, that confession made a difference.[49] Nonetheless, what was ultimately significant was that Rhinelanders *perceived* they were discriminated against and, as the liberal Benzenberg observed, that they wished to govern themselves.[50] This was hardly surprising given the survival of the deeply ingrained notion of an '*Indignatsprinzip*' – the principle that public positions should be held by natives – that had been a matter of conflict between *Land* and princes under the Old Regime.

This sentiment was strongest in the former imperial cities, whose elites preserved a degree of autonomy even under French rule. Like Frankfurt and Hamburg, which successfully preserved their independence in 1815, the Rhenish cities united around a common bourgeois ideology that sought to diminish internal social divisions and present a united front against intrusions by the territorial state.[51] In both Aachen and Cologne, voices were raised following Napoleon's fall calling for their restoration as independent mini-states within a re-established Reich. They used the expulsion of the French as an excuse to briefly restore their old civic symbols and unfurl their ancient banners.[52] Berlin had other plans, though these were at first concealed by promises to respect constitutional order and local customs. Misunderstanding resulted in conflict, especially in the Rhineland's largest city, Cologne. In August 1815, Cologne's municipality presented its extensive demands to Hardenberg. These included calls for the re-establishment of the archdiocese, the location of the planned Rhenish university in the city, the return of treasures stolen by the French or, if these had been lost, by the transfer of other artistic objects held in Paris, compensation for losses suffered by private individuals at the hands of the French, and compensation for endowments lost by church-schools and hospitals. More fundamentally, Cologne's representatives referred to the city's 'constitutional rights', and stated that the city deserved an appropriate degree of representation amongst the Prussian estates when these were finally established. Why, they

---

[49] John R. Gillis, *The Prussian Bureaucracy in Crisis 1840–1860. Origins of an Administrative Ethos* (Stanford, 1971), pp. 35–6, 207–8.

[50] Johann Friedrich Benzenberg, *Wünsche und Hoffnungen eines Rheinländers* (Paris, 1815), p. 25.

[51] Lothar Gall, 'Vom alten zum neuen Bürgertum. Die mitteleuropäische Stadt im Umbruch 1780–1820', in idem (ed.), *Vom alten zum neuen Bürgertum. Die mitteleuropäische Stadt im Umbruch 1780–1820* (*Historische Zeitschrift* Beiheft 14, Munich, 1991), pp. 16–17.

[52] Ladoucette to Montalivet, 4 March 1814, AN, F^{IC}III Roër 4, no. 326. For civic patriotism in Cologne, see also *Kölnische Zeitung*, 1 February, 19 April, 7 July 1814.

argued, should the imperial cities not receive the same privileges as the mediatised nobility, whose special status the Congress of Vienna recognised? Cologne's representatives concluded by requesting that their city's territory be expanded so that it would enjoy greater success in exercising its old privileges.[53]

Prussia had no intention of restoring the imperial cities' old privileges. Instead, it imposed the same bureaucratic control as the French had attempted in their final years. The realisation of what the future held came in 1816, when Berlin transferred police powers in larger Rhenish cities from their mayors to centrally appointed police-presidents who were usually Protestant, East-Elbian and all too ready to justify local fears of *Junker* methods. Hardenberg viewed this reform as a practical means of providing employment for 'old Prussians' dismissed by the cash-strapped eastern cities, whilst the police minister ominously justified the reform on the grounds that the Rhineland needed officials 'experienced in the police methods of the old provinces'.[54] In the Rhineland, the imposition was viewed as an attack on local autonomy comparable to the Napoleonic special police commissioners. It brought to the surface all the points of conflict between periphery and centre, such as the balance between old and new Prussians, Protestants and Catholics, and the relative virtues of Prussian and French institutions.[55] It also exposed differences within the Prussian administration. Solms-Laubach, whose views approximated Stein's, supported the reform and opposed Napoleonic institutions largely out of hatred of all things French.[56] Solms-Laubach's reform-minded colleagues disagreed with attempts to introduce eastern institutions, and instead urged that account be taken of Rhenish 'peculiarities'. They argued that police needed to be familiar with local conditions and that those from the East-Elbian provinces would do more harm than good. They also insisted that candidates should be Catholic, because of the numerous religious processions they needed to police, and suggested they should be drawn from the local judiciary, which enjoyed great respect. The tradition of civic autonomy in cities such

---

[53] GStA, rep. 89, nr. 14673, 'Denkschrift für die Stadt Köln im Julius 1815 nach der zweiten Eroberung von Paris Seiner Durchlaucht. dem Fürsten von Hardenberg von den an Seine Majestät abgesandten Deputirten überreicht'.

[54] Wittgenstein to Solms-Laubach, 13 April 1816, GStA, rep. 77, tit. 669, nr. 1, bd. 1, nos. 5–6.

[55] Hardenberg to Wittgenstein, 4 April 1816, *ibid.*, nos. 1–2. See also Hardenberg to Wittgenstein, 19 July 1816 and Struensee (police-director of Magdeburg) to Wittgenstein (21 October 1816), *ibid.*, nos. 50, 61 respectively.

[56] Solms-Laubach to Bülow (minister of finance) and Schuckmann, 31 May 1816, GStA, rep. 77, tit. 50, nr. 50, nos. 4–12. Also, Solms-Laubach to Wittgenstein, 24 June 1816, GStA, rep. 77, tit. 669, nr. 1, bd. 1, nos. 17–30.

as Cologne, they warned, had been weakened but not destroyed by the French.[57]

Berlin ignored the advice. Conflict and confusion resulted, as it soon proved impossible to legally reconcile French local government with Prussian police. Schuckmann and Wittgenstein exploited this to call for the total abolition of all French institutions, something opposed by the provincial authorities, who argued that Napoleonic institutions were more rigorous, comprehensive and harmonious than those in Prussia.[58] Meanwhile, Cologne's new mayor, Mylius – a prefectoral councillor under French rule, whose influence, according to the provincial authorities, extended throughout the region – refused to recognise the legality of the police commissioner's appointment in his city, arguing that as mayor he represented the historic rights of Cologne. He submitted the proposed government reforms to the city council as the only legitimate authority that might approve them.[59] This elicited a furious response from Berlin, which viewed the mayor's assertions as undermining the legality of Prussian rule. Taken to their logical conclusion, they implied that royal legislation was only valid if passed by an elected assembly like the French Corps Législative.[60] Cologne's new police commissioner, Struensee, for his part complained that the Rhineland was full of francophile lawyers adept at exploiting legal technicalities.[61] The interior and police ministers shared this assessment, and argued that the King had clearly expressed his intention to administer the western territories according to Prussian forms, an assertion Hardenberg rejected.[62]

Mylius and Cologne's councillors then drafted a memorandum condemning Berlin's policies and reminding the government that 'the larger and better part of the inhabitants here have not forgotten what the citizenry formerly represented, right up to the time of the French upheaval', and that they had hoped to see their rights extended, not limited.[63] The city council officially registered its pain at seeing powers transferred to 'a police-president subordinated to the state', a reform that made an 'extremely disadvantageous impression' on public opinion, as 'according to the ancient constitution, the burghers of the city of Cologne submitted to the civic authority of their fellow citizens', and that it could 'not be the intention

---

[57] *Ibid.*, nos. 74–6.   [58] *Ibid.*, nos. 73–7, 105–8.
[59] Extract from Mylius's report, dated 21 February 1817, *ibid.*, nos. 130–2.   [60] *Ibid.*, nos. 133–9.
[61] Struensee to Wittgenstein, 9 February 1817, GStA, rep. 77, tit. 669, nr. 1, bd. 1, nos. 116–17, 124–9, 141–3.
[62] *Ibid.*, nos. 146–7.   [63] The memorandum was dated 20 May 1817, *ibid.*, nos. 230–8.

of the Prussian government to change something based on these ancient rights... before the introduction of the new constitution'.[64] Thus were old, parochial concerns for the preservation of civic privilege explicitly linked to the 'modern', liberal demand for a constitution, though as yet to no avail: the police reform was confirmed and plans for constitutional representation shelved. Mylius resigned, and became an appeals court judge in 1819. From this position within the judiciary, he continued to vex Berlin into the 1830s. Cologne's experience was by no means unique. Elsewhere in western and southern Germany, where urban traditions were strong, liberals exploited older civic traditions in their struggle against the state. Old rights were reinterpreted as guaranteeing liberal freedoms. Thus were the first generation of liberals able to widen their social base, attracting those less impressed by political abstractions than by deeply ingrained civic republican sentiment.[65]

Napoleon's law codes served as a substitute constitution for the Prussian Rhineland before 1848, and were defended vigorously. They fulfilled a similar function in the Bavarian Palatinate and Hessian territories to the south. As the *Mainzer Zeitung* reported in 1817: 'The inhabitants of this side [of the Rhine] expect no more from an all-Hessian constitution than what we already possess.'[66] In November 1814, the Prussian government indicated that the Allgemeines Landrecht (ALR) should be reintroduced in the former Hohenzollern duchies in place of the French codes. The ALR, promulgated in 1794, was an ambiguous legacy of Frederick the Great's reign. According to Robert Berdahl, it resembled an 'archaeological excavation' with various layers representing different periods with but a 'hint of the future' to attract those hoping for reform.[67] Amongst the numerous sections not hinting at the future were the 152 paragraphs concerned with offences against honour, which stipulated higher punishments for commoners insulting nobles on the principle that different social groups had innate moral characteristics. For Rhinelanders this was absurd. The fact that the ALR ultimately

[64] Minutes of the municipal council of Cologne, 5 September 1817, *ibid.*, nos. 265–8.

[65] For a judicious survey of recent research into the linkages (or lack of them) between older civic traditions and nineteenth-century German liberalism, see Elisabeth Fehrenbach, 'Bürgertum und Liberalismus. Die Umbruchsperiode 1770–1815', in Lothar Gall (ed.), *Bürgertum und bürgerlich-liberale Bewegung in Mitteleuropa seit dem 18. Jahrhundert* (*Historische Zeitschrift* Sonderheft Band 17, Munich, 1997), pp. 1–62.

[66] *Mainzer Zeitung* 140 (18 December 1817).

[67] Robert M. Berdahl, *The Politics of the Prussian Nobility: The Development of a Conservative Ideology 1770–1848* (Princeton, 1988), p. 98.

undermined the concept of orders by justifying them pragmatically was of small comfort to those already accustomed to equal citizenship, as enshrined in the French codes.[68]

Sack resisted pressure from the conservative justice minister, Kircheisen, to replace the Napoleonic codes, claiming that as governor-general he only obeyed instructions from Hardenberg. He vigorously supported French judicial procedures, reporting to Frederick William that juries worked well even in criminal cases, and that they enjoyed widespread public support.[69] Other reformers shared his assessment, and published their positive experiences of Napoleonic procedures, notably the strength of the civilian administration vis-à-vis the military, and the principle of the rule of law.[70] Hardenberg responded to these reports constructively by suspending the introduction of the ALR and despatching a fact-finding mission to investigate the judiciary in the Rhineland. This was led by Christoph Wilhelm Sethe, one of Sack's numerous brothers-in-law. Sethe spent the summer of 1815 interviewing Rhenish jurists, who overwhelmingly supported the retention of the Napoleonic system.[71] Hardenberg, taking note, set up a special law commission (*Immediat Justizkommission*) in June 1816, again chaired by Sethe, and subordinated it to a newly appointed minister for the revision of legislation, the pro-reform Karl Friedrich von Beyme, thereby outflanking Kircheisen. The latter was supported in his opposition to the law commission by Kamptz, Wittgenstein and Schuckmann. The interior minister in particular feared the Napoleonic codes' preservation in the west would morally contaminate the entire Monarchy. In early 1816, he even attempted to retroactively annul civil marriages conducted according to French law on the grounds that 'we are dealing with a people who, under the rhetoric of liberal toleration, have been dragged to and thrown in the excrement of revolutionary immorality', and that Prussia needed to 'present itself as a strict, religious moral judge, rather than reinforce previous indifference'.[72]

---

[68] The classic account of the ambiguous ALR remains Reinhart Koselleck, *Preußen zwischen Reform und Revolution. Allgemeines Landrecht, Verwaltung und soziale Bewegung von 1791 bis 1848* (Stuttgart, 1967).

[69] Sack to Frederick William III, 15 November 1815, GStA, rep. 89, 13607, 'Acta betr. Zustand der Rheinprovinz 1814–19', nos. 5–14. See also Ilja Mieck, 'Die Integration preußischer Landesteile französischen Rechts nach 1814/15', in Otto Büsch and Monika Neugebauer-Wölk (eds.), *Preussen und die Revolutionäre Herausforderung seit 1789* (Berlin, 1991), p. 357.

[70] Johann Daniel Ferdinand Neigebaur, *Darstellung der provisorischen Verwaltung am Rhein vom Jahr 1813 bis 1819* (Cologne, 1821), pp. 281–2.

[71] Ernst Landsberg (ed.), *Die Gutachten der Rheinischen-Immediat-Justiz-Kommission und der Kampf um die rheinische Rechts- und Gerichtsverfassung 1814–1819* (Bonn, 1914), pp. xxx–xxxv.

[72] *Ibid.*, p. xxxviii.

Hardenberg fended off such opposition whilst the law commission actively solicited lawyers for their views on constitutional, administrative and judicial matters, and even encouraged ordinary Rhinelanders to present their grievances over abuses committed by 'old Prussian' officials and policemen.[73] Reformers in the provincial administration similarly enlisted local support to reinforce their own constitutional demands in reports to Berlin.[74] The western provincial governors – Solms-Laubach (Jülich-Cleves-Berg), Ingersleben (Lower Rhine) and Vincke (Westphalia) – in particular stressed their status as spokesmen for the peculiar interests of their provinces, against the opposition of the interior and police ministers, who wished to subordinate them to their own ministries. This was in keeping with the provincial governors' self-image as representatives of local interests in lieu of parliamentary institutions.[75] Rhinelanders were thus mobilised as auxiliaries in the struggle against Prussian conservatism. Thanks in part to this support, Sethe's commission successfully completed its work and made its recommendations, which were enshrined in the Cabinet order of 19 November 1818. This preserved French law in the Rhineland until the general revision of law within the Monarchy as a whole, something that would occur only at the end of the century.[76]

The preservation of Napoleonic forms ensured that the judiciary remained overwhelmingly Rhenish in terms of personnel, as 'old Prussian' jurists lacked education in French methods. Native lawyers and judges subsequently emerged as the most important defenders of the French legacy, upon whose survival their own careers depended. Former students of the French law school in Koblenz were especially prominent in employing their pens in the following years in defence of what soon became known as Rhenish law.[77] They rejected the tendency of some in Berlin who viewed the French period as an illegal interregnum. Instead, they clung on to Napoleonic codes that for them fulfilled a quasi-constitutional function.

Their opponents identified them as carriers of the revolutionary contagion which had infected the west, whose population was dominated by 'sophistic lawmongers'.[78] Kamptz, the future justice minister – whom one

---

[73] *Ibid.*, pp. lxii–lxiii.

[74] Rüdiger Schütz, *Preußen und die Rheinlande. Studien zur preußischen Integrationspolitik im Vormärz* (Wiesbaden, 1979), pp. 178–9.

[75] Rüdiger Schütz, 'Zur Eingliederung der Rheinlande', in Peter Baumgart (ed.), *Expansion und Integration. Zur Eingliederung neugewonnener Gebiete in den preußischen Staat* (Cologne and Vienna, 1984), pp. 206–9.

[76] Landsberg, *Gutachten*, pp. xxxix, xlv–xlvi, lii–liii, lx–lxi.

[77] Luitwin Mallmann, *Französische Juristenausbildung im Rheinland 1794–1814. Die Rechtschule von Koblenz* (Cologne and Vienna, 1987), pp. 176–7.

[78] Landsberg, *Gutachten*, p. xli.

senior Rhenish judge referred to as the 'lie made flesh' – feared that 'old Prussia' itself might be corrupted by French principles via the western judiciary, which he denounced less on technical grounds and more for reasons of 'national character'. Juries, he argued, suited the superficial French but not the Germans, who were less influenced by appearances. He advised Rhinelanders to reconform to 'German customs, German attitudes and the German way of thinking', and hoped that 'old Prussians' might counter French influences and help propagate 'German virtues and habits'.[79] He welcomed the closure of the Napoleonic law school in Koblenz in 1817, and the absence of a chair in French law in Bonn (one was created only in 1844). Friedrich Karl von Savigny, the greatest Prussian jurist of his age, expressed similar hostility to the Napoleonic codes (at least initially), and advised the government against employing men 'with a one-sided predilection for French law'.[80]

Kircheisen similarly condemned the jury system, stating it represented class justice, not the right of individuals to be tried by their peers. He subsequently attempted to undermine the system by making difficulties over how juries were selected. According to the Napoleonic Code d'instruction criminelle, juries were chosen from amongst a clearly defined group of 'notables': members of the electoral colleges, the 300 top tax-payers per department, holders of doctorates and other approved professional qualifications, notaries, businessmen paying large amounts of patent tax, and so on. Following the abolition of the electoral colleges and changes to the tax system, these provisions became redundant and necessitated modification. Initially, the district governors took a free hand in selecting juries, but not according to any fixed rules or criteria, and this gave opponents of the French structures a new opportunity to attack them per se. Rhenish jurists and the Rhenish appeal court in Cologne responded by attempting to formulate new criteria for jury selection, criteria that represent an interesting example of the various moral virtues contemporaries associated with 'bourgeois values'. These were eventually agreed and approved by Berlin. As under the French, the numbers eligible for jury service represented a small fraction of the total population. In the district of Düsseldorf, for example, only 723 were eligible as jurors, out of a population of 72,774.[81]

Despite powerful opposition, 'Rhenish law' survived, and even won some converts, including Savigny himself. Over the following decades lawyers

[79] Kamptz, *Annalen*, I (1817), part I, pp. 292–3, 297.   [80] Mallmann, *Juristen*, pp. 163–4.
[81] Dirk Blasius, 'Der Kampf um die Geschworenengerichte im Vormärz', in Hans-Ulrich Wehler (ed.), *Sozialgeschichte Heute. Festschrift für Hans Rosenberg zum 70. Geburtstag* (Göttingen, 1974), pp. 153–4.

from 'old Prussia' increasingly entered the Rhenish judiciary. Eventually, about 40 per cent of all judges from the eastern provinces served in the Rhineland for some time. Most returned to the east, impressed by the Napoleonic system's strengths.[82] So, when in 1843 the revision of the ALR was sufficiently close to completion for Berlin to submit it to the provincial estates, it was hardly surprising that the response in the Rhineland was hostile. Yet again, the old arguments were aired and the revised ALR rejected on the familiar grounds that it threatened the jury system, allowed for corporal punishment and undermined equality. That the ALR punished property crimes more leniently than the Napoleonic code hardly endeared it to the Rhenish elite; yet their opposition received vigorous support from the wider community, as demonstrated in the petitioning campaign organised in defence of the existing system. Yet again, the entire *Bürgertum* could unite in defence of the French legacy.[83] Following the 1848 revolutions it was the Rhenish system that provided the model for Prussia and the rest of Germany.

Berlin's decision in 1818 to preserve French law in the Rhineland came at a time of heightened political tension throughout Germany, especially in the west, where radicals remained active despite the *Rheinischer Merkur*'s suppression. Görres remained an embittered thorn in the side of the Prussian government and exploited his dismissal as director of education in Koblenz to allege discrimination against Catholics. He played a prominent role in the 1817 petitioning campaign in support of a constitution, a movement that developed out of the poverty relief associations founded the previous year.[84] His native Koblenz presented its petition, signed by over 3,000 individuals, to Hardenberg in January 1818, during the chancellor's visit. The provincial government gave its tacit support to this exercise – which also occurred in Aachen, Cleves, Cologne and Trier – and overturned attempts by conservative county commissioners (*Landräte*) to block the collection of signatures. The petition itself reminded Frederick William of his promise to grant a constitution.[85]

---

[82] Christina von Hodenberg, *Die Partei der Unparteiischen. Der Liberalismus der preußischen Richterschaft, 1815–1848/49* (Göttingen, 1996), p. 80.

[83] Blasius, 'Geschworenengerichte', pp. 154–6.

[84] Joseph Görres, *In Sachen der Rheinprovinzen und in eigener Angelegenheit* (Stuttgart, 1822), pp. 45–58, 77–9, 258–61.

[85] Görres's account, dated 24 January 1818 and entitled 'Die Übergabe der Adresse der Stadt Koblenz und der Landschaft an S. Majestät den König in öffentlicher Audienz bei S. Durch. dem Fürsten Staatskanzler am 12. Januar 1818', appears as a separately paginated supplement at the end of Joseph Görres, *Deutschland und die Revolution* (Koblenz, 1819).

Hardenberg, according to Görres's account, accepted Koblenz's petition in good grace. He explained that provincial assemblies needed to be
formed before the creation of an all-Prussian parliament, and admitted
that his government faced great difficulties in uniting the Monarchy's dis-
parate territories under one constitution, a problem under discussion at
the highest levels. Other grievances presented by the delegates concerned
the plight of the Catholic Church, burden of military service, lack of press
freedom, problems faced by industry and the quartering burdens in garrison towns. The delegates went on to praise certain Napoleonic institutions, especially French legal procedures. Görres claimed this represented
a transformation of public opinion, which previously had opposed French
institutions because of the evil motivating force behind them. People now
favoured the French system as 'the better, animated form' as against the
'ponderous, paralysing' Prussian system 'imposing itself' from outside. As
a result, complained Görres, Rhinelanders faced the outrageous accusation
of being francophile by Prussian conservatives.[86]

Görres's role in the petitioning campaign hardened the conservatives'
determination to neutralise him. They increasingly enjoyed the support of
Frederick William, who did not share Hardenberg's equanimity over the
campaign and criticised the provincial government for allowing it. The King
condemned Görres's subsequent published account of it as indicative of the
'utmost pernicious intrigues in the Rhine provinces'.[87] Matters reached a
climax the following year. On 23 March 1819 the conservative playwright,
August von Kotzebue, was assassinated in Mannheim by a student, Karl
Sand. Sand turned out to be a member of a *Burschenschaft*, a movement
that had started in Jena in 1815 when it became clear that patriotic hopes for
the reordering of Germany had lost out to Metternich's agenda. Kotzebue's
murder had serious repercussions throughout Germany. Metternich exploited Frederick William's consternation at the outrage by meeting him
at Teplitz in July and persuading him that constitutions were one short
step away from revolution. A few months later, Metternich, with Prussian
support, cajoled the rest of the Germanic Confederation into passing the
Karlsbad Decrees, a series of repressive laws that imposed strict supervision
over universities to ensure youth would not be poisoned 'by [the] spread
of harmful ideas which might subvert public peace and order, and undermine the foundations of the existing states'. Complementary measures
included tighter press restrictions and co-operation between the states in

---

[86] Görres, 'Übergabe', p. 44. Görres, in the Koblenz address, also praised the old estates of the electorate
    of Trier, and refuted claims that they were rotten or out of date.
[87] Levinger, 'Hardenberg', p. 267. See also Görres, *Deutschland*, pp. 69–70, and idem, *Sachen*, p. 108.

enforcing censorship, plus the creation of a federal investigative bureau in Mainz to root out subversion. The swing towards reaction contributed to a government crisis in Berlin leading to the dismissal of the reforming ministers Beyme (legislation), Boyen (war) and Humboldt (estate affairs), and triumph for the conservatives.[88]

Reaction aggravated centre–periphery tensions over the French legacy in the Rhineland. In 1819, Görres published another polemic, *Deutschland und die Revolution*, in which he condemned the 'corrosive poison of senseless, despotic principles of government' and ridiculed the imposition of 'freedom' through Cabinet order instead of a constitution. The trust of the Rhenish provinces had been lost, he wrote, as their inhabitants rejected the Prussian 'bureaucratic/arbitrary state'. Paris was now the liberal capital of the world and Berlin overcome by 'spiritual influenza'.[89] The Prussian government decided to arrest Görres, who sensibly left the Rhineland and moved to Frankfurt. Berlin requested his extradition, but Görres managed to flee to Strasbourg, from where he continued his polemics safely beyond the Prussian authorities' reach. His subsequent publications accused Berlin of breaking all its promises to Rhinelanders and of employing despotic Napoleonic police methods, the only defence against which was the Rhenish judicial system.[90]

Görres's attacks, though embarrassing, where at least in the open. More dangerous, from Berlin's viewpoint, were the activities of secret societies, especially those centred on Bonn's new university. The government appointed Arndt professor of history at Bonn in August 1818, but was greatly annoyed a month later when he published a piece (the fourth part of *Geist der Zeit*) critical of the police. Wittgenstein presented a copy to Frederick William, who as a result seriously considered abandoning the foundation of the university. Hardenberg persuaded him otherwise, and the university opened as planned on 18 October. Arndt was now on probation and himself recognised the danger from the '*Wittgenstein-Kampzianer*'. These bided their time and then struck during the crackdown following Kotzebue's murder. On 15 July 1819 Prussian police conducted a thorough early-morning search of Arndt's house in Bonn, seizing a large number of papers. A hundred '*Burschen*' gathered around the house during the search and greeted the police with whistles and cat-calls as they emerged. Despite petitions from provincial governor Solms-Laubach, Berlin followed the advice of the federal investigative bureau and suspended Arndt in November 1820. He

---

[88] For a general overview of the swing towards reaction in Berlin, and the wider context, see James J. Sheehan, *German History 1770–1866* (Oxford, 1993 pbk edn), pp. 420–3.
[89] Görres, *Deutschland*, pp. 3, 23, 38, 67–8, 96, 115–16.   [90] Görres, *Sachen*, pp. 150–63, 203–29.

was only rehabilitated in 1840, following the accession of Frederick William IV.[91]

Arndt and Görres were the most prominent victims of the German-wide '*Demagogenverfolgung*' ('persecution of the demagogues'). Both Metternich and his advisor, Friedrich von Gentz, who had been closely involved in drafting the Karlsbad Decrees, blamed the revolutionary subversion on Stein, whom they accused of supporting German 'Jacobins' along the Rhine when head of the Central Administration.[92] Kamptz and Wittgenstein suspected that senior Prussian officials in the Rhenish provinces, including Solms-Laubach, encouraged or at least shielded subversive elements and 'patriotic' societies such as the *Tugendbund* and Jahn's gymnastics associations, which had been founded during the Wars of Liberation to renew 'morality, religion and public spirit'. At least one 'German society' appeared in the Rhineland, in Kreuznach, in October 1814, though it was not a success and dissolved in early 1816.[93] Frederick William III had always viewed such societies suspiciously, even when directed against Napoleon, and reports reaching him from the Rhineland after 1819 increased his paranoia over their activities in the strategically vulnerable western provinces.

The most detailed report devoted to sedition was the 469-page piece completed by the federal investigative bureau and entitled, 'Reports on political activity on the Rhine, in particular, in Bonn' (*Vorträge über das politische Treiben am Rhein ins besonders zu Bonn*). The report stated that Bonn university had been identified at an early stage by the 'party' 'working towards the political reconstruction of Germany' as a centre for influencing youth. Most alarming of all, the report accused senior figures, including Gneisenau, Gruner and Solms-Laubach, as having known about or even sponsored various organisations set up 'to work upon the spirit of Rhenish youth'. These organisations included the gymnastics societies, whose activities on the Rhine culminated in a festival in Bonn held on 31 March 1817, the first major event of its kind in the region.[94] Koblenz, Gneisenau's headquarters and subsequently capital of the unified *Rheinprovinz*, was also identified as a centre of subversion and subject to special investigation after Karlsbad. An especially worrying report sent to the interior ministry in late 1822 identified a secret society in the city 'where one expresses oneself strongly on current affairs', and complained of intrigue, secret symbols and

---

[91] Edith Ennen, *Ernst Moritz Arndt, 1769–1860* (Bonn, 1968), pp. 22–8. Karl Heinz Schäfer, *Ernst Moritz Arndt als politischer Publizist. Studien zur Publizistik, Pressepolitik und kollektivem Bewußtsein im frühen 19. Jahrhundert* (Bonn, 1974), pp. 113 n., 143, 212–16. *Allgemeine Deutsche Biographie*, 1, pp. 541–8.

[92] Schäfer, *Arndt*, pp. 215–16.　　[93] *Ibid.*, pp. 227 n., 228.

[94] GStA, rep. 77, tit. 17, nr. 55, vol. 1, pp. 13–16, 45, 51–2, 81.

another society – 'Rhenanie' – whose members (mainly university teachers and students) wore bands coloured red, blue, black and green. Berlin was alarmed. Significantly, the ministry advised the local police commander not to notify the provincial authorities of its findings, but instead to employ an official with 'laudable, loyal devotion to the state' who was guaranteed to make further enquiries.[95] Meanwhile, Rhinelanders closely associated with the 'patriots' found their careers in government service effectively ended.[96]

The conservatives, triumphant in Berlin after 1819, subsequently sought to undermine the 1818 settlement preserving the Napoleonic codes. This was facilitated by the fact that the law commission's conclusions were never officially published, though they became generally known. Nonetheless, the government's acceptance of the commission's original findings in 1818 made it politically impossible to reopen the question fully. Instead, the newly constituted government adopted salami tactics, slicing away at the codes with individual measures, such as the Cabinet orders of 20 August 1819 and 6 March 1821 that decreed that all crimes against the state would henceforth be tried under the ALR, even if committed in the Rhineland.[97]

A more fundamental challenge to the essentially bourgeois Rhenish social order came with the native nobility, which Berlin now identified as a tool for integrating the western provinces on the east's terms. As already noted, French rule damaged the southern Rhenish nobility far more than its northern counterpart, whose revenues, consisting of money-rents from tenants, remained untouched by the abolition of 'feudalism'. 'Feudalism' could hardly be reintroduced after 1814, though the successor governments agreed to return *unsold* nationalised secular properties to their former owners. There were few of these left, however, as revealed by the investigation conducted into the fate of Metternich's former holdings along the Moselle.[98] Most had long since been sold, and disentangling the precise status of all such properties, whether sold or unsold, proved a time-consuming affair. The northern nobility, which was territorial (mediated), had not been affected by revolutionary sequestration, unlike the imperial nobility to the south. However, even before the Revolution, the northern nobles had owned only a relatively small proportion of the land. This had

---

[95] Interior ministry to the commander of the gendarmerie, Koblenz, 14 December 1822, GStA, rep. 77, tit. 17, nr. 54, nos. 1–4.
[96] Klein, *Personalpolitik*, pp. 23–5; Landeshauptarchiv Koblenz (LHAK), Bestand 403, 4134, nos. 1–3, 5, 7–9, 11, 17–21, 25–8.
[97] Landsberg, *Gutachten*, pp. cxxvii–cxxviii.   [98] LHAK, Bestand 350, 103, no. 5.

not changed fundamentally with the subsequent sale of the vast properties confiscated from the Catholic Church. Even in its reconstituted form, the Rhenish nobility as a whole represented a social foundation for rule that was both extremely thin and unevenly distributed. Nonetheless, this class showed skill in presenting its case at the Congress of Vienna, receiving influential support from Stein. It turned liberal calls for constitutional government into an argument for the restoration of noble estates. Ironically, the Rhenish nobility, as a united, cohesive group, never existed under the Old Regime, but only emerged in 1814/15 to present its case for 'restoration'.[99] Though it would have preferred to see the restoration of its old privileges, it recognised the need for some accommodation with the modern state and constitutional arrangements. This pragmatism, and synthesis of modernity and tradition – 'calculating pseudo-modernity' – typified Germany's subsequent development.

Powerful elements in Berlin, centred around the Crown Prince and Stein, favoured the reconstitution of the nobility as the basis of the Rhenish social order. In this they were opposed by Hardenberg and most of the provincial bureaucracy, which favoured equal citizenship, with civil servants alone mediating relations between the individual and state. Reform-minded bureaucrats posted to the west lost no opportunity in publicly humiliating ex-Rhenish nobles who insisted on recognition of their former titles. Whether conservatives deceived themselves as to the isolation and insignificance of the Rhenish nobility is not clear. They should have lost their illusions during the petitioning campaign of 1817–18, when the great majority of Rhinelanders supported 'French' equality, and rejected the noble submission drafted largely by Stein that seemed to reject the legality of Napoleonic rule and imply that lands contained inherent values that were inviolable even by international treaty.[100] Frederick William nonetheless wished to reconstitute the Rhenish nobility, stating in his Cabinet order of 6 March 1821 that only one 'internal state law' existed within the Monarchy, and that this law recognised nobility. This provoked opposition from the provincial administration, which argued that the nobility remained abolished in the Rhineland. The police minister, Wittgenstein, responded by informing

---

[99] Christof Dipper, 'Der rheinische Adel zwischen Revolution und Restauration', in Helmuth Feigl and Willibald Rosner (eds.), *Adel im Wandel. Vorträge und Diskussionen des elften Symposions des Niederösterreichischen Instituts für Landeskunde, Horn, 2.–5. Juli 1990* (Vienna, 1991), p. 100.

[100] Christof Dipper, 'Die Reichsritterschaft in napoleonischer Zeit', in Eberhard Weis (ed.), *Reformen im rheinbündischen Deutschland* (Munich, 1984), pp. 66–74, 104–6. Horst Lademacher, 'Der Niederrheinische und Westfälische Adel in der Preussischen Verfassungsfrage', *Rheinische Vierteljahrsblätter* 31 (1966–7), pp. 442–54. See also Sack's circular, dated October 1815, LHAK, Bestand 355, no. 76.

the provincial governor, Ingersleben, that the King's opinion was that public law recognised nobility, and that since the Rhineland was Prussian, the nobility should again be recognised.[101] The Rhenish district administrations countered that no registers existed listing those of noble status, and then argued that the royal Cabinet order did not re-establish nobility, but only decreed that those French laws and institutions incompatible with the rest of the Monarchy might be revised sometime in the future by individual measures. Until that time, they insisted, nobility remained illegal under Rhenish law, and those employing 'pretended' titles continued to face fines of 100 francs.[102]

It was in this context that five constitutional commissions laboured from 1817 to 1822 to give Frederick William III's promise of 1815 institutional form.[103] The fruit of this labour ripened in the provincial-estates laws of 1823 and 1824, which created assemblies for each of Prussia's nine provinces. The Rhenish provincial assembly comprised four estates. The first was composed of former unmediated nobles, a status enjoyed by a mere five families. The heads of these sat by right in the assembly. The other three estates elected twenty-five representatives each, making a grand total of eighty deputies. The second estate contained representatives of owners of privileged landed estates. The cities were represented in the third estate, and small landowners in the fourth. This basic structure remained intact until 1887.[104]

This arrangement failed to meet liberal expectations. Amongst the wider Rhenish population the provincial assembly was ridiculed as the '*Narrentag*', or 'fools' assembly'. It had no budgetary powers; there were severe restrictions on the reporting of its debates; its convocation depended upon royal will, not constitutional law. Representation by estate contradicted equality and gave undue political weight to the insignificant nobility: the deputies from the cities of Aachen and Cologne, for example, represented 120 times more constituents and thirty-four times more tax revenue than representatives of the second estate. Wealthy businessmen discovered they were without representation. In the district of Düsseldorf, this was the case for industrialists with enterprises enjoying a turnover estimated at 30 million *Thaler*, and paying 150,000 in trade tax. Owners of vast amounts of 'non-privileged' land, paying thousands of *Thaler* in tax, found themselves excluded from the second estate, whose members might

---

[101] Wittgenstein to Ingersleben, 8 November 1823, LHAK, Bestand 403, 9710, nos. 35–7.

[102] *Ibid.*, nos. 39–48.   [103] Schütz, 'Eingliederung', pp. 215–17.

[104] Gustav Croon, *Der Rheinische Provinziallandtag bis zum Jahre 1874. Im Auftrage des Rheinischen Provinzialausschusses* (Bonn, 1974: reproduction of Düsseldorf, 1918 edn), pp. 30–5.

pay little more than seventy-five *Thaler* in land tax. Similarly unpopular were the over-complicated indirect electoral procedures for the third and fourth estates: voters from the latter needed to nominate electors, who in turn elected district electors, who then elected the deputies. Voters, electors and actual representatives of both the third and fourth estates needed to pass precisely graded tax thresholds. The government prevented troublesome intellectuals, lawyers and officials from elbowing their way into the assembly via the fourth estate by the selective enforcement of the regulation stipulating that only those who derived their income from the ownership of the land itself (and not from some other profession) might sit amongst this group.[105]

Despite limitations, the provincial assembly, which convened in Düsseldorf for four weeks every two years, contributed to the formation of public opinion. Amongst the important issues it debated in the 1820s, 30s and 40s were Church–state relations, Jewish emancipation and local government reform. It supervised public finance, scrutinising whether the west was being overburdened to subsidise the east. The first assembly, which convened in October 1826, sat for a total of seventy-one days, resisting attempts by the provincial governor to curtail its passionate discussion of Rhenish law. The assembly served as a platform for liberals challenging the provincial bureaucracy for leadership of the reform movement.

As for the nobility, the seating arrangement adopted in the assembly reflected its isolation rather than elevation. It was only whilst preparing for the first assembly that Prussian officials discovered just how few former landed estates eligible for privileged status had survived.[106] Undaunted, Berlin pressed ahead, and reconstituted a Rhenish nobility, with its titles, arms and entailed estates, in a series of Cabinet orders between 1826 and 1828. This occurred in the teeth of popular hostility and opposition from the judiciary and provincial government.[107] Ironically, the latter was entrusted with the time-consuming task of digging up evidence to justify individual claims to noble status.[108] This amounted to what one provincial governor described as rummaging through the junk room, and what the prominent liberal David Hansemann condemned as experimentation in the western provinces to see how 'feudal leftovers' might reconcile themselves with modern society.[109] By April 1834, the administration had unearthed enough

[105] *Ibid.*, pp. 30–41.   [106] Dipper, 'Reichsritterschaft', p. 60.

[107] Dipper, 'Adel', pp. 98–106.   [108] LHAK, Bestand 403, 9710 and 9754.

[109] For the governor's comment, see Schütz, *Preußen*, p. 182. Hansemann's observation was made in his lengthy memorandum of 31 December 1830, reproduced in Joseph Hansen (ed.), *Rheinische Briefe und Akten zur Geschichte der politischen Bewegung 1830–1850* (2 vols., Bonn, 1919–42), I, p. 76.

evidence to recognise the claims of twenty-four counts, 190 *Freiherrn*, and 492 other nobles in the *Rheinprovinz*.[110]

The consciously bourgeois self-perception of the urbanised Rhenish elite, who set the social and cultural tone for the *Rheinprovinz* as a whole, remained undiminished throughout the nineteenth century. It was immunised by its economic strength against feelings of inferiority towards the re-established nobility.[111] Nor were the professions cowed into modifying their self-consciously liberal outlook by aping the nobility. The judiciary in particular held out, its egalitarian *mentalité* symbolised by Sethe's decision, as president of the Rhenish supreme appeal court, to turn down a patent of ennoblement. Those few nobles who joined the judiciary were 'bourgeoisified' in terms of marriage patterns and lifestyle.[112] Nor was there any difference between Rhinelanders and 'old Prussians' in this respect, as many of the latter who decided to enter the Rhenish judiciary as unpaid trainees did so precisely because they were dissatisfied with the eastern system and wished to study Napoleonic institutions.[113] They reinforced rather than undermined an ethos hostile to anything that challenged legal equality.

An example of this ethos came in June 1828, when the Crown Prince of Hessen, Frederick William (a nephew of Frederick William III), was ordered to present himself before Bonn's justice of the peace. The summons arose from a dispute with a builder contracted to extend his private residence in the city. Significantly, the district government of Cologne, to which Bonn belonged, supported the JP's actions, arguing that there were no privileged courts in the Rhineland, and that Prussian law compelled foreign princes to recognise the particular laws of the various provinces when visiting as private individuals. The administration rejected the accusation that the summons had employed 'the coarsest expressions'; any other form would have been illegal. The outraged Crown Prince naturally ignored the summons, and the commander of the regiment providing his honour guard enquired of the provincial governor what he should do when the local police arrived

[110] LHAK, Bestand 403, 9710, nos. 1–34, 'Verzeichnis derjenigen Individuen, deren Ansprüche auf adliche Prädicate bis jetzt anerkannt worden sind'. The Rhenish district with the largest number of nobles was Düsseldorf, located on the right bank, with close to 300 listed. Trier district, on the other hand, only produced a dozen individuals suitable for inclusion on the list. Aachen and Cologne counted between 150 and 200 each. LHAK, Bestand 403, 9754, nos. 63–6 (Trier), 83–130 (Aachen), 149–238 (Düsseldorf), 301–40 (Cologne). Unfortunately, there is a non-locatable gap in this *Bestand*, which presumably contained figures for the district of Koblenz.

[111] Hans-Peter Schwarz, *Konrad Adenauer. A German Politician and Statesman in a Period of War, Revolution and Reconstruction*, vol. 1: *From the German Empire to the Federal Republic, 1876–1952* (Oxford and Providence, 1995), p. 20.

[112] Hodenberg, *Partei*, pp. 11ff.   [113] *Ibid.*, pp. 79–80.

with an arrest warrant.[114] The affair provoked outrage in Berlin, where the foreign ministry could not help but marvel at the zeal with which the Rhenish judiciary ruthlessly interpreted the law to the letter in such cases. The matter was eventually resolved when the government proposed that the Crown Prince nominate a representative to settle the matter privately, or before the *Kammergericht* in Berlin, which had jurisdiction in affairs involving Prussian princes, an arrangement he accepted.[115]

The attempt to integrate the two fundamentally opposed systems that co-existed in Prussia's eastern and western halves inevitably caused instability. When combined with social hardship, associated with the birth-pangs of industrialisation, a potentially revolutionary situation came into being that required only a Parisian spark to explode. The first years of Prussian rule, when the region was exposed to British competition, were especially painful in places like Aachen, located next to the new Dutch tariff barrier. One consequence of this hardship was anglophobia.[116] Another was the accusation that Prussia's policies sacrificed the interests of the western provinces for the east. That the Rhenish economy would experience painful readjustment with the collapse of Napoleon's Continental System could hardly be blamed upon the Prussians, though Berlin might be criticised for underestimating the problem. This, despite the fact that Prussia had already acquired information on the region's economy through industrial espionage during the Napoleonic period. Berlin believed in free trade, and would only countenance restrictions to this in support of industries that over the longer term could compete without assistance. Beyond that, the government sponsored information exchange on best practice, supported industrial espionage to speed technology transfer, and encouraged manufacturers such as the Cockerills to found new factories throughout the Monarchy.[117] The liberal trade policy, enshrined in the customs law of 1818, certainly provoked complaints from manufacturers (though not merchants) and was subsequently amended in 1824/5. To its credit, Berlin invested considerable diplomatic effort in diminishing Dutch customs barriers. With respect to monetary policy, Prussia maintained a stable currency,

[114] LHAK, Bestand 403, 3936, nos. 1–2, 9–11, 13–16.
[115] Ministry of foreign affairs to Ingersleben, 16 July 1828, and the Kurprinz to Ingersleben, 16 August 1828, LHAK, Bestand 403, 3936, nos. 17–19, 25.
[116] Oscar J. Hammen, 'Economic and Social Factors in the Prussian Rhineland in 1848', *The American Historical Review* 54 (1949), pp. 829–30.
[117] Koltes, *Rheinland*, pp. 336–40.

though foreign coin continued to circulate in the Rhineland for decades after 1815.[118]

As for fiscal policy, the new tax regime introduced in 1820 was favourable to manufacturing, as most of the burden fell on land. Industrial cities such as Krefeld paid about half the per capita rate of tax of administrative centres like Bonn and Koblenz. The controversy over whether the Rhineland was fiscally exploited rumbled on in a number of publications, notably David Hansemann's *Preußen und Frankreich*, published in 1833. This compared (unfavourably) Prussian fiscal policies with those of the French, and concluded that Berlin overtaxed its westernmost province by up to a quarter. Recent research that has also taken account of government expenditure – bureaucrats' salaries, investment in roads, spending on education, and military expenditure covering not only the maintenance of 18,000 troops in the region, but also major works on fortifications like at Ehrenbreitstein – has rejected the notion that the Rhineland was exploited to finance development in the east. Only about one-sixth of revenue raised in the Rhineland went to the centre, with the rest spent in the region.[119]

Statistical surveys of the 1820s suggest that the economic geography of the Rhineland emerged little changed from the postwar recession. The painful readjustment after 1815 had the arguably beneficial effect of eliminating under-capitalised enterprises founded in the Napoleonic period, many of which sold shoddy products compared to the competition. Firmly rooted establishments that sold top-quality products enjoying a Europe-wide reputation, such as eau de Cologne, survived and then flourished. Wuppertal and Berg remained centres of metallurgy, Krefeld a centre for textiles, and the district of Aachen for mining, metallurgy and cloth making. Technology was slowly making an impact: by 1818, Düsseldorf district counted eighteen and Aachen fifteen steam engines, though there were none elsewhere in the *Rheinprovinz*. Putting-out, not concentration into manufactories, remained the norm for the dominant industrial branch, textiles: half of the cotton and two-thirds of woollen processing occurred in rural areas. Only the silk industry was predominantly urban. This pattern was beginning to change in the 1820s, a decade that witnessed dramatic growth

---

[118] Johann Joseph Eichhoff, *Betrachtungen über den XIX. Artikel der deutschen Bundesakte nebst Andenkungen, wie in Gefolge desselben dem Handelsverkehr zwischen den Verschiedenen Bundesstaaten Erleichterung zu verschaffen* (Wiesbaden, 1820), pp. 10–11.

[119] Wolfgang Zorn, 'Preußischer Staat und rheinische Wirtschaft (1815–1830)', in *Landschaft und Geschichte. Festschrift für Franz Petri zu seinem 65. Geburtstag am 22 Februar 1968* (Bonn, 1970), pp. 552–60.

in at least some sectors, notably in mining: in Aachen district, the tonnage of coal mined rose from 138,908 tonnes in 1822 to 160,408 in 1828; in Saarbrücken, the figures were 126,607 and 216,497 respectively. The output of raw iron from Saarbrücken increased from 3,068 to 4,591 tonnes in the same period, and from 603 to 3,702 in Düren. Another measure of commercial activity, revenues raised through trade tax, shows a similar increase: for the *Rheinprovinz* as a whole, the take rose from 300,352 *Thaler* to 392,449 between 1822 to 1829, with the northern districts registering the largest increases. The north/south gap was widening. Of the non-metallurgical and non-mining sectors, cotton and silk registered the highest growth whilst wool and linen stagnated. As for the impact of mechanisation and increased productivity on industrial wages, evidence from nearby Verviers suggests there was none: wage rates for adults in the textile sector remained constant for the first four decades of the century, whilst prices rose.[120]

Agriculture also made advances and recovered from the damage inflicted by military movements in 1813–15 thanks to higher commodity prices. Rhenish agriculture was efficient by Prussian standards, with an average yield of produce per acre 75 per cent higher than the Monarchy as a whole, and over 300 per cent higher than East Prussia. By the 1820s, the potato had emerged as the dominant staple (700,000+ tonnes in an average year), outstripping rye (200,000+ tonnes), wheat (70,000 tonnes), barley (60,000) and oats (250,000 tonnes).[121] The overall product of Rhenish agriculture and forestry, including commercial crops such as tobacco, flax and rapeseed, amounted to 30 million *Thaler* per annum. Prussian statistics fail to provide a comparable figure for manufacturing and commerce, but it appears that these sectors now accounted for a significantly higher figure. A contemporary estimate for the commercial and industrial product of the district of Düsseldorf alone in 1830 was 30 million *Thaler*, and for the district of Cologne just over 2 million. The *Rhineland* was now a mixed, not a primarily agricultural, economy.[122]

Despite overall progress, one sector suffered substantially in these years: viticulture. This was a significant sector, employing 50,000 people and supporting another 150,000 dependants, together representing a tenth of the *Rheinprovinz*'s 2 million inhabitants. Early on, Berlin identified this sector for fiscal exploitation. However, at least in return Rhenish viticulture

[120] Wolfgang Zorn, 'Die wirtschaftliche Struktur der Rheinprovinz um 1820', *Vierteljahrsschrift für Sozial- und Wirtschafsgeschichte* 54 (1967), pp. 289–324. For wage rates in Verviers, see Joel Mokyr, *Industrialization in the Low Countries, 1795–1850* (New Haven, 1976), pp. 183–4, 187.

[121] E. G. Zitzen, *Die Grundlagen der rheinischer Landwirtschaft* (Cologne, 1939), p. 21.

[122] Zorn, 'Struktur', p. 309.

benefited from preferential access to the Prussian market. This ended in 1828, with the Prusso-Hessian customs agreement. Hessian wine, which was cheaper to produce, now flooded onto the market, and Nassau's accession to the union in 1835 aggravated the situation further. The growing plight of the Rhenish vintners brought other grievances to the fore: the fact that the tax on vineyards took as its base year one that had witnessed an uncommonly good harvest; that consumption taxes were structured so they could not be passed on to consumers; the unscrupulousness of wine merchants, who spread rumours about the quality of the wine to depress the price so as to purchase it cheap; or the perceived ruthlessness of Jewish money lenders. The vintners plight highlighted social problems associated with the disappearance of common property rights, an issue that attracted the attention of the young Karl Marx.[123] Vintners were especially dependent upon wood from commons not only as a source of fuel, but also for barrels and stakes. Unfortunately, the Prussian state encouraged the swiftest possible liquidation of communal debts, with the result that common lands and woods were privatised. Wood prices soared. This resulted in real hardship, especially during cold winters, as revealed by reports of epidemics of gastric fever.

Rural poverty provoked social conflict, including anti-Semitism, a problem that attracted the attention of the 1826/7 *Landtag*. It also encouraged rural crime, especially wood theft. This reached such proportions in the 1820s and 1830s that the government completed several investigations that provide our best source for this phenomenon. In 1834, of the 30,038 crimes tried in Rhenish courts, 26,749, or over 89 per cent, were wood theft, the incidence of which rose dramatically in the following years, peaking at 72,918 in 1847. Rural society distinguished morally between property that was manifestly the result of labour, whose theft was unacceptable, and natural items such as wood. This distinction is reflected by the fact that wood theft was a crime committed disproportionately by women and children. The provisions of the Code pénal, whose severity shocked some Prussian officials, made no such distinction. The harshness of the proscribed sentences, coupled with the fact that more than half the crimes that came before Rhenish juries in this period were crimes against property, and that these juries were selected from the highest tax-payers, provoked not only the condemnation of Marx, but also criticism from the eminent jurist Savigny. In their eyes, defence of 'Rhenish' law was chiefly about narrow class interest.

---

[123] Hans Pelger, 'Karl Marx und die rheinpreußische Weinkrise', *Archiv für Sozialgeschichte* 13 (1973), pp. 309–75.

This assessment was unfair, and ignored cases in which juries acted in favour of defendants and against brutal forestry guards. Perhaps the most famous of these – at least in terms of the stir it caused in the Prussian *Rheinprovinz* at the time – was the acquittal by a jury, amidst popular jubilation, of two peasants who had been accused of shooting a particularly brutal forester near Trier in 1845.[124]

It was in this socio-economic climate that news reached the region in July 1830 of revolution in Paris. The French contagion quickly spread into neighbouring Belgium, where a revolt against Dutch rule erupted in late August. The violent separation of a Catholic region from a Protestant state with which it had been unwillingly lumped could not fail to have repercussions across the border. On 30 August serious riots occurred in Aachen. More than any Rhenish city, Aachen had changed significantly since 1815 thanks to industrialisation, boasting in 1830 a dozen modern manufactories. During the riots, a wealthy manufacturer's house was destroyed, and the Prussian military momentarily lost control. For the first time in Germany, the red flag was unfurled.[125] Order was eventually restored by a hastily mobilised civic guard amidst fighting that left seven dead, numerous injured and resulted in 150 arrests. Unlike in 1848, the Prussian state remained intact and responded over the following weeks by deploying 2,690 troops, including cavalry and artillery, to the city.

As one would expect from the Prussians, a thorough investigation now followed, and the conclusions provide an insight into social conflict within this city.[126] Trouble started on 28 August, before news of the Belgian disturbances, when workers at Nellesen's textile manufactory protested against their pay being docked for shoddy work. The Prussian government, which

---

[124] For Marx's assessment of the wood-theft question, see Karl Marx and Friedrich Engels, *Karl Marx Friedrich Engels Werke* (edited by the Institut für Marxismus-Leninismus beim ZK der SED, 3rd edn, Berlin, 1974), 1, pp. 109–47. For the statistics on wood theft, see Dirk Blasius, *Bürgerliche Gesellschaft und Kriminalität. Zur Sozialgeschichte Preußens im Vormärz* (Göttingen, 1976), pp. 29, 43–8, 122–6. For the debate on juries, see Dirk Blasius, 'Kampf', pp. 154–6. More generally, Heinrich Rubner, *Forstgeschichte im Zeitalter der industriellen Revolution* (Berlin, 1967). For a contemporary source, T. C. Banfield, *Industry of the Rhine* (2 vols., London, 1846–8), 1: *Agriculture: Embracing a View of the Social Condition of the Rural Population of That District*, p. 28. The case of the two peasants acquitted by the Trier Assizes in late 1845 is taken from Sperber, *Rhineland Radicals*, p. 76.

[125] Michael Sobania, 'Das Aachener Bürgertum am Vorabend der Industrialisierung', in Lothar Gall (ed.), *Vom alten zum neuen Bürgertum. Die mitteleuropäische Stadt im Umbruch 1780–1820* (*Historische Zeitschrift* Beiheft 14, Munich, 1991), p. 227.

[126] The conclusions of the Prussian investigation into Aachen's disturbances provide the main source for Heinrich Volkmann, 'Wirtschaftlicher Strukturwandel und sozialer Konflikt in der Frühindustrialisierung. Eine Fallstudie zum Aachener Aufruhr von 1830', in Peter Christian Ludz (ed.), *Soziologie und Sozial-Geschichte* Sonderheft 16/1972 (Opladen, 1972), pp. 550–65, upon which the following paragraph is based.

eschewed any meaningful factory legislation to prevent the worst abuses, tolerated such practices, which were common. On this occasion, industrial fines sparked a dangerous situation when rumours filtered in of successes achieved by textile workers in neighbouring Belgium. The arrival of manufacturers from Belgium seeking refuge added to the tension. On 30 August, Aachen's textile workers marched on Nellesen's establishment to claim their full wages and the abolition of fines. Elements who had joined the protest attempted to storm the factory, but were held back by the workers themselves until the authorities arrived. These, far from calming matters, exacerbated the situation before fleeing in the face of the crowd that started chanting '*Auf nach Cockerill*' ('On to Cockerill's!'). The mass then proceeded to the property of this representative of industrial wealth, which they wrecked in a ritual of Luddite destruction. This having been achieved, the crowd identified its next target, the city prison, and proceeded to release imprisoned 'brothers'. Significantly, almost 90 per cent of prisoners were serving 'correctional' sentences for crimes such as wood theft. These might be viewed seriously by the Prussian authorities and Aachen's elite, but appeared justified by the poor, especially in the light of that year's crop failure and increase by a third in the price of rye bread that August. It was at this stage that the 230-strong civic guard intervened, and put down the uprising.

Thus had a protest against a specific industrial practice, initiated by a small number of workers, spiralled into a wider demonstration against poverty. Industrial workers who had, after all, prevented the storming of Nellesen's establishment, were not involved in the later actions against Cockerill's residence and the prison. Indeed, the number of active participants in this violence was small, numbering no more than 100. This number swelled to perhaps 4,000, representing an eighth of Aachen's population, if passive participants and sympathetic onlookers are included. Of the hardcore, as represented in the fifty-four subsequent convictions, half were youths aged between fifteen and twenty. Most were unemployed or under-employed labourers from the needle and textile industries, with the rest mainly young unskilled craftsmen, especially from the building trade. These represented very much the bottom of the social pile. The *Bürgertum* remained cohesive. The main social division was located within the lower class, not between the lower and middle classes. Industrial workers, apart from their involvement in the beginning, subsequently found themselves on neither side of the conflict, whilst craftsmen were to be found both amongst the rioters and the civic guard.

Cologne's *Bürgertum* similarly remained cohesive during disturbances that occurred following the arrival of news of Aachen's events on the night of 31 August, though on this occasion it appears to have instigated the trouble directed at the Prussian authorities. Certainly, police reports of Cologne's disturbances suggest it was more than a bread riot, and point to the openly anti-government spirit of the city's elite, which led the other classes in ridiculing the Prussian authorities. Large crowds gathered on city squares, chanting: 'Long live Napoleon and the Constitution.' Significantly, the Rhenish appeal court was the only government institution that explicitly met with the crowd's approval. The crowd eventually dispersed, but reassembled the next evening in even greater strength, but again dispersed without major incident. On the third day the 25th infantry regiment arrived from Koblenz and re-established order.[127]

Berlin, fearing revolution, appointed Prince William governor-general of the Rhineland and Westphalia with extraordinary powers. The government also instructed its officials to minimise contacts with representatives of the 'rebellious' Belgian regime, lest such intercourse offend Prussia's 'honour'.[128] Significantly, both Ingersleben and Prince William identified Cologne's police commissioner, Struensee, and his 'predilection for drastic measures', as responsible for the trouble (Struensee's original appointment in 1816, as noted earlier, had sparked bitter protests from the city government). Both favoured his transfer out of the province, as he was hated by the judiciary, Catholic Church and members of the 'highest estate'.[129] Struensee defended himself and blamed the disturbances on the army's absence and the revolutionary spirit spreading from France and Belgium. This had emboldened the masses into demonstrating openly against unpopular taxes. It was at this point that events took a sinister turn, he reported, with the 'party' composed of the city's elite allegedly turning the mob against the Prussian police. The hatred of this 'party', Struensee claimed, had frequently manifested itself since the beginning of his appointment in various incidents. Despite his defence, Ingersleben succeeded in getting Struensee out by sending him on a fact-finding tour of prisons in the eastern provinces.[130]

Struensee's transfer represented a defeat for his conservative supporters in Berlin, including the justice minister, Kamptz, who distrusted the provincial administration. To investigate possible connections between Rhinelanders and foreign revolutionary emissaries, Berlin dispatched a

---

[127] LHAK, Bestand 403, 4163, nos. 49–50.   [128] LHAK, Bestand 403, 96, nos. 3–6, 51–4, 99–100.
[129] LHAK, Bestand 403, 4163, nos. 31–2, 35–6, 57–60.   [130] *Ibid.*, nos. 33–5, 39–48, 83–5, 89–90.

special police agent, Schnabel, to the province. The provincial governor and his subordinates viewed Schnabel as another representative of eastern reaction, entrusted with the task of spying on themselves. The suspicion was not unfounded. Secret police reports despatched from the *Rheinprovinz* to Berlin in the 1830s betrayed a mixture of mistrust and contempt for the senior provincial officials in place, a sentiment fully reciprocated.[131] The result was the continuation into the 1830s and 1840s of centre–periphery conflict within the Prussian administration. This provided an opening for a new generation of Rhenish liberal who now came of age, led by the businessmen David Hansemann, Gustav Mevissen and Ludolf Camphausen. They would increasingly assume leadership of the movement not only to preserve the Rhineland's unique institutions, but see their extension to the rest of Germany.[132]

The 1830 disturbances in the *Rheinprovinz* failed to escalate into full-blown revolution mainly because the core of the Prussian Monarchy remained calm. Berlin could therefore rapidly deploy military force to nip problems in the bud. Similarly, the Bavarians eventually mastered the even more dramatic upsurge in their Rhenish possessions. Here too centre–periphery tension had been brewing since the beginning of Bavarian rule and worsened after 1828 when King Ludwig I signalled a more conservative, clerical course with the appointment of Eduard von Schenk as minister of the interior and of cults. This shift represented a provocation for the largely Protestant Rhineland-Palatinate, and it was against this context that news broke of the French revolution of July 1830. Munich responded with reaction, a course challenged by the Bavarian *Landtag*. Here Palatine deputies – notably, the lawyers Christian Culmann and Friedrich Schüler – played a leading role in the liberal opposition, but seemed to have achieved little by late 1831 when a frustrated King Ludwig dissolved the body. However, salvation for the liberals and democrats came with the Rhineland-Palatinate's French institutions. The dissolution of the *Landtag* left the free press as the sole organ through which the opposition could effectively express itself and in the Rhineland-Palatinate it escaped government repression thanks to the protection afforded by the legal system. This extended not only to local newspapers, but also to the increasing number of radical papers that relocated from elsewhere in Bavaria to escape censorship. These collectively founded the 'Association for the Support of a

---

[131] See, for example, the secret police report, dated 3 September 1833, GStA, rep. 89, nr. 16157, 2–4.
[132] For an examination of the ideas of the most famous – though, through his attachment to *Realpolitik*, uncharacteristic – *Vormärz* Rhenish liberal, see Alan Kahan, 'Liberalism and *Realpolitik* in Prussia, 1830–52: The Case of David Hansemann', *German History* 9 (1991), pp. 281–307.

Free Press' (Vaterlandsvereins zur Unterstützung der freien Presse), a creation that quickly took root and spread until its branches covered southern Germany and extended to the north; there was even a section in Paris, which boasted Heinrich Heine amongst its members.

Political conflict over representation and press freedom overlay deepening economic hardship in the Rhineland-Palatinate. This, coupled with broader centre–periphery conflicts that revolved around confession and fiscal policy, contributed to the radicalisation of broader social groups. An explosion resulted on 27 May 1832 with the Hambach Fest, a great public festival that represented the highpoint of early German liberalism. Like their counterparts in Berlin, conservatives in Munich blamed the political agitation on former Rhenish servants of Napoleon. During the Hambach *Fest* itself, the Bavarian government even feared that veterans of Napoleon's army might lend military muscle to the moderate calls of intellectuals and journalists addressing the crowds.[133] Characteristically for this period, the event's political potential hinged upon the ability of liberal activists to make a connection between their demands for the overthrow of the existing political order, and the grievances of the ordinary people. These grievances, according to the investigation conducted by the Bavarian authorities following the event, were directed less against the Monarchy in the abstract but rather against individual officials who were especially unpopular. Popular engagement with the 'high' political agenda and theorising of the radical (and for the majority inaudible) speakers who addressed the crowd at Hambach, in contrast, remained minimal. It was not that the masses were apolitical, but rather that their political consciousness was rooted elsewhere.[134] Nonetheless, French institutions gave this consciousness expression. In the words of the Bavarian army's commander, Field-Marshal Wrede, in his letter to Metternich shortly after Hambach, it was these institutions 'that contained the poison within themselves'. Metternich, of course, needed no convincing, and exploited the festival to initiate yet another crackdown against opposition movements throughout Germany, whilst in Bavaria a reaction set in against the 'palatinisation' of the state.[135]

Prussia annexed the Rhineland at a time when the Monarchy's future course remained undetermined. The reforms initiated by Stein and Hardenberg

---

[133] Walther Klein, *Der Napoleonkult in der Pfalz* (Munich and Berlin, 1934), p. 14.

[134] Karl H. Wegert, *German Radicals Confront the Common People. Revolutionary Politics and Popular Politics 1789–1849* (Mainz, 1992), pp. 102ff., 144–71.

[135] Wrede to Metternich, 31 July 1832. Quoted in Heiner Haan, 'Kontinuität und Diskontinuität in der pfälzischen Beamtenschaft im Übergang von der französischen zur bayerischen Herrschaft (1814–1818)', *Jahrbuch für westdeutsche Landesgeschichte* 2 (1976), pp. 308–9.

in response to Prussia's defeat by Napoleon remained incomplete. Would Berlin continue down the path of reform? The expansion of the Monarchy westwards through the incorporation of provinces previously within the Napoleonic orbit offered to breathe new life into the process. For conservatives, in contrast, the danger of contamination by an alien set of values now presented itself. In the Rhineland, prejudices against Prussian militarism and brutality – prejudices that predated the Napoleonic period – came to the fore. The confessional question, which further divided the largely Catholic population from an essentially Protestant state, also undermined attempts at integration. That said, this issue was not paramount in the first decades of Prussian rule, when hierarchy and state found many areas of co-operation. It was only in the 1830s that relations collapsed under the burden of the mixed-marriages crisis.

More important than religion in determining relations between centre and periphery was the French legacy. Initially, reform-minded Prussian officials played a crucial role in ensuring that this was not immediately swept aside. This should never be forgotten. Beyond that, defence of 'French' institutions potentially united a broad social coalition within the region itself. Too often, preservation of the French legacy has been seen in Marxist terms of class conflict. Certainly, wealthy liberal businessmen had an interest in seeing most Napoleonic institutions preserved. However, there was more to these institutions than the protection of property. For many Rhinelanders, the French legacy provided a defence against the arbitrary exercise of authority that was, rightly or wrongly, associated with 'Prussian methods'. As we saw in previous chapters, Napoleonic rule, far from making Rhinelanders used to authoritarianism, endowed them with a new set of institutions that blunted it. Chief amongst these was the law.

CHAPTER 10

Reflections

This study examines the diffusion of political ideas and institutions. Several conclusions can now be drawn. Popular suspicion of new ideas and institutions in the Rhineland in the revolutionary era cannot be ascribed to apathy or ignorance, even though such an interpretation was shared by successive waves of reformers, radicals and revolutionaries, and has entered the historiography. Nor can unease at externally imposed innovation be dismissed as conservative parochialism or unquestioning satisfaction with the existing order, as this underplays the indigenous conflicts that distinguished this period. Historical research has revealed the extent of these under the Old Regime, though their continuation through the superficially depoliticised Napoleonic and Restoration periods may come as a surprise. Their survival illustrates the degree of continuity that existed between those two great revolutionary decades, the 1780s and 1840s.

Discontent with the existing order in the 1780s and 1790s, coupled with suspicion of radical alternatives, led to various moderate reform proposals that one might label 'third way' were that phrase not encumbered by modern connotations. In any case, that bland term is fundamentally inaccurate in this context, as it implies location on the modern political spectrum, and not to the alternative order of Reich, *Land* and *Stadt* which shaped the Rhineland's political culture. This culture was vibrant, capable of evolution, receptive to external influences and able to thrive within new institutional settings.

Napoleon, who straddled the old and new order, is central to this study. At one level, Napoleon was less significant than is sometimes claimed. He did not mark a new beginning if that implies the elimination of earlier traditions. Nor can Napoleonic rule be reduced to a simple account of state imposed 'social-disciplining' that inexorably ground down local resistance. Throughout, the sources have revealed the effectiveness of resistance to 'social-disciplining', and also the willingness of the Napoleonic state to accommodate this. Napoleonic government emerges as more pragmatic, and as more dependent upon local elites, than is recognised in accounts that focus simply on the awesome administrative structures. These proved impressive on paper, but in practice underwent modification when confronted with the challenges of governing a recently annexed peripheral region with a largely alien culture.

This study emphasises the Napoleonic state's limitations. It does not intend to diminish the significance of French rule. This was of huge significance, for several reasons. One was that some French institutions gained a surprising degree of popular support. Superficially, this seems bizarre, given that the Napoleonic order apparently represented the antithesis of what Rhinelanders were used to. Yet, several factors allowed the new regime to gain acceptance, including its very flexibility and fragility. Furthermore, Napoleon followed upon a brief but disastrous period of military occupation characterised by the arbitrary exercise of power. More fundamentally, some Napoleonic institutions, including the various representative councils and electoral colleges – bodies which cannot be dismissed as a sham – suited the existing political culture very well. Most significant of all in this respect was the judiciary: the codes and multi-tiered system of courts with their oral proceedings and juries. Napoleon's state was a *Rechtsstaat*, where executive action was confined by procedural regulations. This holds true, despite the occasional spectacular acts of arbitrariness committed at the highest levels.[1] For Napoleon jealously reserved such arbitrary discretion for himself, whilst binding his subordinates with guidelines. Furthermore, he established institutions that enabled citizens to gain redress if these were deviated from. For Rhinelanders, long accustomed to the checks provided by representative estates and imperial courts, such institutional protection against arbitrariness was immensely important. This sentiment was exposed by later Prussian investigation of the pros and cons of the French legal system: what Rhinelanders really appreciated was the transparent and equitable court procedures rather than the laws themselves, which in many respects were harsher than the Prussian alternative. As the liberal David Hansemann observed in the 1830s, Rhinelanders cared more about equality – by which he meant equitable treatment by public authorities – than liberty.

Napoleonic institutions, like those of the old *Reich*, provided protection against the arbitrariness Rhinelanders experienced under occupation in the 1790s, and which most associated with the eastern monarchies. With respect to these, Rhenish prejudices remained remarkably consistent. They were

[1] Isser Woloch, *Napoleon and His Collaborators. The Making of a Dictatorship* (New York and London, 2001), p. 56.

shared by a broad social spectrum, and were indeed an integral part of what it meant to be a Rhinelander. Now, for the eighteenth century, much of the historiography interprets this as clinging on to outmoded rights in the face of 'modernisation' as was being imposed from above in the 'enlightened' monarchies to the east. For the nineteenth century, in contrast, the same values appear as a progressive and liberal defence of the concept of due process against monarchical and ministerial despotism. Of course, such a shift did not occur within Rhenish *mentalités*. Rather, it is the consequence of a theoretical framework that identifies the absolute monarchies as the sole repositories of progress during the Old Regime, and the liberal bourgeoisie as the bearers of modernity in the nineteenth century. Such a framework – a linear model, in which the path to modernity proceeds from the late medieval/early-modern world of rights and privileges to the nineteenth-century world of constitutions and liberties, and *of necessity passes through an intervening phase of enlightened absolutism* – makes no sense within the Rhenish context.

The Napoleonic period should not be viewed in Weberian terms, as bureaucratic modernisation forced through against 'traditional' opposition. What is true is that Napoleon provided a new institutional framework through which *existing* values were updated and could be expressed more effectively in a region that had already embarked upon the transition from corporations to class. In achieving this, French institutions also transposed to a wider territorial stage the values previously formed in the context of *Land* and *Stadt*. A comment by Peter Heinrich Merkens, deputy to the Rhenish *Landtag* of 1833, encapsulates this process: 'The era of the petty town burgher has given way to that of the citizen' ('Die Zeit der Pfahl- und Spießbürger ist der Zeit des Staatsbürgers gewichen').[2] Here lies Napoleon's significance.

Napoleonic institutions struck deep roots in the Rhineland and gained widespread acceptance. Such support facilitated their survival in the hostile climate of the Restoration. For whilst their initial preservation after 1814/15 depended upon a small number of pro-reform Prussian, Bavarian and Hessian officials, it seems unlikely that these would have prevailed in the longer term had the French legacy represented some unpopular foreign imposition. For that was how conservatives within Prussia and the other successor states sought to portray Napoleonic institutions. They feared they carried within them the germs of revolution that would infect the rest of

---

[2] Quoted from Friedrich Lenger, 'Bürgertum und Stadtverwaltung in rheinischen Grossstädten des 19. Jahrhunderts. Zu einem vernachlässigten Aspekt bürgerlicher Herrschaft', in Lothar Gall (ed.), *Stadt und Bürgertum im 19. Jahrhundert* (Munich, 1990), p. 102.

Germany. Hence their determination to destroy the French legacy in the Rhineland after 1815.

Political struggle between two competing visions therefore distinguished the Restoration and *Vormärz*: the one was monarchical and aristocratic, the other constitutional and broadly *Bürgerlich*. The failure of full-blown revolution to break out in 1830/32 suggested the continued triumph of the former. However, in the Rhineland at least, that quintessentially liberal French institution, the jury, blunted the conservative counter-offensive that followed those years. Not only did Rhenish jurors acquit the participants in the Hambach Fest, but the open court proceedings gave wider publicity to the politics they espoused. Similar acquittals of political agitators occurred over the following years. Karl Marx, for example, the most famous Rhenish agitator of all, was twice cleared by juries of alleged press offences. This hardly modified his opinion that juries dispensed class justice, an assessment that does not square with the evidence. In practice, jurors defended civil liberties, and would continue to do so even after the 1848 revolutions, as the numerous acquittals in political cases over the following years illustrate.[3] Not surprisingly, radicals elsewhere in Germany identified 'Rhenish' judicial institutions as their favoured model, and when the Europe-wide crisis of the 1840s led to revolution in 1848, these served as a model for the so-called liberal 'March ministries' that came to power (and in which Rhenish liberals, including many jurists, played a prominent role).[4] Briefly, in 1848, it appeared that the constitutional values of the west had triumphed over the monarchical east.

Events in the Rhineland in 1848 were bound up with the early career of Karl Marx. At first glance, it seems difficult to connect Marx's political beliefs with the region's traditions. Certainly, his doctrinaire belief in class struggle runs at odds with the picture presented here, with its emphasis upon

[3] Jonathan Sperber, *Rhineland Radicals. The Democratic Movement and the Revolution of 1848–1849* (Princeton, 1993 pbk edn), pp. 101–2, 265.

[4] In Prussia, the new ministry appointed by Frederick William IV in March 1848 was dominated by two liberal Rhenish businessmen, Camphausen and Hansemann. In addition, the Rhenish merchant and banker Hermann von Beckerath held the finance portfolio in the all-German *Reich* government that was established later that year. Meanwhile, Rhenish lawyers took over the justice ministries in Hessen and Bavaria, and there presided over the introduction of French-style judicial proceedings throughout those states. Furthermore, 100 of the 500 members of the Frankfurt pre-parliament were native Rhinelanders, a disproportionately large number. Significantly, the overwhelming majority of these delegates came from the towns and cities, reflecting the essentially urban flavour of politics in the Rhineland; only ten of the hundred came from rural areas, in which three-quarters of the population still lived. James J. Sheehan, 'Liberalism and the City in Nineteenth-century Germany', *Past & Present* 51 (1971), p. 122 n. 12. For a recent contribution on the business elite, see James M. Brophy, *Capitalism, Politics, and Railroads in Prussia, 1830–1870* (Columbus, OH, 1998).

a broad-based social coalition uniting around common hostility to the arbitrary exercise of state power. Marx's Left-Hegelian philosophical abstractions hardly contributed to the formation of this coalition. Yet, as Jonathan
Sperber reveals in his book on 1848, Marx rarely mixed philosophy with
practical politics and, as a practical politician in 1848, he acted very much as
a Rhinelander. Far from playing up class war, Marx did everything he could
to contribute to the formation of a socially broad-based political alliance
founded upon common hostility to monarchical authority and the bureau-
cratic/military apparatus through which it was exercised. Marx avoided
actions that might jeopardise this objective, such as attacking the Roman
Catholic Church.[5] Instead, he followed the precepts already outlined in his
Communist Manifesto, written in collaboration with another Rhinelander,
Friedrich Engels. This demanded the overthrow of the existing East-Elbian,
aristocratic, 'Prussian' order by a broad-based bourgeois-led coalition. For
this to succeed, working-class consciousness needed to be diminished, not
increased. Indeed, the *Communist Manifesto* went so far as to accuse so-
called 'true socialists' – those engaged in class war – of aiding and abetting
Prussian absolutism. When, in the course of 1848, Marx seized control of
the Workers' Association of Cologne, he used it as a mechanism to attach
the city's lower classes to the broader democratic movement, and not to
engage in independent working-class politics. The subsequent struggles he
was personally involved in, such as the tax boycott of November 1848, were
definitely directed against the bureaucratic and military apparatus of the
state.[6]

Radicals like Marx were not alone in exploiting anti-Prussian sentiment.
Catholic-clericals, occupying the other end of the political spectrum, and
moderate liberals, did the same. Centre–periphery conflict, pitting outlying
regions against dynastic cores to which they had been unwillingly attached
at the beginning of the century, lay at the heart of much of what occurred
in Germany in 1848. Certainly, this centre–periphery dimension was of
overriding importance in the entire Rhineland, including Rhine-Hessen
and the Bavarian Palatinate as well as the Prussian *Rheinprovinz*. Friedrich
Engels recognised the revolutionary potential of this situation when he
stated at a provincial democratic congress in 1848: 'The character trait of
the Rhineland is hatred of Prussianism, especially the Prussianism of the
state officials; this sentiment will, hopefully, continue.' Demands in 1848
for the creation of a German nation should be viewed within this context.
At least within the Rhineland, they stemmed from a hope of rescue from

---

[5] Sperber, *Rhineland Radicals*, p. 303.   [6] *Ibid.*, pp. 300–1.

alien dynastic states, and not from any desire for submergence within a larger territorial unit. Confessional differences often reinforced this sentiment, but were not of fundamental importance. What was crucial was the deficit of legitimacy suffered by the dynastic states within newly acquired regions. Nor was this deficit quickly overshadowed by social conflict as the 1848 revolutions progressed. Rather, it remained at the forefront to the bitter end. It provided the glue that held together a broad social coalition, and this survived into 1849. For far from betraying the revolution as later Marxist interpretations argue, the Rhineland's bourgeois elite remained vociferous in demanding political change. Cologne's well-established notables, for example, meeting in defiance of the Berlin authorities in early 1849, yelled 'German! German! Secession from Prussia!' when prompted by a speaker with the question of whether they wanted to be German or Prussian.[7]

Accounts that (unconvincingly, in my opinion) privilege the social dynamic behind the 1848 revolutions have often distinguished between the northern and southern Rhineland, contrasting the more radical south with the moderate north. A differing social structure – a south dominated by a relatively homogeneous middling bourgeoisie versus a north distinguished by a small elite of wealthy capitalists – has sometimes been proffered as an explanation for this. Other explanations have looked back to the 1790s, and sought to establish familial connections between the Middle Rhine radicals of the 1840s with the Mainz Jacobins. None of this is convincing as compared to the most straightforward explanation: the Prussian state was simply better at crushing disorder than its southern counterparts. For ultimately, the revolutions of 1848/9 collapsed not because of social divisions or weakness within the Rhineland, but because of the deployment by Prussia of overwhelming military force. Military power, which throughout Germany remained at the princes' disposition and rested upon the unshaken dynastic loyalty of the mainly rural populations of the core provinces, ended the revolutions.[8]

In many respects, the defeat experienced by progressive forces in 1848/49 was less dramatic than previously thought. At least in the Rhineland, the liberal bourgeoisie was not cowed into political inaction by the threat of social revolution or government repression. For example, it vigorously protested Berlin's re-establishment in 1851 of the provincial *Landtag* in its old form. The broad-based social coalition founded around opposition to the state's

---

[7] *Ibid.*, p. 360.
[8] Whilst the western regiments of the Prussian and Bavarian armies proved unreliable in 1848/9, those recruited from the core eastern provinces remained loyal. *Ibid.*, pp. 247–8, 398–9.

heavy-handed methods remained intact.[9] However, the 1850s witnessed three developments that would lead to a fracturing of this coalition and the emergence of radically altered political alignments: first, rapid industrialisation; second, the rise of political Catholicism; and third, the shift of focus away from provincial and towards national (that is, Prussian) politics. The old battle centred on French institutions receded, not least because Prussia emerged from the mid-century crisis with a constitution, thereby finally fulfilling Frederick William III's promise of 1815. In any case, by now the survival of important elements of the Napoleonic legacy was assured within the region. Indeed, 'Rhenish' institutions had helped shape development throughout Prussia, especially in judicial matters. Furthermore, in 1866 Bismarck introduced a greater measure of provincial self-government in Prussia as part of a readjustment made necessary by the annexation of new territories following the Austro-Prussian war. By 1900, the year when an all-German code finally (and uncontroversially) superseded the French laws in the Rhineland, the struggles of the Restoration and *Vormärz* seemed irrelevant and distant. The old centre–periphery conflicts had long since been submerged under the new mass party politics that straddled regional boundaries.

That is not to say that differences between the Prusso-German state and its western marches disappeared entirely. As late as 1866, Prussian officers referred to the Rhineland as 'conquered territory'.[10] For the predominantly bourgeois Rhenish elite, the values of the Hohenzollern court (from which it remained largely excluded) were as alien as before. It was surprisingly immune from 'aristocratisation', thanks to self-confidence in its own values.[11] This is well illustrated by an anecdote concerning the formidable Madame Neven du Mont of Cologne, wife of a leading liberal politician and councillor in the city. When, during a line-up at a reception given by the visiting Emperor William II the lord chamberlain announced, 'Your Majesty, the nobility ends here,' Madame du Mont responded with similar decisiveness, 'But here, your Majesty, is where the money begins.'[12] This

[9] Simon Hyde, 'Hans Hugo von Kleist-Retzow and the Administration of the Rhine-Province during the "Reaction" in Prussia, 1851–1858' (Oxford D.Phil., 1993), pp. 123–81, 239–40, 305.

[10] Franz Petri and Georg Droege, *Rheinische Geschichte in drei Bänden* (3 vols., Düsseldorf, 1976–9), 2, pp. 666ff.

[11] For the aristocratic exclusivity of the Prussian court under Frederick William IV, see David E. Barclay, *Frederick William IV and the Prussian Monarchy 1840–1861* (Oxford, 1995), pp. 109, 219–22. More generally, on the durability of bourgeois values in nineteenth-century Germany, see Jürgen Kocka (ed.), *Bürgertum im 19. Jahrhundert: Deutschland im europäischen Vergleich* (3 vols., Munich, 1988), 1, p. 68.

[12] Hans-Peter Schwarz, *Konrad Adenauer. A German Politician and Statesman in a Period of War, Revolution and Reconstruction*, vol. 1: *From the German Empire to the Federal Republic, 1876–1952* (Providence and Oxford, 1995), p. 20.

arrogance echoed the earlier comments by Schaaffhausen, about marrying into a poor family. Ensconced within the municipal administrations of the larger cities and shielded from mass politics by the plutocratic three-tier voting system pioneered in the region, the bourgeois elite could afford to feel smug.

For the majority, religion remained the defining element in their culture. In the early nineteenth century, religion generally acted as a cohesive force, binding the elite to the masses. It helped bridge social differences. Certainly, there were some divisions. Sectarian differences obviously divided Catholics and Protestants, though these were more pronounced at the popular than at the elite level. Within the Catholic laity, divisions also existed, as we saw in the deacons' reports sent to Archbishop Spiegel. According to these, liberal bourgeois Catholics tended to sneer at the popular piety of the masses, and involved themselves in religious festivities mainly to assert their social superiority rather than for spiritual reasons. Liberal Catholic bourgeois felt more comfortable with their social equals from the Protestant and even Jewish communities with whom they mixed socially and co-operated politically. As such, there was no unbridgeable chasm between liberalism and Catholicism. Indeed, both could come together in their opposition to the Prussian state.

This changed after the 1850s. Those two forces that had shaped Rhenish culture over the centuries – urban culture and the Catholic Church – moved apart. Liberalism, which was rooted in the city, became increasingly incompatible with what it saw as Catholic 'obscurantism'. Scientific certainty, and especially the evolutionary theories of Darwin, pulled free-thinking liberals in one direction, and the uncompromising doctrinal developments of Pius IX's pontificate coupled with a revival in popular piety pulled Catholics in the other. Liberal Catholics faced an awful dilemma. Germany's unification by Prussia in 1871 and the accompanying attempt to construct a national canon in which Catholics found no place compounded this dilemma for some, but also ensured that the majority would rally around their co-religionists rather than their social equals during the so-called *Kulturkampf* that now followed.[13] At one level, this battle was fought out between Church and state, and is in particular associated with a series of legislative measures taken by the Prussian government between 1871 and 1876. The most important of these were the so-called 'May Laws' of 1873, through which the state assumed greater control over the Catholic clergy. Whilst Pope Pius IX

---

[13] During the Austro-Prussian war of 1866, Austrian propaganda propagated a confessional view of the conflict, and even called on Catholics to refuse to serve in the Prussian army. This propaganda appears to have met with success in some parts of the Rhineland. Margaret Lavinia Anderson, *Windthorst. A Political Biography* (Oxford, 1981), p. 98.

threatened to excommunicate anyone observing the laws, the government acted vigorously against clergy who refused to obey them, so that by 1876 ten out of twelve Prussian bishops (including the Archbishop of Cologne and Bishop of Trier) were either under arrest or in exile, and 1,400 parishes (representing one-third of the total) were without incumbents. For many free-thinking liberals, like the National Liberal politician Rudolf Virchow (himself a Rhinelander), who originally coined the phrase *Kulturkampf*, the conflict represented a profounder clash of 'civilisations'.

Politically, the *Kulturkampf* proved a godsend for political Catholicism (as represented by the fledgling Centre Party) in the Rhineland and a disaster for liberalism. For the vast majority of Catholic Rhinelanders, the heavy-handed actions of the Prussian government transformed the conflict that liberals recognised – a conflict between cultures – into a far more familiar struggle against the authoritarian state. Certainly, this was how the leaders of the Centre Party sought to portray the conflict as they mastered the politics of moral outrage focused on the abuse of executive power. In this, they could resurrect all the old anti-Prussian stereotypes. This tactic proved successful in rallying many liberal Catholics, who were frankly embarrassed by Pius IX's pontificate. Liberals, in contrast, encountered grave ideological difficulties on the terrain selected by the Centre Party. They faced the choice of either supporting Bismarck's heavy-handed methods or else siding with a culture they found profoundly threatening. The majority opted for the former route; indeed, many National Liberals criticised the Prussian government for not being tough enough in its pursuit of the *Kulturkampf*. Left Liberals, in contrast, though equally strong in their opposition to Catholic 'obscurantism', expressed some unease at government actions.[14]

The Centre's tactics brought electoral rewards in the Rhineland and elsewhere. In the 1874 *Reichstag* elections, the Centre attracted an estimated 83 per cent of the Catholic vote in Germany as a whole and achieved an especially high degree of voter mobilisation in the *Rheinprovinz*. On a broader level, the *Kulturkampf* encouraged the expansion of a counter-culture in the Rhineland that was opposed to the official culture of the newly founded Kaiserreich, and from which Protestants were excluded. Well might National Liberal supporters of Bismarck, like the historian Heinrich von Treitschke, fume about the Rhineland as the 'region of the crosier'. Sectarian divisions within the region, as in Germany as a whole, tended to widen rather than narrow in the final decades of the nineteenth

---

[14] David Blackbourn, *Marpingen. Apparitions of the Virgin Mary in Nineteenth-Century Germany* (New York, 1994), pp. 263–7.

century. This, despite Bismarck's abandonment of the *Kulturkampf* in 1878/9 and repeal of the last May Laws in 1885. Liberals emerged with nothing to show for their loyalty to the government, apart from internal divisions and a falling share of the vote. In the first half of the nineteenth century, the Rhineland served as a liberal stronghold; by the century's end, liberalism was of marginal political importance and lingered in the cities thanks only to plutocratic voting systems. These in turn would disappear along with the Kaiserreich in 1918.

The *Kulturkampf*'s impact on the Rhineland's position as a component of the Hohenzollern Monarchy is rather complicated. On one level, it demonstrated what many Rhinelanders viewed as inherent Prussian authoritarianism. Confessional conflict delayed the day when the majority of the region's inhabitants would ever feel any *emotional* attachment to the Monarchy. The feeling was mutual, as indicated by William II's description of his Catholic subjects several decades later as being 'without a Fatherland'. Instead, Rhenish Catholics, like their co-religionists elsewhere in the *Reich*, retreated into their own counter-culture, which survived the Hohenzollerns' fall.[15] Indeed, this counter-culture arguably stood them in good stead, as it provided immunisation from the kind of trauma felt by many other Germans at the establishment of a republic in 1918. It was no accident that Rhinelanders, of all Germans over the following fifteen years, were amongst those least likely to gravitate towards the political extremes.

A dominant Prussia within Germany outlived the Hohenzollerns, and the majority of Rhinelanders remained loyal to this entity and rejected the separatist agenda supported by France in the 1920s. Respect for Prussian institutions contributed to this sentiment. For whilst the *Kulturkampf* of half a century earlier had prevented the development of any emotional bond between the Hohenzollern Monarchy and its western periphery, it paradoxically reinforced the belief that the Prussian state now met the standards expected of a *Rechtsstaat*. Certainly, this is the impression left by David Blackbourn's analysis of the Marian apparitions in the Rhenish village of Marpingen in the mid-1870s, an episode that in microcosm brought to the boil the various conflicts of the *Kulturkampf*. For whilst the executive arm of the state behaved with a degree of arbitrary ruthlessness, the Prussian courts (eventually) intervened and unravelled the fragile legal basis of government

---

[15] For more on this, see the fascinating study, Ute Schneider, *Politische Festkultur im 19. Jahrhundert. Die Rheinprovinz von der französischen Zeit bis zum Ende des Ersten Weltkrieges (1806–1918)* (Essen, 1995).

actions.[16] The courts, together with parliamentary institutions in Berlin, provided a mechanism for redress, and this ultimately neutered separatist tendencies. The concept of the *Rechtsstaat* – something derived not from the belief in parliamentary sovereignty, nor from the concept of a division of powers, nor even from an enunciation of basic civil rights, but from the notion that executive power must never be exercised arbitrarily – remained the benchmark against which all government was measured. Prussia, thanks in part to institutions that owed much to the French, ultimately met this standard.

[16] Popular confidence in the judiciary's rulings in the Rhineland during the *Kulturkampf* was reinforced by the fact that the proportion of native Catholics within this institution was significantly higher than in the administrative bureaucracy. Indeed, some National Liberals complained that this coloured legal judgements. Blackbourn, *Marpingen*, p. 276.

Bibliography

MANUSCRIPT SOURCES

AG: ARCHIVES DE L'ARMÉE DE TERRE (VINCENNES)

4YB Special military academy.
B^{13} General military correspondence.
C^{10} First Empire: state of the military divisions.
M Manuscripts of the archives of the Ministry of War.
$X^{k}41$ Special formations: *Légion des Francs du Nord.*

AN: ARCHIVES NATIONALES (PARIS)

29 AP Private archives: Roederer papers.
AF IV Archives of the executive: imperial secretariat of state.
BB Payments to the ministry of justice.
C National (legislative) assemblies.
D Missions of the peoples' representatives. Committees of the assemblies.
F^{1a} Ministry of the interior: general administration. General affairs.
F^{1b}II Ministry of the interior: general administration. Administrative personnel. Departmental series.
F^{1c}I Ministry of the interior: miscellaneous documents. Public opinion.
F^{1c}III Ministry of the interior: public opinion and elections. Departmental series.
F^{1c}V Ministry of the interior: general councils. Departmental series.
F^{1e} Ministry of the interior: annexed or dependent territories.
F^{7} General police.
F^{9} Military affairs.

BN: BIBLIOTHÈQUE NATIONALE (PARIS)

(Manuscrits), FM Manuscripts relating to freemasonry.

GSTA: GEHEIMES STAATSARCHIV PREUßISCHER KULTURBESITZ, BERLIN-DAHLEM

Rep. 74 Chancellery of state.

Rep. 77   Ministry of the interior (including the ministry of police, 1814–19).
Rep. 89   Privy Civil Cabinet.

HASK: HISTORISCHES ARCHIV DER STADT KÖLN (COLOGNE)

Bestand 10   Transition from French to Prussian rule.
Bestand 890   Documents relating to the (French) government commissioner generals.
Bestand 1018   Boisserée papers.
Bestand 1123   Wittgenstein papers.
Bestand 1134   Klespe papers.
FV   French administration.

HSTAD: HAUPTSTAATSARCHIV DÜSSELDORF

Generalgouvernement vom Nieder- und Mittel-rhein.
Kleve-Kammer.
Kurköln II.
Lande zwischen Maas und Rhein.
Microfilm A54: *Etat des services des fonctionnaires du département de la Roër fourni au Commissaire du Gouvernement dans les nouveaux Départemens de la rive gauche du Rhin pendant le mois de Germinal an 8.*
Oberpräsidium Köln.
Roërdepartement.

HSTAD: HAUPTSTAATSARCHIV DÜSSELDORF
(ZWEIGSTELLE SCHLOSS KALKUM)

Notarial records.

LHAK: LANDESHAUPTARCHIV KOBLENZ

Bestand 241   Rhin-et-Moselle department.
Bestand 241ff.   French interim administration.
Bestand 256   Rhin-et-Moselle department.
Bestand 276   Sarre department.
Bestand 349   General government of the Middle Rhine.
Bestand 350   General government of the Lower and Middle Rhine.
Bestand 353   Sarre department.
Bestand 354   General government of the Sarre department.
Bestand 355   Allied transitional administrations.
Bestand 371   Austro-Bavarian joint administration (LAK).
Bestand 403   Prussian Rhine Province.

STAA: STADTARCHIV AACHEN

Bestand RAII General documents.
Handschriften: Französische Zeit.

PRINTED PRIMARY SOURCES

Adress-Kalender von den im Fürstenthum Minden, Grafschaft Ravensberg, Grafschaft Teklenberg, Grafschaft Lingen, Herzogthum Cleve, Grafschaft Moers, Herzogthum Geldern, Fürstenthum Ostfriesland und Fürstenthum Neufchatel befindlichen hohen und niederen Collegien, Instanzen und Expeditionen, Magistraten, Universitäten, Kirchen, Schulen, Stiften, Klöstern, und in öffentlichen Aemtern stehenden Personen, auf das Jahr 1797 (1797).

Allgemeines Landrecht für die Preussischen Staaten von 1794. Textausgabe (Frankfurt a. M., 1970).

Almanach Départemental de la Roër pour l'année 1806 (Aachen, 1806).

Almanach du Département de la Roër pour l'année 1808 (Aachen, 1808).

Almanach du Roër (Aachen, 1813).

Alpen, Heinrich Simon van, *Geschichte des fränkischen Rheinufers, was es war und was es itzt ist* (2 vols., Cologne, 1802).

Annuaire du département de la Roër pour l'année... (Aachen, 1809–13).

Antwort auf die infame Druckschrift Beschwerden gegen die Munizipal-Verwaltung zu Rheinberg (Cologne, 1800).

Archenholz, J. W. von, 'Briefe über den gegenwärtigen Zustand der deutsch-französischen Rheinländer', *Minerva* 1 (1802).

Archives Parlementaires de 1787 à 1860. Recueil complet des débats législatifs et politiques des chambres françaises. Imprimé... sous la direction de MM. I. Mavidal et E. Laurent, etc., 1st series (1787–99), (Paris, 1868–).

Archives Parlementaires de 1787 à 1860. Recueil complet des débats législatifs et politiques des chambres françaises. Imprimé... sous la direction de MM. I. Mavidal et E. Laurent, etc., 2nd series (1800–1860), (Paris, 1862–).

Arndt, Ernst Moritz, *Noch ein Wort über die Franzosen* (Leipzig, 1814).

Banfield, T. C., *Industry of the Rhine* (2 vols., London, 1846–8).

Benzenberg, Johann Friedrich, *Wünsche und Hoffnungen eines Rheinländers* (Paris, 1815).

Bönnisches Intelligenzblatt.

Boost, Johann Adam, *Was waren die Rheinländer als Menschen und Bürger, und was ist aus ihnen geworden?* (Mainz, 1819).

Bormann, Karl Theodor Friedrich, and Alexander von Daniels (eds.), *Handbuch der für die königlich-preußischen Rheinprovinzen verkündigten Gesetze, Verordnungen und Regierungsbeschlüsse aus der Zeit der Fremdherrschaft* (8 vols., Cologne, 1833–45).

Botzenhart, Erich (ed.), *Freiherr vom Stein. Briefe und amtliche Schriften* (8 vols., Stuttgart, 1959–70).

Braubach, Max (ed.), *Joseph Görres, Gesammelte Schriften*, vol. 1: *Politische Schriften der Frühzeit, 1795–1800* (Cologne, 1928).

Bulletin des lois de l'Empire Français, 4th series (Paris, April/May 1804–March 1814).

Cardauns, H., and R. Müller (eds.), *Die rheinische Dorfchronik des Johann Peter Delhoven aus Dormagen, 1783–1823* (Cologne, 1926).

Clercq, Alexandre de, *Recueil des traités de la France* (23 vols., Paris, 1861–1919).

Codes de l'Empire Français (Paris, 1813).

Demian, J. A., *Geographisch-statistische Darstellung der deutschen Rheinlande, nach dem Bestande vom 1. August 1820* (Koblenz, 1820).

Dodd, C. E., *An Autumn Near the Rhine; or, Sketches of Courts, Society, Scenery, & c. in Some of the German States Bordering the Rhine* (London, 1818).

Dorsch, Anton Joseph, *Statistique du département de la Roër* (Cologne, 1804).

Eichhoff, Johann Joseph, *Mémoire sur les quatre départemens réunis de la rive gauche du Rhin, sur le commerce et les douanes de ce fleuve* (Paris, 1802/3).

Eichhoff, Johann Joseph, *Topographisch-statistische Darstellung des Rheins, mit vorzüglicher Rücksicht auf dessen Schifffahrt und Handlung, bisherigen Zustand seiner polizeilichen Verfassung, deren mögliche Verbesserung und Ausdehnung auf die übrigen grossen Ströme, womit er theils schon in Verbindung steht, theils noch gebracht werden könnte* (Cologne, 1814).

Eichhoff, Johann Joseph, *Betrachtungen über den XIX. Artikel der deutschen Bundesakte nebst Andenkungen, wie in Gefolge desselben dem Handelsverkehr zwischen den Verschiedenen Bundesstaaten Erleichterung zu verschaffen* (Wiesbaden, 1820).

Fallersleben, Hoffmann von, *Mein Leben* (Hannover, 1868).

Galisset, C. M., *Corps du droit français ou recueil complet des lois, décrets, ordonnances, sénatus-consultes, règlements, avis du conseil d'état, rapports au roi, instructions ministérielles, etc., publiés depuis 1789 jusqu'à nos jours* (11 vols., Paris, 1833–52).

Golbery, Sylv.-Meinrad Xavier de, *Considérations sur le département de la Roër, suivies de la notice d'Aix-la-Chapelle et de Borcette. Ouvrage composé d'après les recherches de l'Auteur et les documents réunis dans les archives de la préfecture* (Aachen, 1811).

Görres, Joseph, *Deutschland und die Revolution* (Koblenz, 1819).

Görres, Joseph, *In Sachen der Rheinprovinzen und in eigener Angelegenheit* (Stuttgart, 1822).

Handbuch über den Königlich-Preussischen Hof und Staat für das Jahr 1818 (Berlin, 1818).

Hansemann, David, *Preussen und Frankreich: Staatwirtschaftlich und politisch, unter vorzüglicher Berücksichtigung der Rheinprovinz* (Leipzig, 1833).

Hansen, Joseph (ed.), *Quellen zur Geschichte des Rheinlandes im Zeitalter der französischen Revolution 1780–1801* (4 vols., Bonn, 1931–8).

Hansen, Joseph (ed.), *Rheinische Briefe und Akten zur Geschichte der politischen Bewegung 1830–1850* (2 vols., Bonn, 1919–42).

Hauterive, Ernest d' (ed.), *La Police secrète du Premier Empire: Bulletins quotidiens adressés par Fouché à l'Empereur, 1804–1810* (5 vols., Paris, 1908–64).

Heyderhoff, Julius (ed.), *Benzenberg. Der Rheinländer und Preusse 1815–1823. Politische Briefe aus den Anfängen der Preussischen Verfassungsfrage* (Bonn, 1928).

Hoogen, Jacob, *Durch welche Mittel läßt sich in den vier Departementen am linken Rheinufer Anhänglichkeit an die Verfassung, und Liebe zum Vaterlande bewirken?* (Cologne, 1801).

Hubatsch, Walther, *Heinrich Friedrich Karl Freiherr vom und zum Stein, Briefe und amtliche Schriften* (10 vols., Stuttgart, 1957–74).

Hugo, Victor, *Le Rhin. Lettres à un ami* (2 vols., Paris, 1912 Nelson edn).

Journal des Nieder- und Mittel-Rheins (Aachen, 1814–15).

Die jüngsten Scenen zu Kölln am Rhein. Ein Beitrag zum jetzigen Kriege. Aus Briefen und sonstigen Quellen gesammelt von einem ihrer gewesenen Mitbürger (Cologne, 1797).

Kalender für den Kreis und die Stadt Köln auf das Schaltjahr nach der Geburt unseres Herrn Jesu Christi 1816 (Cologne, 1816).

Kamptz, K. A. von (ed.), *Annalen der Preußischen inneren Staats-Verwaltung* (23 vols., Berlin, 1817–39).

Keil, Anton, *Handbuch für Maire und Adjuncten, für Polizey-Commissare, Gemeinde-Räthe, Steuer-Empfänger und Vertheiler, Spital- und Armenverwalter, Pfarrer, Kirchen-Räthe und Kirchenmeister, Feld- und Forsthüter und Geschäftsmänner. Zweyte ganz umgearbeitete und vermehrte Auflage* (2 vols., Cologne, 1811–13).

Klebe, Albert, *Reise auf dem Rhein durch die teutschen Staaten von Frankfurt bis zur Grenze der Batavischen Republik, und durch die Französischen Departemente des Donnersbergs des Rheins u. der Mosel und der Roër im Sommer und Herbst 1800* (Frankfurt a. M., 1801).

Klebe, Albert, *Reise auf dem Rhein durch die teutschen und französischen Rheinländer nach Achen und Spaa* (2nd edn, Frankfurt a. M., 1806).

Klein, Adolf, and Justus Bockemühl (eds.), *1770–1815. Weltgeschichte am Rhein erlebt. Erinnerungen des Rheinländers Christoph Wilhelm Heinrich Sethe aus der Zeit des europäischen Umbruchs* (Cologne, 1973).

Kölnische Zeitung.

König, Heinrich (ed.), *Denkwürdigkeiten des Generals Eickemeyer* (Frankfurt a. M., 1845).

Koppe, Johann Gottlieb, *Die Stimme eines Preußischen Staatsbürgers in den wichtigsten Angelegenheiten dieser Zeit* (Cologne, 1815).

Kopstadt, Johann Adolf, *Über Cleve. In Briefen an einen Freund aus den Jahren 1811 und 1814* (Frankfurt a. M., 1822).

Kurtrierisches Intelligenzblatt.

Ladoucette, Jean Charles François de, *Voyage fait en 1813 et 1814 dans le pays entre Meuse et Rhin, suivi de notes, avec une carte géographique* (Paris and Aachen, 1818).

Mainzer Zeitung.

Marshall, Henry, *Hints to young Medical Officers of the Army on the Examination of Recruits; . . . with official documents and the regulations for the inspection of Conscripts for the French and Prussian Armies* (London, 1828).

Marx, Karl and Friedrich Engels, *Karl Marx Friedrich Engels Werke* (edited by the Institut für Marxismus-Leninismus beim ZK der SED, 3rd edn, Berlin, 1974).

Le Moniteur Universel.

Moser, Friedrich Carl von, *Über die Regierung der geistlichen Staaten in Deutschland* (Frankfurt a. M. and Leipzig, 1787).

Möser, Johann Jacob, *Von der Reichsstättischen Regiments-Verfassung (= Neues Teutsches Staatsrecht, Bd. 18)* (Frankfurt a. M. and Leipzig, 1772).

Müller, P. A., *Statistisches Jahrbuch für die deutschen Länder zwischen dem Rhein, der Mosel und der französischen Grenze auf das Jahr 1815* (Mainz, 1815).

Napoleon I, *Correspondance de Napoléon Ier publiée par ordre de l'empereur Napoléon III* (32 vols., Paris, 1858–69).

Neigebaur, Johann Daniel Ferdinand, *Darstellung der provisorischen Verwaltung am Rhein vom Jahr 1813 bis 1819* (Cologne, 1821).

Neigebaur, Johann Daniel Ferdinand, *Statistik der Preußischen Rhein = Provinzen, in den drei Perioden ihrer Verwaltung: 1) Durch das General = Gouvernement vom Niederrheine; 2) Durch jenes vom Nieder = und Mittelrheine; 3) Nach Ihrer jetzigen Begränzung und wirklichen Vereinigung mit dem Preußischen Staate. Aus officiellen Quellen. Von einem Preußischen Staatsbeamten* (Cologne, 1817).

Rang- und Quartier-Liste der Königlich Preußischen Armee für das Jahr 1819 (Berlin, 1819).

Recensement de la Population de la Mairie d'Aix-la-Chapelle dressé en conformité de l'árrêté de Monsieur le Préfet du Département Chevalier de la Légion d'Honneur, Baron de l'Empire en dâte du 16 Juin mille huit cent douze (Aachen, 1812).

Recueil de réglemens pour les pays d'entre Meuse et Rhin, et Rhin et Moselle publiés par le commissaire du Gouvernement (Mainz, 1800).

Recueil des actes de la préfecture du département de la Roër (11 vols., Aachen, 1802/3–13).

Réglemens de LAL∴. du secret des Trois Rois A L'O∴. de Cologne (Cologne, 1811).

Rheinischer Merkur.

Sack, Johann August, *Reglement über die Einrichtung einer Bürger-Militz im Gouvernement des Nieder-Rheins* (Cologne, 1814).

Schehl, Karl, *Mit der großen Armee 1812 von Krefeld nach Moskau. Erlebnisse des niederrheinischen Veteranen Karl Schehl, Krefeld* (Düsseldorf, 1912).

Schönebeck, J. B. K., *Das Gesetzbuch der reinen Vernunft, oder kurze Darstellung dessen, was die Vernunft allen Menschen zur Regel ihres Betragens und zur Sicherung ihrer Glückseligkeit vorschreibt* (Bonn, 1787).

Scotti, Johann Josef, *Sammlung der Gesetze und Verordnungen, welche in den ehemaligen Herzogthümern Jülich, Cleve und Berg und in dem vormaligen Herzogthum Berg über Gegenstände der Landeshoheit, Verfassung, Verwaltung und Rechtspflege ergangen sind. Vom Jahr 1475 bis zu der am 15. April 1815 eingetretenen Königlich Preußischen Landes-Regierung* (Düsseldorf, 1821).

Scotti, Johann Josef, *Sammlung der Gesetze und Verordnungen, welche in dem vormaligen Churfürstentum Trier über Gegenstände der Landeshoheit, Verfassung, Verwaltung und Rechtspflege ergangen sind, vom Jahre 1350 bis zur Reichs-Deputations-Schluss-mässigen Auflösung des Churstaates Trier am Ende des Jahres 1802* (3 vols., Düsseldorf, 1832).

Shée, Henri, *Situation de l'administration civile dans les quatre nouveaux départemens sur la rive gauche du Rhin, à l'époque du premier Brumaire an 8* (Mainz, 1800). *Sind die Beschwerden der Beerbten im Canton Rheinberg gegen die Munizipal-Verwaltung gegründet und dorften einige Gutsbesitzer aus Drüptstein freund-schaftlich zusammen kommen, um über die Entledigung dieser Beschwerden sich zu besprechen* (1800).

Steffens, Wilhelm (ed.), *Briefwechsel Sacks mit Stein und Gneisenau (1807/17)* (Stettin, 1931).

Wasserfall, Peter, *Annuaire historique et statistique consacré au département de la Roër* (1799/1800).

Wiebeking, E. F., *Essays on the History of the States of the Palatinate, with Particular Reference to the Duchy of Jülich and Berg, 1742–92* (Heidelberg and Mannheim, 1793).

Young, Arthur, *Travels in France during the Years 1787, 1788 and 1789* (edited with an introduction by Jeffry Kaplow, Gloucester, Mass., 1976).

SECONDARY WORKS

Allgemeine Deutsche Biographie (56 vols., Leipzig, 1875–1912).

Ammerich, Hans, *Landesherr und Landesverwaltung. Beiträge zur Regierung von Pfalz-Zweibrücken am Ende der Alten Reiches* (Saarbrücken, 1981).

Anderson, Margaret Lavinia, *Windthorst. A Political Biography* (Oxford, 1981).

Andrae, Uwe, *Die Rheinländer, der Revolution und der Krieg 1794–1798* (Düsseldorf, 1994).

Aretin, Karl Otmar Freiherr von, 'Friedrich Karl. Der letzte Kurfürst-Erzbischof von Mainz', in Christoph Jamme and Otto Pöggeler (eds.), *Mainz – 'Centralort des Reiches'. Politik, Literatur und Philosophie im Umbruch der Revolutionszeit* (Stuttgart, 1986).

Aretin, Karl Otmar Freiherr von, *Heiliges Römisches Reich 1776–1806* (2 vols., Wiesbaden, 1967).

Augstein, Rudolf, *Konrad Adenauer* (London, 1964).

Bär, Max, *Die Behördenverfassung der Rheinprovinz seit 1815* (Bonn, 1919).

Barclay, David E., *Frederick William IV and the Prussian Monarchy 1840–1861* (Oxford, 1995).

Bargeton, René, *Les Préfets du 11 Ventôse an VIII au 4 septembre 1870* (Paris, 1981).

Barkhausen, Max, 'Government Control and Free Enterprise in Western Germany and the Low Countries in the Eighteenth Century', in Peter Earle (ed.), *Essays in European Economic History 1500–1800* (Oxford, 1974).

Bass, Hans-Heinrich, 'Hungerkrisen in Posen und im Rheinland 1816/17 und 1847', in Manfred Gailus and Heinrich Volkmann (eds.), *Der Kampf um das tägliche Brot. Nahrungsmangel, Versorgungspolitik und Protest 1770–1990* (Opladen, 1994).

Bazillion, Richard J., 'State Bureaucracy and the Modernization Process in the Kingdom of Saxony, 1830–1861', *German History* 13 (1995).

Becker-Jákli, Barbare, *Die Protestanten in Köln. Die Entwicklung einer religiösen Minderheit von der Mitte des 18. bis zur Mitte des 19. Jahrhunderts* (Cologne, 1983).

Behrens, Klaus (ed.), *Publizistik der Mainzer Jakobiner und ihrer Gegner. Revolutionäre und gegenrevolutionäre Proklamationen und Flugschriften aus der Zeit der Mainzer Republik 1792/93. Zum 200. Jahrestag des Rheinisch-Deutschen Nationalkonvents und der Mainzer Republik* (Mainz, 1993).

Bell, David, 'Nation-building and Cultural Particularism in Eighteenth-century France: the Case of Alsace', *Eighteenth-Century Studies* 21 (1987–8).

Berdahl, Robert M., *The Politics of the Prussian Nobility: The Development of a Conservative Ideology 1770–1848* (Princeton, 1988).

Berding, Helmut, 'Französische Reformpolitik aus revolutionärem Anspruch in später preußischen Gebieten 1794 bis 1814', in Otto Büsch and Monika Neugebauer-Wölk (eds.), *Preußen und die revolutionäre Herausforderung seit 1789* (Berlin, 1991).

Berding, Helmut, *Napoleonische Herrschafts- und Gesellschaftspolitik im Königreich Westfalen 1807–1813* (Göttingen, 1973).

Bergengrün, Alexander, *David Hansemann* (Berlin, 1901).

Berger, Stefan, 'Prussia in History and Historiography from the Nineteenth to the Twentieth Centuries', in Philip G. Dwyer (ed.), *Modern Prussian History 1830–1947* (Harlow, 2001).

Bergeron, Louis, and G. Chaussinand-Nogaret, *Les 'Masses de granit': cent mille notables du Premier Empire* (Paris, 1979).

Berkner, Lutz K. and Franklin F. Mendels, 'Inheritance Systems, Family Structure, and Demographic Patterns in Western Europe, 1700–1900', in Charles Tilly (ed.), *Historical Studies in Changing Fertility* (Princeton, 1978).

Berney, Arnold, 'Reichstradition und Nationalstaatsgedanke (1789–1815)', *Historische Zeitschrift* 140 (1929).

Bertaud, J. P., 'Napoleon's Officers', *Past & Present* 112 (1986).

Best, Geoffrey, *War and Society in Revolutionary Europe, 1770–1870* (London, 1982).

Biro, Sydney Seymour, *The German Policy of Revolutionary France. A Study in French Diplomacy during the War of the First Coalition 1792–1797* (Cambridge, Mass., 1957).

Blackbourn, David, *Marpingen. Apparitions of the Virgin Mary in Nineteenth-Century Germany* (New York, 1994).

Blanning, T. C. W., *The French Revolution in Germany. Occupation and Resistance in the Rhineland 1792–1802* (Oxford, 1983).

Blanning, T. C. W., *The French Revolutionary Wars 1787–1802* (London, 1996).

Blanning, T. C. W., 'German Jacobins and the French Revolution', *The Historical Journal* 23 (1980).

Blanning, T. C. W., *Joseph II* (London, 1994).

Blanning, T. C. W., *The Origins of the French Revolutionary Wars* (London, 1986).

Blanning, T. C. W., *Reform and Revolution in Mainz 1743–1803* (Cambridge, 1974).

Blasius, Dirk, *Bürgerliche Gesellschaft und Kriminalität. Zur Sozialgeschichte Preußens im Vormärz* (Göttingen, 1976).

Blasius, Dirk, 'Der Kampf um die Geschworenengerichte im Vormärz', in Hans-Ulrich Wehler (ed.), *Sozialgeschichte Heute. Festschrift für Hans Rosenberg zum 70. Geburtstag* (Göttingen, 1974).

Blaufarb, Rafe, 'The *Ancien Régime* Origins of Napoleonic Social Reconstruction', *French History* 14 (2000).

Blickle, Peter, 'Kommunalismus, Parlamentarismus, Republikanismus', *Historische Zeitschrift* 242 (1986).

Blickle, Peter, *Landschaften im Alten Reich. Die staatliche Funktion des gemeinen Mannes in Oberdeutschland* (Munich, 1973).

Bluche, F., *Le Bonapartisme: aux origines de la droite autoritaire, 1800–1850* (Paris, 1980).

Bockenheimer, Karl Georg, *Franz Konrad Macke. Bürgermeister von Mainz (1756–1844)* (Mainz, 1904).

Bödeker, H. E., 'Journals and Public Opinion: the Politicization of the German Enlightenment in the Second Half of the Eighteenth Century', in Eckhart Hellmuth (ed.), *The Transformation of Political Culture. England and Germany in the Late Eighteenth Century* (London, 1990).

Boldt, Hans, and Reinhart Koselleck, 'Staat und Souveränität', in Otto Brunner, Werner Conze and Reinhart Koselleck (eds.), *Geschichtliche Grundbegriffe* (8 vols., Stuttgart, 1972–97), vol. 6.

Borck, H. G., *Der schwäbische Reichskreis im Zeitalter der französischen Revolutionskriege (1792–1806)* (Stuttgart, 1970).

Bosl, Karl, *Die Geschichte der Repräsentation in Bayern. Landständische Bewegung, landständische Verfassung, Landesausschuß und altständische Gesellschaft* (Munich, 1974).

Bosl, Karl and Karl Möckl (eds.), *Der moderne Parlamentarismus und seine Grundlagen in der ständischen Repräsentation* (Berlin, 1977).

Bourdon, Jean, 'La Contrebande à la frontière de l'Est en 1811, 1812, 1813', *Annales de l'Est* 5th series, 2nd year, no. 4 (1951).

Boyer, Ferdinand, 'Les Conquêtes scientifiques de la Convention en Belgique et dans les Pays Rhénans (1794–1795)', *Revue d'Histoire Moderne et Contemporaine* 18 (1971).

Braubach, Max, *Kurköln. Gestalten und Ereignisse aus zwei Jahrhunderte rheinischer Geschichte* (Münster, 1949).

Braubach, Max, *Max Franz von Österreich, letzter Kurfürst von Köln und Fürstbischof von Münster* (Münster, 1925).

Braudel, Fernand, *The Identity of France* (2 vols., London, 1988–90).

Bredin, Jean-Denis, *Sieyès. La clé de la Révolution française* (Paris, 1988).

Breuilly, John, 'The National Idea in Modern German History', in idem (ed.), *The State of Germany. The National Idea in the Making, Unmaking and Remaking of a Modern Nation-State* (London and New York, 1992).

Breuilly, John, 'State-building, Modernization and Liberalism from the Late Eighteenth Century to Unification: German Peculiarities', *European History Quarterly* 22 (1992).

Broers, Michael, *Europe under Napoleon 1799–1815* (London, 1996).

Broers, Michael, 'Revolution and Vendetta: Patriotism in Piedmont, 1794–1821', *The Historical Journal* 33 (1990).

Brophy, James M., *Capitalism, Politics, and Railroads in Prussia, 1830–1870* (Columbus, OH, 1998).

Brophy, James M., 'Mirth and Subversion: Carnival in Cologne', *History Today* 47, 7 (1997).

Brubaker, Rogers, *Citizenship and Nationhood in France and Germany* (London, 1992).

Brües, Eva, *Die Rheinlande. Unter Verwendung des von Ehler W. Grashoff gesammelten Materials* (Munich, 1968).

Brunner, Otto, Werner Conze and Reinhart Koselleck (eds.), *Geschichtliche Grundbegriffe* (8 vols., Stuttgart, 1972–97).

Buddruss, Eckhard, 'Die Deutschlandpolitik der Französischen Revolution zwischen Traditionen und revolutionärem Bruch', in Karl Otmar Freiherr von Aretin and Karl Härter (eds.), *Revolution und konservatives Beharren. Das alte Reich und die Französische Revolution* (Mainz, 1990).

Buddruss, Eckhard, *Die französische Deutschlandpolitik 1756–1789* (Mainz, 1995).

Büsch, Otto, *Militärsystem und Sozialleben im Alten Preussen 1713–1807. Die Anfänge der sozialen Militarisierung der preußisch-deutschen Gesellschaft* (Berlin, 1962).

Buschbell, Gottfried, 'Aus der Franzosenzeit in Krefeld', *Annalen des historischen Vereins für den Niederrhein* 115 (1929).

Carl, Horst, 'Die Aachener Mäkelei 1786–1792. Konfliktregelungmechanismen im alten Reich', Sonderdruck aus *Zeitschrift des Aachener Geschichtsvereins* 92 (Aachen, 1985).

Carl, Horst, *Okkupation und Regionalismus. Die preußischen Westprovinzen im Siebenjährigen Krieg* (Mainz, 1993).

Carsten, F. L., *Princes and Parliaments in Germany. From the Fifteenth to the Eighteenth Century* (Oxford, 1959).

Chandler, David, *The Campaigns of Napoleon* (London, 1993 edn).

Church, Clive, *Revolution and Red Tape. The French Ministerial Bureaucracy* (Oxford, 1981).

Church, Clive, 'The Social Basis of the French Central Bureaucracy under the Directory 1795–1799', *Past & Present* 36 (1967).

Clack, Gordon, 'The Nature of Parliamentary Elections under the First Empire: the Example of the Department of Mont-Tonnerre', *Francia* 12 (1984).

Clack, Gordon, 'The Prefecture of Jeanbon Saint-André in the Department of Mont-Tonnerre, 1802–13' (Oxford D.Phil., 1970).

Clark, Christopher M., *The Politics of Conversion. Missionary Protestantism and the Jews in Prussia 1728–1941* (Oxford, 1995).

Clarkson, L. A., *Proto-industrialization: The First Phase of Industrialization?* (Basingstoke, 1985).

Clemens, Gabriele, *Immobilienhändler und Spekulanten: die sozial- und wirtschaftsgeschichtliche Bedeutung der Grosskäufer bei den Nationalgüterversteigerungen in den rheinischen Departements (1803–1813)* (Boppard am Rhein, 1995).

Cobb, R. C., *The Police and the People: French Popular Protest, 1789–1820* (Oxford, 1970).

Coels von der Brügghen, Luise Freiin von (ed.), 'Das Tagebuch des Gilles-Leonard von Thimus-Goudenrath, 1772–1799', *Zeitschrift des Aachener Geschichtsvereins* 60 (1939).

Coing, Helmut, 'Die Französische Rechtsschule zu Koblenz', in *Festschrift für Franz Wieacker zum 70. Geburtstag* (Göttingen, 1978).

Connelly, Owen, *Napoleon's Satellite Kingdoms* (New York and London, 1965).

Conrady, Alexander, *Die Rheinlande in der Franzosenzeit 1750–1815* (Stuttgart, 1922).

Conze, Werner, and Jürgen Kocka (eds.), *Bildungssystem und Professionalisierung in internationalen Vergleichen* (Stuttgart, 1985).

Crook, Malcolm, *Napoleon Comes to Power: Democracy and Dictatorship in Revolutionary France, 1795–1804* (Cardiff, 1998).

Croon, Gustav, *Der Rheinische Provinziallandtag bis zum Jahre 1874. Im Auftrage des Rheinischen Provinzialausschusses* (Bonn, 1974: reproduction of Düsseldorf, 1918 edn).

Croot, Patricia and David Parker, 'Agrarian Class Structure and Economic Development', *Past & Present* 78 (1978).

Crouzet, François, 'Wars, Blockade, and Economic Change in Europe, 1792–1815', *Journal of Economic History* 24 (1964).

Dainville, François de, and Jean Tulard, *Atlas administratif de l'empire Français d'après l'atlas rédigé par ordre du Duc de Feltre en 1812* (Geneva and Paris, 1973).

Dann, Otto, *Nation und Nationalismus in Deutschland 1770–1990* (Munich, 1993).

Deeters, Joachim, 'Das Bürgerrecht der Reichsstadt Köln seit 1396', *Zeitschrift der Savigny-Stiftung für Rechtsgeschichte* 104 (1987).

Deutsches biographisches Archiv microform: eine Kumulation aus 254 der wichtigsten biographischen Nachschlagewerke für den deutschen Bereich bis zum Ausgang des neunzehnten Jahrhunderts (Munich, 1982).

Diefendorf, Jeffry M., *Businessmen and Politics in the Rhineland, 1789–1834* (Princeton, 1980).

Diestelkamp, Bernhard, *Rechtsfälle aus dem alten Reich: denkwürdige Prozesse vor dem Reichskammergericht* (Munich, 1995).

Dilcher, Gerhard, 'Vom ständischen Herrschaftsvertrag zum Verfassungsgesetz', *Der Staat* 27 (1988).

Dippel, Horst, 'Möglichkeiten und Grenzen des sozialen Aufstiegs im Napoleonischen Rheinland. Die Maires des Arrondissements Köln, 1801–1813', *Zeitschrift für historische Forschung* 18 (1991).

Dippel, Horst, 'Der Verfassungsdiskurs im ausgehenden 18. Jahrhundert und die Grundlegung einer liberaldemokratischen Verfassungstradition in Deutschland', in idem (ed.), *Die Anfänge des Konstitutionalismus in Deutschland. Texte deutscher Verfassungsentwürfe am Ende des 18. Jahrhunderts* (Frankfurt a. M., 1991).

Dipper, Christof, 'Probleme einer Wirtschafts- und Sozialgeschichte der Säkularisation in Deutschland (1803–1813)', in Armgard von Reden-Dohna (ed.), *Deutschland und Italien im Zeitalter Napoleons* (Wiesbaden, 1979).

Dipper, Christof, 'Die Reichsritterschaft in napoleonischer Zeit', in Eberhard Weis (ed.), *Reformen im rheinbündischen Deutschland* (Munich, 1984).

Dipper, Christof, 'Der rheinische Adel zwischen Revolution und Restauration', in Helmuth Feigl and Willibald Rosner (eds.), *Adel im Wandel. Vorträge und Diskussion des elften Symposions des Niederösterreichischen Instituts für Landeskunde, Horn, 2.–5. Juli 1990* (Vienna, 1991).

Dotzauer, Winfried, *Freimaurergesellschaften am Rhein. Aufgeklärte Sozietäten auf dem linken Rheinufer vom Ausgang des Ancien Régime bis zum Ende der napoleonischen Herrschaft* (Wiesbaden, 1977).

Doyle, William, *Jansenism. Catholic Resistance to Authority from the Reformation to the French Revolution* (Basingstoke, 2000).

Droz, Jacques, *L'Allemagne et la Révolution française* (Paris, 1949).

Droz, Jacques, *Le Libéralisme Rhénan 1815–1848* (Paris, 1940).

Dufraisse, Roger, 'La Contrebande dans les départements réunis de la rive gauche du Rhin à l'époque napoléonienne', *Francia* 1 (1973).

Dufraisse, Roger, 'La Crise économique de 1810–1812 en pays annexé: l'exemple de la rive gauche du Rhin', *Francia* 6 (1978).

Dufraisse, Roger, '"Élites" anciennes et "élites" nouvelles dans les pays de la rive gauche du Rhin à l'époque napoléonienne', in idem, *L'Allemagne à l'époque napoléonienne. Questions d'histoire politique, économique et sociale* (Bonn and Berlin, 1992).

Dufraisse, Roger, 'L'Influence de la domination française sur l'économie du Palatinat', in idem, *L'Allemagne à l'époque napoléonienne. Questions d'histoire politique, économique et sociale* (Bonn and Berlin, 1992).

Dufraisse, Roger, 'L'Installation de l'institution départementale sur la rive gauche du Rhin (4 novembre 1797–23 septembre 1802)', in idem, *L'Allemagne à l'époque napoléonienne. Questions d'histoire politique, économique et sociale* (Bonn and Berlin, 1992).

Dufraisse, Roger, 'Les Notables de la rive gauche du Rhin à l'époque napoléonienne', *Revue d'histoire moderne et contemporaine* 18 (1970).

Dufraisse, Roger, 'Les Populations de la rive gauche du Rhin et le service militaire à la fin de l'Ancien Régime et à l'Époque Révolutionnaire', *Revue Historique* 231 (1964).

Dufraisse, Roger, 'De quelques conséquences économiques et sociales de la domination française sur les régions du Rhin inférieur 1794–1814', in Peter Hüttenberger and Hansgeorg Molitor (eds.), *Franzosen und Deutsche am Rhein 1789–1918–1945* (Essen, 1989).

Dufraisse, Roger, 'Sarre', 'Mont-Tonnerre', 'Rhin-et-Moselle' and 'Roër', in Louis Bergeron and Guy Chaussinand-Nogaret (eds.), *Grands Notables du premier empire* (vol. 3, Paris, 1978).

Dufraisse, Roger, 'Une Rébellion en pays annexé: le «soulèvement» des gardes nationales de la Sarre en 1809', *Bulletin de la Société d'Histoire Moderne* 14th series, no. 10, 68th year (1969).

Duguit, L., H. Monnier and R. Bonnard, *Constitutions et lois politiques de la France depuis 1789* (Paris, 1952).

Dumont, Franz, *Die Mainzer Republik von 1792/93. Studien zur Revolutionierung in Rheinhessen und der Pfalz* (Alzey, 1982).

Dunan, Marcel, *Napoléon et l'Allemagne. Le système continental et les débuts du royaume de Bavière 1806–1810* (Paris, 1942).

Durand, Charles, *Les Auditeurs au conseil d'état de 1803 à 1814* (Aix-en-Provence, 1958).

Ebeling, Dietrich, *Bürgertum und Pöbel. Wirtschaft und Gesellschaft Kölns im 18. Jahrhundert* (Cologne and Vienna, 1987).

Effertz, Peter, 'Die Kartenaufnahme der Rheinlande durch Tranchot', *Rheinische Vierteljahrsblätter* 54 (1990).

Eisenhardt, Ulrich, *Aufgabenbereich und Bedeutung des Kurkölnischen Hofrats in den letzten zwanzig Jahren des 18. Jahrhunderts. Ein Abriß der Behördenorganisation und des Gerichtswesens im Kurfürstentum Köln* (Cologne, 1965).

Ellis, Geoffrey, *Napoleon's Continental Blockade: the Case of Alsace* (Oxford, 1981).

Ellis, Geoffrey, 'Rhine and Loire: Napoleonic Elites and Social Order', in G. Lewis and C. Lucas (eds.), *Beyond the Terror: Essays in French Regional and Social History, 1794–1815* (Cambridge, 1983).

Ellul, Jacques, *Propaganda. The Formation of Men's Attitudes* (translated from the French by Konrad Kellen and Jean Lerner; with an introduction by Konrad Kellen, New York, 1968).

Emsley, Clive, *Napoleonic Europe* (London, 1993).

Engelbrecht, Jörg, 'Grundzüge der französischen Verwaltungspolitik auf dem linken Rheinufer (1794–1814)', in Christof Dipper, Wolfgang Schieder and Reiner Schulze (eds.), *Napoleonische Herrschaft in Deutschland und Italien – Verwaltung und Justiz* (Berlin, 1995).

Engelhardt, Ulrich, 'Zum Begriff der Glückseligkeit in der kameralistischen Staatslehre des 18. Jahrhunderts', *Zeitschrift für historische Forschung* 8 (1981).

Engerand, L., *L'Opinion publique dans les provinces rhénanes et la Belgique, 1789–1815* (Paris, 1919).

Ennen, Edith, *Ernst Moritz Arndt, 1769–1860* (Bonn, 1968).

Erdmann, Claudia, *Aachen im 1812. Wirtschafts- und sozialräumliche Differenzierung einer frühindustriellen Stadt* (Aachen, 1986).

Erkens, Marcel, *Die französische Friedengerichtsbarkeit 1789–1814 unter besonderer Berücksichtigung der vier rheinischen Departements* (Cologne, Weimar and Vienna, 1994).

Essers, Karl, *Zur Geschichte der kurkölnischen Landtage im Zeitalter der französischen Revolution (1790–1797)* (Gotha, 1909).

Evertz, Wilfried, *Seelsorge im Erzbistum Köln zwischen Aufklärung und Restauration 1825–1835* (Cologne, Weimar and Vienna, 1993).

Faber, Karl-Georg, *Andreas van Recum 1765–1828. Ein rheinischer Kosmopolit* (Bonn, 1969).

Faber, Karl-Georg, *Die Rheinlande zwischen Restauration und Revolution. Probleme der Rheinischen Geschichte von 1814 bis 1848 im Spiegel der zeitgenössischen Publizistik* (Wiesbaden, 1966).

Faber, Karl-Georg, 'Verwaltungs- und Justizbeamte auf dem linken Rheinufer während der französischen Herrschaft. Eine personengeschichtliche Studie', in *Aus Geschichte und Landeskunde, Forschungen und Darstellungen. Fritz*

Steinbach zum 65. Geburtstag gewidmet von seinen Freunden und Schülern (Bonn, 1960).

Favier, Jean, *et al.*, *Chronicle of the French Revolution* (London, 1989).

Fehrenbach, Elisabeth, 'Bürgertum und Liberalismus. Die Umbruchsperiode 1770–1815', in Lothar Gall (ed.), *Bürgertum und bürgerlich-liberale Bewegung in Mitteleuropa seit dem 18. Jahrhundert* (*Historische Zeitschrift* Sonderheft Band 17, Munich, 1997).

Fehrenbach, Elisabeth, 'Der Einfluss des Napoleonischen Frankreich auf das Rechts- und Verwaltungssystem Deutschlands', in Armgard von Reden-Dohna (ed.), *Deutschland und Italien im Zeitalter Napoleons. Deutsch-Italienisches Historikertreffen in Mainz, 29 Mai–1 Juni 1975* (Wiesbaden, 1979).

Fehrenbach, Elisabeth, 'Rheinischer Liberalismus und gesellschaftliche Verfassung', in Wolfgang Schieder (ed.), *Liberalismus in der Gesellschaft des deutschen Vormärz* (Göttingen, 1983).

Fehrenbach, Elisabeth, *Traditionelle Gesellschaft und revolutionäres Recht. Die Einführung des Code Napoléon in den Rheinbundstaaten* (Göttingen, 1974).

Feldenkirchen, Wilfried, 'Aspekte der Bevölkerungs- und Sozialstruktur der Stadt Köln in der Französischen Zeit (1794–1814)', *Rheinische Vierteljahrsblätter* 44 (1980).

Feldenkirchen, Wilfried, 'Der Handel der Stadt Köln im 18. Jahrhundert (1700–1814)' (Bonn D.Phil., 1975).

Finzsch, Norbert, 'Zur "Ökonomie des Strafens": Gefängniswesen und Gefängnisreform im Roërdépartement nach 1794', *Rheinische Vierteljahrsblätter* 54 (1990).

Forrest, Alan, *Conscripts and Deserters. The Army and French Society during the Revolution and Empire* (Oxford, 1989).

François, Etienne, *Koblenz im 18. Jahrhundert. Zur Sozial- und Bevölkerungsstruktur einer deutschen Rezidenzstadt* (Göttingen, 1982).

François, Etienne, 'Villes d'Empire et Aufklärung', in Pierre Grappin (ed.), *L'Allemagne des lumières. Périodiques, correspondances, témoignages* (Metz, 1982).

François, Etienne, 'Die Volksbildung am Mittelrhein im ausgehenden 18. Jahrhundert. Eine Untersuchung über den vermeintlichen "Bildungs-Rückstand" der katholischen Bevölkerung Deutschlands im Ancien Régime', *Jahrbuch für westdeutsche Landesgeschichte* 2 (1976).

Friedrich, Klaus, *Marc Antoine Berdolet (1740–1809), Bischof von Colmar, erster Bischof von Aachen. Sein Leben und Wirken unter besonderer Berücksichtigung seiner pastoralen Vorstellung* (Mönchengladbach, 1973).

Friedrichs, Christopher R., 'Urban Conflicts and the Imperial Constitution in Seventeenth-Century Germany', *Journal of Modern History* 58 (supplement) (1986).

Furet, François, *Revolutionary France 1770–1880* (Cambridge, Mass., 1992).

Gabel, Helmut, *Widerstand und Kooperation. Studien zur politische Kultur rheinischer und maasländischer Kleinterritorien (1648–1794)* (Tübingen, 1995).

Gagliardo, John G., *Germany under the Old Regime 1600–1790* (London, 1991).

Gagliardo, John G., *Reich and Nation. The Holy Roman Empire as Idea and Reality, 1763–1806* (Bloomington, 1980).

Gailus, Manfred and Heinrich Volkmann (eds.), *Der Kampf um das tägliche Brot. Nahrungsmangel, Versorgungspolitik und Protest 1770–1990* (Opladen, 1994).

Gall, Lothar (ed.), *Bürgertum und bürgerlich-liberale Bewegung in Mitteleuropa seit dem 18. Jahrhundert* (*Historische Zeitschrift* Sonderheft Band 17, Munich, 1997).

Gall, Lothar, 'Liberalismus und "Bürgerliche Gesellschaft". Zu Charakter und Entwicklung der liberalen Bewegung in Deutschland', *Historische Zeitschrift* 220 (1975).

Gall, Lothar (ed.), *Stadt und Bürgertum im Übergang von der traditionalen zur modernen Gesellschaft* (Munich, 1993).

Gall, Lothar (ed.), *Vom alten zum neuen Bürgertum. Die mitteleuropäische Stadt im Umbruch 1780–1820* (*Historische Zeitschrift* Beiheft 14, Munich, 1991).

Gates, David, *The Napoleonic Wars 1803–1815* (London, 1997).

Gellner, Ernest, *Nations and Nationalism* (Oxford, 1983).

Gerschler, Walter, *Das preußische Oberpräsidium der Provinz Jülich-Kleve-Berg in Köln 1816–1822* (Cologne, 1967).

Gerteis, Klaus, 'Bildung und Revolution: Die deutschen Lesegesellschaften am Ende des 18. Jahrhunderts', *Archiv für Kultur-Geschichte* 53 (1971).

Gerth, Hans, *Bürgerliche Intelligenz um 1800: Zur Soziologie des deutschen Frühliberalismus* (Göttingen, 1976).

Gestrich, Andreas, *Absolutismus und Öffentlichkeit: Politische Kommunikation in Deutschland zu Beginn des 18. Jahrhunderts* (Göttingen, 1994).

Gill, John H., *With Eagles to Glory. Napoleon and his German Allies in the 1809 Campaign* (London, 1993 reprint).

Gillis, John R., *The Prussian Bureaucracy in Crisis 1840–1860. Origins of an Administrative Ethos* (Stanford, 1971).

Godechot, Jacques, *France and the Atlantic Revolution of the Eighteenth Century, 1770–1799* (New York, 1965).

Godechot, Jacques, *La Grande Nation. L'expansion révolutionnaire de la France dans le monde 1789–1799* (2 vols., Paris, 1956).

Godechot, Jacques, *Les Institutions de la France sous la Révolution et l'Empire* (Paris, 1951).

Godechot, Jacques, 'L'Opposition du Premier Empire dans les conseils généraux et les conseils municipaux', in *Mélanges offert à G. Jacquemyns* (Brussels, 1968).

Godechot, Jacques, 'Sens et importance de la transformation des institutions révolutionnaires à l'époque napoléonienne', *Revue d'histoire moderne et contemporaine* 17 (1970).

Goecke, Rudolf, 'Ein Beitrag zur Stimmung der Bevölkerung am Niederrhein 1797–1798', *Annalen des historischen Vereins für den Niederrhein* 39 (1883).

Goeters, J. F. Gerhard, 'Neubegründung evangelischer Gemeinden in der Rheinprovinz während der Franzosenzeit', *Monatshefte für evangelische Kirchengeschichte des Rheinlandes* 39 (1990).

Gothein, Eberhard, 'Verfassungs- und Wirtschaftsgeschichte der Stadt Cöln vom Untergange der Reichsfreiheit bis zur Errichtung des Deutschen Reiches', in Stadt Köln, *Die Stadt Cöln im ersten Jahrhundert unter Preußischer Herrschaft. 1815 bis 1915* (Cologne, 1915).

Grab, Alexander, 'Army, State, and Society: Conscription and Desertion in Napoleonic Italy (1802–1814)', *The Journal of Modern History* 67 (1995).

Grab, Walter, *Norddeutsche Jakobiner. Demokratische Bestrebungen zur Zeit der Französischen Revolution* (Frankfurt a. M., 1967).

Graumann, Sabine, *Französische Verwaltung am Niederrhein. Das Roërdepartement 1798–1814* (Essen, 1990).

Gross, Hanns, *Empire and Sovereignty. A History of the Public Law Literature in the Holy Roman Empire, 1599–1804* (Chicago and London, 1975 reprint).

Gürtler, Heinz, *Deutsche Freimaurer im Dienste napoleonischer Politik: die Freimaurer im Königreich Westfalen 1807–1813* (Struckum, 1988 reprint).

Haan, Heiner, 'Die bayerische Personalpolitik in der Pfalz von 1816/18 bis 1849', *Jahrbuch für westdeutsche Landesgeschichte* 3 (1977).

Haan, Heiner, 'Kontinuität und Diskontinuität in der pfälzischen Beamtenschaft im Übergang von der französischen zur bayerischen Herrschaft (1814–1818)', *Jahrbuch für westdeutsche Landesgeschichte* 2 (1976).

Haasis, Helmut, *Deutscher Jakobiner: Mainzer Republik und Cisrhenan, 1792–1798* (Mainz, 1981).

Haasis, Helmut, *Morgenröte der Republik. Die linksrheinischen deutschen Demokraten 1789–1849* (Frankfurt a. M., Berlin and Vienna, 1984).

Hammen, Oscar J., 'Economic and Social Factors in the Prussian Rhineland in 1848', *The American Historical Review* 54 (1949).

Hammerstein, Notker, *Aufklärung und katholisches Reich. Untersuchungen zur Universitätsreform und Politik katholischer Territorien des Heiligen Römischen Reichs deutscher Nation im 18. Jahrhundert* (Berlin, 1977).

Hardtwig, Wolfgang, 'Der deutsche Weg in die Moderne. Die Gleichzeitigkeit des Ungleichzeitigen als Grundproblem der deutschen Geschichte 1789–1871', in Wolfgang Hardtwig und Harm-Hinrich Brandt (eds.), *Deutschlands Weg in die Moderne. Politik, Gesellschaft und Kultur im 19. Jahrhundert* (Munich, 1993).

Härter, Karl, *Reichstag und Revolution 1789–1806. Die Auseinandersetzung des immerwährenden Reichstags zu Regensburg mit den Auswirkungen der Französischen Revolution auf das alte Reich* (Göttingen, 1992).

Hartung, Fritz, *Deutsche Verfassungsgeschichte vom 15. Jahrhundert bis zur Gegenwart* (Leipzig and Berlin, 1922).

Hartung, Fritz, *Studien zur Geschichte der preussischen Verwaltung* (3 vols., Berlin, 1942–8).

Hashagen, Justus, *Das Rheinland und die französische Herrschaft. Beiträge zur Charakteristik ihres Gegensatzes* (Bonn, 1908).

Hastings, Adrian, *The Construction of Nationhood. Ethnicity, Religion and Nationalism* (Cambridge, 1997).

Hecker, Hellmuth, *Staatsangehörigkeit im Code Napoléon als europäisches Recht: die Rezeption des französischen Code Civil von 1804 in Deutschland und Italien in Beziehung zur Staatsangehörigkeit* (Hamburg, 1980).

Heckscher, Eli F., *The Continental System. An Economic Interpretation* (Oxford, 1922).

Hegel, Eduard, *Geschichte des Erzbistums Köln*. Vol. 4: *Das Erzbistum Köln zwischen Barock und Aufklärung vom Pfälzischen Krieg bis zum Ende der französischen Zeit 1688–1814* (Cologne, 1979).

Henderson, W. O., *Britain and Industrial Europe 1750–1870. Studies in British Influence on the Industrial Revolution in Western Europe* (Liverpool, 1954).

Henn, Volker, 'Die soziale und wirtschaftliche Lage der rheinischen Bauern im Zeitalter des Absolutismus', *Rheinische Vierteljahrsblätter* 42 (1978).

Henn, Volker, 'Zur Lage der rheinischen Landwirtschaft im 16. bis 18. Jahrhundert', *Zeitschrift für Agrargeschichte und Agrarsoziologie* 21 (1973).

Hentschel, Uwe, 'Revolutionserlebnis und Deutschlandbild', *Zeitschrift für historische Forschung* 20 (1993).

Herborn, Wolfgang, 'Der Graduierte Ratsherr. Zur Entwicklung einer neuen Elite im Kölner Rat der frühen Neuzeit', in Heinz Schilling and Hermann Diederiks (eds.), *Bürgerliche Eliten in den Niederlanden und in Nordwestdeutschland. Studien zur Sozialgeschichte des europäischen Bürgertums im Mittelalter und in der Neuzeit* (Cologne, 1985).

Herrmann, Ulrich, *Die Bildung des Bürgers. Die Formierung der bürgerlichen Gesellschaft und die Gebildeten im 18. Jahrhundert* (Münich, 1990).

Herrmann, Alfred, 'Die Stimmung der Rheinländer gegenüber Preußen 1814/16', *Annalen des historischen Vereins für den Niederrhein* 115 (1929).

Hersche, Peter, 'Intendierte Rückständigkeit: Zur Charakteristik des geistlichen Staates im Alten Reich', in Georg Schmidt (ed.), *Stände und Gesellschaft im Alten Reich* (Stuttgart, 1989).

Hettling, Manfred, *Reform ohne Revolution. Bürgertum, Bürokratie und kommunale Selbstverwaltung in Württemberg von 1800 bis 1850* (Göttingen, 1990).

Heyer, Uwe, 'Die politische Führungsschicht der Stadt Jülich im 18. Jahrhundert', *Beiträge zur Jülichen Geschichte* 58 (1990).

Historische Kommission bei der Bayerischen Akademie der Wissenschaft, *Quellen zu den Reformen in den Rheinbundstaaten* (Munich, 1992).

Historisches Archiv der Stadt Köln, *Die französischen Jahre. Ausstellung aus Anlaß des Einmarsches der Revolutions Truppen in Köln am 6. Oktober 1794* (Cologne, 1994).

Hodenberg, Christina von, *Die Partei der Unparteiischen. Der Liberalismus der preußischen Richterschaft, 1815–1848/49* (Göttingen, 1996).

Hofmeister-Hunger, Andreas, *Pressepolitik und Staatsreform. Die Institutionalisierung staatlicher Öffentlichkeitsarbeit bei Karl August von Hardenberg (1792–1822)* (Göttingen, 1994).

Hofmeister-Hunger, Andreas, 'Provincial Political Culture in the Holy Roman Empire. The Franconian Margravates of Ansbach and Bayreuth', in Eckhart

Hellmuth (ed.), *The Transformation of Political Culture. England and Germany in the Late Eighteenth Century* (London, 1990).

Holborn, Hajo, *A History of Modern Germany. The Reformation* (London, 1965).

Holthausen, Heinrich, *Verwaltung und Stände des Herzogtums Geldern preußischen Anteils im 18. Jahrhundert* (Geldern, 1916).

Holtman, Robert B., *The Napoleonic Revolution* (Baton Rouge, 1950).

Houdaille, J., 'Le Problème des pertes de la guerre', *Revue d'histoire moderne et contemporaine* 17 (1970).

Huber, Ernst Rudolf, *Deutsche Verfassungsgeschichte seit 1789* (3 vols., Stuttgart, Berlin, Cologne and Mainz, 1957–63).

Hudemann-Simon, Calixte, *L'Etat et la santé: la politique de santé publique ou "police médicale" dans les quatre départements rhénans, 1794–1814* (Sigmaringen, 1995).

Hudemann-Simon, Calixte, *L'Etat et les pauvres: l'assistance et la lutte contre la mendicité dans les quatre départements rhénans, 1794–1814* (Sigmaringen, 1997).

Hudemann-Simon, Calixte, 'Réfractaires et déserteurs de la Grande Armée en Sarre (1802–1813)', *Revue Historique* 277 (1987).

Hudemann-Simon, Calixte, 'Wohlfahrts-, Armen- und Gesundheitswesen in der Saarregion 1794–1813', *Jahrbuch für westdeutsche Landesgeschichte* 17 (1991).

Hughes, Michael, *Early Modern Germany, 1477–1806* (London, 1992).

Hughes, Michael, 'The Imperial Aulic Council ("Reichshofrat") as Guardian of the Rights of Mediate Estates in the Later Holy Roman Empire: Some Suggestions for Further Research', in Rudolf Vierhaus (ed.), *Herrschaftsverträge, Wahl-Kapitulationen, Fundamentalgesetze* (Göttingen, 1977).

Huyskens, Albert, 'Die Aachener Annalen aus der Zeit von 1770 bis 1803', *Zeitschrift des Aachener Geschichtsvereins* 59 (1939).

Hyde, Simon, 'Hans Hugo von Kleist-Retzow and the Administration of the Rhine-Province during the "Reaction" in Prussia, 1851–1858' (Oxford D.Phil., 1993).

Ingrao, Charles W., *The Hessian Mercenary State. Ideas, Institutions, and Reform under Frederick II, 1760–1785* (Cambridge, 1987).

Jeismann, Michael, *Das Vaterland der Feinde. Studien zum nationalen Feindbegriff und Selbstverständnis in Deutschland und Frankreich 1792–1918* (Stuttgart, 1992).

Joulia, Antoinette, 'Der Departementalverein Ober-Ems (1812). Ein Erbe der Aufklärung oder ein Produkt des napoleonischen Dirigismus?', *Osnabrücker Mitteilungen* 78 (1971).

Juillard, Étienne, *L'Europe rhénane. Géographie d'un grand éspace* (Paris, 1968).

Julku, Kyösti, *Die revolutionäre Bewegung im Rheinland am Ende des achtzehnten Jahrhunderts.* Vol. 1: *Die Anfänge der revolutionären Bewegung von etwa 1770 bis zum Beginn der Revolutionskriege* (Helsinki, 1965).

Just, Wilhelm, *Verwaltung und Bewaffnung im westlichen Deutschland nach der Leipziger Schlacht 1813 und 1814* (Göttingen, 1911).

Kahan, Alan, 'Liberalism and *Realpolitik* in Prussia, 1830–52: The Case of David Hansemann', *German History* 9 (1991).

Kann, Robert A., *The Problem of Restoration. A Study in Comparative Political History* (Berkeley and Los Angeles, 1968).

Käss, Ludwig, *Die Organisation der allgemeinen Staatsverwaltung auf dem linken Rheinufer durch die Franzosen während der Besetzung 1792 bis zum Frieden von Lunéville (1801)* (Mainz, 1929).

Kermann, Joachim, *Die Manufakturen im Rheinland 1750–1833* (Bonn, 1972).

Keßler, A., 'Düren 1797: Die Absetzung des Magistrats und der Aufbruch in eine neue Zeit', *Dürener Geschichtsblätter* 43 (1967).

Kielmansegg, Graf Peter von, *Stein und die Zentralverwaltung 1813/14* (Stuttgart, 1964).

Kisch, Herbert, 'The Impact of the French Revolution on the Lower Rhine Textile Districts. Some Comments on Economic Development and Social Change', *Economic History Review* 2nd series, 15 (1962–3).

Klein, August, *Die Personalpolitik der Hohenzollernmonarchie bei der Kölner Regierung. Ein Beitrag zur preußischen Personalpolitik am Rhein* (Düsseldorf, 1967).

Klein, W., *Der Napoleonkult in der Pfalz* (Munich and Berlin, 1934).

Knudsen, Jonathan B., *Justus Möser and the German Enlightenment* (Cambridge, 1986).

Kocka, Jürgen (ed.), *Bürgertum im 19. Jahrhundert: Deutschland im europäischen Vergleich* (3 vols., Munich, 1988).

Kohn, Hans, *Prelude to Nation-States. The French and German Experience, 1789–1815* (Princeton, 1967).

Koltes, Manfred, *Das Rheinland zwischen Frankreich und Preußen. Studien zu Kontinuität und Wandel am Beginn der preußischen Herrschaft (1814–1822)* (Cologne, 1992).

Körber, Esther-Beate, *Görres und die Revolution. Wandlungen ihres Begriffs und ihrer Wertung in seinem politischen Weltbild 1793 bis 1819* (Husum, 1986).

Koselleck, Reinhart, *Preußen zwischen Reform und Revolution. Allgemeines Landrecht, Verwaltung und soziale Bewegung von 1791 bis 1848* (Stuttgart, 1967).

Koselleck, Reinhart, and Klaus Schreiner (eds.), *Bürgerschaft. Rezeption und Innovation der Begrifflichkeit vom hohen Mittelalter bis in 19. Jahrhundert* (Stuttgart, 1994).

Krämer, Wolfgang (ed.), *Reichsgräfin Marianne von der Leyen, geb. von Dalberg. Leben, Staat, Wirken* (Saarbrücken, 1937).

Kraus, Thomas R., *Auf dem Weg in die Moderne. Aachen in französischer Zeit 1792/93, 1794–1814. Handbuch-Katalog zur Ausstellung im 'Krönungssaal' des Aachener Rathauses vom 14. Januar bis zum 5. März 1995* (Aachen, 1994).

Kuhn, Axel, *Jakobiner im Rheinland: der Kölner konstitutionelle Zirkel von 1798* (Stuttgart, 1976).

Kurschat, Wilhelm, *Das Haus Friedrich & Heinrich von der Leyen in Krefeld. Zur Geschichte der Rheinlande in der Zeit der Fremdherrschaft 1794–1814* (Frankfurt a. M., 1933).

La Vopa, Anthony J., 'Specialists against Specialization: Hellenism as Professional Ideology in German Classical Studies', in Geoffrey Cocks and Konrad H. Jarausch (eds.), *German Professions, 1800–1950* (New York and Oxford, 1990).

Lademacher, Horst, 'Der Niederrheinische und Westfälische Adel in der Preussischen Verfassungsfrage', *Rheinische Vierteljahrsblätter* 31 (1966–7).

Lahrkamp, Monika, *Münster in Napoleonischer Zeit 1800–1815* (Münster, 1976).

Landsberg, Ernst (ed.), *Die Gutachten der Rheinischen-Immediat-Justiz-Kommission und der Kampf um die rheinische Rechts- und Gerichtsverfassung 1814–1819* (Bonn, 1914).

Lenger, Friedrich, 'Bürgertum und Stadtverwaltung in rheinischen Großstädten des 19. Jahrhunderts. Zu einem vernachlässigten Aspekt bürgerlicher Herrschaft', in Lothar Gall (ed.), *Stadt und Bürgertum im 19. Jahrhundert* (Munich, 1990).

Levinger, Matthew, *Enlightened Nationalism. The Transformation of Prussian Political Culture, 1806–1848* (Oxford, 2000).

Levinger, Matthew, 'Hardenberg, Wittgenstein, and the Constitutional Question in Prussia 1815–22', *German History* 8 (1990).

Leyhausen, Wilhelm, *Das höhere Schulwesen in der Stadt Köln zur französischen Zeit [1794–1814]* (Bonn, 1913).

Lipgens, Walter, *Ferdinand August Graf Spiegel und das Verhältnis von Kirche and Staat, 1789–1835. Die Wende vom Staatskirchentum zur Kirchenfreiheit* (2 vols., Münster, 1965).

Longy, *La Campagne de 1797 sur le Rhin* (Paris, 1909).

Lyons, Martyn, *France under the Directory* (Cambridge, 1975).

Lyons, Martyn, *Napoleon Bonaparte and the Legacy of the French Revolution* (Basingstoke, 1994).

Macartney, C. A., *The Habsburg Empire 1790–1918* (London, 1971 edition).

McPhee, Peter, 'A Case-study of Internal Colonization: the Francisation of Northern Catalonia', *Review* 3 (1980).

Mallmann, Luitwin, *Französische Juristenausbildung im Rheinland 1794–1814. Die Rechtsschule von Koblenz* (Cologne and Vienna, 1987).

Mann, Michael, *The Sources of Social Power*. Vol. 1: *A History of Power from the Beginning to A.D.1760* (Cambridge, 1978).

Mansel, Philip, *The Court of France 1789–1830* (Cambridge, 1988).

Mathy, Helmut, 'Anton Joseph Dorsch, 1758–1819', *Mainzer Zeitschrift* 62 (1967).

Mathy, Helmut, 'Moguntia academica von der Spätaufklärung über die Große Revolution bis zum Ende der französischen Herrschaft', in Christoph Jamme and Otto Pöggeler (eds.), *Mainz – 'Centralort des Reiches'. Politik, Literatur und Philosophie im Umbruch der Revolutionszeit* (Stuttgart, 1986).

May, Georg, *Seelsorge an Mischehen in der Diözese Mainz unter Bischof Ludwig Colmar. Ein Beitrag zum Kirchenrecht und Staatskirchenrecht im Rheinland unter französischer Herrschaft* (Amsterdam, 1974).

Meinecke, Friedrich, *The Age of German Liberation, 1795–1815* (Berkeley and London, 1977).

Mergel, Thomas, *Zwischen Klasse und Konfession: Katholisches Bürgertum im Rheinland 1794–1914* (Göttingen, 1994).

Mestwerdt, Georg, *Zur clevischen Geschichte aus der Zeit der französischen Herrschaft, 1795–1798* (Cleves, 1895).

Mettele, Gisela, 'Kölner Bürgertum in der Umbruchszeit (1776–1815)', in Lothar Gall (ed.), *Vom alten zum neuen Bürgertum. Die mitteleuropäische Stadt im Umbruch 1780–1820* (Munich, 1991).

Mieck, Ilja, 'Die Integration preußischer Landesteile französischen Rechts nach 1814/15', in Otto Büsch and Monika Neugebauer-Wölk (eds.), *Preussen und die Revolutionäre Herausforderung seit 1789* (Berlin, 1991).

Milz, H., *Das kölner Großgewerbe von 1750–1835* (Cologne, 1962).

Mokyr, Joel, *Industrialization in the Low Countries, 1795–1850* (New Haven, 1976).

Molitor, Hansgeorg, 'Bewegungen im deutsch-französischen Rheinland um 1800', *Jahrbuch für westdeutsche Landesgeschichte* 6 (1980).

Molitor, Hansgeorg, 'Die Juden im französischen Rheinland', in Jutta Bohnke-Kollwitz *et al.* (eds.), *Köln und das rheinische Judentum. Festschrift Germania Judaica 1959–1984* (Cologne, 1984).

Molitor, Hansgeorg, 'La Vie religieuse populaire en Rhénanie Française, 1794–1815', in Bernard Plongeron (ed.), *Practiques religieuses dans l'Europe révolutionnaire (1770–1820). Actes du colloque, Chantilly 27–29 novembre 1986* (Paris, 1988).

Molitor, Hansgeorg, *Vom Untertan zum administré. Studien zur französischen Herrschaft und zum Verhalten der Bevölkerung im Rhein-Mosel-Raum von den Revolutionskriegen bis zum Ende der Napoleonischen Zeit* (Wiesbaden, 1980).

Molitor, Hansgeorg, 'Zensur, Propaganda und Überwachung zwischen 1780 und 1815 im mittleren Rheinland', in *Vom alten Reich zu neuer Staatlichkeit. Alzeyer Kolloquium, 1979: Kontinuität und Wandel im Gefolge der Französischen Revolution am Mittelrhein* (Wiesbaden, 1982).

Mücke, Gustav, *Die geschichtliche Stellung des Arrondissements und seines Verwalters zur Zeit der napoleonischen Herrschaft, dargestellt an dem Leben und Wirken Karl Ludwig von Keverbergs als Unterpräfekt in Cleve* (Bonn, 1935).

Muir, Rory, *Tactics and the Experience of Battle in the Age of Napoleon* (New Haven and London, 1998).

Müller, Alwin, 'Das Sozialprofil der Juden in Köln (1808–1850)', in Jutta Bohnke-Kollwitz *et al.* (eds.), *Köln und das rheinische Judentum. Festschrift Germanica Judaica 1959–1984* (Cologne, 1984).

Müller, Horst, *Fürstenstaat oder Bürgernation. Deutschland 1763–1815* (Berlin, 1989).

Müller, Jürgen, *Von der alten Stadt zur neuen Munizipalität. Die Auswirkungen der Französischen Revolution in den linksrheinischen Städten Speyer und Koblenz* (Koblenz, 1990).

Müller, Klaus, 'Städtische Unruhen im Rheinland des späten 18. Jahrhunderts. Ein Beitrag zur rheinischen Reaktion auf die Französische Revolution', *Rheinische Vierteljahrsblätter* 54 (1990).

Müller-Hengstenberg, Herbert, 'Werbung, Rekrutierung und Desertion beim kurkölnischen Militär im 18. Jahrhundert', *Annalen des historischen Vereins für den Niederrhein* 195 (1992).

Neipperg, R. Graf von, *Kaiser und schwäbischer Kreis (1714–1733). Ein Beitrag zu Reichsverfassung. Kreisgeschichte und kaiserlicher Reichspolitik am Anfang des 18. Jahrhunderts* (Stuttgart, 1991).

Neue Deutsche Biographie (Berlin, 1953–).

Neugebauer-Wölk, Monika, 'Reich oder Republik? Pläne und Ansätze zur republikanischen Neugestaltung im alten Reich 1790–1800', in Heinz Duchhardt and Andreas Kunz (eds.), *Reich oder Nation? Mitteleuropa 1780–1815* (Mainz, 1998).

Nicolini, Ingrid, *Die politische Führungsschicht in der Stadt Köln gegen Ende der Reichsstädtischen Zeit* (Cologne and Vienna, 1979).

Nicolson, Harold, *The Congress of Vienna. A Study in Allied Unity: 1812–22* (London, 1989 edn).

Nipperdey, Thomas, *Germany from Napoleon to Bismarck 1800–1866* (translated by Daniel Nolan, Dublin, 1996).

Nipperdey, Thomas, *Gesellschaft, Kultur, Theorie* (Göttingen, 1976).

Nolte, Paul, *Gemeindebürgertum und Liberalismus in Baden 1800–1850: Tradition, Radikalismus, Republik* (Göttingen, 1994).

Obenaus, Herbert, *Anfänge des Parlamentarismus in Preußen bis 1848* (Düsseldorf, 1984).

Oestreich, Gerhard, 'Zur Vorgeschichte des Parlamentarismus: ständische Verfassung, landständische Verfassung und landschaftliche Verfassung', *Zeitschrift für historische Forschung* 6 (1979).

Oncken, Herrmann, *Die historische Rheinpolitik der Franzosen* (Stuttgart and Gotha, 1922).

Palmer, Alan, *Bernadotte. Napoleon's Marshal, Sweden's King* (London, 1990).

Palmer, Alan, *Metternich. Councillor of Europe* (London, 1997 pbk edition).

Palmer, R. R., *The Age of the Democratic Revolution. A Political History of Europe and America, 1760–1800* (2 vols., Princeton, 1959–64).

Pange, Jean de, *Les Libertés rhénanes* (Paris, 1922).

Papke, Gerhard, *Von der Miliz zum stehenden Heer. Wehrwesen im Absolutismus [1648–1789]* (Munich, 1979).

Papst, Klaus, 'Bildungs- und Kulturpolitik der Franzosen im Rheinland zwischen 1794 und 1814', in Peter Hüttenberger and Hansgeorg Molitor (eds.), *Franzosen und Deutsche am Rhein 1789–1918–1945* (Essen, 1989).

Paret, Peter, *Yorck and the Era of Prussian reform* (Princeton, 1966).

Pelger, Hans, 'Karl Marx und die rheinpreußische Weinkrise', *Archiv für Sozialgeschichte* 13 (1973).

Perrot, Jean-Claude, and Stuart J. Woolf, *State and Statistics in France 1789–1815* (New York, 1984).

Petre, F. L., *Napoleon at Bay 1814* (London, 1977 edn).

Petri, Franz, 'Preußen und das Rheinland', in Walter Först (ed.), *Das Rheinland in preussischer Zeit* (Cologne and Berlin, 1965).

Petri, Franz and Georg Droege, *Rheinische Geschichte in drei Bänden* (3 vols., Düsseldorf, 1976–9).

Piereth, Wolfgang, *Bayerns Pressepolitik und die Neuordnung Deutschlands nach den Befreiungskriegen* (Munich, 1999).

Pollard, Sidney, *Peaceful Conquest. The Industrialization of Europe 1760–1970* (Oxford, 1981).

Ponteil, Felix, *Napoléon Ier et l'organisation autoritaire de la France* (Paris, 1956).

Popkin, Jeremy, 'Buchhandel und Presse in napoleonischen Deutschland', *Archiv für Geschichte des Buchwesens* 26 (1986).

Post, John D., 'A Study in Meteorological and Trade Cycle History: The Economic Crisis Following the Napoleonic Wars', *The Journal of Economic History* 34, 2 (1974).

Press, Volker, 'Landstände des 18. und Parlamente des 19. Jahrhunderts', in Helmut Berding and Hans-Peter Ullmann (eds.), *Deutschland zwischen Revolution und Restauration* (Düsseldorf, 1981).

Press, Volker, 'Die Reichsstadt in der altständischen Gesellschaft', in Johannes Kunisch (ed.), *Neue Studien zur frühneuzeitlichen Reichsgeschichte* (*Zeitschrift für historische Forschung* Beiheft 3, Berlin, 1987).

Raab, Heribert, *Clemens Wenzeslaus von Sachsen und seine Zeit (1739–1812).* Vol. 1: *Dynastie, Kirche und Reich im 18. Jahrhundert* (Freiburg, Basel and Vienna, 1962).

Radkau, Joachim, 'Holzverknappung und Krisenbewußtsein im 18. Jahrhundert', *Geschichte und Gesellschaft* 9 (1983).

Ramsey, Matthew, *Professional and Popular Medicine in France, 1770–1830* (Oxford, 1988).

Reinhard, Marcel, 'La Statistique de la population sous le Consulat et l'Empire', *Population* 5, 1 (1950).

Reuter, Timothy, *Germany in the Early Middle Ages c. 800–1056* (London, 1991).

Riedel, Matthias, *Köln – ein römisches Wirtschaftszentrum* (Cologne, 1982).

Rieger, Ute, *Johann Wilhelm von Archenholz als 'Zeitbürger'. Eine historsch-analytische Untersuchung zur Aufklärung in Deutschland* (Berlin, 1994).

Rödel, Walter, 'Demographische Entwicklung in Deutschland und Frankreich', in Helmut Berding, Etienne François and Hans-Peter Ullmann (eds.), *Deutschland und Frankreich im Zeitalter der Revolution* (Frankfurt a. M., 1989).

Roider Jr., Karl A., *Baron Thugut and Austria's Response to the French Revolution* (Princeton, 1987).

Rokkan, Stein, 'Territories, Centres, and Peripheries: Toward a Geoethnic-Geoeconomic-Geopolitical Model of Differentiation within Western Europe', in Jean Gottmann (ed.), *Centre and Periphery. Spatial Variation in Politics* (Beverly Hills and London, 1980).

Rokkan, Stein, and Derek Urwin, *Economy, Territory, Identity: Politics of West European Peripheries* (London, 1983).

Rosenberg, Hans, *Bureaucracy, Aristocracy and Autocracy. The Prussian Experience 1660–1815* (Cambridge, Mass., 1958).

Rothenberg, Gunther E., *Napoleon's Great Adversaries. The Archduke Charles and the Austrian Army, 1792–1814* (London, 1982).

Rovère, Julien, *Les Survivances françaises dans l'Allemagne Napoléonienne 1815–1914* (Paris, 1918).

Rowe, Michael, 'Between Empire and Home Town: Napoleonic Rule on the Rhine, 1799–1814', *The Historical Journal* 42 (1999).

Rowe, Michael, 'Divided Loyalties: Sovereignty, Politics and Public Service in the Rhineland under French Occupation, 1792–1801', *European Review of History* 5 (1998).

Rowe, Michael, 'Forging "New-Frenchmen": State Propaganda in the Rhineland, 1794–1814', in Bertrand Taithe and Tim Thornton (eds.), *Propaganda* (Stroud, 1999).

Rublack, Hans-Christoph, 'Political and Social Norms in Urban Communities in the Holy Roman Empire', in Kaspar von Greyerz (ed.), *Religion, Politics and Social Protest. Three Studies on Early Modern Germany* (London, 1984).

Rubner, Heinrich, *Forstgeschichte im Zeitalter der industriellen Revolution* (Berlin, 1967).

Sagnac, Philippe, *Le Rhin français pendant la Révolution et l'Empire* (Paris, 1918).

Schaab, Mainrad, *Geschichte der Kurpfalz*. Vol. 2: *Neuzeit* (Stuttgart, 1992).

Schaaf, Erwin, 'Sozioökonomische Funktionen der Volksschule und Gewerbeschule im Raum Trier-Koblenz vom aufgeklärten Absolutismus bis zur Mitte des 19. Jahrhunderts', *Jahrbuch für westdeutsche Landesgeschichte* 4 (1978).

Schäfer, Karl Heinz, *Ernst Moritz Arndt als politischer Publizist. Studien zur Publizistik, Pressepolitik und kollektivem Bewußtsein im frühen 19. Jahrhundert* (Bonn, 1974).

Schama, Simon, *Patriots and Liberators. Revolution in the Netherlands 1780–1813* (London, 1992 edn).

Scheel, Heinrich, *Deutscher Jakobinismus und deutsche Nation: ein Beitrag zur nationalen Frage im Zeitalter der grossen Französischen Revolution* (Berlin, 1966).

Scheel, Heinrich (ed.), *Die Mainzer Republik* (2 vols., Berlin, 1975–81).

Schieder, Theodor, 'Zur Theorie der Führungsschichten in der Neuzeit', in Hans Hubert and Günther Franz (eds.), *Deutsche Führungs-Schichten in der Neuzeit: eine Zwischenbilanz. Büdinger Vorträge 1978* (Boppard am Rhein, 1980).

Schieder, Wolfgang (ed.), *Säkularisation und Mediatisierung in den vier rheinischen Departements 1803–1813: Edition des Datenmaterials der zur veräussernden Nationalgüter* (5 vols., Boppard am Rhein, 1991).

Schlieper, Inge, 'Die Diskussion um die territoriale Neuordnung des Rheinlandes 1813–1815' (Cologne D.Phil., 1971).

Schmitt, Friedrich, *Das Mainzer Zunftwesen und die französische Herrschaft. Ein Beitrag zur Charakteristik ihres Gegensatzes* (Darmstadt, 1929).

Schmitt, Friedrich, *Die provisorische Verwaltung des Gebietes zwischen Rhein, Mosel und französischer Grenze durch Österreich und Bayern in den Jahren 1814–1816* (Meisenheim, 1962).

Schmitz, Wilhelm, *Die Misch-Mundart in den Kreisen Geldern (südlicher Teil), Kempen, Erkelenz, Heinsberg, Geilenkirchen, Aachen, Gladbach, Krefeld, Neuss und Düsseldorf, sowie noch mancherlei* (Dülken, 1893).

Schneid, Frederick C., *Soldiers of Napoleon's Kingdom of Italy. Army, State and Society, 1800–1815* (Boulder, Colo., 1995).

Schneider, Ute, *Politische Festkultur im 19. Jahrhundert. Die Rheinprovinz von der französischen Zeit bis zum Ende des Ersten Weltkrieges (1806–1918)* (Essen, 1995).

Schroeder, Paul, *The Transformation of European Politics, 1763–1848* (Oxford, 1994).

Schuck, Gerhard, *Rheinbundpatriotismus und politische Öffentlichkeit zwischen Aufklärung und Frühliberalismus. Kontinuitätsdenken und Diskontinuitätserfahrung in den Staatsrechts- und Verfassungsdebatten der Rheinbundpublizistik* (Stuttgart, 1994).

Schulte, F., *Die Entwicklung der gewerblichen Wirtschaft in Rheinland-Westfalen im 18. Jahrhundert* (Cologne, 1959).

Schultheis-Friebe, Marieluise, 'Die französische Wirtschaftspolitik im Roër-Departement 1792–1814' (Bonn D.Phil., 1969).

Schulze, Winfried, 'Vom Gemeinnutz zum Eigennutz. Über den Normenwandel in der ständischen Gesellschaft der Frühen Neuzeit', *Historische Zeitschrift* 243 (1986).

Schumacher, Alois, *Idéologie révolutionnaire et pratique politique de la France en Rhénanie de 1794 à 1801. L'Exemple du pays de Trèves* (Paris, 1989).

Schütz, Rüdiger, *Preußen und die Rheinlande. Studien zur preußischen Integrationspolitik im Vormärz* (Wiesbaden, 1979).

Schütz, Rüdiger, 'Zur Eingliederung der Rheinlande', in Peter Baumgart (ed.), *Expansion und Integration. Zur Eingliederung neugewonnener Gebiete in den preußischen Staat* (Cologne and Vienna, 1984).

Schwarz, Hans-Peter, *Konrad Adenauer. A German Politician and Statesman in a Period of War, Revolution and Reconstruction.* Vol. 1: *From the German Empire to the Federal Republic, 1876–1952* (Providence and Oxford, 1995).

Schwennicke, Andreas, 'Der Einfluß der Landstände auf die Regelungen des Preußisches Allgemeinen Landrechts von 1794', in Günter Birtsch and Dietmar Willoweit (eds.), *Reformabsolutismus und ständische Gesellschaft. Zweihundert Jahre Preußisches Allgemeines Landrecht* (Berlin, 1998).

Scott, S., and B. Rothaus (eds.), *Historical Dictionary of the French Revolution, 1789–1799* (Westport, 1985).

Sheehan, James J., *German History 1770–1866* (Oxford, 1993 pbk edn).

Sheehan, James J., 'Liberalism and the City in Nineteenth-century Germany', *Past & Present* 51 (1971).

Sheehan, James J., 'State and Nationality in the Napoleonic Period', in John Breuilly (ed.), *The State of Germany. The National Idea in the Making, Unmaking and Remaking of a Modern Nation-State* (London, 1992).

Shinn, Jerry, *Savoir scientifique et pouvoir social. L'Ecole polytechnique, 1794–1914* (Paris, 1980).

Siemann, Wolfram, *The German Revolution of 1848–49* (Basingstoke, 1998).

Siemann, Wolfram, *Vom Staatenbund zum Nationalstaat. Deutschland 1806–1871* (Munich, 1995).

Simms, Brendan, *The Impact of Napoleon. Prussian High Politics, Foreign Policy and the Crisis of the Executive, 1797–1806* (Cambridge, 1997).

Simms, Brendan, *The Struggle for Mastery in Germany, 1779–1850* (London, 1998).

Smets, Josef, 'De la coutume à la loi. Le pays de Gueldres de 1713 à 1848' (Montpellier III Doctorat d'Etat, 1994).

Smets, Josef, 'Freiheit, Gleichheit, Brüderlichkeit. Untersuchungen zum Verhalten der linksrheinischen Bevölkerung unter der französischen Herrschaft', *Rheinische Vierteljahrsblätter* 59 (1995).

Smets, Josef, *Les Pays rhénans (1794–1814): le comportement des Rhenans face à l'occupation française* (Bern, 1997).

Smets, Josef, 'Von der "Dorfidylle" zur preußischen Nation. Sozialdisziplinierung der linksrheinischen Bevölkerung durch die Franzosen am Beispiel der allgemeinen Wehrpflicht (1802–1814)', *Historische Zeitschrift* 262 (1996).

Smith, Helmut Walser, *German Nationalism and Religious Conflict. Culture, Ideology, Politics, 1870–1914* (Princeton, 1995).

Sobania, Michael, 'Das Aachener Bürgertum am Vorabend der Industrialisierung', in Lothar Gall (ed.), *Vom alten zum neuen Bürgertum. Die mitteleuropäische Stadt im Umbruch 1780–1820* (*Historische Zeitschrift* Beiheft 14, Munich, 1991).

Soboul, Albert (ed.), *Dictionnaire historique de la Révolution Française* (Paris, 1989).

Soboul, Albert, *La Révolution française* (Saint-Amand, 1992 edn).

Spencer, Elaine Glovka, 'Regimenting Revelry; Rhenish Carnival in the Early Nineteenth Century', *Central European History* 28 (1995).

Sperber, Jonathan, *Popular Catholicism in Nineteenth-Century Germany* (Princeton, 1984).

Sperber, Jonathan, *Rhineland Radicals. The Democratic Movement and the Revolution of 1848–1849* (Princeton, 1993 pbk edn).

Springer, Max, *Franzosenherrschaft in der Pfalz* (Stuttgart and Leipzig, 1926).

Stamm-Kuhlmann, Thomas, *König in Preußens großer Zeit. Friedrich Wilhelm III. Der Melancholiker auf dem Thron* (Berlin, 1992).

Steffens, Wilhelm, 'Die linksrheinischen Provinzen Preußens unter französischer Herrschaft 1794–1802', *Rheinische Vierteljahrsblätter* 19 (1954).

Stein, Wolfgang Hans, 'Die Ikonographie der rheinischen Revolutionsfeste', *Jahrbuch für westdeutsche Landesgeschichte* 15 (1989).

Steuer, Heiko, *Das Wappen der Stadt Köln* (Cologne, 1981).

Stolleis, Michael (ed.), *Recht, Verfassung und Verwaltung in der frühneuzeitlichen Stadt* (Cologne, 1991).

Strassoldo, Raimondo, 'Centre-periphery and System-Boundary: Culturological Perspectives', in Jean Gottmann (ed.), *Centre and periphery. Spatial Variation in Politics* (Beverly Hills and London, 1980).

Strauss, Gerald, 'The Holy Roman Empire Revisited', *Central European History*, 11 (1978).

Tann, Jennifer and M. J. Breckin, 'The International Diffusion of the Watt Engine, 1775–1825', *Economic History Review* 31 (1978).

Taylor, Peter Keir, *Indentured to Liberty. Peasant Life and the Hessian Military State* (Ithaca, N.Y. and London, 1994).

Theuringer, Thomas, *Liberalismus im Rheinland. Voraussetzungen und Ursprünge im Zeitalter der Aufklärung* (Frankfurt a. M., 1998).

Tilly, Richard, *Financial Institutions and Industrialization in the Rhineland 1815–1870* (Madison and London, 1966).

Toni, Diederich, *Die alten Siegel der Stadt Köln* (Cologne, 1980).

Torsy, Jakob, *Geschichte des Bistums Aachen während der französischen Zeit (1802–1814)* (Bonn, 1940).

Treitschke, Heinrich von, *History of Germany in the Nineteenth Century* (translated by Eden Paul and Cedar Paul, London, 1915).

Tulard, Jean (ed.), *Dictionnaire Napoléon* (Paris, 1987).

Tulard, Jean, *Le Grand Empire* (Paris, 1982).

Tulard, Jean, 'Problèmes sociaux de la France impériale', *Revue d'histoire moderne et contemporaine* 17 (1970).

Turner, R. Steven, 'The "Bildungsbürgertum" and the Learned Professions in Prussia, 1770–1830: The Origins of a Class', *Histoire Sociale* 13 (1980).

Vallée, Gustav, *Le Compte général de la conscription de A. A. Hargenvilliers* (Paris, 1937).

Vanden Heuvel, Jon, *A German Life in the Age of Revolution: Joseph Görres, 1776–1848* (Washington, D.C., 2000).

Vann, J. A., *The Swabian Kreis. Institutional Growth in the Holy Roman Empire, 1648–1715* (Brussels, 1975).

Vierhaus, Rudolf, 'Land, Staat und Reich in der politischen Vorstellungswelt deutscher Landstände im 18. Jahrhundert', *Historische Zeitschrift* 223 (1976).

Volkmann, Heinrich, 'Wirtschaftlicher Strukturwandel und sozialer Konflikt in der Frühindustrialisierung. Eine Fallstudie zum Aachener Aufruhr von 1830', in Peter Christian Ludz (ed.), *Soziologie und Sozial-Geschichte* Sonderheft 16 (Opladen, 1972).

Vollheim, Fritz, *Die provisorische Verwaltung am Nieder- und Mittelrhein während der Jahre 1814–1816* (Bonn, 1912).

Voss, Jürgen, *Deutsch-französische Beziehungen im Spannungsfeld von Absolutismus, Aufklärung und Revolution. Ausgewählte Beiträge* (Bonn and Berlin, 1992).

Voth, Hans-Joachim, 'The Prussian Zollverein and the Bid for Economic Superiority', in Philip G. Dwyer (ed.), *Modern Prussian History 1830–1947* (Harlow, 2001).

Wagner, Elisabeth, 'Revolution, Religiosität und Kirchen im Rheinland um 1800', in Peter Hüttenberger and Hansgeorg Molitor (eds.), *Franzosen und Deutsche am Rhein 1789–1918–1945* (Essen, 1989).

Walker, Mack, *German Home Towns: Community, State, General Estate, 1648–1871* (New York, 1971).

Weber, Eugen, *Peasants into Frenchmen. The Modernization of Rural France 1870–1914* (London, 1977).

Weber, Max, *The Theory of Social and Economic Organization* (Oxford, 1964 edition).

Wedel, Hasso von, 'Heinrich von Wittgenstein (1797–1869)', *Rheinische Lebensbilder* 8 (1980).

Wegert, Karl H., *German Radicals Confront the Common People. Revolutionary Politics and Popular Politics 1789–1849* (Mainz, 1992).

Wehler, Hans-Ulrich, *Deutsche Gesellschaftsgeschichte*. Vol. 1: *1700–1815* (Munich, 1987).

Weis, Eberhard, 'Der aufgeklärte Absolutismus in den mittleren und kleinen deutschen Staaten', in idem (ed.), *Deutschland und Frankreich um 1800. Aufklärung, Revolution, Reform* (Munich, 1990).

Weis, Eberhard, 'Der Illuminatenorden (1776–1786). Unter besonderer Berücksichtigung der Fragen seiner sozialen Zusammensetzung, seiner politischen Ziele und seiner Fortexistenz nach 1786', in idem (ed.), *Deutschland und Frankreich um 1800. Aufklärung – Revolution – Reform* (Munich, 1990).

Weis, Eberhard, 'Kontinuität und Diskontinuität zwischen den Ständen des 18. Jahrhunderts und den frühkonstitutionellen Parlamenten von 1818/1819 in Bayern und Württemberg', in idem (ed.), *Deutschland und Frankreich um 1800. Aufklärung – Revolution – Reform* (Munich, 1990).

Weis, Eberhard, 'Ländliche und städtische Unruhen in den linksrheinischen deutschen Gebieten von 1789 bis 1792', in idem (ed.), *Deutschland und Frankreich um 1800. Aufklärung – Revolution – Reform* (Munich, 1990).

Weiss, John H., 'Bridges and Barriers: Narrowing Access and Changing Structure in the French Engineering Profession, 1800–1850', in Gerald L. Geison (ed.), *Professions and the French State 1700–1900* (Philadelphia, 1984).

Wende, Peter, *Die geistlichen Staaten und ihre Auflösung im Urteil der zeitgenössischen Publizistik* (Lübeck and Hamburg, 1966).

Westerholt, Egon Graf von, *Lezay Marnesia. Sohn der Aufklärung und Präfekt Napoleons (1769–1814)* (Meisenheim am Glan, 1958).

Wetzler, Peter, *War and Subsistence. The Sambre and Meuse Army in 1794* (New York, 1985).

Wilson, Peter H., *German Armies. War and German Politics, 1648–1806* (London, 1998).

Wilson, Peter H., 'Social Militarization in Eighteenth-Century Germany', *German History* 18 (2000).

Wilson, Peter H., *War, State and Society in Württemberg, 1677–1793* (Cambridge, 1995).

Wohlfeil, Rainer, *Spanien und die deutsche Erhebung 1808–1814* (Wiesbaden, 1965).

Woloch, Isser, *Napoleon and his Collaborators. The Making of a Dictatorship* (New York and London, 2001).

Woloch, Isser, 'Napoleonic Conscription: State Power and Civil Society', *Past & Present* 111 (1986).

Woloch, Isser, *The New Regime. Transformations of the French Civic Order, 1789–1820s* (New York and London, 1994).

Woolf, Stuart, 'French Civilisation and Ethnicity in the Napoleonic Empire', *Past & Present* 124 (1989).

Woolf, Stuart, *Napoleon's Integration of Europe* (London, 1991).

Wraskaja, N. S., *A. G. F. Rebmann. Leben und Werke eines Publizisten zur Zeit der grossen französischen Revolution* (Heidelberg, 1907).

Wright, Vincent, *Les préfets du second empire* (Paris, 1973).

Wunder, Bernd, *Geschichte der Bürokratie in Deutschland* (Frankfurt a. M., 1986).

Wunder, Bernd, *Privilegierung und Disziplinierung: die Entstehung des Berufsbeamtentums in Bayern und Württemberg (1780–1825)* (Munich, 1978).

Wunder, Bernd, 'Rolle und Struktur staatlicher Bürokratie in Frankreich und Deutschland', in Helmut Berding, Etienne François and Hans-Peter Ullmann (eds.), *Deutschland und Frankreich im Zeitalter der Französischen Revolution* (Frankfurt a. M., 1989).

Würtenberger, Thomas, 'Staatsverfassung an der Wende vom 18. zum 19. Jahrhundert', in *Wendemarken in der deutschen Verfassungsgeschichte* (*Der Staat. Zeitschrift für Staatslehre, öffentliches Recht und Verfassungsgeschichte* Beiheft 10, 1993).

Zitzen, E. G., *Die Grundlagen der rheinischen Landwirtschaft* (Cologne, 1939).

Zorn, Wolfgang, 'Preußischer Staat und rheinische Wirtschaft (1815–1830)', in *Landschaft und Geschichte. Festschrift für Franz Petri zu seinem 65. Geburtstag am 22 Februar 1968* (Bonn, 1970).

Zorn, Wolfgang, 'Die wirtschaftliche Struktur der Rheinprovinz um 1820', *Vierteljahrsschrift für Sozial- und Wirtschaftsgeschichte* 54 (1967).

Zückert, Hartmut, 'Republikanismus in der Reichsstadt des 18. Jahrhunderts', *Aufklärung* 4 (1989).

Index

NEW STUDIES IN EUROPEAN HISTORY

Books in the series

Royalty and Diplomacy in Europe, 1890–1914
RODERICK R. MCLEAN

Catholic Revival in the Age of the Baroque
Religious Identity in Southwest Germany, 1550–1750
MARC R. FORSTER

Helmuth von Moltke and the Origins of the First World War
ANNIKA MOMBAUER

Peter the Great
The Struggle for Power, 1671–1725
PAUL BUSHKOVITCH

Fatherlands
State Building and Nationhood in Nineteenth-Century Germany
ABIGAIL GREEN

The French Second Empire
An Anatomy of Political Power
ROGER PRICE

Origins of the French Welfare State
The Struggle for Social Reform in France, 1914–1947
PAUL V. DUTTON

Ordinary Prussians
Brandenburg Junkers and Villagers, 1500–1840
WILLIAM W. HAGEN

Liberty and Locality in Revolutionary France
Six Villages Compared
PETER JONES

Vienna and Versailles
The Courts of Europe's Dynastic Rivals, 1550–1780
JEROEN DUINDAM

From *Reich* to State
The Rhineland in the Revolutionary Age, 1780–1830
MICHAEL ROWE